Maida Heatter's
Book of
Great Desserts

ALSO BY
MAIDA HEATTER

Maida Heatter's Book of Great Cookies
(1977)

Maida Heatter's Book of Great Chocolate Desserts
(1980)

Maida Heatter's New Book of Great Desserts
(1982)

Maida Heatter's Book of Great American Desserts
(1985)

Maida Heatter's Greatest Dessert Book Ever
(1990)

Maida Heatter's Brand-New Book of Great Cookies
(1995)

Maida Heatter's Book of Great Desserts

DRAWINGS BY
TONI EVINS

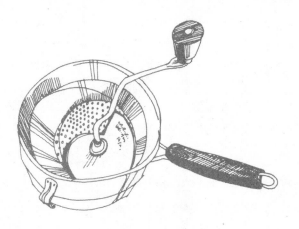

**Andrews McMeel
Publishing**

Kansas City

00 01 02 RDH 10 9 8 7 6 5 4 3 2

Originally published in 1974 by Alfred A. Knopf, Inc., New York, in slightly different form.

LIBRARY OF CONGRESS CATALOGING-IN-PUBLICATION DATA
Heatter, Maida.
    Maida Heatter's book of great desserts / drawings by Toni Evins.
      p. cm.
    Originally published : New York : Knopf, 1974.
    Includes index.
    ISBN 0-8362-7861-5 (hardcover)
    1. Desserts. I. Title. II. Title: Book of great desserts.
  TX773.H35 1999
  641.8'6—dc21   98-45993
                                                CIP

Design by BTDnyc

ATTENTION: SCHOOLS AND BUSINESSES
Andrews McMeel books are available at quantity discounts with bulk purchase for educational, business, or sales promotional use. For information, please write to: Special Sales Department, Andrews McMeel Publishing, 4520 Main Street, Kansas City, Missouri 64111.

Contents

Author's Note

This is the first book I wrote. It was originally published in 1974 and has been in print since then. At first it was published by Knopf and then by Random House. In May of 1998, it received a great honor. It was inducted into the James Beard Cookbook Hall of Fame. I received a call from the Beard organization telling me about the award (once a year, one book receives this honor). They invited me to attend the event and informed me that I would be called on stage and I should plan on making an acceptance speech.

It was a formal event. There were about two thousand people there. Barbara Lazaroff introduced me with much hullabaloo and great fanfare.

I walked onto the stage—to a standing ovation. It bowled me over. I think I told everyone that I loved them—and then I reached into my bag and pulled out a brownie. I gave it to Barbara. Then I reached in for more—and threw them to the audience. I could not believe what happened. In the audience were Julia Child, Jacques Pepin, Martha Stewart (and her mother), Madeleine Kamman, Daniel Boulud, etcetera. The most sophisticated food people in the country. I had brought about fifty brownies. I wished I had more. The crowd went wild. They all wanted brownies. They jumped up and down and laughed and screamed and called out "Here—throw one here." I'm a terrible ball player. My aim is lousy. I'm sorry I didn't have a better aim and more brownies.

When I ran out of brownies I received several propositions. The deal was "a hundred dollars for one of those brownies" I could have made a bundle. However, here's the recipe for the brownies I brought. It is from *Maida Heatter's Brand-New Book of Great Cookies* (Random House, 1995).

These are made at a swanky Palm Beach deli, and I got the recipe (without the mints) from a Palm Beach newspaper.

I hope you like this additional recipe—and all the rest of the book.

HAPPY DESSERTS,

Maida Heatter

1999
Miami Beach, Florida

Palm Beach Brownies
with Chocolate-Covered Mints

At a party that Mr. and Mrs. David Brinkley gave in Miami Beach, I was introduced to Mrs. Tip O'Neill. She heard my name and without hesitation she said, "Palm Beach Brownies." This has happened to me many times. The recipe for Palm Beach Brownies is one of the two or three most popular recipes in all of my books.

The original recipe is in my chocolate book, with this introduction: "The biggest, thickest, gooiest, chewiest, darkest, sweetest, mostest-of-the-most . . . with an almost wet middle and a crisp-crunchy top." This recipe is the same as the original, but I have added a layer of chocolate-covered mints in the middle. The mints stay whole (they don't melt), and they look and taste gorgeous.

The baked cake should be refrigerated for at least a few hours, or overnight, or frozen for an hour or two before it is cut into bars.

8 ounces unsweetened chocolate
8 ounces (2 sticks) unsalted butter
8 ounces (2 generous cups) walnuts
5 eggs graded "large"
2 teaspoons vanilla extract
½ teaspoon almond extract
¼ teaspoon salt
1 tablespoon plus 1 teaspoon powdered instant espresso
    (I use Medaglia d'Oro from an Italian grocery store)
3¾ cups sugar
1⅔ cups sifted unbleached flour
2 14- or 15.4-ounce bags York chocolate-covered
    peppermint patties, unwrapped

Adjust an oven rack one third up from the bottom and preheat oven to 425 degrees. Line a 9 x 13 x 2-inch pan as follows: Invert the pan and center a 17-inch length of aluminum foil, shiny side down, over the pan. (If you are using a Magic Line® pan that has straight sides and square corners, use heavy-duty foil or the sharp corners will tear it. This is a wonderful pan and makes beautiful brownies.) With your hands, press down on the sides and corners of the foil to shape it to the pan. Remove the foil. Turn the pan right side up. Place the foil in the pan and very carefully press it into place in the pan. Now, to butter the foil, place a piece of butter (additional to that in ingredients) in the pan, and put the pan in the oven. When the butter is melted, use a pastry brush or a piece of crumpled plastic wrap to spread the butter all over the foil. Set the prepared pan aside.

Place the chocolate and the butter in the top of a large double boiler over hot water on moderate heat, or in a 4- to 6-cup heavy saucepan over low heat. Stir occasionally, until the chocolate and butter are melted. Stir to mix. Remove from the heat and set aside.

Break the walnuts into large pieces; set aside.

In the large bowl of an electric mixer, beat the eggs with the vanilla and almond extracts, salt, espresso, and sugar at high speed for 10 minutes. On low speed add the chocolate mixture (which may still be warm) and beat only until mixed. Then add the flour and again beat on low speed only until mixed. Remove the bowl from the mixer.

Stir in the nuts.

Spoon half the mixture (about 3½ cups) into the prepared pan and smooth the top.

Place a layer of the mints, touching each other and the edges of the pan, all over the chocolate layer. Cut some mints to fill in large spaces on the edges. (You will not use all the mints. There will be some left over.)

Spoon the remaining chocolate mixture all over the pan and smooth the top.

Bake for 35 minutes, reversing the pan front to back once during baking to insure even baking. At the end of 35 minutes the cake will have a firm crust on top, but if you insert a toothpick in the middle it will come out wet and covered with chocolate. Nevertheless, it is done. Do not bake any longer.

Remove the pan from the oven; let stand until cool. Cover the pan with a cookie sheet and invert the pan and the sheet. Remove the pan and foil lining.

Cover the cake with a length of wax paper and another cookie sheet and invert again, leaving the cake right side up.

Now the cake must be refrigerated for a few hours or overnight before it is cut into bars.

When you are ready to cut the cake, use a long, heavy knife with a sharp blade, either serrated or straight—try both. Cut the cake into quarters. Cut each quarter in half, cutting through the long sides. Finally, cut each piece into 4 bars, cutting through the long sides. (I think these are better in narrow bar shapes than in squares.)

Pack in an airtight box, or wrap individually in clear cellophane, wax paper, or foil.

These freeze perfectly and can be served very cold or at room temperature.

Notes: When you remove the cake from the pan you might see burned and caramelized edges. (You might not—it depends on the pan.) If you do, you can leave them on or cut them off. I have friends who say that this is the best part. I cut them off, but then I can't resist eating them.

These are huge! For some occasions you might want to cut them smaller. They are equally delicious, and sometimes they seem more appropriate.

P.S. *Once upon a time . . . I was in the brownie business. I made the original Palm Beach Brownies (without the mints) and sold them to the Jordan Marsh department store here in Miami. I wrapped them individually in clear cellophane and then packaged them in white boxes with clear plastic tops. I wrote the recipe by hand and had it Xeroxed. Each box contained a dozen brownies and the recipe. Business was great, but it took up almost all my time. When I started writing cookbooks, I had to quit the brownie business. But it was great while it lasted.*

Variation

Recently, I was invited to bake cookies for an event held by the American Institute of Wine and Food. It was a South Sea Islands dinner held at the Kampong in Coconut Grove, Florida. The Kampong is the former home of Dr. David Fairchild, botanist, horticulturist, and America's foremost plant collector. He named his home after the many kampongs he visited throughout South Asia.

I made up these Bali Hai Brownies. I used the above recipe without the walnuts and the mints. I added the following ingredients, just stirred into the dough:

6 ounces crystallized ginger, cut in ¼- to ½-inch pieces
10 ounces (about 3 packed cups) shredded coconut
10 ounces (2 generous cups) whole macadamia nuts (I use the
    Mauna Loa nuts that come in a jar—they are roasted and salted.)

The brownies were lush, moist (like thick macaroons), exotic, and dramatic (the whole macadamias were startling). The recipe is extravagant—the ingredients are expensive. The brownies are extraordinary.

The ginger is optional. The flavor is delicious, but the brownies are equally fabulous with or without it.

Acknowledgment

People often ask me how I started to cook, and I'm startled. It was so natural, part of life. That was because of my mother, a most unusual woman. She could do almost anything and did everything well. She was a great cook and true gourmet. Every meal was an occasion . . . the menu planned with care, the table set beautifully and arranged with an artist's eye. Whether or not she had help, she did most of the cooking herself because she loved it. And she imparted that love to me. We were very close and there was hardly a day that we didn't talk, either in person or on the telephone, usually about food. For me, life's problems seem less important and easier to cope with while trussing a chicken, chopping onions, kneading a yeast dough, or icing a cake. And all seems well to me when popovers and soufflés rise to magnificent heights. My mother taught me that cooking is an act of love—and a beautiful, mountainous escape.

Introduction

This is not intended to be a complete book of every dessert recipe. Most of these are desserts that I prepared daily for many years. They were for my husband's restaurant (called Inside), but I made them in my kitchen at home and Ralph transported them twice a day. You will find that the number of servings indicated will provide large portions—because that is what the customers wanted. And since it was important to have desserts that would remain fresh so that they would still be good at dinner if they weren't all eaten at lunch, there is an abundance of recipes that can be made ahead of time. I hope you won't be disappointed if you look for something (such as fruit pie for instance) and find that it is not included, but that is probably the reason.

I kept a daily chart of the number of portions of each dessert sold at the restaurant each day, and just as a matter of interest Raspberry-Strawberry Bavarian was always the leader. Chocolate Mousse Heatter came in second, and Black-and-White Cheesecake and Queen Mother's Cake tied for third.

I have cooked and tested every one of the recipes in this book over and over so that they are worked out perfectly. But in order for these recipes to work for you as they do for me, it is of the utmost importance that you follow every direction exactly. Many instructions might seem trivial, arbitrary, or unimportant, but there really is a practical reason for everything.

If a recipe says to line a cookie sheet with aluminum foil, it is not because I am a fuddy-duddy and care about keeping cookie sheets clean. The foil is essential to keep the cookies from sticking. In some recipes, such as Oatmeal Wafers or Benne Seed Wafers, you would encounter disaster without the foil. With it, if you are like me, you will squeal with joy at the ease, fun, and satisfying excitement of peeling the foil from the smooth, shiny backs of the cookies.

If a recipe includes directions to refrigerate for at least 10 hours or longer (see Flan), it is because the custard would collapse if it were served sooner. With adequate baking and chilling time it will hold its shape like a smooth cheesecake, and serving it (to say nothing of eating it) will be a sensuous thrill.

If Pecan Buttercrunch is not allowed to stand for the specified time after it comes out of the oven, it will ooze when you try to cut it into portions. And if the Brownies are cut too soon they will squash.

I could go on and on, but please, take my word for it. Read the recipes carefully and follow them exactly.

I wish you good luck with this book. I have had pleasure, satisfaction, moments of pride, and even some of sheer ecstasy with these recipes. And I wish you the same.

1974
Miami Beach, Florida

Maida Heatter's
Book of
Great Desserts

Ingredients

BUTTER

Whenever butter is called for it means sweet, unsalted butter.

To Clarify Butter

Clarified butter may be used for buttering pans and is good for frying crêpes or pancakes; it lessens the chances of sticking and is less likely to burn. It will keep indefinitely in the refrigerator.

To make a large amount: Place any amount of cut-up sweet butter in a saucepan, preferably a wide, shallow one rather than a deep, narrow one, and large enough to allow the butter to bubble up. Cook without stirring over medium heat. Turn down the heat and let it cook slowly for about 5 minutes. With a large spoon, carefully skim the foam off the top. Do not disturb the milky substance in the bottom. Let the butter cool for 5 minutes or so and then, very gently, pour the clear butter off the top and discard the milky residue.

To make a small amount (¼ to ½ pound): The following is Craig Claiborne's method. Place the cut-up butter in a heatproof glass measuring cup (a 1-cup size for ¼ pound of butter; the 2-cup size for ½ pound of butter); put it in a 250-degree oven until the butter is melted. Skim off the foam. Carefully pour the clarified butter off the top and discard the milky residue.

When clarified, butter loses one fourth of its original volume.

CHOCOLATE

Kinds of Chocolate

Unsweetened Chocolate. Also called baking chocolate or bitter chocolate.

Sweet, Semisweet, Bittersweet, and Extra-Bittersweet. Generally interchangeable in cooking and baking, depending on your taste and on the availability of chocolates.

Semisweet Chocolate Morsels, Chips, or Bits. Made by Nestlè, Baker, Hershey, and others. I seldom use them in cooking or baking (although many people do with excellent results), except for making one of the greatest cookies of all, Toll House Cookies. The recipe for those cookies is printed on the package of Nestlè's Chocolate Morsels.

Milk Chocolate. I seldom use milk chocolate in cooking or baking. When I do, it is used cut up, like morsels (for chocolate chip cookies).

Compound Chocolate. Real chocolate contains cocoa butter. Compound chocolate contains some shortening other than cocoa butter. Real chocolate should be tempered for certain uses (tempering is a lengthy and technical process of melting and cooling the chocolate). Compound chocolate does not have to be tempered.

It does not discolor or streak after being melted with no other ingredients (as real chocolate will), and it will set up (harden) faster than real chocolate.

There are many brands. One, made by Nestlè, is available in wafers by the pound from Sweet Celebrations in Minneapolis, Minnesota ([800] 328-6722).

There is a compound chocolate made by Semper in Sweden. I think it is very good. It comes in 11-pound bars. I get it in Miami from L. Karp's ([305] 652-3171).

I use compound chocolate most especially for making Mushroom Meringues (page 272), but also for Chocolate Cones (page 513), Chocolate Leaves (page 515), Chocolate Slabs (page 516), and Chocolate Cigarettes (page 517). These items can also be made with real chocolate but not as easily (unless the chocolate is tempered, which is a long story).

Cocoa. Any unsweetened cocoa may be used in baking and cooking, but I prefer Dutch process. It has nothing to do with Holland or the Dutch—it has been treated with alkali to neutralize the natural acids. It is darker than other cocoa and, to my taste, has a richer and better flavor. I use Droste.

Lindt Thins (5-ounce box). These are 1½ inch square, paper-thin pieces of semisweet or milk chocolate. They are meant for eating as candy, but are great for decorating. Any desserts that have been prepared in individual portions and topped with whipped cream, or any of the pies or icebox desserts that have been topped with whipped cream, may be decorated with some of the squares, standing them upright or on an angle in the whipped cream.

To Melt Chocolate

When melting chocolate with no other ingredient, the container in which you are melting it *must* be absolutely dry. Even the merest drop of moisture will cause the chocolate to "tighten." (If it should "tighten," stir in 1 tablespoon of homogenized vegetable shortening for each 3 ounces of chocolate.) Melt it in the top of a double boiler over hot, but not boiling water. The reason for this is that boiling water might bubble up and get into the chocolate. People who have a microwave tell me that is the best way of all to melt chocolate.

Chocolate should melt slowly—it burns easily. To be sure chocolate doesn't get overheated and burn, it is always advisable to remove it from over the hot water before it is completely melted and then stir it until it is entirely melted and smooth.

COFFEE

Instant coffee in a recipe means dry—powdered, chunks, or granules.

Instant coffee powder will dissolve more easily than chunks or granules. If you happen to have one of the other two on hand, it is easy to powder it yourself. Whirl some in the blender, then strain it and return the coarse part to the blender until it is all powdered. Medaglia d'Oro instant espresso is finely powdered and works very well. It is generally available at specialty food stores and/or Italian markets.

CREAM

Half-and-half has from 10½ to 18 percent butterfat. Light cream and coffee cream both have from 18 to 30 percent butterfat. Whipping cream has from 30 to 36 percent. And heavy whipping cream has from 36 to 40 percent.

To Whip Cream

Heavy cream may be whipped with an electric mixer, a rotary beater, or a large, balloon-type wire whisk (the same kind as described for beating egg whites [page xxiii]). It will whip more easily and give better results if the cream, bowl, and beaters are cold. The bowl should be metal (but not copper), as that gets and stays colder. Place the bowl and beaters in the refrigerator or the freezer until just before using them. If the room is very warm, the bowl in which you are whipping the cream should be placed in a larger bowl of ice and water.

Do not overbeat or the cream will lose its smooth texture; if you beat even more it will turn into butter (see recipe on page xx). If you use an electric beater, a handy safeguard is to stop beating before the cream is completely whipped and then finish the job with a wire whisk. This allows less chance for overbeating.

It is best not to whip cream too far ahead of time. However, if you do, cover and refrigerate it and then check it before serving. It will probably have separated slightly and the bottom will be watery. But it may be reincorporated easily by mixing very briefly—a wire whisk is best.

To Make Butter

To make quick, homemade butter (delicious and such fun), beat 1 pint of heavy cream at high speed until the liquid begins to separate. Then reduce the speed to prevent the cream from spattering, and continue to beat until the butter separates from the milk. Pour through a strainer and then return the solid part to the mixing bowl. Add ice water, about as much as there was buttermilk, and mix at lowest speed (it will splash) to wash the butter. Drain again, then mix again with fresh ice water. Drain this, too, then stir the butter briefly in the strainer to remove any trapped milk. You may want to add a scant ¼ teaspoon of salt, as this quick, homemade butter tastes a bit flat without it.

One pint of cream will make ½ pound (1 cup) of butter, but you can use this same process with as much cream as you want. Pack the butter into a crock or any covered container, or roll it in wax paper and shape it into a roll or block.

EGGS

Size

These recipes are all based on the use of eggs graded large or extra-large.

To Open Eggs

If directions call for adding whole eggs one at a time, they may all be opened ahead of time into one container and then poured into the other ingredients, approximately one at a time. Do not open eggs directly into the batter—you wouldn't know if a piece of shell had been included.

To Separate Eggs

A new bride, when faced with the direction "separate eggs," placed them carefully on the table about 4 inches apart, and wondered how far they should be from each other.

Eggs separate more safely when they are cold.

Place three small bowls in front of you, one for the whites and one for the yolks. The third one might not be needed, but if you should break the yolk when opening an egg, just drop the whole thing into the third bowl and save it for some other use.

When cracking the shell it is important not to use too much pressure or you will break the yolk at the same time.

There are many gadgets available for separating the yolks from the whites. The most common is cup-shaped with small openings in the bottom. The egg is cracked over the form set on a small bowl—the yolk stays in the top section and the white runs through the holes. Some cooks can do the same thing by opening the egg directly on the palm of a hand and letting the white run through their fingers into a bowl while the yolk remains in their hand.

The most popular method is to tap the side of the egg firmly on the edge of a bowl to crack the shell. Then, holding the egg in both hands, separate the two halves of the shell, letting some of the white run out into a bowl. Now pour the yolk back and forth from one half of the shell to the other, letting all of the white run out. Drop the yolk into the second bowl.

As each egg is separated the white should be transferred to another container, because if you drop all of the whites into one container there is a chance that the last egg might have a broken yolk, which could spoil all of the whites. Generally, a bit of yolk or shell can be removed with an empty half shell.

To Freeze Egg Whites

Leftover egg whites may be kept covered in the refrigerator for a few days or they may be frozen. I prefer to freeze them individually in ovenproof glass custard cups. When they are frozen, run hot water over the back of the cups (or place the cups in shallow hot water) until the frozen white falls out. Then wrap them individually in plastic wrap. To thaw, remove the number you want, transfer them to a cup or bowl, and let them stand at room temperature or place them in a very slightly warm oven. One cup of egg whites is made up of the whites of 6 extra-large or jumbo eggs, 8 large ones, or 10 medium.

Frozen egg whites are handy to have for recipes such as the Mushroom Meringues (page 272) or the filling for Black Velvet (page 337).

To Beat Egg Whites

Egg whites may be beaten with an electric mixer, a rotary eggbeater, or a large balloon-type wire whisk. Both the bowl and beater must be perfectly clean and dry. Just a bit of oil or grease will prevent the whites from inflating properly.

If you use an electric mixer or a rotary beater, be careful not to use a bowl that is too large or the whites will be too shallow to get the full benefit of the beater's action. Also, if you use an electric hand mixer or rotary beater, keep moving it around in the bowl. If you use a mixer on a stand, use a rubber spatula frequently to push the whites from the sides of the bowl into the center.

If you use a wire whisk, use one that is at least 4 inches wide at the top and that has many thin wires instead of fewer heavy ones, and beat in an unlined copper bowl, if you have one. (You may use glass, china, or stainless steel, but do not beat egg whites in aluminum or plastic.) To prepare the copper bowl, it should be treated before using as follows: Put 1 or 2 teaspoons of salt in the bowl and rub thoroughly with half a lemon, mixing the lemon juice into the sale. Rinse with hot water (no soap) and dry.

The beaten whites will have a better—creamier—consistency if you beat some of the sugar into the whites as they begin to hold a shape.

Do not beat egg whites ahead of time. They must be folded in immediately after they are beaten. If it is a cake that you are making, it must then be placed in the oven right away.

Do not overbeat the whites or they will become dry and you won't be able to fold them in without losing the air you have beaten in. Beat only until they hold a shape or a point—"stiff but not dry."

FLOUR

With only one or two exceptions these recipes call for sifted flour. This means that it should be sifted immediately before it is measured. If the flour is not sifted, or if it is sifted long before it is to be used, it packs down and 1 cup is liable to contain a few spoonfuls more than 1 cup of flour sifted immediately before measuring. If you have one, use a double or triple sifter; otherwise sift the flour twice. Sift onto a piece of paper, sifting a bit more than you will need. Use a metal measuring cup. Spoon the sifted flour lightly into the cup. Do not shake the cup or pack or press the flour down; just scrape any excess off the top with a metal spatula or any flat-sided implement. It is not necessary to wash a flour sifter, just shake it out firmly and store in a plastic bag.

SUGAR

When sugar is called for in these recipes, unless it is qualified it means granulated white sugar.

Sugar should be measured in the same metal cups as those recommended for flour. If granulated sugar is lumpy it should be strained before it is used. Brown sugar and confectioners sugar are best strained also. (Hard lumps in brown sugar will not disappear in mixing or baking.) Unlike flour, though, sugars may all be strained ahead of time and you may do several pounds at once. Use a very large strainer set over a large bowl and press the sugar through with your fingertips.

Confectioners Sugar

I would rather strain than sift it. Maybe it is easier or maybe it is just habit. However, when I open a box I work it through a large strainer set over a bowl and use my fingertips to press the sugar through the strainer. Then I transfer it for storage.

To sprinkle confectioners sugar over a cake or cookies, use a small strainer. This makes it very easy to control the amount and placement of the sugar.

Vanilla Sugar

To make vanilla sugar, fill a covered jar (about 1-quart size) with confectioners sugar and bury 1 or 2 split vanilla beans in it. Cover tightly, and let stand for at least a few days before using. As the sugar is used it may be replaced. The vanilla beans will continue to flavor the sugar for several months. Vanilla sugar adds a lovely flavor when strained over cakes and cookies.

NUTS

Over 2 ounces, I've given weights as well as measure for nuts; if measure only is given, weight is under 2 ounces.

To Store

All nuts should be stored in the freezer or refrigerator. Always bring them to room temperature before using, and smell them and taste them—rancid nuts would ruin a whole cake or an entire batch of cookies.

To Blanch

To blanch almonds: Cover almonds with boiling water. Let them stand until the water is cool enough to touch. Pick out the almonds one at a time, and squeeze each one between thumb and forefinger to squirt off the skin. As each one is skinned, place it on a towel to dry. Then spread the almonds in a single layer in a shallow baking pan and bake in a 200-degree oven for half an hour or so until they are dry. Do not let them brown. If the almonds are to be split or sliced or slivered, cut them one at a time immediately after removing the skin. Bake to dry as above. Sliced almonds are those that have been cut into very thin slices. Slivered almonds are the fatter, oblong, "julienne"-shaped pieces.

To *blanch hazelnuts:* Spread the hazelnuts on a baking sheet and bake at 350 degrees for 15 minutes or until the skins parch and begin to flake off. Then, working with a few at a time, put them in a large strainer or a colander and rub them with a stiff brush. Most of the skin will come off. Pick out the nuts and discard the skins. Don't worry about the few little bits of skin that may remain.

To *blanch pistachio nuts:* In a small saucepan bring a few inches of water to a boil. Drop the nuts (no more than ¼ to ½ cup of them at a time, as the skin is difficult to remove after the nuts have cooled) into the boiling water and let them boil for only a few seconds. They will lose their color if boiled for too long. Remove one nut and pinch the skin off with your fingers. If it slides off easily, immediately drain them all and turn them out onto a paper towel. While they are still warm pinch off the skins. Now they may be either slivered with a small paring knife or chopped into pieces that are coarse or almost as fine as a powder.

To Decorate with Pistachios

Chopped green pistachio nuts are an attractive and elegant topping when sprinkled lightly on whipped cream or cake icings (before the icing is dry).

Buy shelled, unsalted green pistachios. These are not readily available, but specialty nut shops and wholesale nut dealers carry them.

The nuts are green or yellow-green with reddish-purple skin. It is not essential to remove the skin, as the nuts may be chopped skin and all and the color won't be disturbing. However, the skin can be removed (see above) if you want a more elegant product and have the time to do it.

After the nuts have been blanched and skinned, some chefs heat the nuts in a moderate oven to crisp them. If you are a perfectionist you might want to do so, but be very careful not to leave them in too long or they may lose their color.

To Grind Nuts

When the instructions say "ground" it means that the nuts should be reduced to a powder, the consistency of coarse flour. Chopped nuts are much less fine and are left in visible pieces.

To grind nuts in a food processor use the metal chopping blade. If possible, always add some of the flour called for in the recipe. If the recipe does not have any flour, use some of the sugar called for. It will help to prevent the nuts from becoming oily. And do not overprocess.

DATES AND RAISINS

Raisins and dates must be fresh and soft—baking will not soften them. They may be softened by steaming them in a vegetable steamer or a strainer over boiling water, covered, for about 5 minutes. Dates and raisins should be stored in the refrigerator or freezer.

ORANGE AND LEMON RIND

When grating orange or lemon rind, if your grater has different-shaped openings, it is best to grate the rind on the side with the small, round openings, rather than the diamond-shaped ones.

Equipment

BAIN MARIE

When baking custards, puddings, some cheesecakes, or other dishes in a large pan of hot water (bain marie), if the large pan is made of aluminum, the hot water will discolor it. To prevent this, add ½ teaspoon cream of tartar for each quart of water. Just drop it in; no need to stir.

A CERTAIN CAKE PAN

When this book was originally published many of the recipes called for a 9 by 3-inch loose-bottomed tube cake pan with an 11-cup capacity. Years ago the manufacturers stopped making this size. But GOOD NEWS! Bridge Kitchenware has just arranged to carry this pan again. Call (800) 274-3435 or, in New York City, (212) 838-1901.

DOUBLE BOILER

Some directions call for a double boiler, perhaps a larger or smaller one than you have. If necessary, you can create a double boiler by placing the ingredients in a heatproof bowl over a saucepan of shallow hot water. The bowl should be wide enough so that its rim rests on the rim of the saucepan and the bowl is supported above the water.

ELECTRIC MIXERS

I use an electric mixer on a stand, the type that comes with two different-size bowls. Mine is a Sunbeam. However, these recipes may be followed with other equipment. My mother loved her Kitchen Aid mixer, the type with only one bowl. Many people have excellent results with an electric hand mixer. Susan, my mother's cook for 35 years, beat egg whites with a tree branch, in spite of a fantastically well-equipped kitchen. In the country she picked a fresh one as she needed it; in the city she always washed it carefully and put it away.

If you have an electric mixer, I recommend that you buy one or two extra sets of beaters. If you do much baking and dessert-making, you will find that it will save washing time and make the work much easier. An additional set of mixer bowls is also nice to have. Extra beaters and bowls are available wherever mixers are sold.

Because I use an electric mixer on a stand, I have given directions for beating times based on this type of mixer; a handheld mixer might take longer. If you are not using a mixer on a stand, when directions call for "small bowl of electric mixer" use a bowl with a 7-cup capacity. When directions are for "large bowl of electric mixer" use one with a 4-quart capacity.

Some of these recipes would be too much work without any mixer. Others, especially many of the cookies, may be made using your bare hands for creaming and mixing. Don't be afraid to use your hands.

MEASUREMENTS

To Measure Heat: Oven Thermometer

Success in baking depends on many things. One of the most important is correct oven temperature. Most gas and electric companies are helpful in checking your oven temperature for you. I also suggest that you buy an oven thermometer, preferably a mercury thermometer. Hardware stores sell them.

Measuring Cups

Glass measuring cups with the measurements marked on the sides and the 1-cup line below the top are only for measuring liquids. With the cup at eye level, fill carefully to exactly the line indicated. To measure dry ingredients, use the metal cups that come in sets of four: ¼ cup, ⅓ cup, ½ cup, and 1 cup. Fill to overflowing and then scrape off the extra with a metal spatula, a dough scraper, or the flat side of a large knife. If you are measuring flour do not pack it down.

Measuring Spoons

Standard measuring spoons must be used for correct measurements. They are sold in sets of four: ¼ teaspoon, ½ teaspoon, 1 teaspoon, and 1 tablespoon. When being used for dry ingredients, fill to overflowing and then scrape off the excess with a small metal spatula or the flat side of a knife.

PASTRY BAGS

The best pastry bags are those made of canvas and coated on one side only with plastic. The small opening generally has to be cut a bit larger to allow the metal tubes to fit. It is easier to work with a bag that is too large rather than one that is too small.

PASTRY BRUSHES

There are different types of pastry brushes. Use a good one, or the bristles will come out while you are using it. Generally, the flat brush with bristles about ¾ inch long is practical and does a good job. Sometimes I use an artist's watercolor brush in a large size; it is softer and there are times when I prefer it.

RUBBER SPATULAS

Rubber spatulas are almost indispensable—not plastic; they are not flexible enough. Use rubber spatulas for folding, for some stirring, for scraping bowls, pots, etc. I suggest that you have several. They are made in three sizes, of which I find "medium" the most useful and most generally available. I have very little, if any, use for the smallest, which is called a bottle scraper. The largest is marvelous for folding large amounts of whipped cream or beaten egg whites.

TURNTABLE

If you ice a cake—either occasionally or often—you will be able to do a much better job (it will be smooth and professional-looking in no time) if you have a cake-decorating turntable. You will be glad if you do. If you don't have one now you will thank me if I influence you to get one. You will say, "Wow—this is a joy—how did I get along without it—why didn't you tell me sooner?"

I am surprised that all kitchen shops don't carry them. They don't, but Bridge Kitchenware does. Call (800) 274-3435 or, in New York City, (212) 838-1901.

Procedures

BEFORE YOU BAKE

1. Read the recipe completely. Make sure that you have everything you will need, including the correct-size baking pan.
2. Remove butter, cream cheese, eggs from the refrigerator.
3. Adjust oven racks and preheat oven.
4. Prepare the pan according to directions.
5. Grind or chop nuts.
6. Sift flour (and other dry ingredients) onto a large piece of paper.
7. Open eggs (separate them if necessary).
8. Measure all the other ingredients and organize them into the order called for in the recipe.

CAKES

To Prepare the Cake Pan

I use butter, which I spread on the pan with a piece of crumpled wax paper or plastic wrap. Occasionally I also spray the buttered pan with Pam or another non-stick spray.

Baking parchment has been coated on both sides with silicone to prevent sticking. It comes in sheets or in a roll. It is available in hardware stores and most kitchen shops.

To line a pan with baking parchment: Place the pan right side up on the paper and trace around it. If it is a tube pan, stick the pencil into the tube and trace the opening. Cut the paper with scissors. After you have cut the opening for the tube, cut short lines radiating from the tube hole about ½ inch deep and ¼ inch apart to insure a smooth fit. If you do much baking, cut several pieces of paper at once and keep a supply on hand.

For most recipes (but not all) I prefer to coat the buttered pan with bread crumbs rather than flour. Put a few spoonfuls of crumbs (or flour, when specified) into the prepared pan. Holding the pan over a piece of paper, tilt it in all directions. Tap the pan and shake it back and forth until it is completely coated. Invert the pan over the paper and shake out the excess crumbs or flour. It should be a thin, even coating.

Naturally use unseasoned bread crumbs, which all food stores carry. Or make your own by removing the crust from white bread and drying in a low oven (225 degrees) until it is completely dry and crisp. Then break it up coarsely and grind it in the food processor. If necessary, strain the bread crumbs through a coarse strainer and return any chunks to the processor. Store bread crumbs in an airtight container.

Timing

The minute you put the cake into the oven set a timer, if you have one. But even if you do, write down the time that it should be finished. Good insurance.

It is important not to overbake cakes, or they become dry. There are several ways to test for doneness, but the tests vary with different cakes. (All of these recipes indicate which test or tests to use.) Some cakes will come slightly away from the sides of the pan when done, the top of others will spring back when touched lightly with your fingertip, while still others must be tested with a cake tester. Cake testers are available in hardware stores and kitchen-equipment shops. A cake tester is a 6-inch piece of thin wire with a ring at the top for ease in handling, or for hanging. The wire should be inserted gently, straight down into the middle of the cake, going all the way to the pan. Withdraw it gently. If it comes out clean, the cake is done. If some moist batter clings to the tester, the cake needs to be baked longer. Test in two or three places to be sure.

Or test with a toothpick or a thin wooden skewer.

To Freeze Cakes

All of the cakes in this book may be frozen before icing (individual layers should be wrapped separately or they will stick together), and most of them can also be frozen after, except where indicated in individual recipes. (For instance, 7-Minute Icing doesn't freeze.) Iced cakes should be frozen unwrapped and then, when firm, they should be wrapped airtight—plastic wrap is best for this.

If you freeze a cake on a plate and then want to remove it from the plate to wrap it, there should be wax paper or baking parchment between the cake and the plate or else they will stick together.

Having frozen every freezable recipe in this collection, I find that contrary to general opinion it is better to thaw iced cakes before removing the wrapping.

They sweat while thawing. If they have been unwrapped the moisture collects on the cake. If they have not been unwrapped, the moisture collects on the outside of the wrapping.

Even if the cakes are not iced, I prefer to allow all cakes to thaw before unwrapping.

To Prepare the Cake Plate

When you are ready to ice a cake, begin by tearing off a 10-inch length of wax paper or baking parchment. Fold it crossways into four parts, then cut through the folds with a knife, making four 10 x 3-inch strips. Place them in a square on the cake plate to protect it. As soon as the cake is iced remove the paper, pulling each strip out by a narrow end and leaving the cake plate clean.

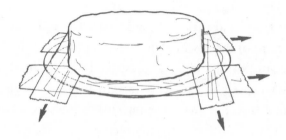

FOLDING

Ingredients are folded together rather than mixed when it is necessary to retain air that has been beaten into one or both of the mixtures. If one of the mixtures is heavy, first actually stir in a bit of the lighter mixture. Then, with a rubber spatula (or occasionally on lowest speed of an electric mixer), gradually fold the remaining light mixture into the heavier mixture as follows:

Place part of the light mixture on top.

With a rubber spatula: Rounded side down, cut down through the center to the bottom, then toward you against the bottom of the bowl, then up against the side, and finally out over the top, bringing the heavier ingredients from the bottom over the top. Rotate the bowl slightly with your other hand. Repeat cutting with the rounded side of the spatula down, rotating the bowl a bit after completing each cut. Continue only until both mixtures are combined. Try to make every motion count—do not handle any more than necessary.

With an electric mixer: I do not recommend an electric mixer for folding beaten egg whites or whipped cream. However, flour may be folded into a well-beaten egg-and-sugar mixture with an electric mixer if you are careful not to overmix. Use lowest speed and with a rubber spatula constantly push the ingredients from the sides of the bowl toward the center, mixing only until the flour is incorporated.

USING INGREDIENTS
To Bring Ingredients to Room Temperature
In individual recipes I have indicated the very few times I actually bring ingredients to room temperature before using. Otherwise they may be used right out of the refrigerator. If butter is too hard, cut it into small pieces, and let it stand only until it can be worked with.
To Add Dry Ingredients Alternately with Liquid
Always begin and end with dry ingredients. The procedure is generally to add about one third of the dry ingredients, half of the liquid, the second third of the dry, the rest of the liquid, and finally the last third of the dry.

Use the lowest speed on an electric mixer for this. After each addition mix only until smooth. If your mixer is the type that allows for a rubber spatula to be used while it is in motion, help the blending along by using the rubber spatula to scrape around the sides of the bowl. If the mixer does not allow room, or if it is the handheld kind, stop it frequently and scrape the bowl with the spatula.

Tortes

The difference between a torte and a cake is not clear. Experts differ in their definitions. Basically *torte* or *torta* is a European word meaning cake, and, because many European cakes are often made without flour, a torte is often defined as a cake without flour. (Ground nuts or bread crumbs might take the place of the flour.)

But it's all very complicated, especially as many classic torte recipes do call for flour. For instance, Dobosh Torte and Sacher Torte both do. (Incidentally, Sacher Torte is not included in this collection of recipes because, if you want a dense chocolate cake, I think that Queen Mother's Cake is so much better. To further complicate the subject, Queen Mother's Cake, although it is called a cake, is included in the torte section because it has no flour.) And many classic desserts called tortes are really neither cakes nor tortes. Linzer Torte, for example, is really a tart or a European pie.

Therefore, the recipes in this section are here for one of two reasons: either they are classically called tortes, or they are made without, or almost without, flour.

And a final fillip—Chocolate Mousse Torte, which is included here because it is made without flour, is really a kind of pie.

O.K.?

Linzer Torte

TWO 9-INCH TORTES, EACH 8 PORTIONS

Making a Linzer Torte is a big-time craft. The satisfaction is great—I love it! Taking this beautiful creation out of the oven is a thrill.

This is a classic, traditional, very famous Austrian cake. It is made in a shallow cake pan. It has a delicious crust made with ground nuts and spices. It is filled with jam, and is topped with a gorgeous lattice made of the crust mixture.

CRUST
> 1 pound (4½ cups) walnuts
> 3 cups sifted all-purpose flour
> 2 teaspoons cinnamon
> ½ teaspoon powdered cloves
> ¼ teaspoon salt
> 10 ounces (2¼ sticks) butter, cut up
> 1⅔ cups sugar
> 1 egg plus 1 egg yolk
> Finely grated rind of 1 large lemon (or 2 small)

Adjust rack one-third up from bottom of oven. Preheat oven to 400 degrees. Butter two 9 x 1¾-inch round layer-cake pans, preferably pans with removable bottoms (see Note). Line the bottoms with parchment paper cut to fit. Butter the paper.

Place the nuts in the bowl of a food processor fitted with the metal chopping blade. Add ½ cup of the flour (reserve remaining 2½ cups flour). Process for 15 seconds until the nuts are ground fine.

Put remaining flour, cinnamon, cloves, and salt in a large mixing bowl. With a pastry blender cut in the butter until the mixture resembles coarse crumbs. Stir in the sugar and walnuts. Mix the egg and egg yolk slightly and add along with the lemon rind. Work the dough with your hands a bit, and then turn it out onto a large board or smooth surface and squeeze it between your fingers until it holds together. Now "break off" the dough as follows:

Form it into a slightly flattened ball. Start at the further end of the dough, and using the heel of your hand, push off small pieces (about 2 tablespoons), pushing it against the work surface and pushing away from you. Continue pushing off, or breaking, until all the dough has been broken off. Re-form the dough and "break" it off one more time.

Divide the dough in half, and then in half again. Form each quarter into a ball. Place one of the quarters in each pan (reserve remaining two rounds). Press each one into place with your fingers. (If the dough is sticky dip your fingers in flour as necessary.) Press evenly and firmly over the bottoms of the pans and about 1¼ to 1½ inches up on the sides. Don't worry about making a smooth or level edge on the sides. That will be filled in later.

Bake these shells both on the same rack for about 15 minutes or until they barely begin to color.

While the shells are baking roll each of the remaining rounds of dough between two large pieces of wax paper to about ¼- to ⅜-inch thickness and about 10 inches in diameter. Leave both pieces of wax paper on the dough. Slip a cookie sheet under it and place in the freezer for 10 to 15 minutes (or a little longer in the refrigerator) until the dough is well chilled.

Meanwhile, remove baked shells from the oven. Reduce oven temperature to 350 degrees and raise the rack to one third of the way from the top of the oven.

FILLING
    ¼ cup fine, dry bread crumbs
    24 ounces (2 cups) seedless raspberry jam

Sprinkle about 2 tablespoons of the bread crumbs evenly over the bottom of each shell.

Stir the jam until it is soft and spread 1 cup in each shell. Set filled shells aside.

Remove the dough one at a time from the freezer (or refrigerator) and from the cookie sheet. Place it on a large board. Remove the top piece of wax paper. Use a small, sharp knife and cut the dough, cutting through the bottom wax paper at the same time, into strips ½ to ¾ inch wide. Lift each strip by the wax paper ends. Starting in the middle of the torte, flip one strip over the top of the jam. Peel off the wax paper. Cut the ends of the dough by pressing them on the sides of the pan. Place the strips ½ to ¾ inch apart, crisscrossing them on an angle to make a lattice top with diamond-shaped openings. Use the left-over pieces of dough to fill in the empty spaces between the strips around the edges. (The unbaked strips and the baked rim will blend together.) Press the outer edge with your fingertips or a spatula to level it. Score the rim with a fork. The top of the rim will be about ¼ inch below the top of the pan. Repeat with the remaining ball of dough for the remaining shell.

TOPPING

    1 egg yolk
    1 teaspoon water
    5 ounces (1 cup) slivered almonds (slivered almonds are the oblong,
        "julienne"-shaped pieces)

Make a glaze by mixing egg yolk and water. Brush it all over pastry strips and border. Sprinkle ½ cup almonds evenly over each torte. Bake both on the same rack for 1 hour or so until crust and almonds are well browned.

Remove from oven. Cool in pans on racks only until cool enough for you to handle but still warm. When removing tortes from pans, if the sides stick release them carefully with a small, sharp knife. The sides are crisp, and heavy handling will crack them. However, if you have used a loose-bottomed pan you will probably be able to release the sides by gently pushing the bottom up.

In order to remove the tortes without losing the loose almonds on top, cover torte with clear wrap or foil. Place cake rack on top. Invert. Remove pan and paper lining. Place cake plate or rack over the torte. Invert again, right side up, and remove clear wrap or foil. Let stand overnight before serving.

Optional: Sprinkle tops generously with confectioners sugar through a fine strainer.

Note: This recipe will make one large Linzer Torte in an 11- or 12-inch shallow pan, or a large quiche pan with fluted sides and removable bottom. I've made it in a variety of unconventional forms and pans. In any event, it must be made in a shallow pan, and the bottom must be lined with paper or the torte will stick to the pan.

Dobosh Torte

12 PORTIONS

This is a famous and fabulous specialty of Hungarian baking, although the Austrians claim it as well. It is made of very very thin layers of sponge cake with chocolate filling and icing. Traditionally, the cake has seven layers. I made a fifty-layer Dobosh Torte for my mother and father's fiftieth wedding anniversary. Spectacular! It was about 12 inches high. To serve portions I cut down about 3 inches into the cake, so each portion had about thirteen layers. I don't remember how many batches I made in order to have enough layers— but it was many. I have made many Dobosh Tortes in different widths and different heights.

I love to make it.

I love to serve it.

I love to eat it.

Warning! You need a large work area—a lot of time—and much patience. If you wish, start this ahead of time and freeze the layers before filling and icing.

> 7 eggs, separated, plus 3 egg yolks
> 1 pound (3½ cups) confectioners sugar
> ¾ cup sifted all-purpose flour
> 1 tablespoon lemon juice
> ⅛ teaspoon salt

To prepare for baking seven cake layers (the usual number): Cut seven pieces of baking parchment, each about 11 inches square. Trace a 9–inch circle on each paper. Turn the papers upside down. Butter an area a little larger than the traced circle (which will show through). Sift flour over the buttered papers; shake and tilt the papers to shake off excess flour. Set papers aside.

Place rack in the center of the oven and preheat to 450 degrees.

In the large bowl of an electric mixer at high speed, beat the ten egg yolks for a few minutes until they are pale lemon-colored. Reduce speed and gradually add sugar. Increase speed to high again and beat for 5 minutes until very thick. Reduce speed and gradually add the flour, then again increase it to high and beat for 5 minutes more (mixture will be almost stiff), scraping the bowl occasionally with a rubber spatula. Mix in the lemon juice and remove from mixer. (The mixture will be very thick—use your fingers to get it all off the beaters.)

In a clean bowl with clean beaters, beat the seven egg whites with the salt until they hold a point—stiff, but not dry. Since the yolk mixture is very thick, actually stir a few spoonfuls of the whites in to lighten it a bit. Then fold in a few large spoonfuls three or four times until the mixture lightens.

Gently fold in the remaining whites.

Although a Dobosh Torte is generally seven layers high, I pride myself on the number and thinness of my layers. If you only make seven layers, that's perfectly all right—trying for more is one of my own personal hang-ups. With a large serving spoon, place two or three large spoonfuls of the batter on one of the pieces of prepared paper. Using an offset spatula or the back of the spoon, spread the batter thin, slowly rotating the paper with your left hand as you spread the batter with your right hand. Make it thin but do not leave any holes in it. A 1/4-inch thickness should give you seven layers. Do not make the edges too thin. Follow the lines closely, but don't worry—the edges may be trimmed later.

Slide a cookie sheet under the paper and bake for 5 to 7 minutes or until the top is golden brown with dark brown spots. If the layers are thicker than mine are, they will take longer to bake. If they are not baked long enough they will stick to the paper. Repeat with remaining layers.

When a layer is baked and out of the oven, lift the corners of the paper and invert onto a rack. Peel off the paper and immediately invert the layer onto another rack to cool, right side up. (If you let the layer cool upside down it will stick to the rack.) When you run out of racks, layers may cool on smooth toweling that has been dusted with confectioners sugar. When you run out of room, cooled layers may be stacked if you sprinkle the tops lightly with confectioners sugar and place wax paper between them.

Cooled layers may be trimmed to even the edges. Working on a board, place an 8½-inch or 9-inch pot cover or cake pan on the layer. Cut around with a small sharp knife or trace with the knife and then cut with scissors.

Prepare the following:

FILLING AND ICING FOR DOBOSH TORTE

½ pound semisweet or bittersweet chocolate
½ pound (2 sticks) butter
1 teaspoon vanilla extract
3 egg yolks
2 tablespoons confectioners sugar

Melt the chocolate in the top of a small double boiler over hot water on moderate heat. Remove from heat, stir until smooth, and set aside to cool completely.

In small bowl of electric mixer beat the butter until soft. Add vanilla and egg yolks and beat well. Add sugar and cooled chocolate. Beat until thoroughly mixed, scraping the bowl with a rubber spatula.

Place four strips of baking parchment or wax paper around the outer edges of a cake plate. Place one cake layer on the plate and with a long, narrow metal spatula spread with a thin layer of the chocolate filling. If you have made more than seven layers, the filling must be spread *very* thin, in order to have enough for all. Place another layer on top, adjusting it carefully so that the edges are lined up evenly. Continue icing the layers, stacking them as evenly as possible. If necessary, trim the edges again.

Spread the remaining chocolate smooth around the sides first and then over the top.

Remove paper strips by pulling each one out by a narrow end (see page xxxi) and refrigerate cake for at least several hours to set the icing. Store in refrigerator and serve cold.

Notes:

1. This is a very firm cake; use a sharp, heavy knife for serving.
2. Dobosh Torte is traditionally made with a layer of caramelized sugar on top. I prefer it this way with icing on top—it is easier to prepare, easier to serve, easier to eat, and, to my taste, very delicious.

Chocolate Mousse Torte

6 TO 8 PORTIONS

You make chocolate mousse, refrigerate part of it, and bake part of it in a pie plate. After baking, the mousse will settle in the center. Cool it, and then place the refrigerated mousse on the baked mousse. Refrigerate it again and then top it with whipped cream.

When I sent this recipe to my friend Craig Claiborne, he gave it a full page in the *New York Times* magazine section. It then became the 1972 Dessert of the Year.

If there are any other *New York Times* Desserts of the Year I haven't heard of them. This is special!

8 ounces semisweet chocolate
1 tablespoon instant coffee
¼ cup boiling water
8 eggs, separated
⅔ cup sugar
1 teaspoon vanilla extract
⅛ teaspoon salt

Adjust rack to center of oven. Preheat oven to 350 degrees. Butter a 9-inch round ovenproof glass pie plate. Dust it with fine, dry bread crumbs. Set aside.

Place chocolate in the top of a small double boiler over hot water. Dissolve the coffee in the boiling water and pour it over the chocolate. Cover and let stand over low heat, stirring occasionally with a small wire whisk until the chocolate is almost melted. Remove chocolate from heat and continue to stir until smooth. Set aside to cool slightly.

In the small bowl of an electric mixer beat the yolks at high speed for about 5 minutes, until they are pale lemon-colored and thickened. Gradually add ⅓ cup of the sugar (reserve remaining ⅓ cup of sugar) and continue to beat at high speed for 5 minutes more until very thick. Add the vanilla and chocolate, beating slowly and scraping the bowl with a rubber spatula until blended.

Remove from mixer. In the large bowl of electric mixer beat the whites with the salt until they hold soft peaks. Add the reserved sugar and beat until the whites hold firm peaks or are stiff but not dry. Gradually, in two or three small additions, fold half of the whites into the chocolate (do not be too thorough) and then fold the chocolate into the remaining whites, folding only until no whites show. Handling as little as possible, gently remove and set aside about 4 cups of the mousse. Turn the balance into the pie plate; it will barely reach the top. Very gently spread level and place in oven to bake.

Cover reserved mousse and refrigerate.

When mousse has baked 25 minutes turn off the heat. Leave it in the oven for 5 minutes more. Then remove from oven and cool on a rack. (Mousse will rise during baking and then, while cooling, it will settle in the center, leaving a high rim.)

When completely cool, remove reserved mousse from refrigerator. Handling as little as possible, place the refrigerated mousse in the center of the shell of baked mousse. Mound it slightly higher in the center, but be careful to handle as little as possible or it will lose the air beaten into it.

Refrigerate for at least 2 to 3 hours.

TOPPING

1½ cups heavy cream
1½ teaspoons vanilla extract
⅓ cup confectioners sugar

In a chilled bowl with chilled beaters, whip above ingredients until they hold a definite shape. Spread over the unbaked part of the mousse, excluding the rim. Refrigerate.

Optional: Coarsely grate some semisweet chocolate over the top.

Notes:

1. Another and very attractive way of applying the whipped cream: Use a pastry bag fitted with a medium star tube and, as Jean Hewitt did when she prepared this torte to be photographed for the *New York Times*, form a lattice pattern over the top of the pie and a border around the edge.

2. Place the pie plate on a folded napkin (on a platter or cake plate) to hold the plate steady when serving.

Queen Mother's Cake

12 PORTIONS

This was in my first book and in my chocolate book. It is one of the most popular recipes in all of my books and is the one cake I make more often than any other. I originally got the recipe in 1962 from a food column by Clementine Paddleford in the *New York Herald Tribune*.

The story is that Jan Smeterlin, the eminent Polish pianist, loved to cook. And he collected recipes. This is one that was given to him on a concert tour in Austria.

When the Queen Mother was invited to tea at the home of some friends of the Smeterlins, the hostess baked the cake according to Smeterlin's recipe. The Queen Mother loved it and asked for the recipe. Then—as the story goes—she served it often at her royal parties. Including the time she invited the Smeterlins to her home. (Incidentally, the Queen Mother and I corresponded with each other about this recipe. She is charming.)

It is a flourless chocolate cake that is nothing like the flourless chocolate cakes that are so popular today. It is not as heavy or dense. This has ground almonds and the texture is almost light, although it is rich and moist. It is divine.

I recently became a cover girl when *Saveur* magazine put this cake on its cover (November 1997) and the picture showed my hand putting Chocolate Cigarettes on the cake.

6 ounces (scant 1½ cups) blanched or unblanched almonds
6 ounces semisweet chocolate, cut into small pieces
¾ cup sugar
6 ounces (1½ sticks) unsalted butter
6 eggs, separated
⅛ teaspoon salt
1 teaspoon lemon juice

First toast the almonds in a single layer in a shallow pan in a 350 degree oven for 12 to 15 minutes, shaking the pan a few times, until the almonds are lightly colored and have a delicious smell of toasted almonds when you open the oven door. Set aside to cool.

Adjust a rack one-third up in the oven and preheat oven to 375 degrees. Butter the bottom and sides of a 9 x 3-inch springform pan and line the bottom with a round of baking-pan liner paper cut to fit. Butter the paper. Dust the pan all over with fine, dry bread crumbs, invert over paper, and tap lightly to shake out excess. Set the prepared pan aside.

Place the chocolate in the top of a small double boiler over warm water on moderate heat. Cover until partially melted, then uncover and stir until just melted and smooth. Remove the top of the double boiler and set it aside until tepid or room temperature. Place the almonds and ¼ cup of the sugar (reserve remaining ½ cup sugar) in a food processor fitted with a metal chopping blade. Process very well until the nuts are fine and powdery. Stop the machine once or twice, scrape down the sides, and continue to process. Process for at least a full minute. I have recently realized that the finer the nuts are, the better the cake will be. Set aside the ground nuts.

In the large bowl of an electric mixer beat the butter a bit until soft. Add ¼ cup of the sugar (reserve remaining ¼ cup sugar) and beat to mix. Add the egg yolks one at a time, beating and scraping the sides of the bowl as necessary until smooth. On low speed add the chocolate and beat until mixed. Then add the processed almonds and beat, scraping the bowl, until incorporated.

Now the whites should be beaten in the large bowl of the mixer. If you don't have an additional large bowl for the mixer, transfer the chocolate mixture to any other large bowl.

In the large bowl of the mixer, with clean beaters, beat the egg whites with the salt and lemon juice, starting on low speed and increasing it gradually. When the whites barely hold a soft shape, reduce the speed a bit and gradually add the remaining ¼ cup sugar. Then, on high speed, continue to beat until the whites just barely hold a straight point when the beaters are slowly raised. Do not overbeat.

Stir a large spoonful of the whites into the chocolate mixture to soften it a bit.

Then, in three additions, fold in the remaining whites. Do not fold thoroughly until the last addition and do not handle any more than necessary.

Turn the mixture into the prepared pan. Rotate the pan a bit briskly from left to right in order to level the batter.

Bake for 20 minutes at 375 degrees and then reduce the temperature to 350 degrees and continue to bake for an additional 50 minutes (total baking time is 1 hour and 10 minutes). Do not overbake; the cake should remain soft and moist in the center. (The top might crack a bit—it's O.K.)

The following direction was in the original recipe, and although I do not understand why, I always do it. Wet and slightly wring out a folded towel and place it on a smooth surface. Remove the cake pan from the oven and place it on the wet towel. Let stand until tepid, 50 to 60 minutes.

Release and remove the sides of the pan (do not cut around the sides with a knife—it will make the rim of the cake messy). Now let the cake stand until it is completely cool, or longer if you wish.

The cake will sink a little in the middle; the sides will be a little higher. Use a long, thin, sharp knife and cut the top level. Brush away loose crumbs.

Place a rack or a small board over the cake and carefully invert. Remove the bottom of the pan and the paper lining. The cake is now upside down; this is the way it will be iced. Place four strips of baking-pan liner paper (each about 3 x 12 inches) around the edges of a cake plate. With a large, wide spatula, carefully transfer the cake to the plate; check to be sure that the cake is touching the papers all round (in order to keep the icing off the plate when you ice the cake).

If you have a cake-decorating turntable or a Lazy Susan, place the cake plate on it.

ICING

½ cup whipping cream
2 teaspoons powdered instant espresso or coffee (see Note)
8 ounces semisweet chocolate, cut into small pieces

Scald the cream in a 5- to 6-cup saucepan over moderate heat until it begins to form small bubbles around the edges or a thin skin on top. Add the dry espresso or coffee and whisk to dissolve. Add the chocolate and stir occasionally over heat for 1 minute. Then remove the pan from the heat and whisk or stir until the chocolate is all melted and the mixture is smooth.

Let the icing stand at room temperature, stirring occasionally, for about 15 minutes or a little longer, until the icing barely begins to thicken.

Then, stir it to mix, and pour it slowly over the top of the cake, pouring it onto the middle. Use a long, narrow metal spatula to smooth the top and spread the icing so that a little of it runs down the sides (not too much—the icing on the sides should be a much thinner layer than on the top). With a small, narrow metal spatula, smooth the sides.

Remove the strips of paper by pulling each one out toward a narrow end (see page xxxi).

Note: I use Medaglia d'Oro instant espresso.

Optional: Chocolate Cigarettes (see page 517), whipped cream, and fresh raspberries. Decorate the cake or individual portions with the optional chocolate cigarettes. Place a mound of optional whipped cream (lightly sweetened with confectioners sugar and lightly flavored with vanilla extract) on one side of each portion on individual dessert plates, and a few optional raspberries on the other side of each portion.

Truffles Torte

12 PORTIONS

Chocolate three ways (cake, icing, and truffles). The cake (rich, intense, dense, moist, almost flourless), the icing (smooth, silken, creamy), and truffles. Yum!

> 7 ounces (2 cups) pecans
> 3 tablespoons sifted all-purpose flour
> 4 ounces semisweet chocolate
> 2 ounces unsweetened chocolate
> 6 ounces (1½ sticks) butter
> ¾ cup sugar
> 5 eggs, separated
> 3 tablespoons Baileys Irish Cream Liqueur, or any liquor
> Pinch of salt

Adjust rack to center of oven. Preheat oven to 350 degrees. Butter bottom and sides of a 9 x 2- or 3-inch springform pan. Line the bottom with a round of baking parchment cut to fit. Butter the parchment. Dust the pan all over lightly with fine, dry bread crumbs.

Place pecans and flour in bowl of food processor fitted with the metal chopping blade. Process for about 30 seconds until the pecans are very fine. Set aside.

Melt both chocolates together in top of double boiler over hot water on moderate heat. Set aside to cool slightly.

In the small bowl of an electric mixer beat the butter a bit until softened. Add ½ cup of the sugar (reserve remaining ¼ cup sugar) and beat for a minute or two. Add the yolks one at a time, beating after each. On low speed add the chocolate and liqueur or liquor. Transfer to a large bowl and stir in the nuts.

In the large bowl of the electric mixer, with clean beaters beat the whites with the salt until they hold a soft peak. On low speed slowly add the reserved sugar. Then beat on high speed until the whites just barely hold a straight peak or are stiff but not dry.

The chocolate mixture will be quite thick. First stir a rather large spoonful of the whites in to lighten it a bit. Then, in a few additions—small at first—gently fold in the balance of the whites.

Turn into the cake pan and spread the top smooth (but don't handle it any more than necessary).

Bake for 1 hour. Remove from oven. Cool in the pan on a rack for about 15 minutes. Then remove the sides of the pan, cover cake with a rack, and invert. Remove the bottom of the pan and the parchment lining. Let the cake cool upside down.

While cake is baking or cooling, make the truffles, or they may be made ahead of time and kept at room temperature for a day or frozen for a longer time.

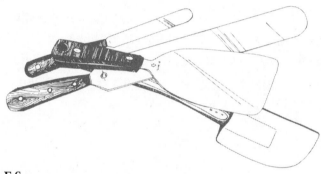

TRUFFLES

3 ounces semisweet chocolate
2 tablespoons butter, at room temperature
1 egg yolk
Optional: 1 teaspoon Baileys Irish Cream Liqueur, or any liquor
Unsweetened cocoa

In top of small double boiler set over hot water on moderate heat, melt the chocolate. Remove chocolate from heat. With a small wire whisk beat in the butter, then the yolk, and the optional liqueur or liquor. Beat until smooth. Let stand, stirring occasionally, until mixture thickens slightly. (It may be stirred very briefly over ice water.) Drop in twelve mounds on wax paper. Let stand for about half an hour to an hour until firm enough to handle.

Strain some cocoa onto a piece of wax paper or parchment. Have another piece of paper ready for the finished truffles. Coat your hands lightly with cocoa. Roll each truffle into an uneven ball. Roll it around in the cocoa. Place it on the wax paper. Continue to cocoa your hands as necessary. (If necessary, reroll truffles in cocoa before placing them on the cake.)

Place four strips of wax paper or parchment around the edges of a cake plate. Gently transfer the cake to the plate, bottom up.

ICING

6 ounces semisweet chocolate
¼ pound (1 stick) butter
1 egg yolk
1 tablespoon Baileys Irish Cream Liqueur, or any liquor

Melt chocolate in top of double boiler over hot water on moderate heat. Set aside to cool.

In the small bowl of an electric mixer beat the butter until slightly softened. Beat in the chocolate, yolk, and liqueur or liquor. Beat briefly at high speed. Pour it all onto the top of the cake. Smooth over top and sides of cake. Place truffles evenly around top of cake, one to a portion. Remove paper strips by pulling each one out by a narrow end (see page xxxi).

Helen McCully's French Chocolate Torte

6 PORTIONS

This divine cake, small and chic, is a specialty of my good friend Helen McCully, the food editor of *House Beautiful*. When Helen sent this recipe to me she said it was "the best of all."

    4 ounces semisweet chocolate
    ¼ cup fine, dry bread crumbs
    5 ounces (1 cup) almonds
    ¼ pound (1 stick) butter
    ⅔ cup sugar
    3 eggs
    Finely grated rind of 1 large orange

Adjust rack to center of oven and preheat oven to 375 degrees. Butter an 8-inch round layer-cake pan. Line the bottom with parchment paper. Butter the paper. Dust all over with fine, dry bread crumbs. (These are in addition to those called for in the list of ingredients.)

In the top of a small double boiler over hot water on moderate heat, melt the chocolate. Remove pan from heat and set aside to cool slightly.

In a food processor, process the bread crumbs and the almonds together until the almonds are ground fine—about 15 seconds. In the small bowl of an electric mixer, beat the butter until slightly softened. Gradually add the sugar and beat at moderately high speed for a few minutes. Beat in the eggs one at a time, beating well after each and scraping the bowl with a rubber spatula as necessary to keep mixture blended. It will look curdled—O.K. On lowest speed add the chocolate, bread crumbs, and almonds, beating only until smooth. Remove from mixer and stir in orange rind.

Turn into prepared pan. Spread the top level. Bake in preheated oven for 25 minutes. The center of the cake will be soft and moist and will not seem thoroughly baked; this is correct.

Remove from oven and cool in pan on a rack for about 30 minutes. With a small, sharp knife cut around edge of cake to release. Place rack over cake and invert. Remove pan and paper. Let stand until completely cool. The cake will be soft. Either let it stand for a few hours or refrigerate it briefly until firm.

Place four strips of wax paper or parchment around the edges of a cake plate. The cake is very fragile; with a wide metal spatula carefully transfer it to the plate, bottom up. Brush away any loose crumbs.

GLAZE

  2 ounces unsweetened chocolate
  2 ounces semisweet chocolate
  2 ounces ($\frac{1}{2}$ stick) butter
  2 teaspoons honey
  Optional: $\frac{1}{4}$ cup toasted, slivered almonds (see Note), or 6 pieces of choco-
      late-covered candied orange rind

Place both chocolates, butter, and honey in the top of a small double boiler over hot water on moderate heat. Cook, stirring occasionally, until melted and smooth. Remove from heat.

Replace the water in the bottom of the double boiler with ice water, deep enough to touch the upper section. Place glaze over ice water and stir briefly and constantly only until it cools and barely begins to thicken very slightly. Watch it carefully so that it doesn't harden.

Pour over top of cake. With a long, narrow metal spatula spread it smooth over the top, letting some run down on the sides a bit. With a small, narrow metal spatula smooth the sides. Remove the paper strips, gently pulling each piece out by a narrow end (see page xxxi).

Optional: Before the glaze hardens, garland the rim of the cake with toasted, slivered almonds, placing them close together, or with six pieces of chocolate-covered orange rind (one on each portion).

Note: "Slivered" almonds are those cut in squarish oblongs, or "julienne." To toast them, bake in a small shallow pan in the center of a preheated 350 degree oven. Shake pan occasionally until nuts are lightly browned, about 7 to 8 minutes.

Chocolate Applesauce Torte with Kumquats

10 PORTIONS

1 cup fine, dry bread crumbs
1½ teaspoons baking powder
6 eggs, separated
1 cup sugar
2 tablespoons unsweetened cocoa
½ cup sweetened or unsweetened applesauce
Finely grated rind of 1 large orange
⅛ teaspoon salt

Adjust two oven racks to divide the oven into equal thirds. Preheat oven to 350 degrees. Butter three round 9-inch layer-cake pans, and dust all over lightly with fine, dry bread crumbs. (These are in addition to those called for in the recipe.) Set aside.

Place bread crumbs in a small bowl. Through a fine strainer add the baking powder. Stir well to mix and set aside.

In small bowl of electric mixer beat the egg yolks for 1 minute. Gradually add ¾ cup of the sugar (reserve remaining ¼ cup sugar) and beat at high speed for 5 minutes until thick. On lowest speed add the cocoa and the applesauce. Then add the bread crumbs, scraping the bowl with a rubber spatula and beating only until smooth. Remove from mixer. Stir in orange rind. Set aside.

In large bowl of electric mixer beat the egg whites with the salt until the whites hold a soft shape. Add the reserved sugar and beat until the whites barely hold firm peaks or are stiff but not dry. Fold about one-third of the whites into the cocoa mixture and then fold the cocoa mixture gently into the remaining whites until no whites show.

Turn into prepared pans. Tilt pans gently to level batter. Bake 18 to 20 minutes or until tops spring back when lightly touched and layers begin to come away from sides of pans.

Remove from oven and let stand for about 3 minutes. Cover each pan with a rack and invert. Let stand for a minute or so until layers fall out of pans. If layers are stuck to the sides anywhere, release them with a small knife. Remove pans. Cover each layer with another rack and invert again to finish cooling, right side up. Layers will be thin, only about ¾ inch high.

Place four strips of parchment or wax paper around the edges of a cake plate. Place one layer of cake on plate. Prepare the following:

KUMQUAT CREAM
    1 10-ounce jar preserved kumquats
    ¼ cup brandy, or dark rum
    3 cups heavy cream
    ⅔ cup confectioners sugar
    1 tablespoon vanilla extract

Thoroughly drain the kumquats in a strainer set over a bowl. Mix ¼ cup of the drained kumquat syrup with the brandy or rum and set aside.

On a board, with a small, sharp knife, cut the kumquats roughly into quarters. Carefully remove the pits. Chop the kumquats into small dice, about ⅛ inch. Set aside.

In a large, chilled bowl with chilled beaters, whip the cream with the sugar and vanilla until it holds a shape and is firm enough to be used as filling and icing.

Brush one third of the kumquat and brandy or rum syrup over the first layer of cake. Spread with a thick layer of the whipped cream. Sprinkle with one third of the kumquats. Cover with the second layer of cake; brush second layer with syrup, spread with whipped cream, sprinkle with kumquats. Top with third layer and remaining syrup. Spread the remaining whipped cream over the sides and top. Sprinkle remaining kumquats evenly over the top. Remove paper strips by pulling each one out by a narrow end (see page xxxi).

Refrigerate for several hours before serving for flavors to blend. Serve very cold.

Optional: Some of the whipped cream may be reserved to be piped on the finished cake, using a pastry bag and a star tube, and piping the cream in a ruffle (after removing the paper strips) around the base and the rim.

Note: In the absence of kumquats you might use ¼ to ½ cup of Grand Marnier for brushing the cake layers and either use the whipped cream alone or top it with coarsely cut walnuts or pecans.

Small Walnut Torte

This is an Old World, classic Hungarian torte. In other words—this is wonderful.

5 ounces (1¼ cups) walnuts
3 tablespoons cornstarch
½ teaspoon baking powder
4 eggs, separated
½ cup sugar
1 tablespoon lemon juice
⅛ teaspoon salt

Adjust rack to center of oven. Preheat oven to 350 degrees. Butter two 8-inch round layer-cake pans. Line the bottoms with parchment paper. Butter the papers and dust lightly with fine, dry bread crumbs.

Place walnuts, cornstarch, and baking powder in bowl of food processor fitted with metal chopping blade. Process about 25 seconds until nuts are fine. Set aside.

In the small bowl of an electric mixer at high speed beat the yolks and ¼ cup of the sugar (reserve remaining ¼ cup sugar) for 10 minutes until very thick. On low speed, add the lemon juice and the nut mixture. Remove from mixer.

Beat egg whites with the salt until they hold a soft shape. Add the reserved sugar and beat until whites barely hold firm peaks or are stiff but not dry. The yolk mixture will be very stiff. In order to lighten it a bit, actually stir in two to three spoonfuls of the beaten whites.

Divide the mixture between the prepared pans (layers will be thin). Spread gently to level. Bake 25 to 30 minutes or until tops spring back when lightly touched and cakes come away from sides of pans. Remove from oven and let stand for 2 or 3 minutes.

If necessary, cut around the sides to release. Cover each layer with a rack and invert. Remove pans and papers. Cover with racks and invert again to cool completely right side up. Prepare Bittersweet Chocolate Icing.

BITTERSWEET CHOCOLATE ICING
6 ounces semisweet, bittersweet, or extra-bittersweet chocolate
¼ pound (1 stick) butter
1 egg

Break up chocolate and place in top of small double boiler over hot water on moderate heat to melt. Remove from hot water and set aside to cool to tepid. In small bowl of electric mixer, beat the butter to soften it a bit. Beat in the egg. (Mixture will not be smooth.) Add the chocolate and beat, scraping the bowl with a rubber spatula, until very smooth and slightly lightened in color.

Place four strips of wax paper or parchment around the edges of a cake plate. Place one layer on the plate, upside down. With a long, narrow metal spatula, cover with about one third of the icing. Place second layer on, right side up. Cover top and sides with the remaining icing, spreading with a small metal spatula around the sides.

Remove wax paper strips by pulling each one out by a narrow end (see page xxxi). Refrigerate. Serve cold.

Optional: Some of the icing may be reserved and used with a pastry bag and a star tube to decorate the torte, or the top and/or sides of the torte may be covered with chopped walnuts. Or place 6 to 8 large walnut halves around the top.

Swedish Almond Torte

This is easy and foolproof—you can do it in an hour or two—and you will have a beautiful, classic, delicious, and impressive Swedish torte.

PASTRY

1⅔ cups sifted all-purpose flour
1¼ teaspoons baking powder
¼ cup sugar
¼ pound (1 stick) cold butter, cut into 6 pieces
1 egg

Butter a round cake pan measuring 9 x 1½ inches. Line the bottom with a round of baking parchment and butter the paper.

Sift together flour and baking powder into a bowl. Stir in the sugar. With a pastry blender cut in the butter until the mixture resembles coarse crumbs. Stir egg slightly with a fork and, using the fork, stir it into the flour mixture. Turn it onto a board or smooth surface and knead slightly until it holds together. "Break" the dough by pushing off a small amount of the dough (about 2 tablespoons) with the heel of your hand, pressing the piece against the work surface and pushing away from you. Continue until all the dough has been pushed off. Re-form the dough and push it off, or "break" it again. Form the dough into a ball. Flatten slightly.

Place dough between two sheets of wax paper. With a rolling pin roll gently, working from the center out, in all directions. Roll into a circle 11½ to 12 inches in diameter. Work quickly or the dough will become sticky. (If that should happen, chill it a bit.)

Remove top piece of wax paper. Carefully invert dough into the cake pan. Remove remaining wax paper. Press the dough firmly into place against the bottom and sides. If it is sticky, flour your fingertips. Cut off any excess and use it to patch any low or empty spots. Cut dough even with top of cake pan. Set aside.

FILLING

¼ cup fine, dry bread crumbs

1 cup fruit preserves, jam, or jelly (thick and seedless)

Sprinkle bread crumbs evenly over pastry. Stir preserves to soften slightly. Drop the preserves in small mounds, close together, over the bread crumbs, and with the back of a teaspoon spread smooth. Refrigerate while preparing the topping.

Adjust oven rack one third of the way up from the bottom. Preheat oven to 325 degrees.

TOPPING

5 ounces (1 cup) blanched almonds

1 cup confectioners sugar

¼ pound (1 stick) butter

½ teaspoon almond extract

2 eggs

Finely grated rind of 1 lemon

Place the almonds in a food processor fitted with a metal chopping blade. Add ¼ cup of the sugar (reserve remaining ¾ cup sugar) and process for about half a minute until the nuts are fine. Set aside. In small bowl of electric mixer beat the butter to soften it a bit. Add reserved sugar and beat to mix. Add almond extract and 1 egg. Beat until smooth, scraping bowl with a rubber spatula as necessary to keep mixture smooth. On lowest speed gradually add the ground almonds and then the remaining egg. Beat until smooth. Remove from mixer. Stir in lemon rind. Spread this topping evenly over filling. The rim of the pastry shell should extend slightly above the topping.

Bake 1 hour and 20 minutes or until top is well browned. Remove from oven and place on a rack to cool completely. (While cooling, the torte will sink a bit in the center.) Cover with a rack and invert. Remove pan and paper. Cover with another rack and invert again, leaving torte right side up.

Prepare the following glaze:

GLAZE

½ cup confectioners sugar
1 scant tablespoon lemon juice
1 teaspoon tasteless salad oil (such as safflower or corn oil)
Optional: Toasted, sliced almonds

Place the sugar, lemon juice, and salad oil in a small bowl. With a rubber spatula mix until completely smooth. Glaze should be the consistency of thick cream sauce. If necessary, adjust with additional sugar or lemon juice or a bit of water.

Pour the glaze over the topping, and with a pastry brush spread a thin coating of it over the topping only, not the crust. If glaze settles heavily in the center of the torte, remove excess with the brush.

While the glaze is still wet it may be sprinkled with a few spoonfuls of the optional toasted, sliced almonds.

Let torte stand at least 3 to 4 hours or overnight before serving.

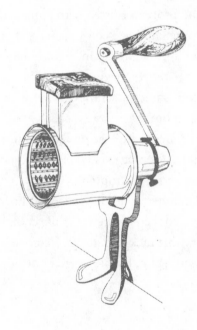

Royal Viennese Walnut Torte

12 TO 16 PORTIONS

Cakes don't get more regal than this.

When I was in Seattle on a book tour the food editor of a Seattle paper told me that he was a trained pastry chef, and when he took the final exam at the culinary school he attended, the biggest part of the exam was to make this cake. He passed with flying colors, and the cake has since become his favorite.

And so I guess that after you make it—and have great results—you will be a qualified pastry chef—or food editor.

This is not a quickie, and is not for beginners.

You will need a large bowl (at least 8-quart capacity) for folding the ingredients together.

> 1 pound (4½ cups) walnuts
> 2 cups sugar
> ½ cup strained unsweetened cocoa powder (preferably Dutch process)
> 12 eggs, large or extra-large, separated
> ½ teaspoon salt

The three layers for this cake should not be baked too high or too low in the oven or they will burn. Adjust two racks to divide the oven into thirds, and preheat to 350 degrees. Butter three 9-inch layer-cake pans. Line the bottoms with rounds of baking parchment cut to fit. Butter the papers and the sides. Dust all over with fine, dry bread crumbs, and set aside.

Place the walnuts and ½ cup of the sugar (reserve remaining 1½ cups sugar) in the bowl of a food processor fitted with the metal chopping blade. Process for 15 seconds only—no longer (if you process it even a bit too long it will make the nuts oily and lumpy). Add the cocoa and pulse the machine very few times. Scrape down the sides, pulse again only a bit. Transfer the mixture to a bowl and stir with a fork to finish mixing the ingredients. Set aside.

In the small bowl of an electric mixer beat the egg yolks at high speed for about 3 minutes. Reduce the speed and gradually add 1 cup of the sugar (reserve remaining ½ cup sugar). Increase the speed to high again and continue to beat for 5 minutes more until thick and pale. Remove from the mixer and transfer to a mixing bowl with at least an 8-quart capacity. Set aside.

In the large bowl of the electric mixer (with clean beaters) beat the egg whites and the salt until they hold a soft shape. On low speed gradually add the remaining ½ cup sugar and then continue to beat on high speed until the whites hold a firm point when the beaters are raised, or are stiff but not dry. Do not overbeat. Remove from the mixer.

With a large rubber spatula fold half of the nut mixture into the yolks, and then, in the following order, fold in one-third of the whites, the remaining half of the nut mixture, half the remaining whites, and then the balance of the whites. With all this folding, do not fold even once more than necessary, and do not fold until completely blended until the last addition—and then, just barely.

Divide the batter among the prepared pans. Spread the tops level with the bottom of a large spoon.

Bake two pans on one rack and one pan on the other, without placing one directly over another. Bake for about 50 minutes until the tops spring back when gently pressed with a fingertip and the layers come away slightly from the sides of the pans. (During baking the layers will rise and then sink a little—it's O.K.)

Remove the pans from the oven. Cover each pan with a rack and invert but do not remove the pans until they are cool enough to be handled. Then, cut around the edges to release, invert onto a rack, remove pan (do not remove the paper linings until you are ready to ice the cake), and then invert onto another rack to cool right side up.

Prepare the following buttercream for filling and icing:

COFFEE BUTTERCREAM

6 egg yolks, large or extra-large
½ cup sugar
3 tablespoons dry instant coffee
½ cup boiling water
1 pound (4 sticks) butter
1 teaspoon vanilla extract
3 tablespoons dark rum or cognac
Optional: additional rum or cognac (for sprinkling on the layers)

Place the yolks in the top of a small double boiler. Beat a little with a small wire whisk just to mix. Gradually stir in the sugar. Dissolve the coffee in the boiling water, and gradually whisk it into the yolk mixture.

Place over warm water on low-medium heat. The water must not touch the top of the double boiler and it must not boil or the mixture will curdle—be careful! Cook, stirring and scraping the pot constantly with a rubber spatula for 10 to 15 minutes until the mixture thickens to a soft custard consistency, and reaches 170 to 175 degrees on a candy thermometer. Now, to stop the cooking, quickly turn the mixture into a bowl—preferably a metal bowl. Place the bowl of custard into a larger bowl of ice and water. Stir frequently until the mixture is cool.

Beat the butter in the large bowl of an electric mixer to soften it a bit. Gradually add the cooled custard mixture, the vanilla, and the 3 tablespoons of rum or cognac, and beat well until very smooth and lighter in color. (If necessary, refrigerate the mixture to firm it a bit and then beat it again.)

Just before icing the cake, peel the papers away from the layers.

Place four strips of baking parchment around the edges of a large, flat cake plate. Place the first layer on the plate right side up, checking to be sure that it touches the papers all around. Optional additional rum or cognac may be sprinkled over each layer before spreading with buttercream. The filling must be spread thin or you won't have enough to cover the top and sides of the cake. Use a long, narrow metal spatula to spread a thin layer of the filling. Continue stacking layers right side up.

When the layers are in place, brush the sides of the cake to remove any loose crumbs. Then cover the sides and finally the top with the buttercream, spreading it smooth.

If you wish, reserve some of the buttercream and, with a pastry bag fitted with a small star tube, form a ruffled border on the top rim of the cake. If you still have some of the buttercream you might want to form another row around the base of the cake.

Remove the paper strips by pulling each one out by a narrow end (see page xxxi).

Refrigerate and serve cold.

Optional: If you wish, coat the sides of the cake with chopped walnuts. The pieces should be rather fine. Apply them with the palm of your hand and with your fingers before removing the paper strips.

Mocha Pecan Torte
(Mexican)

10 PORTIONS

12 ounces (3½ cups) pecans
3 tablespoons sifted all-purpose flour
1 teaspoon baking powder
1½ cups sugar
6 eggs, separated
2 tablespoons instant coffee
⅛ teaspoon salt

Adjust rack to the center of the oven. Preheat oven to 350 degrees. Butter two 9-inch layer-cake pans. Line the bottoms with parchment paper cut to fit. Butter the paper and dust with fine, dry bread crumbs.

Place the nuts, flour, baking powder, and ½ cup of the sugar (reserve remaining 1 cup sugar) in the bowl of a food processor fitted with the metal chopping blade. Process until the nuts are fine. Set aside.

In the small bowl of an electric mixer beat egg yolks at high speed for about 3 minutes until pale lemon-colored. Reduce speed while gradually adding instant coffee and ½ cup of the sugar (reserve remaining ½ cup sugar). Increase speed to high again and beat for 5 minutes until very thick. Remove from mixer and set aside.

In large bowl of electric mixer (with clean beaters) beat egg whites with the salt until the whites hold a soft peak. Gradually add the reserved sugar and beat until they hold a firm peak or are stiff but not dry. In three additions, fold about three-quarters of the whites into the yolks. Pour the yolks over the balance of the whites and fold together—don't be too thorough. Pour all of the egg mixture over the nut mixture and fold gently only until blended.

Divide batter between prepared pans. Level tops with spatula. Bake 35 to 40 minutes or until tops spring back when lightly touched, and layers barely begin to come away from sides of pans.

Invert onto racks, but do not remove cake pans. Let cool for about 10 minutes. Then, if necessary, cut around cakes to release, cover with racks, and invert; remove pans and papers, cover with racks, and invert again to finish cooling right side up.

FILLING AND ICING FOR MOCHA PECAN TORTE
3 ounces (¾ stick) butter
4 ounces unsweetened chocolate
1 tablespoon plus 1 teaspoon instant coffee
2 cups confectioners sugar
⅓ cup milk
2 eggs
1 teaspoon vanilla extract
Optional: crème de cacao, Kahlúa, or cognac

Place butter and chocolate in top of small double boiler over hot water on moderate heat. Stir until melted. Add instant coffee and stir to dissolve. Remove from heat and set aside to cool.

In a small mixer bowl, mix sugar, milk, eggs, and vanilla. Place in a larger bowl half filled with ice and cold water. Add cooled chocolate and beat at high speed for 3 to 4 minutes, scraping bowl occasionally with a rubber spatula until mixture becomes fluffy and light in color and the consistency of whipped butter—stiff enough to hold its shape.

Place four strips of paper around edge of cake plate. Place first layer upside down. If you wish, brush with optional crème de cacao, Kahlúa, or cognac. Spread with filling about ½ inch thick. Cover with top layer, right side up. Again, brush with optional liqueur. Spread icing smooth over top and sides of cake (see note). Cut carefully between bottom of cake and paper strips, and then remove paper by pulling each strip out by a narrow end (see page xxxi).

Refrigerate for 2 to 3 hours or more before serving.

Optional: Reserve a bit of the icing to use with a pastry bag fitted with a small star tube and form a border around the upper rim and another around the base of the cake. Or with the bag and star tube form ten rosettes around the top of the cake and place a large pecan half upright in each.

Note: If you have a turntable or Lazy Susan to work on, the icing may be spread smooth. If not, it might be easier to fluff it in irregular peaks with a spatula or the back of a spoon.

Royal Norwegian Macaroon Torte

12 OR MORE PORTIONS

This is a classic.

PASTRY

    2 cups sifted all-purpose flour
    2 teaspoons baking powder
    ¼ teaspoon salt
    ½ cup sugar
    ½ pound (2 sticks) butter
    1 egg
    Finely grated rind of 1 large lemon

Sift together flour, baking powder, and salt into a large bowl. Stir in the sugar. With a pastry blender, cut in the butter until mixture resembles coarse crumbs. With a fork, beat the egg lightly just to mix and stir it in along with lemon rind. Turn out onto a large board or smooth surface. Squeeze between your hands two or three times and then knead briefly with the heel of your hand only until the mixture holds together and leaves the board clean. Divide the dough in half and wrap one half in wax paper. Flatten slightly and refrigerate.

Place the other half in the center of an unbuttered 9-inch square cake pan. With floured fingertips press it out to cover the bottom and to rise 1 inch up the sides of the pan. Place in freezer or refrigerator while you prepare filling.

Adjust rack one-quarter up from bottom of oven. Preheat oven to 375 degrees.

FILLING

½ pound (1⅔ cups) blanched almonds, ground fine (see pages xxiv and xxv; for this recipe they do not have to be strained)

2 cups confectioners sugar

1 egg white

¼ cup light rum

¼ teaspoon almond extract

3 drops green food coloring

½ cup thick apricot preserves

Place the nuts and 1 cup of the sugar (reserve remaining 1 cup sugar) in the bowl of a food processor fitted with the metal chopping blade. Process for about half a minute until the nuts are fine. Add the remaining sugar, the egg white, rum, almond extract, and food coloring and pulse/process to mix until smooth.

Remove pastry shell from freezer or refrigerator. Stir the preserves slightly to soften and spread over the pastry, leaving ½-inch border around the edge of the pan.

Drop the filling over the preserves by small spoonfuls. The mounds should touch each other and ought to cover the bottom and touch the sides of the crust. But it is all right if a bit of the preserves or bottom crust show through in a few spots.

Remove remaining half of pastry from refrigerator. Working quickly, roll between two pieces of wax paper into a 9-inch square. Remove top piece of paper. Using another 9-inch square pan over the rolled pastry, or a 9-inch

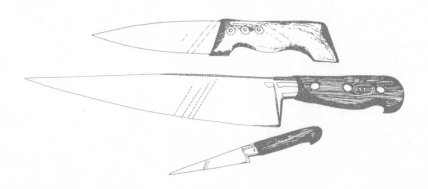

square of wax paper as a pattern, cut off any uneven edges. Save trimmings to fill in where needed. If dough has become sticky, chill it briefly in the freezer.

Invert over filled torte and ease it gently into place. Remove wax paper. If necessary, trim the edges with a small, sharp knife, pressing the pastry trimmings into any gaps.

Bake 1 hour and 10 minutes or until top is well browned and torte begins to come away from sides of pan. Cool to room temperature in cake pan on a rack.

With a small, firm, sharp knife cut around edges to release. Cover with a rack or cookie sheet and invert. Remove pan. Cover with another rack or cookie sheet and invert again, leaving torte right side up.

The torte must be refrigerated or placed briefly in the freezer until it is well chilled before it can be cut. Transfer to a cutting board.

With a very sharp, long, thin knife cut into oblongs, thin slices, or small squares. Serve at room temperature.

Carrot-Nut Torte

This is not the usual carrot cake. No way. This has no flour. No butter. No oil. It is an elegant European torte with a light, moist texture and a light, spicy flavor. It is special. And it has a solid white glaze on top that looks best if you put it on a few hours before serving.

> Finely grated rind of 1 large lemon
> 3 tablespoons lemon juice
> 6 ounces (1¼ cups) almonds
> 1 cup very finely grated carrots, tightly packed (about 3 medium-size carrots) (see Note 1)
> ¾ cup fine, dry bread crumbs
> ¼ teaspoon mace
> 1 teaspoon baking powder
> 6 eggs, separated
> 1¼ cups sugar
> ⅛ teaspoon salt

Adjust rack one-third up from the bottom of the oven. Preheat oven to 350 degrees. Butter an 8 x 3-inch springform pan. Line the bottom with parchment paper. Butter the paper and dust it all over with fine, dry bread crumbs (in addition to those called for in the recipe).

Mix lemon rind and juice and set aside. Grind the almonds in a food processor fitted with the metal chopping blade for 20 to 30 seconds until fine. Place grated carrots and almonds in a large bowl and stir or toss with your fingers to mix thoroughly. Place bread crumbs in a small bowl and, through a fine strainer, add mace and baking powder. Stir to mix. Add to the carrot-almond mixture and, with a rubber spatula, mix thoroughly. Set aside.

In small bowl of electric mixer at high speed, beat the yolks about 3 minutes until they are pale lemon-colored. Reduce the speed and gradually add ¾ cup of the sugar (reserve remaining ½ cup sugar). Increase speed to high again and beat for 5 minutes more until very thick. Remove from mixer and stir in rind and juice. Add to carrot mixture and mix thoroughly with a rubber spatula.

Beat egg whites with the salt until they hold a soft shape. On low speed gradually add the reserved sugar. Then beat on high speed until the whites hold a point or are stiff but not dry. In three or four additions (small at first) fold them into the carrot mixture. (When folding, grated carrots will collect on edge of rubber spatula. To remove them, reverse the spatula frequently, first folding with the curved edge down, and then with the straight edge down.) Fold only until no whites show.

Turn into prepared pan. The pan will be almost full. If necessary, shake pan gently to level batter. Bake 1 hour or until a cake tester comes out dry and the top springs back when lightly touched. Cool torte in pan on a rack for about 30 minutes. The center of the cake will sink a little. AOK.

With a sharp knife, pressing firmly against the sides of the pan, cut around the sides to release. Remove sides of pan. Cover torte with a rack, invert, and remove bottom of pan and paper. Cover with another rack and invert again to finish cooling right side up.

When completely cool use a long, thin, sharp knife and cut the top level. Place four strips of wax paper or baking parchment around the edges of a cake plate and gently transfer the torte, bottom side up. Prepare glaze a few hours before serving.

GLAZE
      1¾ cups confectioners sugar
      1 tablespoon lemon juice
      1 to 2 tablespoons boiling water

In a small bowl, stir all of the ingredients very thoroughly to mix well, adjusting amount of liquid or sugar to make a mixture about the consistency of thick cream sauce. If it is too thin it will run. Pour it on the torte and with a long, narrow metal spatula smooth it over the top only. If a bit runs down the sides leave it that way; do not spread. Remove paper strips, pulling each one out by a narrow end (see page xxxi). Let stand several hours for the glaze to set.

Optional: Before the glaze sets, decorate the rim with lightly toasted whole almonds, or whole glazed red cherries; or place one or more (depending on their size) marzipan carrots on top.

Notes:
1. There is no need to peel the carrots. Just wash them and grate on a grater with small, round—not diamond-shaped—openings.
2. Do not freeze this torte after glazing it—the glaze becomes wet after thawing.

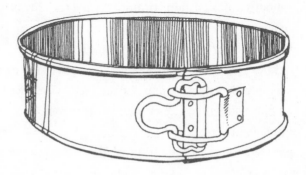

Chocolate Cakes and Layer Cakes

CHOCOLATE CAKE SQUARES
(Grandma Hermalin's)   42

CHOCOLATE CAKE SQUARES
(Lydia Pinkham's)   44

FUDGE CAKE WITH FUDGE   46

WALNUT FUDGE PIE À LA MODE WITH HOT FUDGE SAUCE   48

PALM BEACH CHOCOLATE LAYER CAKE   50

PALM BEACH CHOCOLATE TUBE CAKE   52

SOUR CREAM CHOCOLATE LAYER CAKE   54

DEVIL'S FOOD CAKE   56

MONTANA MOUNTAIN CAKE   58

RUM CREAM LAYER CAKE   60

RUM CHOCOLATE LAYER CAKE   64

COCONUT LAYER CAKE   67

Chocolate Cake Squares

(Grandma Hermalin's)

9 PORTIONS

> 1 cup sifted all-purpose flour
> 1 teaspoon baking soda
> ½ teaspoon baking powder
> ⅛ teaspoon salt
> ¼ pound (1 stick) butter
> 1 teaspoon vanilla extract
> 1 cup sugar
> 1 egg
> ½ cup powdered, unsweetened cocoa
> ½ cup milk
> 1 tablespoon instant coffee
> ½ cup boiling water

Adjust oven rack one-third up from the bottom of the oven. Preheat oven to 350 degrees. Butter a 9-inch square cake pan and dust the bottom only, very lightly, with fine, dry bread crumbs.

Sift together flour, baking soda, baking powder, and salt. Set aside.

In small bowl of electric mixer beat the butter a bit to soften. Add vanilla and sugar and beat for a minute or two. Beat in the egg. On lowest speed, add the cocoa. Then, in this order, gradually add one-half of the milk, one-half of the dry ingredients, remaining milk, and remaining dry ingredients, scraping bowl frequently with a rubber spatula all during mixing. Mix only until smooth after each addition.

Dissolve the instant coffee in the boiling water. While it is still hot, add it very gradually on lowest speed to the chocolate mixture. Beat only until smooth. Batter will be thin. Turn it into the prepared pan. Bake 40 minutes or until top springs back when lightly touched. Cool in pan on a rack for about 10 minutes. Cover with a rack and invert. Remove pan. Cover with another rack and invert again to finish cooling right side up. Prepare the following icing:

ICING

4 ounces semisweet chocolate (see Note)
2 ounces (½ stick) butter, cut in 4 pieces

In the top of a small double boiler over hot water on moderate heat, melt the chocolate. Remove top of double boiler. With a small wire whisk beat in the butter, one piece at a time, beating until each piece is thoroughly incorporated before adding the next.

This icing may be used immediately, or, if it is too thin, place the pan into ice water and stir constantly until icing thickens very slightly, but watch it closely to see that it doesn't harden. It should still be fluid when used.

Pour it over the cake and smooth with a long, narrow, metal spatula.

Note: If you like bittersweet chocolate, substitute 1 ounce of unsweetened chocolate for 1 ounce of the semisweet chocolate.

Chocolate Cake Squares

(Lydia Pinkham's)

9 PORTIONS

Lydia Pinkham was best known for her cure-all vegetable compound and her many activities in all the women's rights movements of her time. But first and last she was a good old-fashioned cook and housekeeper. Her recipe for chocolate cake does not contain any of her patent medicine.

> ¼ pound (1 stick) butter
> 1 teaspoon vanilla extract
> 1 cup sugar
> ¼ teaspoon salt
> 1 egg
> 2 tablespoons powdered, unsweetened cocoa
> 1 teaspoon baking soda
> 1 cup buttermilk
> 1½ cups sifted all-purpose flour

Adjust rack to center of oven. Preheat oven to 350 degrees. Butter an 8- or 9-inch square pan and dust the bottom only with fine, dry bread crumbs.

In small bowl of electric mixer beat the butter a bit to soften. Add vanilla, sugar, and salt and beat for a minute or two. Beat in the egg, scraping bowl with a rubber spatula as necessary until smooth. On lowest speed beat in the cocoa.

In a small bowl stir the baking soda into the buttermilk to dissolve and then gradually beat it into the batter. The mixture will look curdled—O.K.

On lowest speed, gradually add the flour, scraping the bowl with the rubber spatula and beating only until smooth.

Turn into prepared pan. Smooth the top and run the batter up on the sides a bit, leaving it slightly lower in the center.

Bake 40 minutes or until top springs back when lightly touched and cake begins to come away from sides of the pan. Remove from oven and cool in pan for about 5 minutes. Cover with a rack and invert. Remove pan. Cover with another rack and invert again to finish cooling right side up. Prepare the following icing:

ICING

    6 ounces semisweet chocolate
    3 tablespoons butter
    1 egg plus 1 egg yolk

In the top of a small double boiler over hot water on moderate heat, melt the chocolate. Transfer melted chocolate to small bowl of electric mixer. Cool slightly for a minute or two. Add butter, egg, and yolk and beat on slow speed only until smooth, thick, and shiny. Do not overbeat. It should stay dark; additional beating will lighten the color.

Turn all the icing onto the top of the cake and with a long, narrow metal spatula spread over the top only (not the sides). Then, with the tip of a small spoon, pull it up in small peaks, making even rows that completely cover the top of the cake.

Fudge Cake with Fudge

12 TO 16 PORTIONS

> 4 ounces unsweetened chocolate
> ½ cup hot water
> 1¾ cups sugar
> 2 cups sifted cake flour
> 1 teaspoon baking soda
> ¼ teaspoon salt
> ¼ pound (1 stick) butter
> 1 teaspoon vanilla extract
> 3 eggs
> ⅔ cup milk

Adjust racks to divide oven in thirds. Preheat oven to 350 degrees. Butter two 9-inch square cake pans.

Place chocolate and hot water in top of small double boiler over hot water on moderate heat. Cook, stirring occasionally, until chocolate is melted and mixture is smooth. Mix in ½ cup of the sugar (reserve remaining 1¼ cups) and continue to cook 2 minutes longer, stirring with a rubber spatula to keep mixture smooth. Remove top of double boiler and set aside.

Sift together flour, baking soda, and salt. Set aside. In large bowl of electric mixer beat the butter a bit to soften. Add vanilla and reserved 1¼ cups sugar and beat for about a minute or two. Scrape the bowl with a rubber spatula as necessary to keep mixture smooth. Beat in eggs one at a time, beating until thoroughly incorporated after each addition. On lowest speed alternately add sifted dry ingredients in three additions and milk in two additions, scraping the bowl with the spatula as necessary and beating only until smooth after each addition. Add the chocolate mixture (don't worry if it is still warm) and beat only until smooth.

Divide evenly between prepared pans. Tilt pans gently to level batter. Bake 30 to 40 minutes or until the tops spring back when lightly touched and cakes come away from sides of pans.

Cool cakes in pans for 5 minutes. Cover with racks or cookie sheets and invert. Remove pans. Cover with racks and invert again to cool right sides up.

Place the bottom layer upside down on a platter or board. Prepare the following fudge for filling and icing:

FUDGE
   3 cups sugar
   1 cup milk
   Pinch of salt
   3 tablespoons light corn syrup
   4 ounces unsweetened chocolate, coarsely cut
   5$\frac{1}{3}$ tablespoons butter
   2 teaspoons vanilla extract

Place sugar, milk, salt, corn syrup, and chocolate over moderate heat in a heavy saucepan with at least a 3-quart capacity (see Note 1). Bring slowly to the boil, stirring occasionally with a wooden spoon or spatula until the sugar is dissolved and the chocolate is melted. Insert a candy thermometer in the saucepan and let the syrup boil until the temperature reaches 232 degrees (or until the syrup forms a very soft ball in cold water).

Immediately, in order to stop the cooking, transfer to a large mixing bowl. Cut the butter into small pieces and add. Replace the thermometer and let mixture stand without stirring until the temperature drops to 110 degrees. (This might take as long as 1 hour.)

Add the vanilla. With a heavy wooden spatula stir and beat for 3 to 5 minutes until this heavy mixture thickens a bit more. Do not wait too long. You are making fudge; it will harden quickly and it must be spread before it hardens. Work very quickly—spread about half the fudge roughly on the bottom layer, cover with top layer placed right side up so that both flat sides meet in the center, and spread fudge on top. Do not try to spread it on the sides, but just let some of it run down unevenly.

Notes:
1. If the saucepan is too small, the syrup will boil over.
2. If the fudge icing becomes too thick and stiff, add boiling water, a few drops at a time, to soften it to the right consistency.
3. To make Fudge Squares, ice the layers separately and do not stack them on top of each other.
4. Serve as is, or à la mode (with ice cream), or all the way—with a bowl of ice cream, a bowl of whipped cream, and a bowl of walnut halves or fresh strawberries. And chocolate sauce?

Walnut Fudge Pie à la Mode with Hot Fudge Sauce

6 TO 8 PORTIONS

Although this is called a pie, it does not have a crust. It is a dense choco-late cake, almost like Brownies baked in a pie plate.

    2 ounces unsweetened chocolate
    ¼ pound (1 stick) butter
    1 teaspoon vanilla extract
    1 cup sugar
    2 eggs, separated
    2 tablespoons hot water
    ⅓ cup sifted all-purpose flour
    ½ cup walnuts, cut in medium-size pieces
    Pinch of salt

Adjust rack to center of oven. Preheat oven to 350 degrees. Line a 9-inch oven-proof glass pie plate with a large piece of aluminum foil. (See directions for crumb crust, page 350, for lining a pie plate with aluminum foil.) Brush the foil well with soft or melted butter.

In the top of a small double boiler over hot water melt the chocolate. Remove from heat and set aside.

In small bowl of electric mixer beat the butter to soften it a bit. Add the vanilla and ¾ cup of the sugar (reserve remaining ¼ cup sugar) and beat for a minute or two. Beat in the egg yolks and then the chocolate. When smooth add the hot water and then the flour, scraping bowl with a rubber spatula as necessary and beating only until smooth. Remove from mixer and stir in the walnuts.

Beat the whites with the salt until they hold a soft shape. Add the reserved sugar and continue to beat until stiff but not dry, and fold them into the choco-late mixture. Turn into pie plate and spread the top level.

Bake 35 minutes. During baking the cake will rise and then sink—correctly. The top will have formed a crust but it will be soft inside. Cool in the plate on a rack. When completely cool, let stand for about ½ to 1 hour to become firm and then cover with a cookie sheet or a rack and invert. Remove pie plate and aluminum foil. Replace pie plate over pie and invert again.

Just before serving place scoops of ice cream on the top of the pie; or place a ring of whipped cream (1 cup heavy cream beaten with ¼ cup confectioners sugar and 1 scant teaspoon vanilla) around the edge and fill the center with ice cream.

With this, pass Hot Fudge Sauce (page 503), or any other chocolate sauce. Luscious.

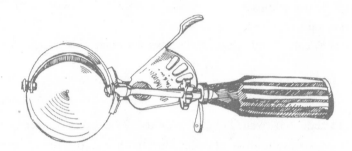

Palm Beach Chocolate Layer Cake

10 PORTIONS

3 ounces unsweetened chocolate
2 cups sifted cake flour
1 teaspoon baking soda
½ pound (2 sticks) butter
1 teaspoon vanilla extract
1 pound (2¼ cups, firmly packed) dark brown sugar
2 eggs
1 cup boiling water

Adjust rack to center of oven. Preheat oven to 375 degrees. Butter two round 9-inch layer-cake pans and dust all over lightly with fine, dry bread crumbs. Set aside.

Melt chocolate in the top of a double boiler over hot water, then set aside to cool. Sift together flour and baking soda and set aside.

In large bowl of electric mixer beat the butter a bit to soften it. Add vanilla. Gradually add the sugar and beat for a minute or two, scraping the bowl with a rubber spatula as necessary. Beat in the eggs and then the melted chocolate. Beat until smooth. On lowest speed alternately add the sifted dry ingredients in three additions and the boiling water, very gradually at first, in two additions, scraping the bowl as necessary with the rubber spatula.

It is a very thin liquid batter. Divide between prepared pans. Bake 30 minutes or until cakes come away from sides of pans and tops spring back when lightly touched.

Cool in pans on racks for about 5 minutes. Cover with racks and invert. Remove pans. Cover with racks and invert again to finish cooling right side up.

When cool, place one layer upside down on a cake plate protected with four strips of wax paper or baking parchment. Prepare the following:

PALM BEACH CHOCOLATE FILLING AND ICING

5 ounces unsweetened chocolate
3 ounces (¾ stick) butter
1 pound (3½ cups) confectioners sugar
2 eggs
1 tablespoon hot water
1 teaspoon vanilla extract

In a small, heavy saucepan over low heat, melt the chocolate and butter. Transfer to large bowl of electric mixer. Add all remaining ingredients at once. Starting at low speed and gradually increasing to high, beat until smooth, scraping bowl as necessary with a rubber spatula.

Use immediately, as icing forms a crust very quickly. Work quickly. Spread about one third over bottom layer (it will be a rather thin layer of filling). Cover with top layer, placed right side up so that both flat sides meet in the center. Pour remainder of icing over the top and quickly spread it on the top and sides of the cake.

Remove paper strips by pulling each one out by a narrow end (see page xxxi).

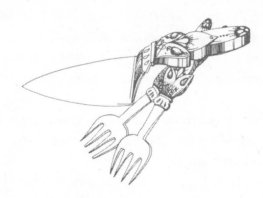

Palm Beach Chocolate Tube Cake

8 TO 10 PORTIONS

2 cups sifted cake flour
1 teaspoon baking powder
3 ounces unsweetened chocolate
¼ pound (1 stick) butter
1 cup boiling water
2 cups sugar
1 teaspoon vanilla extract
2 eggs, separated
1 teaspoon baking soda
½ cup sour cream
Pinch of salt

Adjust rack one-third up from bottom of oven. Preheat oven to 350 degrees. Butter a 9-inch tube pan. Line the bottom with paper cut to fit and butter the paper. Dust all over very lightly with fine, dry bread crumbs. Set aside.

Sift together flour and baking powder and set aside.

Combine chocolate, butter, and boiling water in a small saucepan over moderate heat. Stir until chocolate and butter are melted. Transfer to large bowl of electric mixer.

Remove and reserve 2 tablespoons of the sugar. Beat remaining sugar and vanilla into warm chocolate mixture. Beat in egg yolks, scraping bowl with rubber spatula to keep mixture smooth.

In a small bowl stir the baking soda into the sour cream and beat it into the chocolate mixture. On lowest speed add the sifted dry ingredients, scraping bowl with the rubber spatula and beating only until smooth. Remove from mixer.

Beat egg whites with salt until they hold a soft shape. Add the reserved sugar and continue to beat until the whites hold a point or are stiff but not dry. Fold a few large spoonfuls of the chocolate mixture into the whites, and then fold the whites into the remaining chocolate mixture.

The batter will be thin. Pour it into prepared pan. Bake for 1 hour or until a cake tester comes out dry and top springs back when lightly touched.

Cool cake in pan on a rack for about 5 minutes. Cover with a rack and invert. Remove pan and paper. Cover with a rack and invert again to finish cooling right side up.

Place cooled cake either side up on a cake plate protected with four strips of wax paper. Prepare the following:

ICING

8 ounces semisweet chocolate
¾ cup sour cream, at room temperature (see Note)
1 egg

Melt chocolate in top of small double boiler over hot water on moderate heat. Transfer to small bowl of electric mixer. Immediately beat in sour cream and egg, scraping the bowl with rubber spatula and beating until smooth.

If mixture is too thin or too soft, let it stand at room temperature for about 10 minutes, stirring occasionally, until very slightly thickened.

Reserve a few tablespoons of the icing and pour the balance over the top of the cake. Spread it over the top and sides.

Apply the reserved icing with a pastry bag fitted with a large star tube, forming 8 to 10 large rosettes on top of the cake; or, with a large spoon, drop 8 to 10 egg-shaped mounds.

Remove wax paper by pulling each strip by a narrow end (see page xxxi).

Note: If the sour cream is too cold, it will set the icing too quickly; it may be softened over hot water and then beaten again until smooth.

Sour Cream Chocolate Layer Cake

12 PORTIONS

3 ounces unsweetened chocolate
½ cup boiling water
2 cups sifted cake flour
1½ teaspoons baking powder
1 teaspoon baking soda
¼ teaspoon salt
6 ounces (1½ sticks) butter
2 teaspoons vanilla extract
1 cup granulated sugar
⅔ cup light brown sugar, firmly packed
3 eggs
1 cup sour cream

Adjust rack to center of oven and preheat oven to 375 degrees. Butter two 9-inch round layer-cake pans and dust both lightly with fine, dry bread crumbs.

In a small, heavy saucepan over low heat melt the chocolate with the boiling water. Stir occasionally with a small wire whisk until smooth. Set aside to cool.

Meanwhile, sift together flour, baking powder, baking soda, and salt. Set aside.

In large bowl of electric mixer beat the butter to soften a bit. Add vanilla, granulated sugar, and light brown sugar and beat well, scraping the bowl with a rubber spatula as necessary to keep mixture smooth. Beat in eggs one at a time, beating well after each.

Stir sour cream and cooled chocolate together until smooth and add to batter, beating only until mixed.

On lowest speed, add the sifted dry ingredients, continuing to scrape the bowl with a rubber spatula. Beat only until smooth.

Turn into prepared pans. With rubber spatula spread tops smooth and then run the batter up on the sides a bit, leaving the batter slightly lower in the centers.

Bake 35 minutes or until tops spring back when lightly touched and layers come away from sides of pans.

Cool in pans for about 5 minutes. Place racks over the cakes and invert. Remove pans. Cover with racks and invert again to cool right side up.

Prepare the following:

FILLING AND ICING
3 ounces unsweetened chocolate
2 tablespoons butter
3/4 cup sour cream
1 teaspoon vanilla extract
1/4 teaspoon salt
1 pound (3½ cups, packed) unsifted confectioners sugar

In top of small double boiler over hot water on low heat, melt chocolate and butter. Stir until smooth and remove from heat to cool completely.

In small bowl of electric mixer at low speed, beat sour cream, vanilla, and salt just to mix. Gradually beat in the sugar, scraping the bowl with a rubber spatula. When smooth, add cooled melted chocolate and beat at high speed for about ½ minute until very smooth.

Place four strips of wax paper or baking parchment around the edges of a cake plate to protect it while icing cake. Place one layer on the plate upside down. Spread with filling. Cover with second layer, right side up so that both bottom sides meet in the center. Cover the sides and then the top with remaining filling and icing, smoothing it with a long, narrow, metal spatula; then, if you wish, use the back of a teaspoon to form swirls and peaks all over the sides and top.

Remove paper by pulling each strip by a narrow end (see page xxxi).

Devil's Food Cake

A high, three-layer black cake with wonderful, fluffy 7-Minute Icing.

> 3 ounces unsweetened chocolate
> 2½ cups sifted cake flour
> 2 teaspoons baking soda
> ½ teaspoon salt
> ¼ pound (1 stick) butter
> 2 teaspoons vanilla extract
> 2½ cups dark brown sugar, firmly packed
> 3 eggs
> ½ cup buttermilk
> 1 cup boiling water

Adjust rack to center of oven. Preheat oven to 375 degrees. Butter three round 8-inch layer-cake pans. Dust bottoms with fine, dry bread crumbs.

Melt chocolate in top of small double boiler over hot water on moderate heat. Set aside. Sift together flour, baking soda, and salt. Set aside. In large bowl of electric mixer beat the butter to soften a bit. Add vanilla and sugar and beat for a minute or two. Beat in eggs one at a time, scraping the bowl with a rubber spatula as necessary to keep mixture blended. Continue to beat for 1 to 2 minutes after the last egg has been added. Beat in melted chocolate. On lowest speed add half of the sifted dry ingredients, then the buttermilk, and then the other half of the dry ingredients, scraping the bowl as necessary with the rubber spatula and beating only until smooth after each addition. Gradually beat in the boiling water.

Batter will be thin. Divide it among the prepared pans.

Bake for 25 minutes or until tops spring back when lightly touched and cakes come away from sides of pans.

Cool cakes in pans for about 5 minutes. Cover with racks or cookie sheets and invert. Remove pans. Cover with racks and invert again to finish cooling right side up.

When layers have cooled completely, use a long, thin, sharp knife to cut off any rises in the tops, making them level.

Place the bottom layer on a cake plate protected with four strips of wax paper or baking parchment around the outer edge. Prepare the following icing:

7-MINUTE ICING
    4 egg whites
    1½ cups sugar
    ¼ cup plus 1 tablespoon cold water
    1 teaspoon cream of tartar
    ⅛ teaspoon salt
    1½ teaspoons vanilla extract

Mix everything except the vanilla in the top of a large double boiler; it must have at least an 8- to 10-cup capacity. Place over hot water on moderate heat. Beat with electric mixer at high speed for about 5 minutes until mixture stands in peaks when beaters are withdrawn. Immediately, in order to stop the cooking, transfer mixture to large bowl of electric mixer. Add vanilla. Beat at high speed until mixture is smooth and stiff. Use immediately.

Stack and frost each layer, then cover sides and top of cake, pulling the icing up in irregular peaks, if you wish.

Remove paper strips, pulling each one out by a narrow end (see page xxxi).

Note: 7-Minute Icing does not freeze well. It is best to ice the cake the day it is to be served.

Montana Mountain Cake

10 PORTIONS

A high three-layer chocolate cake filled and iced with Caramel Coffee 7-Minute Icing.

3 ounces unsweetened chocolate
3 cups sifted cake flour
1½ teaspoons baking soda
½ teaspoon salt
6 ounces (1½ sticks) butter
1½ teaspoons vanilla extract
2¼ cups sugar
3 eggs
1½ cups ice water

For 8-inch pans adjust rack to center of oven. For 9-inch pans adjust two racks to divide oven in thirds. Preheat oven to 375 degrees. Butter three 8- or 9-inch round layer-cake pans and dust them lightly with fine, dry bread crumbs.

Melt the chocolate in top of small double boiler over hot water on moderate heat. Set aside. Sift together flour, baking soda, and salt and set aside. In large bowl of electric mixer beat the butter to soften a bit. Add vanilla and sugar and beat for a minute or two. Beat in eggs one at a time, scraping the bowl with a rubber spatula as necessary to keep the mixture well blended. Continue to beat for 2 to 3 minutes. Beat in the chocolate. On lowest speed alternately add sifted dry ingredients in three additions and ice water in two additions, continuing to scrape the bowl as necessary with the spatula and beating only until smooth after each addition.

Divide batter between prepared pans. Spread tops level and then push the batter up on the sides a bit so that the centers are slightly lower.

Bake 25 to 30 minutes or until tops spring back when lightly touched and cakes begin to come away from the sides of the pans.

Cool in pans for about 5 minutes. Cover with racks or cookie sheets and invert. Remove pans. Cover with racks and invert again to finish cooling right side up.

Place four strips of wax paper or baking parchment around the edges of a cake plate. Place one layer on the plate, right side up. Prepare the following icing:

CARAMEL COFFEE 7-MINUTE ICING

Follow recipe for 7-Minute Icing (page 57) with the following changes: Substitute 1½ cups light brown sugar (or 1 cup dark brown sugar and ½ cup granulated white sugar) for the sugar. Use strong coffee in place of the water (about 1 tablespoon instant coffee dissolved in ¼ cup plus 1 tablespoon hot water).

With a long, narrow, metal spatula spread icing over the layer. Place second layer on right side up. Spread with icing. Top with third layer, also right side up. Spread icing on sides and top.

With the spatula or with the back of a spoon, quickly pull the icing up in definite peaks all over the cake.

Remove wax paper strips by pulling each one out by a narrow end (see page xxxi).

Notes:
1. If you have used 8-inch pans, the finished cake will be about 6 to 7 inches high—startling! You will need large plates for serving.
2. Since 7-Minute Icing does not freeze well, it is best to ice the cake the day you are going to serve it.

Rum Cream Layer Cake

12 PORTIONS

Four light, white layers, generously brushed with rum, filled with whipped cream that is loaded with rum, and it is all covered with chocolate. An heirloom recipe—it is extraordinary.

2 cups sifted cake flour
2 teaspoons baking powder
¼ teaspoon baking soda
¼ teaspoon salt
½ cup orange juice (before squeezing juice, grate and reserve rind of 1 orange to use below)
3 tablespoons light rum
¼ pound (1 stick) butter
¼ teaspoon almond extract
½ teaspoon vanilla extract
1 cup sugar
2 eggs, separated
Finely grated rind of 1 orange

Adjust rack to center of oven. Preheat oven to 350 degrees. Butter two round 9-inch layer-cake pans, line the bottoms with paper, butter and flour the lined pans, and set aside.

Sift together flour, baking powder, baking soda, and salt. Set aside. Combine orange juice and rum and set aside.

In large bowl of electric mixer, beat the butter to soften a bit. Add almond and vanilla extracts, and ¾ cup of the sugar (reserve remaining ¼ cup). Beat for a few minutes until smooth. Add egg yolks. Beat well, scraping bowl with a rubber spatula as necessary to keep mixture smooth. On lowest speed alternately add sifted dry ingredients in three additions, and orange juice–rum mixture in two additions, scraping bowl with the rubber spatula and beating only until smooth after each addition. Remove from mixer and stir in grated orange rind.

In small bowl of electric mixer, on high speed, beat whites (with clean beaters) until they increase in volume and thicken slightly. Gradually add reserved ¼ cup of sugar and continue to beat until whites hold a definite shape—stiff, not dry. Fold into orange mixture.

Turn batter into prepared pans. With a rubber spatula, spread tops level and then run batter up on sides of pans a bit, making layers slightly lower in the centers.

Bake 20 to 23 minutes or until tops spring back when lightly touched and cakes come away from sides of pans. Remove from oven and cool in pans for 2 to 3 minutes. If necessary, cut around sides to release. Cover each layer with a rack, invert, remove pan and paper, cover with another rack, and invert again to finish cooling right side up.

When completely cool, with a long, thin, sharp knife cut each layer in half, making four thin layers. The baked layers will each be about 1 inch high, so that when you cut them you will end up with four ½-inch layers.

RUM CREAM FILLING
   1 tablespoon (1 envelope) unflavored gelatin
   3 tablespoons cold water
   1 cup light rum
   3 cups heavy cream
   ¾ cup confectioners sugar
   1 teaspoon vanilla extract

Sprinkle the gelatin over the water in a small, heatproof cup. Let stand 5 minutes. Stir in ¼ cup of the rum (reserve remaining ¾ cup). Place cup in shallow hot water (about halfway up the side of the cup) in a small saucepan or skillet over low heat until gelatin is dissolved. Remove from heat and set aside.

In large bowl of electric mixer, with bowl and beaters chilled, at high speed beat the cream, sugar, vanilla, and ¼ cup of the rum (reserve remaining ½ cup rum to brush on layers) until the cream barely starts to thicken. Quickly stir one or two spoonfuls of the partially whipped cream into the gelatin, and then add the gelatin all at once to the cream and continue to beat until firm enough to be used as a filling. (Be careful not to overbeat.) Remove from mixer.

The bottom cake layers should be placed upside down and the two top layers right side up, so that both original undersides meet in the center. Place the bottom layer on a cake plate protected with four strips of aluminum foil (see Note 1). Brush with 2 tablespoons of the reserved ½ cup rum. Spread with one third of the filling. Continue with remaining layers, rum, and filling. If any filling extends out beyond the layers, it should be removed.

Chill cake 1 to 2 hours (or more if you wish) in refrigerator, or about ½ hour in freezer, until cream filling is set.

Prepare the following icing:

CHOCOLATE ICING
    4 ounces unsweetened chocolate
    1 cup confectioners sugar
    2 tablespoons hot water
    2 eggs
    3 ounces (¾ stick) butter, at room temperature, cut in 4 pieces

Melt chocolate in top of small double boiler over hot water on moderate heat. Transfer to small bowl of electric mixer. Immediately add sugar, water, and eggs. Beat at moderately high speed until smooth, scraping bowl with a rubber spatula as necessary to keep mixture smooth. Beat in butter, one piece at a time, beating until smooth after each addition.

Pour over top of cake. Work quickly before chilled cake makes icing set. With a long, narrow metal spatula spread smooth, letting it run down the sides, then smooth the sides. Remove the foil strips, gently pulling each one out by a narrow end (see page xxxi).

Refrigerate the cake at least 1 hour before serving. But it may stand, refrigerated, overnight.

Optional: With a long, thin knife, mark the top into twelve portions. Place a Chocolate Cone (see directions, page 513), lying on its side, open end out, on each portion. Or eliminate Chocolate Cones and, before removing the foil strips, press chopped walnuts generously into the sides of the cake (not the top). Or place one large walnut half on each portion.

Notes:

1. Because the layers will be brushed with rum, they will be quite wet and would wet wax paper, which might tear when being removed; aluminum foil will not tear.

2. When filling the layers, if the weight of the cake presses the filling beyond the edge of the cake, spread the filling and chill it briefly in the freezer or refrigerator before covering it with the next layer of cake.

Rum Chocolate Layer Cake

1½ cups sifted cake flour
1½ teaspoons baking powder
¼ teaspoon salt
3 eggs
1½ cups sugar
¾ cup milk
3 ounces (¾ stick) butter
1 teaspoon vanilla extract

Adjust rack to center of oven. Preheat oven to 375 degrees. Butter two round 8-inch layer pans. Line the bottoms with paper. Butter the paper and dust lightly with flour.

Sift together flour, baking powder, and salt. Set aside. In small bowl of electric mixer at high speed, beat eggs until they are light lemon-colored. Reduce speed and gradually add sugar. Increase speed again and continue to beat for 5 minutes until the mixture forms a heavy ribbon when beaters are lifted.

Meanwhile, place milk and butter in a small saucepan over low-medium heat. It is best to have the milk and butter getting hot while you are beating the eggs. Otherwise the beaten eggs have to stand and wait too long. The milk should be quite hot by the time the eggs are beaten so that it doesn't take too long then to bring it to a boil.

After beating eggs for 5 minutes, beat in vanilla and transfer to large bowl of mixer. On low speed add the sifted dry ingredients, scraping the bowl with a rubber spatula as necessary and beating only until smooth.

Bring the milk and butter to a boil and, at low speed, gradually beat into the batter, scraping bowl with spatula. As soon as mixture is smooth turn it into prepared pans. Batter will be thin. Bake 30 to 35 minutes or until layers begin to come away from sides of pans and tops spring back when lightly touched.

Remove from oven. Let stand for a few minutes. If necessary, cut around edges to release. Cover each layer with a rack and invert. Remove pans and papers. Cover with racks and invert again to cool right side up.

When completely cool, using a long, thin, sharp knife, slice each 1-inch layer in half, making four ½-inch layers. Prepare the following buttercream:

RUM CHOCOLATE BUTTERCREAM
12 ounces semisweet chocolate
½ pound (2 sticks) butter
1 teaspoon instant coffee
3 egg yolks, jumbo or extra-large (or 4 large or medium)
½ cup light rum (to be brushed on cooled layers)

In the top of a small double boiler over hot water on moderate heat, melt the chocolate. When partially melted remove from heat and stir until completely melted and smooth. Set aside to cool.

In small bowl of electric mixer beat the butter and coffee to mix. Add yolks individually, beating well after each. Beat in the cooled chocolate, beating until smooth and slightly lightened in color.

Place four strips of aluminum foil (see Note 1) around the edges of a cake plate. (The two bottom layers should be placed upside down and the two top layers right side up so that the two cake bottoms meet in the center.) Place one layer on the plate. Brush bottom layer with about 2 tablespoons of the rum. (Reserve remaining rum.)

Spread the buttercream rather thin over the first layer. Continue with the remaining layers, brushing both sides of each layer with rum and then spreading the tops with buttercream. Reserve about ¾ cup buttercream to ice the top and sides. Then spread the reserved buttercream over the sides and finally over the top. Remove aluminum foil strips, pulling each one gently by a narrow end (see page xxxi).

Refrigerate for 1 to 2 hours to set the buttercream (or overnight if you wish), but remove from refrigerator 15 to 20 minutes before serving.

Notes:

1. Because the layers will be generously brushed with rum, they will be quite wet and would wet wax paper, which might tear when being removed; aluminum foil will not tear.

2. If you wish, reserve some of the icing to decorate the cake, using a pastry bag and a star tube.

Coconut Layer Cake

2½ cups sifted cake flour
1 tablespoon baking powder
¼ teaspoon salt
¼ pound (1 stick) butter
1 teaspoon vanilla extract
1½ cups sugar
2 eggs
1 cup milk
Finely grated rind of 1 large orange (or 2 small)
A few spoonfuls of melted and strained apricot preserves

Adjust rack to center of oven. Preheat oven to 375 degrees. Butter two 9-inch round layer-cake pans. Line the bottoms with paper. Butter the paper and dust all over lightly with flour. Set aside.

Sift together flour, baking powder, and salt and set aside.

In large bowl of electric mixer, beat the butter to soften a bit. Add the vanilla and sugar and beat for a few minutes. Add the eggs and beat until smooth. On lowest speed add the dry ingredients in three additions—alternately with the milk in two additions—scraping the bowl with a rubber spatula as necessary and beating only until smooth after each addition. Remove from mixer and stir in orange rind.

Divide batter between prepared pans. Tilt and shake pans gently to level batter. Bake 25 to 30 minutes or until cakes come away from sides of pans and tops spring back when lightly touched.

Remove from oven. Let stand about 5 minutes. Cover with racks or cookie sheets and invert. Remove pans and papers. Cover with racks and invert again to cool right side up.

When layers have cooled completely, place four strips of wax paper or baking parchment around a cake plate and place one layer on the plate, upside down. Spread with a thin layer of smooth preserves, reserving some for second layer. Prepare following icing:

FLUFFY WHITE ICING
(A different 7-Minute Icing)

> **4 egg whites**
> **¼ cup light corn syrup**
> **2 tablespoons water**
> **2½ cups confectioners sugar**
> **Pinch of salt**
> **1 teaspoon vanilla extract**
> **¼ teaspoon almond extract**

> **8 to 10 ounces (3 to 4 cups) grated coconut (see Note 1)**

Mix all ingredients except vanilla and almond extracts in the top of a large double boiler; it must have at least an 8- to 10-cup capacity. Place over hot water on moderate heat. Beat with an electric mixer at high speed for 5 to 6 minutes until mixture stands in peaks when beaters are lifted.

Immediately, in order to stop the cooking, transfer to large bowl of electric mixer. Add vanilla and almond extracts and beat at high speed for about 5 minutes more, scraping sides and bottom of bowl almost continuously with a rubber spatula, until mixture is smooth and very thick. Use immediately.

Spread one third of the icing on the bottom layer. Sprinkle with one third of the coconut.

Put on second layer, right side up, so that the two cake bottoms meet in the middle. Spread the top with remaining apricot preserves. Use another third of the icing around the sides and then the remaining third on the top. Quickly spread with a long, narrow metal spatula to smooth the top and sides.

With the palm of your hand, press another third of the coconut onto the sides and sprinkle the remaining coconut evenly over the top.

Remove the paper strips, pulling each one out by a narrow end (see page xxxi).

Notes:

1. Fresh coconut, freshly grated, is a rare treat. If possible, use it. (It is available in some frozen food departments and in some health food stores.) Fresh coconut is moist. If you use canned coconut, use the moist type and the most finely shredded.
2. When serving, dip knife in hot water before making each cut to prevent the icing from sticking to the knife.
3. This icing does not freeze well. It is best to ice the cake the day it is to be served.

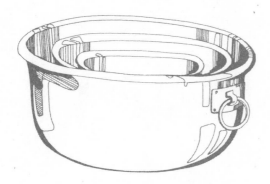

Coffee Cakes, Nut Cakes, Fruit Cakes, and Cakes Made with Fruit

Budapest Coffee Cake

12 PORTIONS

This is one of the most popular recipes in all of my books. I have received love letters and a variety of proposals and propositions all because of this cake. Watch out.

NUT FILLING

3/4 cup firmly packed dark brown sugar

1 tablespoon cinnamon

1 tablespoon powdered, unsweetened cocoa

2 to 3 tablespoons currants or raisins, coarsely chopped (see page xxv)

3 1/2 ounces (1 cup) walnuts, cut fine

In a small bowl stir brown sugar, cinnamon, and cocoa to mix thoroughly. Stir in the currants or raisins and then the walnuts, and set aside.

CAKE BATTER

3 cups sifted all-purpose flour

1 1/2 teaspoons baking powder

1 1/2 teaspoons baking soda

1/2 teaspoon salt

6 ounces (1 1/2 sticks) butter

2 teaspoons vanilla extract

1 1/2 cups sugar

3 eggs

2 cups sour cream

Adjust rack one-third up from the bottom of the oven. Preheat oven to 375 degrees. Butter a 10-inch (12- to 14-cup capacity) Bundt pan. (This is best baked in a Bundt pan, but a tube pan of similar size may be substituted.) Even if the pan is non-stick, it should be buttered for this recipe.

Sift together flour, baking powder, baking soda, and salt. Set aside. In large bowl of electric mixer beat the butter to soften it a bit. Add vanilla and sugar and beat for a minute or two. Add eggs individually, beating until thoroughly incorporated after each. Scrape bowl with a rubber spatula as necessary to keep mixture smooth, and beat briefly at high speed for a minute or so until mixture is very smooth.

On lowest speed alternately add dry ingredients in three additions and sour cream in two additions, continuing to scrape the bowl as necessary with the rubber spatula and beating only until smooth after each addition.

Spread a thin layer of the batter in the bottom of the pan. Sprinkle very generously with about one-third of the nut filling. Continue making layers, four of the batter and three of the filling. The top layer should be batter. It will take a bit of patience to spread the batter thin. It will be easier if the batter is placed on by many small spoonfuls and then spread with the back of the spoon, instead of just being dropped on in two or three large amounts.

Bake for about an hour or until cake tester comes out dry and the top feels firm and springy. Be sure it is done. Remove from oven. Leave cake in pan for 5 minutes, no longer. The cake should be hot when glaze is applied.

Meanwhile, prepare glaze.

GLAZE
  2 cups confectioners sugar
  1 teaspoon vanilla extract
  2 to 3 tablespoons hot milk

In a small bowl, with a rubber spatula, mix sugar with vanilla and about 2 tablespoons of the hot milk. Very gradually add more milk, just a bit at a time, using only enough to make a semifluid mixture about as thick as thick cream sauce.

Cover cake with a rack and invert over a large piece of wax paper or aluminum foil. Remove pan, leaving cake upside down. Immediately pour on the glaze—just pour it on quickly, don't spread it or work over it—and let it run down the sides unevenly.

When the glaze has set, use a large spatula to transfer cake to cake plate. Serve the cake while still slightly warm or after it has cooled completely—even the next day.

Southern Nut Cake

16 OR MORE GENEROUS PORTIONS, EACH 2 OR 3 THIN SLICES

This large cake is almost solid nuts, with just enough batter to hold them together—dramatic, delicious, extravagant. It is best to make this a day ahead.

> 1 pound (4½ cups) walnuts
> 1 pound (4½ cups) pecans
> 3½ cups sifted all-purpose flour
> 2 teaspoons baking powder
> ½ teaspoon mace
> ¼ teaspoon salt
> ¾ cup milk
> ¼ cup brandy or bourbon
> ¾ pound (3 sticks) butter
> 2 cups sugar
> 6 eggs
> Optional: 3 or 4 tablespoons additional brandy or bourbon

Adjust oven rack one-third of the way up from the bottom of the oven. Preheat oven to 325 degrees. Butter a 10 x 4-inch tube pan. Line the bottom with paper cut to fit. Butter the paper and dust all over lightly with fine, dry bread crumbs.

Break or cut the nuts into large pieces. They should *not* be finely chopped. Place the nuts in your largest mixing bowl, 6- to 8-quart capacity. If you don't have a very large mixing bowl, use a saucepan or roasting pan instead.

Sift together flour, baking powder, mace, and salt. Set aside. Combine the milk and ¼ cup brandy or bourbon and set aside.

In large bowl of electric mixer, beat the butter to soften it a bit. Add sugar and beat for a few minutes, scraping the bowl as necessary with a rubber spatula. On moderate speed, add eggs one at a time, beating until thoroughly incorporated after each and scraping the bowl with the rubber spatula as necessary to keep everything well mixed. Increase speed and beat for about 3 minutes until very light and fluffy. Mixture might look curdled at this point—O.K.

On lowest speed alternately add the sifted dry ingredients in three additions and the milk mixture in two, scraping the bowl as necessary with the spatula and beating only until smooth after each addition. Pour the batter over the nuts. Stir with a large wooden spatula or large wooden spoon until the nuts are all coated with the batter. Turn into pan. Spread the top level.

Bake for 1¾ hours or until a cake tester comes out dry. Remove from oven and place cake pan on a rack. Sprinkle or brush optional brandy or bourbon over top of hot cake. Let cake cool in pan for about 20 minutes.

Cover cake with a rack and invert to remove pan and paper. Cover with another rack and carefully invert again to cool. Let cake stand overnight before cutting. Cut with a very sharp knife into thin slices.

Texas Fruit Cake

12 SLICES

T his cake is so thick with fruit and nuts it is almost a confection. Recipe may be multiplied by any number provided you have a very large container for mixing it in. In place of a large bowl use a roasting pan or a dishpan if necessary.

8 ounces (1 cup) pitted dates, left whole
1 cup cut-up candied orange peel, cut in ½-inch pieces, tightly packed
1 cup (4 to 5 slices) candied pineapple, each slice cut in 8 to 10 wedges
½ cup sifted all-purpose flour
8 ounces (2½ cups) mixed walnut and pecan halves, left whole
½ teaspoon baking powder
¼ teaspoon salt
2 eggs, separated
½ cup sugar
½ teaspoon vanilla extract
2 tablespoons bourbon

Adjust oven rack one-third of the way up from the bottom. Preheat oven to 325 degrees. Butter a 9 x 5 x 3-inch loaf pan. Then cut two strips of aluminum foil to line the pan, one for the length and one for the width. Put them into place carefully; the foil should remain smooth. Brush with melted butter and dust lightly with fine, dry bread crumbs. Set aside.

Pick over the dates carefully to see that there are no pits or stems left in them.

Place the dates, orange peel, and pineapple in a large mixing bowl. Add 2 tablespoons of the flour (reserve remaining flour) and toss with your fingers to separate and coat each piece of fruit thoroughly. Add the nuts and toss again. Set aside.

Sift the remaining flour with the baking powder and salt and set aside.

Place the egg yolks in the small bowl of an electric mixer. Remove and reserve 2 tablespoons of the sugar. Add the remaining sugar and beat for about

3 minutes until light. Reduce the speed to low and add the vanilla and bourbon, and then the sifted dry ingredients, scraping the bowl with a rubber spatula, and beating only until smooth.

Beat the egg whites until they hold a soft shape. Add the reserved sugar and continue to beat until the whites hold a firm shape, or are stiff but not dry. Fold the egg whites into the egg yolk mixture.

Pour the batter over the prepared fruit and nuts. Fold together and then transfer to prepared pan. Cover with plastic wrap, and, with your fingers and the palm of your hand, press down very firmly, especially in the corners of the pan. Make the top as level as possible. Remove plastic wrap.

Bake 1½ hours until the cake is semifirm to the touch, covering the top loosely with foil for the last half hour of baking. Remove from oven and cool in pan for 20 minutes. Cover with a rack and invert. Remove pan and aluminum foil. Cover with another rack and invert again to cool, right side up.

When cool, wrap airtight, and refrigerate for at least several hours, or a day or two if you wish. Freeze for longer storage.

It is best to slice the cake in the kitchen, and arrange the slices on a tray, or wrap them individually in clear cellophane. Turn the cake upside down to slice it. Use a very sharp, thin knife. If you have any trouble, hold the knife under running, hot water before cutting each slice. Cut with a sawing motion. It is difficult to cut this cake into very thin slices; for smaller portions cut each slice in half.

Note: Fruit cakes slice best if very cold; I think they also taste best when cold.

P.S. *A few spoonfuls of diced candied ginger is great—along with the other fruits.*

Creole Christmas Cake

16 PORTIONS

Almost 6 pounds of rich butter cake thick with raisins and nuts. This is traditionally served during the Christmas holidays, but please don't wait. I recommend it now—whenever it is.

Finely grated rind of 2 large lemons
½ cup lemon juice
4 cups sifted all-purpose flour
2 teaspoons baking powder
3 cups (1 15-ounce box) seedless raisins (you may use all light raisins but I prefer 2 cups of light and 1 cup of dark)
1¼ pounds (5½ cups) pecans, whole halves or in large pieces
1 pound (4 sticks) butter
2 cups sugar
6 eggs

Adjust rack one-third up from the bottom of the oven. Preheat oven to 325 degrees. Butter 10 x 4-inch tube pan. Line the bottom with paper cut to fit. Butter the paper and dust all over lightly with fine, dry bread crumbs.

Mix the lemon rind and juice and set aside.

Sift together the flour and baking powder into a 6- to 8-quart mixing bowl. If you do not have a large enough bowl, use a saucepan, roasting pan, or a dishpan. Add the raisins and, with your fingers, stir and toss to separate and coat each raisin thoroughly. Stir in the nuts.

In the large bowl of an electric mixer beat the butter to soften it a bit. Add the sugar and beat for about a minute or two. Add the eggs one at a time, scraping the bowl with a rubber spatula and beating after each until thoroughly incorporated. Remove from mixer and stir in the lemon rind and juice. Pour over the raisin-nut mixture and, with a heavy wooden spatula, stir until the flour is completely absorbed.

The batter will be stiff. Spoon it into the prepared pan and spread the top level. Let stand for 10 minutes and then place in preheated oven.

Bake for 1 hour and 50 to 55 minutes until the cake is well browned and a cake tester inserted all the way to the bottom comes out dry.

Remove from oven and let stand for 10 to 15 minutes. Cover with a rack and invert. Remove pan and paper. Cover with a rack and invert again to cool right side up.

When completely cool wrap in plastic wrap or aluminum foil and let stand for at least 10 to 12 hours or freeze for 1 to 2 hours before cutting. Cut in thin slices.

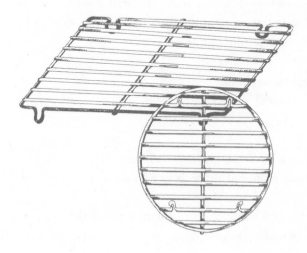

Toasted Almond Butter Cake

8 PORTIONS

A loaf cake that calls for almonds three ways: chopped, ground, and slivered.

⅓ cup blanched almonds, very finely chopped, not ground, for coating the
    pan (if the pieces are not small enough they won't stick to the pan.)
1⅓ cups sifted all-purpose flour
1 teaspoon baking powder
5 ounces (1¼ sticks) butter
½ teaspoon almond extract
1 cup sugar
3 eggs
3 ounces (generous ½ cup) blanched almonds
⅓ cup slivered, blanched almonds (see Note)

Adjust rack about one-third up from the bottom of the oven. Preheat oven to 350 degrees. Generously butter a loaf pan measuring 9 x 5 x 3 inches. Coat it all over with the finely chopped almonds.

Sift flour with baking powder and set aside. In small bowl of electric mixer beat the butter with the almond extract. Gradually add the sugar and beat at high speed for 5 minutes until very light. Scrape the bowl with a rubber spatula as necessary to keep the mixture smooth.

Add the eggs one at a time, beating well after each and beating for 2 minutes after the last one.

Place the 3 ounces of almonds in the bowl of the food processor fitted with the metal chopping blade. Add about 2 tablespoons of the sifted dry ingredients (reserve remaining sifted ingredients) and process for 20 to 30 seconds until the nuts are ground fine.

Add the ground almonds and then the reserved sifted ingredients to the butter mixture and beat only until the mixture is smooth.

Turn into prepared pan. Run batter up on sides of pan a bit, forming a slight trench down the middle.

Sprinkle generously with the slivered almonds, placing them heavily around the outer edges of the cake rather than at the center. Press them a little way into the batter.

Bake 1 hour and 10 minutes or until a cake tester comes out dry. Remove from oven. Cool in pan on a rack for about 15 minutes. Cut around sides to release cake.

To remove the cake from the pan without losing the topping, lay a piece of aluminum foil on top of the cake. Turn it down loosely around the sides. Place a pot holder or folded kitchen towel lightly over the foil. Turn the pan upside down into the palm of your right hand. With your left hand remove the pan and gently place a rack on the cake. Now invert it, right side up, to finish cooling on the rack.

Optional: Top of cooled cake may be sprinkled with confectioners sugar through a fine strainer.

Note: Regarding "slivered" almonds: Almonds cut in thin slices are called "sliced." Those cut in fatter oblongs, or julienne style, are called "slivered." For this recipe the slivered almonds are preferable—sliced almonds would burn. They are available in packages in most supermarkets already cut. Or you can cut them yourself. Uneven pieces look great.

Danish Loaf Cake

2 LOAVES, EACH 6 TO 8 PORTIONS

This unusual recipe starts with whipped cream. It is an old classic and established technique, and has been used for many years—not only in Denmark.

> 3¾ ounces (¾ cup) blanched almonds, very finely chopped, not ground, for coating the pans (if the pieces are not small enough they won't stick to the pans)
> 3 cups sifted all-purpose flour
> 1 tablespoon plus 1 teaspoon baking powder
> ½ teaspoon salt
> 2 cups heavy cream
> 2 teaspoons vanilla extract
> ½ teaspoon almond extract
> 2 cups sugar
> 4 eggs
> 3½ ounces (¾ cup) pignolias (pine nuts)

Adjust oven rack one-third up from the bottom of the oven. Preheat oven to 375 degrees. Heavily butter two 9 x 5 x 3-inch loaf pans. Coat the sides and bottoms of both pans with the finely chopped almonds.

Sift together flour, baking powder, and salt. Set aside. In large bowl of electric mixer, with bowl and beaters chilled, whip the cream with vanilla and almond extracts until it holds a shape. On medium speed quickly beat in the sugar all at once, and then the eggs, one at a time. (Adding the eggs will thin the cream a bit.) On lowest speed add the dry ingredients, scraping the bowl with a rubber spatula as necessary and beating only until smooth. Place about one quarter of the batter in each pan. Spread to level a bit. Sprinkle about 2 tablespoons of the pignolias into each pan. Cover evenly with the remaining batter. Smooth the tops. Sprinkle with remaining pignolias, placing them more heavily around the outer edges than in the center.

Bake 1 hour or until the cakes test done. The tops of the cakes will crack the long way. They are done when the centers of the cracks feel firm and dry when lightly touched, and when a cake tester comes out dry. Place the cake pans on a rack and apply glaze immediately while cakes are still in pans.

GLAZE
⅓ cup kirsch
⅓ cup sugar

Stir kirsch and sugar together immediately before using. (They will not blend—that's O.K.) Brush on hot loaves. Let loaves cool in pans until they are tepid and can be handled comfortably.

With a small, sharp knife cut around the sides to loosen. Do not cut deeply—just around the upper edge.

To remove the cakes from the pans, lay a piece of aluminum foil on each cake and fold down loosely on the sides. Place a pot holder or folded kitchen towel lightly over the foil. Turn the pan upside down into the palm of your right hand. With your left hand remove the pan and gently place a rack on the cake. Now invert it, right side up, to finish cooling on the rack.

Note: This recipe may be easily divided to make only one loaf, but the cake keeps very well for several days or, of course, it may be frozen.

Coffee Cakes, Nut Cakes, Fruit Cakes, and Cakes Made with Fruit   83

Coffee-Walnut Loaf

3½ ounces (1 cup) walnuts, broken into large pieces
1½ cups sifted all-purpose flour
2 teaspoons baking powder
¼ teaspoon salt
¼ pound (1 stick) butter
2 teaspoons vanilla extract
1 tablespoon plus 1 teaspoon instant coffee
1 cup sugar
2 eggs, separated
½ cup milk
½ ounce semisweet chocolate, ground or chopped very fine

Adjust oven rack one-third up from bottom of oven. Preheat oven to 375 degrees. Butter a 9 x 5 x 3-inch loaf pan. Dust pan lightly with fine, dry bread crumbs.

Toss walnuts with 1 teaspoon of the flour and set aside. Sift remaining flour with baking powder and salt. Set aside.

In small bowl of electric mixer beat the butter to soften it a bit. Beat in the vanilla and instant coffee.

Remove and reserve 2 or 3 tablespoons of the sugar. Add remaining sugar and beat for about 2 minutes. Add the egg yolks and continue to beat for another minute or two. On lowest speed alternately add dry ingredients in three additions and milk in two additions, scraping the bowl with a rubber spatula as necessary and beating only until smooth after each addition. Remove from mixer. Stir in the nuts.

In a small bowl beat the egg whites until they hold a soft shape. Add the reserved 2 or 3 tablespoons of sugar and continue to beat until the whites hold a point. Fold them into the batter.

Place about half of the batter in the pan. Spread it level. Sprinkle with the chocolate, and cover with remaining batter. Spread the top level.

Bake 55 minutes to 1 hour or until a cake tester comes out dry. Cool in the pan for 5 to 10 minutes. Cover with a rack and invert. Remove pan and cover with another rack. Invert again to cool.

Carrot Loaf

1 LARGE LOAF

Moist and dark. This is delicious and easy.

2½ cups sifted all-purpose flour
2 teaspoons baking powder
1 teaspoon baking soda
½ teaspoon salt
1 teaspoon cinnamon
5 ounces (1 cup) raisins
3 to 4 medium-size carrots (to make 1 cup grated and packed)
2½ ounces (¾ cup) walnuts, cut or broken into medium-size pieces
1 cup dark brown sugar, firmly packed
2 eggs
1 cup milk
2 ounces (½ stick) melted butter

Adjust rack one-third up from bottom of oven. Preheat oven to 400 degrees. Butter an 8- to 10-cup capacity loaf pan. Dust it very lightly with fine, dry bread crumbs.

Sift together the flour, baking powder, baking soda, salt, and cinnamon and set aside.

Place the raisins in a large mixing bowl and with your fingers separate them thoroughly if stuck together.

Scrub the carrots to clean them—it is not necessary to peel them. Grate them fine on a grater. Pack down into a measuring cup to measure 1 cup, packed. Add carrots, walnuts, and brown sugar to the raisins and stir to mix.

Beat eggs lightly just to mix. Beat in the milk and the melted butter. Stir into the carrot mixture. Add sifted dry ingredients and stir with a rubber spatula, scraping the bowl and mixing only until thoroughly blended.

Turn into prepared loaf pan. Shake gently to level. Bake in preheated oven for 55 to 60 minutes or until a cake tester comes out dry.

Cool in pan on a rack for 5 minutes. Cover with a rack or a small cookie sheet. Invert and remove pan. Cover with a rack and invert again to cool, right side up.

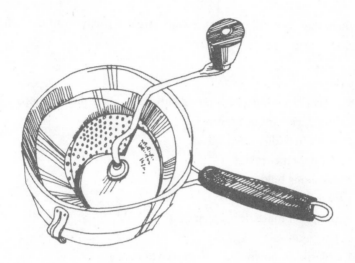

Creole Applesauce Cake with Rum or Brandy

12 TO 18 PORTIONS

A dark date-nut cake. Plan to marinate the raisins and dates for several hours or longer.

    5 ounces (1 cup) raisins
    8 ounces (1 cup, packed) pitted soft dates (each date cut into 3 or 4 pieces)
    1/3 cup dark rum or brandy
    2 cups sifted all-purpose flour
    1 tablespoon cornstarch
    2 teaspoons baking soda
    1 teaspoon cinnamon
    1/2 teaspoon mace or nutmeg
    1/2 teaspoon salt
    1 tablespoon powdered, unsweetened cocoa
    1/4 pound (1 stick) butter
    1 cup sugar
    2 eggs
    15 ounces (1 1/2 cups) applesauce
    7 ounces (2 cups) pecan halves or large pieces
    Optional: Additional rum or brandy

Place raisins and dates in a 2-cup jar with a leakproof cover. Add rum or brandy. Let stand for several hours, or overnight or longer if you wish, turning jar occasionally from side to side and top to bottom.

Adjust rack to center of oven. Preheat oven to 375 degrees. Butter a 9 x 13 x 2-inch pan. Dust it with fine, dry bread crumbs and set aside.

Sift together the flour, cornstarch, baking soda, cinnamon, mace or nutmeg, salt, and cocoa. Set aside.

In large bowl of electric mixer beat the butter to soften it a bit. Add the sugar and beat for a minute or two, scraping the bowl occasionally with a rubber spatula. Add eggs one at a time, beating after each until thoroughly incorporated.

On low speed mix in half of the dry ingredients, then the applesauce, and finally the remaining dry ingredients, scraping the bowl with the rubber spatula as necessary and beating only until incorporated after each addition.

Remove from mixer. Stir in raisins and dates with any remaining rum or brandy, and then stir in the nuts.

Turn the batter into the pan. Spread the top level. Bake 45 to 50 minutes or until top springs back firmly when lightly touched.

Cool in pan on a rack for 10 minutes. Invert onto a rack or cookie sheet. Remove pan and invert again onto a rack to finish cooling right side up. Additional rum or brandy may be sprinkled over the top of the still-warm cake.

Transfer to a cutting board. Cut, preferably with a long, serrated knife, into twelve oblongs. Or cut lengthwise and then across into 1-inch slices and arrange overlapping on a serving tray.

Serve as is or with a spoonful of Ginger Cream (page 499).

Date-Nut Cake Squares

8 ounces (1 cup, packed) pitted soft dates (each date cut into 3 or 4 pieces)
¼ pound (1 stick) butter, at room temperature
1 teaspoon baking soda
1 cup boiling water
1½ cups sifted all-purpose flour
1 teaspoon baking powder
1 egg
1 teaspoon vanilla extract
½ cup sugar
3½ ounces (1 cup) walnuts or pecans, broken into large pieces
Optional: Confectioners sugar

Put dates, butter, and baking soda in a large bowl. Pour on boiling water. Stir until butter melts. Set aside to cool completely.

Adjust rack to center of oven. Preheat oven to 400 degrees. Butter a 9-inch square cake pan.

Sift together flour and baking powder. Set aside. In a small bowl, stir egg, vanilla, and sugar just to mix. When date mixture is cool, stir the egg mixture into it and then the flour mixture. Stir in the nuts. Turn into pan and tilt the pan to level batter.

Bake 25 to 30 minutes or until top is well browned and springs back firmly when lightly touched. Cool in the pan for 5 to 10 minutes. Cover with a rack and invert. Remove pan. Cover with another rack and invert again to cool right side up.

Cover top with confectioners sugar through a fine strainer or with the following caramel icing.

CARAMELIZED SUGAR ICING

⅓ cup heavy cream
3 ounces (¾ stick) butter
2 tablespoons granulated sugar
2 cups confectioners sugar
½ teaspoon vanilla extract
Optional: 9 to 12 walnut or pecan halves

Heat cream and butter in a small saucepan and keep it warm over low heat.

Meanwhile, caramelize the granulated sugar in a medium-size heavy frying pan (9½ to 10 inches in diameter). Stir with a wooden spatula over moderate heat until it turns a rich, golden brown.

Pour hot cream all at once over caramelized granulated sugar. Be careful—it will bubble up hard. Keep stirring over heat until caramel melts and mixture is smooth.

Transfer to small bowl of electric mixer. Add confectioners sugar all at once, then vanilla, and beat only until smooth. If icing is too thick, thin it slightly with just a few drops of additional heavy cream. Use immediately. Pour it over the top of the cake. Quickly spread with a long, narrow metal spatula.

Optional: Mark the top in nine or twelve portions with a long knife, pressing down gently just to score the icing. Top each portion with half a walnut or pecan.

Trinidad Torte

2 cups sifted all-purpose flour
1 teaspoon baking powder
1 teaspoon baking soda
4 ounces (1 generous cup) walnuts
½ pound (2 sticks) butter
1 cup sugar
3 eggs, separated
¾ cup sour cream
Finely grated rind of 1 large orange
Finely grated rind of 2 lemons
⅛ teaspoon salt

Adjust rack one-third of the way up from the bottom of the oven and preheat oven to 350 degrees. Butter a 9 x 2½- or 3-inch springform pan and coat it lightly with fine, dry bread crumbs.

Sift together flour, baking powder, and baking soda. Add a few spoonfuls of the sifted dry ingredients to the nuts. Place in bowl of food processor fitted with the metal chopping blade and process for 20 to 30 seconds until the nuts are ground fine. Set aside.

In small bowl of electric mixer beat the butter to soften it a bit. Remove and reserve about 3 tablespoons of the sugar. Add the remaining sugar to the butter and beat well. Beat in the egg yolks one at a time. On lowest speed, alternately add the sifted dry ingredients in three additions with the sour cream in two additions, scraping the bowl as necessary with a rubber spatula to keep mixture smooth, and beating only until incorporated after each addition.

Transfer to a large bowl. Stir in the nuts and grated rinds.

Beat the whites with the salt until they hold a soft shape. Add the reserved sugar and continue to beat until the whites hold a straight point when the beaters are raised, or are stiff but not dry. Fold them into the batter. Pour into pan and level top by shaking pan briskly back and forth.

Bake 1 hour or until a cake tester comes out dry. A few minutes before removing cake from oven prepare the following glaze:

GLAZE
   ¾ cup sugar
   2 tablespoons orange juice
   2 tablespoons lemon juice

Mix ingredients in a small saucepan. Bring to a boil, stirring occasionally to dissolve the sugar.

When cake is removed from the oven, place the cake pan on a rack, and quickly prick all over the top with a small, sharp knife. Gradually brush the hot glaze over the hot cake until it is all absorbed. Let the cake cool completely in the pan.

When completely cool, remove the sides of the springform. Cover with a rack and invert to remove the bottom of the pan. If the bottom does not lift easily, use a small knife or spatula to release a bit at one edge and then the bottom will slip off. Immediately cover with a cake plate and invert again.

Pumpkin Cake

3 cups sifted all-purpose flour
2 teaspoons baking soda
2 teaspoons baking powder
1 tablespoon cinnamon
½ teaspoon powdered ginger
¼ teaspoon powdered cloves
¼ teaspoon nutmeg
¼ teaspoon allspice
1 teaspoon salt
5 ounces (1 cup) raisins, dark, light, or mixed
3½ ounces (1 cup) walnuts, broken into medium-size pieces
1 1-pound can (2 cups) pumpkin (plain pumpkin, not pie filling)
2 cups sugar
1¼ cups safflower oil, corn oil, or other salad oil (not olive oil)
4 eggs
Optional: Confectioners sugar

Adjust rack one-third up from the bottom of oven and preheat to 350 degrees. Butter a 10 x 4½-inch tube pan. Line the bottom with paper cut to fit and butter the paper.

Sift together the flour, baking soda, baking powder, cinnamon, ginger, cloves, nutmeg, allspice, and salt. Add a tablespoon of the sifted dry ingredients to the raisins in a small bowl. With your fingers, toss the raisins to separate them and coat each one with the dry ingredients. Stir in the nuts and set aside.

In large bowl of electric mixer, place the pumpkin, sugar, and oil. Beat at medium speed until smooth. Add the eggs individually, beating after each until incorporated.

On low speed add the sifted dry ingredients, scraping the bowl with a rubber spatula and beating only until smooth. Remove from mixer. Stir in raisins and nuts.

Turn into the prepared pan. Rotate pan briskly to level top.

Bake 1 hour and 5 minutes or until a cake tester comes out dry. Cool on a rack for about 10 minutes. The baked cake will only fill about three-quarters of the pan.

Cover cake with a rack and invert. Remove pan and paper. Cover with another rack and invert again. Cool right side up on the rack.

When cool, top may be sprinkled with confectioners sugar through a fine strainer.

Serve as is or with a generous spoonful of Ginger Cream (page 499).

Note: Plain canned pumpkin is not always available. At Thanksgiving time, when it is easy to find, I suggest that you stock up on it for this cake, which is delicious all year.

Blueberry Crumb Cake

9 TO 12 PORTIONS

Especially wonderful!

2 cups fresh blueberries

Pick over and wash the blueberries in a large bowl of cold water. Drain in a sieve or colander. Turn them out onto a towel. Pat them lightly with towel to dry. Set aside in a single layer on the towel to dry completely.

TOPPING

$\frac{1}{3}$ cup sifted all-purpose flour

$\frac{1}{2}$ cup sugar

1 teaspoon cinnamon

2 ounces ($\frac{1}{2}$ stick) butter

Adjust rack to the center of the oven. Preheat oven to 375 degrees. Butter a 9-inch square baking pan. Coat it well, bottom and sides, with fine, dry bread crumbs. Set aside.

Prepare the topping: In a small bowl mix flour, sugar, and cinnamon. With a pastry blender cut in the butter until the mixture resembles coarse crumbs. Set aside.

CAKE

2 cups sifted all-purpose flour

2 teaspoons baking powder

$\frac{1}{2}$ teaspoon salt

2 ounces ($\frac{1}{2}$ stick) butter

1 teaspoon vanilla extract

$\frac{3}{4}$ cup sugar

1 egg

$\frac{1}{2}$ cup milk

Finely grated rind of 1 lemon
½ cup walnuts, cut medium fine
Optional: Confectioners sugar

Sift together the flour, baking powder, and salt. Place the dried blueberries in a large bowl. Sprinkle with about 1½ tablespoons of the sifted dry ingredients. Using a rubber spatula, toss and turn gently to flour the blueberries without crushing them. Set aside both the floured berries and also the remaining sifted dry ingredients.

In small bowl of electric mixer, beat the butter to soften it a bit. Beat in vanilla and sugar and beat for 1 minute. Add the egg and beat for 1 minute more. On lowest speed alternately add remaining sifted dry ingredients in three additions and milk in two additions, scraping the bowl with a rubber spatula and beating only until smooth after each addition.

Remove from mixer. Stir in lemon rind. The batter will be stiff. Pour it over the floured blueberries. With a rubber spatula gently fold together until just mixed.

Turn batter into the prepared pan. Spread smooth. Sprinkle walnuts over top, and then sprinkle reserved topping over the nuts.

Bake 50 minutes or until the top is well browned. Cool in the pan for about ½ hour.

Cut around sides of pan to loosen cake.

Cover top of pan with a piece of aluminum foil large enough to fold down around the four sides (in order not to lose any of the topping when the cake is inverted). Over the aluminum foil place a cake rack or cookie sheet. Invert and remove pan. Place cake plate or board upside down on cake and invert again. Remove foil.

This may be served while still warm or at room temperature—it holds its heat for 1 to 1½ hours after being removed from pan. If you wish, before serving cover the top generously with confectioners sugar sifted through a fine strainer.

Prune-Pecan Cake

10 PORTIONS

Moist, a bit spicy, and full of nuts.

1½ cups sifted all-purpose flour
½ teaspoon baking soda
¼ teaspoon salt
1½ teaspoons nutmeg
1¼ cups pitted, stewed prunes (about 15 extra-large prunes)
Finely grated rind of 1 lemon
1½ tablespoons lemon juice
¼ pound (1 stick) butter
1½ cups sugar
2 eggs
⅔ cup buttermilk
½ pound (2¼ cups) pecans, cut or broken into large pieces
Optional: Confectioners sugar

Adjust rack one-third up from the bottom of the oven. Preheat oven to 400 degrees. Butter a 9 x 3½-inch tube pan and line the bottom with paper. Butter the paper. Dust all over lightly with fine, dry bread crumbs.

Sift together flour, baking soda, salt, and nutmeg. Set aside. Cut prunes in quarters. (If they are very small, just cut them in halves.) Spread out on paper toweling to drain. Mix lemon rind and juice and set aside.

In small bowl of electric mixer beat the butter to soften it a bit. Add the sugar and beat well. Add eggs one at a time. Beat for 2 to 3 minutes. On lowest speed add about half of the dry ingredients, then all of the buttermilk, and finally the remaining half of the dry ingredients, scraping the bowl as necessary with a rubber spatula and beating only until smooth after each addition.

Remove from mixer bowl. Turn into a large bowl. Stir in lemon rind and juice, then prunes and nuts. Turn batter into the prepared pan. Rotate pan briskly to level batter.

Bake 1 hour or until cake tester comes out dry and top springs back when lightly touched. Remove from oven and cool in pan on a rack for about 20 minutes. Cover with a rack and invert. Remove pan and paper. Finish cooling on rack, either side up—the top will be flat. Cooled cake may be covered with confectioners sugar through a fine strainer.

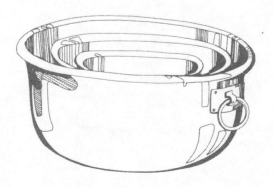

Banana-Nut Cake

10 TO 12 PORTIONS

7 ounces (2 cups) pecan halves or large pieces
2½ cups sifted all-purpose flour
1 teaspoon baking soda
¼ teaspoon salt
3 large or 4 small bananas (to make 1½ to 1¾ cups mashed)
¼ pound (1 stick) butter
1 teaspoon vanilla extract
1½ cups sugar
2 eggs
¼ cup buttermilk

Adjust rack one-third up from the bottom of the oven. Preheat oven to 375 degrees. Butter a 9 x 3½-inch tube pan and dust it all over lightly with fine, dry bread crumbs.

In a small bowl toss the nuts with about 1 tablespoon of the flour to coat them thoroughly. Set aside. Sift remainder of flour with baking soda and salt. Set aside.

In small bowl of electric mixer break up the bananas. Beat them at low speed only enough to mash. You should get 1½ to 1¾ cups. Set aside.

In large bowl of mixer (with same beaters) beat the butter to soften it a bit. Add vanilla and sugar and beat for a few minutes, using a rubber spatula as necessary to keep mixture blended. Add the eggs and continue to beat for 1 to 2 minutes. On lowest speed add half of the dry ingredients, then the buttermilk, and then the remainder of the dry ingredients, continuing to scrape bowl with rubber spatula as necessary. Add mashed bananas, beating only enough to blend. Remove from mixer. Stir in nuts.

Turn batter into prepared pan. Level top by rotating pan briskly back and forth. Bake 1 to 1¼ hours or until cake tester comes out dry.

Cool in pan on a rack for about 10 minutes. Cover with a rack or a small cookie sheet. Invert and remove pan. Cover with a rack and invert again to cool, right side up.

Peaches-and-Cream Rum Cake

8 PORTIONS

RUM SYRUP
¾ cup boiling water
1 cup sugar
½ cup light rum

Stir water and sugar in a 2- to 3-cup saucepan over moderate heat to dissolve the sugar. Boil without stirring for 3 minutes. Remove from heat. Cool to room temperature. Stir in the rum and set aside.

CAKE
1 cup sifted all-purpose flour
1 teaspoon baking powder
¼ teaspoon salt
2 eggs
1 cup sugar
½ teaspoon vanilla extract
½ cup milk
1 tablespoon butter

Adjust rack to center of oven. Preheat oven to 350 degrees. Butter a 9-inch round layer-cake pan and dust it lightly with fine, dry bread crumbs. Set aside.

Sift together the flour, baking powder, and salt. Set aside.

In small bowl of electric mixer beat eggs at high speed for 3 minutes until foamy and light lemon-colored. Gradually add sugar and vanilla and continue to beat at high speed for 5 minutes more until very thick.

Meanwhile, heat milk and butter in a small saucepan, bringing them just to a boil. On lowest speed, very gradually pour the boiling hot milk into the eggs, scraping the bowl with a rubber spatula and beating only until smooth.

Gradually add the sifted dry ingredients, continuing to scrape the bowl with the rubber spatula and beating only until flour is blended.

Turn batter into the prepared pan. Bake ½ hour or until top springs back when lightly touched and cake comes away from sides of pan. Cool in the pan for about 2 minutes. Cover with a rack and invert. Remove pan. Immediately invert again onto a serving plate, which must have a slight rim to keep the rum syrup from running over.

Gradually pour rum syrup all over hot cake until it is absorbed. Set aside to cool completely.

TOPPING

¼ cup apricot preserves
1 tablespoon rum
5 large freestone peaches
¼ cup water
¼ cup sugar

Stir preserves and rum to mix, then spread this over top of cake.

Blanch peaches briefly in boiling water to cover until the skin may be peeled off easily. Peel (see directions on page 472), cut in half from top to bottom, remove pits, and slice each half into eight lengthwise wedges.

In a large skillet bring water and sugar to a boil. Reduce heat to low. Add a single layer of peach slices. Cover and simmer gently for a few minutes. Carefully, with a large spatula, turn peaches. Cover and simmer again very briefly until barely tender.

Gently remove peaches to a towel to drain. Repeat with remaining peaches.

Arrange the peaches overlapping closely in a ring around the top edge of the cake. Fill in the center section with remaining peaches, which may be cut into dice for easier arrangement.

WHIPPED CREAM

1½ cups heavy cream
¼ cup plus 2 tablespoons confectioners sugar
1½ teaspoons vanilla extract
Optional: 2 tablespoons chopped green pistachio nuts, or toasted, sliced
    almonds (see Note)

In a chilled bowl with chilled beaters, whip the cream with sugar and vanilla until cream holds a shape.

Using a pastry bag and a large star tube, press cream into large swirls over center of cake, letting most of the outer ring of peaches show. Refrigerate. This is best when very fresh. It should be served the day it is made.

Before serving, sprinkle optional pistachio nuts or almonds over the whipped cream.

Note: To toast almonds, place them in a shallow pan in a 350 degree oven and stir occasionally until golden.

Walnut-Peach Kuchen

PASTRY

1¼ cups sifted all-purpose flour
¼ teaspoon baking powder
¼ teaspoon salt
¼ cup sugar
2 ounces (½ stick) cold butter, cut in 3 or 4 pieces
1 egg
3 tablespoons walnuts, chopped very fine

Sift together flour, baking powder, salt, and sugar into a bowl. With a pastry blender cut in the butter until the mixture resembles coarse crumbs. Stir the egg lightly with a fork just to mix. With the fork stir it into the above mixture. Stir in the walnuts.

Turn dough out onto a large board or a smooth surface and knead briefly only until the dough is smooth and holds together. Flatten slightly and place in the center of a 9-inch square unbuttered metal cake pan.

If the dough is sticky, dip your fingertips in flour as necessary. Press the dough evenly all over the bottom and about 1¼ inches up on the sides of the pan. See that it isn't too thick in the corners. Cut down any parts that are too high—fill in low parts—but don't worry about getting the top edge exactly even.

Adjust rack one-third up from bottom of oven and preheat oven to 450 degrees.

FILLING

1 tablespoon all-purpose flour
1 teaspoon cinnamon
⅓ cup sugar
4 ounces (1 generous cup) walnuts, cut into medium-size pieces
8 medium-size, ripe freestone peaches
2 tablespoons butter (see Note 1)

Sift together flour, cinnamon, and sugar and set aside. Sprinkle two thirds of the walnuts (reserve remaining 1/3 cup walnuts) over the dough in the pan.

To peel the peaches, place them, a few at a time, in a large pot of rapidly boiling water to cover. They should remain in the water for only a few seconds (a bit longer if they are less ripe), until the skin may be easily peeled off. Have ready a large bowl of cold water. To test, with a slotted spoon transfer a peach to the cold water. Using your fingers and starting at the stem end, peel off the skin. When it comes off easily, transfer all the peaches to the cold water. If you've started to skin a peach and you find it's not ready, replace it in the boiling water, but do not overcook.

After peeling all the peaches, cut them in half from top to bottom, remove pits, and then cut each piece in half again cutting from top to bottom. Drain on toweling.

Place the peach quarters over the walnuts in the pastry shell, alternating them one round-side up, the next round-side down, and fitting them into each other very tightly in even rows.

Sprinkle with reserved ⅓ cup of cut walnuts and then with reserved flour, cinnamon, and sugar mixture. Dot with butter (see Note 1). Cover with a piece of aluminum foil large enough to turn down loosely around the edge.

Bake in 450 degree oven for 30 minutes. Meanwhile, prepare topping.

TOPPING

 2 egg yolks
 ¼ cup heavy cream
 ¼ teaspoon vanilla extract

Stir yolks lightly just to mix, and stir in heavy cream and vanilla.

After cake has baked for 30 minutes, remove the aluminum foil. Without removing pan completely from oven, pour the topping evenly over all the peaches. Reduce oven temperature to 400 degrees. Bake uncovered 25 minutes longer (total baking time: 55 minutes) or until the edge of the crust is well browned.

Remove from oven. Let cool slightly or completely. Cut into portions and, with a wide metal spatula, transfer to a serving plate or individual dessert plates.

Notes:

1. The best way to "dot with butter" is to cut the required amount from frozen butter, cutting in thin slivers or small dice. Refreeze until ready to use.

2. Walnut-Peach Kuchen is best served warm with vanilla ice cream. Warm or not, it is best when very fresh.

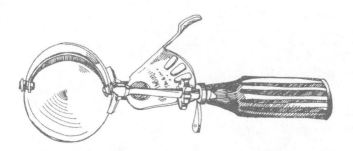

Apple Kuchen

8 TO 10 PORTIONS

⅓ cup light or dark raisins
1¼ cups sifted all-purpose flour
1½ teaspoons baking powder
½ teaspoon salt
¼ cup sugar
2 ounces (½ stick) butter
1 egg
¼ cup milk
1 teaspoon vanilla extract
2½ ounces (¾ cup) walnuts, cut into medium-size pieces

Adjust rack to center of oven. Preheat oven to 400 degrees. Butter a 13 x 9 x 2-inch baking pan.

Place the raisins in a small strainer over a saucepan of shallow boiling water. Cover and let steam for 3 to 5 minutes. Remove from heat and set aside.

Sift together the flour, baking powder, salt, and sugar into a mixing bowl. With a pastry blender cut in the butter until the mixture resembles coarse crumbs.

In a cup or a small bowl, stir the egg just to mix and then stir in the milk.

Add the egg, milk, and vanilla to the flour mixture, stirring with a fork only until the dry ingredients are thoroughly moistened.

Spread the batter evenly in the prepared pan—it will be a thin layer. Sprinkle with the raisins and nuts and set aside.

FILLING

4 medium-large apples (when Rome Beauties are available, they're my first
    choice)
2 ounces (½ stick) butter
¼ cup sugar
1½ teaspoons cinnamon

Peel, quarter, and core the apples. Cut each quarter into about six very thin wedges. Place them, overlapping, in three rows down the length of the cake. If there is a space between the rows, it may be filled in with additional slices placed in the opposite direction. If the apples are small, use one or two more and make four rows of slices.

Melt the butter and brush it over the apples. Mix the sugar and cinnamon, and sprinkle over the butter. Cover the pan loosely with a cookie sheet or a large piece of aluminum foil.

Bake for 35 minutes, removing cookie sheet or foil for the last 5 minutes. Prepare glaze.

APRICOT GLAZE
1/2 cup apricot preserves
2 tablespoons sugar

Strain the preserves and stir in the sugar. In a small saucepan over moderate heat bring the mixture to a boil, stirring constantly. Boil, stirring, for 3 minutes. Immediately brush over the apples.

Serve while still warm or at room temperature, but it is best while very fresh.

Cut cake into eight to ten portions. With a wide metal spatula, transfer portions to a cake platter.

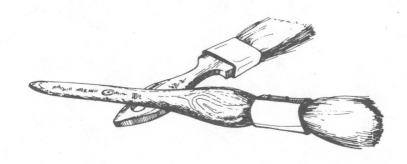

Plain, Loaf, and Other Old-Fashioned Cakes

RUMANIAN SOUR CREAM–RAISIN LOAF CAKE 144

MOOSEHEAD GINGERBREAD 146

JAVA CAKE 148

COPA CAKE 150

Mildred Knopf's Orange Puff Cake

In Mrs. Knopf's marvelous cookbook *The Perfect Hostess Cook Book,**
there is a recipe for a sublime cake. For many years it was my father's
favorite—I made it for him at least once a week. We called it Daddy Cake.
Gabe ate a slice of it every day for years and it always brought forth a smiling
"Ah, there's good news tonight."

The egg whites are beaten on a large platter (mine measures about 18 x
11 inches—it is a turkey platter) with a flat wire whisk. It works, but I
suspect you've never done it before. I never had.

The cake is as light as angel food but more moist. It is extraordinary! It is
not quick or easy—but it is the greatest!

Alfred A. Knopf, the publisher, was Mildred's brother-in-law. And
Mildred's husband, Edwin A. Knopf, was a famous Hollywood producer and
director.

ORANGE PUFF CAKE
(Preheat oven to 325 degrees)

> 1 overrunning cup egg whites (approximately 10 egg whites)
> ¼ teaspoon salt
> 1 teaspoon cream of tartar
> 1⅓ cups sugar
> ⅔ cup water
> 7 egg yolks
> Grated rind of 1 large, deep-colored orange
> 4 tablespoons orange juice
> 1 cup pastry flour

* *The Perfect Hostess Cook Book* was published in 1950 by Alfred A. Knopf.

FIRST: Beat with a flat wire whip 1 overrunning cup of egg whites (approximately 10 egg whites) with ¼ teaspoon salt on a large platter or in a large, wide bowl. When the whites are foamy, add 1 teaspoon cream of tartar, sifting into whites through a small strainer. Continue to beat until the mixture looks moist and shiny and forms peaks when the whip is lifted up.

SECOND: Boil 1⅓ cups sugar and ⅔ cup water until it forms a thread when dropped from a silver fork. (That's 234 degrees on a candy thermometer.)

THIRD: Pour the cooked sugar over the egg whites in a thin stream, holding the pan high enough so as not to scald or curdle the egg whites. This will happen if the sugar syrup is added to the whites too rapidly. Pour with one hand and blend with the other, using silver fork, not the wire whip.

FOURTH: After all the sugar syrup has been added, set the platter or bowl in a pan of cold, shallow water. Continue beating with the flat wire whip until cool, always using a high, lifting stroke to achieve a light texture.

FIFTH: Beat 7 egg yolks until lemon-colored. Add grated rind of 1 large, deep-colored orange and 4 tablespoons orange juice. Mix well and fold gently into the meringue.

SIXTH: Sift 1 cup pastry flour. Measure and resift four times. Sift gently into mixture and fold in with a light, folding motion. Pour the mixture into an angel-food cake pan that has been rinsed in cold water, handling as little as possible. Use a spatula to scrape the bowl clean, then cut through the mixture in the pan with a knife to clear away the air pockets. Bake at 325 degrees for 1 hour. Remove from oven and invert, allowing cake to "hang" until cool. (See Note 1.) Do not place by open window or in drafts, as this causes the cake to shrink.

Notes:

1. Most angel-food pans are equipped with small feet that allow the cake to "hang" (the pan is inverted but the cake does not touch the surface of the table). However, in case your pan is an ordinary tube pan and not a specially made angel-food pan, do not be discouraged. Insert a Coca-Cola bottle into the tube and allow the pan to "hang" supported by the bottle until cool.

2. At first glance, this cake may seem like a lot of trouble, but, believe me, this is the sort of adventure in baking that makes a cook's reputation.

Just follow each direction separately, one at a time, and you will have it done before you know it. It is a superb achievement, and I heartily recommend it as one of the finest cakes in the entire collection.

P.S. *I follow Mrs. Knopf's above directions—however, I use cake flour, and since I do not have a silver fork, I use a stainless steel one. I use a loose-bottomed aluminum (not Teflon) angel-food cake pan that measures 10 x 4 inches, and, although it does have small feet to raise it when inverted, I find it necessary to "hang" the cake over a bottle anyhow, as it has risen so high that the feet do not raise it enough. Incidentally, flat wire whips are generally available in specialty kitchen-equipment shops. (Some of my friends tell me that they make this cake in a large bowl with a large balloon-type whisk. Others make it in an electric mixer, but recently I tried an electric mixer and I do not recommend it for this cake.)*

Use a serrated bread knife to cut the cake and handle very gently so as not to squash this light-as-air creation.

Sponge Cake

8 TO 10 PORTIONS

6 eggs, separated
1 cup sugar
¼ cup lemon juice (before squeezing juice, grate and reserve the rind of 1
    lemon to use below)
1 cup triple-sifted cake flour
⅛ teaspoon salt
Finely grated rind of one lemon

Adjust rack one-third up from bottom of oven. Preheat oven to 350 degrees.

In small bowl of electric mixer beat yolks for 1 minute. On low speed gradually add ¾ cup of the sugar (reserve remaining ¼ cup sugar). Increase speed to high and beat for 5 minutes until very thick. Mix in the lemon juice. On lowest speed gradually add the flour, scraping the bowl with a rubber spatula and beating only until incorporated. Remove from mixer. Stir in grated lemon rind.

In large bowl of electric mixer beat the egg whites with the salt until they hold a soft shape. Add reserved ¼ cup sugar and continue to beat until whites hold a point when beaters are raised or are stiff but not dry. It is important not to overbeat. A safety precaution is to beat the whites with a mixer only until they hold a very soft shape and then finish the beating with a large wire whisk.

Fold one quarter of the whites into the yolks—do not be too thorough. Fold in another quarter. Then fold the yolks into the remaining whites, handling as gently and as little as possible and folding only until the whites have barely disappeared.

Gently turn the batter into an ungreased, loose-bottomed 9 x 3½-inch tube pan. Spread top level.

Bake 50 minutes or until top springs back when lightly pressed with your fingertips. During last 15 minutes of baking it might be necessary to cover top loosely with aluminum foil to prevent overbrowning.

Remove from oven and very carefully invert pan over the neck of a small bottle. Let cake hang until completely cool.

To remove cake from pan, cut around the sides with a firm, sharp knife, pressing firmly against the pan. Do not cut with an up and down motion. An up and down motion marks the side of the cake, but cutting without going up and down, just around the side of the pan without raising and lowering the knife, leaves smooth, beautiful sides. Holding the center tube, lift the bottom of the pan and the cake. Now cut between the bottom of the pan and the cake, pressing the knife firmly against the pan. Cut around the center tube. Cover the cake with a rack and invert to release the cake completely. Cover with another rack and invert again, leaving cake right side up; however, this cake may be served either side up.

Serve as is or with the following icing:

CHOCOLATE ICING
  8 ounces semisweet chocolate
  3 egg yolks
  2 ounces butter (½ stick), at room temperature
  1 tablespoon milk

Break up the chocolate and place it in the top of a large double boiler over hot water on moderately low heat. Cook, stirring with a wooden spoon or spatula, until almost melted. Remove top of double boiler from heat and continue to stir until completely melted and smooth. Let stand for 1 minute and then, beating briskly with the wooden spoon or spatula, add the egg yolks one at a time. Then beat in the butter, 1 tablespoon at a time, and finally, beat in the milk.

Use immediately or, if too thin, let stand at room temperature to thicken slightly.

Place the cake on a plate protected with four strips of wax paper or baking parchment.

Pour the icing over the top of the cake, letting a bit run down on the sides. Leave it that way, or with a long, narrow metal spatula spread on the sides and then the top.

Remove paper strips by pulling each one out by a narrow end (see page xxxi).

Yogurt Cake

10 PORTIONS

3 cups sifted cake flour
2 teaspoons baking powder
¼ teaspoon salt
½ pound (2 sticks) butter
2 cups sugar
5 eggs, separated
1 cup unflavored yogurt
Finely grated rind of 2 large, deep-colored oranges

Adjust rack one-third up from the bottom of the oven. Preheat oven to 375 degrees. Butter a 9 x 3½-inch tube pan. Line the bottom with paper cut to fit. Butter the paper and dust all over lightly with fine, dry bread crumbs.

Sift together flour, baking powder, and salt and set aside. In small bowl of electric mixer beat the butter until it is very soft. Gradually add 1¾ cups of the sugar (reserve remaining ¼ cup sugar) and continue to beat at medium-high speed for about 10 minutes until mixture is almost liquid. Add the yolks one at a time, beating well after each. Scrape the bowl with a rubber spatula as necessary to keep the mixture smooth. Beat in the yogurt. Transfer mixture to large bowl of mixer. On lowest speed gradually add the dry ingredients, scraping the bowl with the spatula and beating only until smooth. Remove from mixer. Stir in orange rind.

Beat the whites until they hold a soft shape. Add reserved ¼ cup sugar and continue to beat until whites hold a straight point, or are stiff but not dry. In two additions fold them into the batter and turn into cake pan. Rotate the pan briskly several times to level the top.

Bake 1 hour and 5 or 10 minutes until a cake tester comes out dry.

If the top of the cake seems to be browning too much, cover it loosely with aluminum foil for the last 15 minutes of baking time.

Cool in pan on a rack for about 15 minutes. Cover with a rack and invert. Remove pan and paper. Again, cover with a rack and invert to cool right side up.

Optional: As soon as the cake is removed from the oven it may be sprinkled lightly with a few spoonfuls of Grand Marnier.

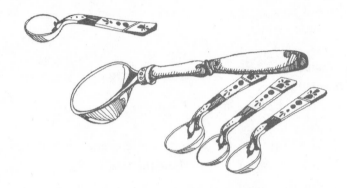

Sour Cream Cake

12 PORTIONS

3 cups sifted all-purpose flour
¼ teaspoon baking soda
½ teaspoon salt
½ pound (2 sticks) butter
2 teaspoons vanilla extract
3 cups sugar
6 eggs
1 cup sour cream
Finely grated rind of 1 large lemon

Adjust oven rack one-third of the way up from the bottom of the oven. Preheat oven to 350 degrees. Butter a loose-bottomed tube pan that measures 9 inches across the top and 3½ inches deep (see Notes). Dust all over with fine, dry bread crumbs.

Sift together flour, baking soda, and salt. Set aside. In large bowl of electric mixer beat the butter to soften it a bit. Add vanilla and gradually add the sugar. Beat for 2 to 3 minutes. Add eggs, two at a time, beating until thoroughly incorporated after each addition, and for 2 to 3 minutes after last addition, scraping the bowl with a rubber spatula as necessary to keep the ingredients well mixed. On the lowest speed add half of the dry ingredients, then all of the sour cream, and then the balance of the dry ingredients, scraping the bowl with the spatula and beating only until smooth after each addition. Remove from mixer. Stir in lemon rind.

Pour into pan. Level top by rotating pan briskly back and forth several times. Bake 1 hour and 30 to 40 minutes or until a cake tester comes out dry.

Cool cake in pan for 10 to 15 minutes. Then cover with a rack and invert. Remove pan (and paper, if it was used). Cover with another rack and invert again to finish cooling right side up.

Notes:

1. If the pan does not have a loose bottom, butter the pan, line the bottom with paper, butter the paper, and dust it all with fine, dry bread crumbs.
2. If the pan is less than 3½ inches deep (if it is only 3¼ inches deep), prepare an aluminum foil collar to extend about 1 inch above the sides—butter about 1 inch of the length before wrapping it around the pan, buttered side up and facing in. Fasten it with straight pins or tie it on.

Austrian Butter Cake

10 TO 12 PORTIONS

It is best to let this yummy cake stand overnight before serving.

 2 cups sifted all-purpose flour
 2 teaspoons baking powder
 ¼ cup cornstarch, unsifted
 ¼ cup potato starch, unsifted
 ¼ teaspoon salt
 1 pound (4 sticks) butter
 1 tablespoon vanilla extract
 1½ cups sugar
 6 eggs
 Finely grated rind of 1 large lemon (or 2 small)

Adjust rack one-third up from the bottom of the oven. Preheat oven to 375 degrees. Butter a 9 x 3½-inch tube pan and dust it with fine, dry bread crumbs.

Sift together flour, baking powder, cornstarch, potato starch, and salt. Set aside. In large bowl of electric mixer beat the butter a bit to soften it. Add vanilla and sugar and beat for 2 to 3 minutes. Add eggs one at a time, beating well after each. Mixture will look curdled at this point—O.K. On lowest speed gradually add the dry ingredients, scraping the bowl with a rubber spatula as necessary to keep mixture smooth. Beat only until blended. Remove from the mixer. With a spatula stir in lemon rind. Spoon batter into prepared cake pan. Spread top level.

Bake 1 hour or until a cake tester comes out dry. Cool in pan on a rack for about 10 to 15 minutes. Cover with a rack and invert. Remove pan. Cover with another rack and invert again to cool right side up.

When completely cool, wrap airtight and let stand overnight before serving.

Buttermilk Spice Cake

12 TO 16 PORTIONS

To make your own buttermilk, warm 1½ cups of regular (sweet) milk over low heat to room temperature (about 70 degrees). Place 1½ tablespoons of lemon juice in a 2-cup glass measuring cup. Then fill it to the 1½-cup line with the room temperature milk, stir, and let stand for 10 minutes. Now you have 1½ cups buttermilk.

3 cups sifted cake flour
1½ teaspoons baking soda
1 teaspoon salt
1½ teaspoons cinnamon
¾ teaspoon nutmeg
¼ teaspoon powdered cloves
6 ounces (1½ sticks) butter
1 teaspoon vanilla extract
1¼ cups firmly packed light brown sugar
1 cup granulated sugar
3 eggs
1½ cups buttermilk
Finely grated rind of 1 lemon

Adjust rack one-third up from the bottom of the oven. Preheat oven to 350 degrees. Butter a 13 x 9 x 2-inch pan and dust it all lightly with fine, dry bread crumbs.

Sift together flour, baking soda, salt, cinnamon, nutmeg, and cloves. Set aside. In large bowl of electric mixer beat the butter to soften it a bit. Add the vanilla and then, gradually, both sugars and beat for 1 to 2 minutes. Add the eggs individually, scraping the bowl as necessary with a rubber spatula and beating well after each. On lowest speed alternately add sifted dry ingredients in three additions and buttermilk in two additions, scraping the bowl with the spatula and beating only until smooth after each addition. Remove from mixer and stir in lemon rind.

Turn into pan and spread top level.

Bake 50 to 55 minutes or until the top springs back when lightly touched and cake begins to come away from sides of pan.

Let cake cool in the pan on a rack for about 15 minutes. Cut around sides to release. Cover with a rack or a cookie sheet and invert. Remove pan. Cover with a rack and invert again to finish cooling.

When completely cool, prepare the following:

BROWN SUGAR ICING
1 cup firmly packed light brown sugar
1/3 cup heavy cream
2 tablespoons butter
Pinch of salt
1/2 teaspoon vanilla extract

In a medium-size saucepan, over moderately low heat, stir the sugar and cream to slowly dissolve the sugar, brushing down the sides occasionally with a wet brush to remove any sugar granules. Stirring constantly, slowly bring the syrup to a boil and let boil for exactly 1 minute. Transfer to small bowl of electric mixer. Add butter and stir to melt. Add salt and vanilla and beat until creamy and slightly thickened. It will still be warm. Immediately pour over the cake and, with a long, narrow metal spatula, spread to cover.

Note: Do not freeze this cake after it has been iced—the icing will become wet when thawed.

East 62nd Street Lemon Cake

Recently this recipe was reprinted in *Saveur*. I gave a copy of the magazine to Devin, the young man who takes care of our swimming pool. The next week he said, "I made the lemon cake and it was great." I said, "Oh, do you bake?"

"No, this was the first cake I ever made."

"Really? I congratulate you—you're wonderful."

He said, "But you don't understand. I don't have an oven. I baked it on the charcoal grill—10 minutes more than the recipe called for. It was perfect."

Wow!

I'm speechless.

The cake got its name because Toni, my daughter, lived on East 62nd Street when she started to make it.

When I sent this recipe to my friend Craig Claiborne, he printed it in the *New York Times*. It became amazingly popular. I heard of many well-known people who started serving it. I heard that Nancy Reagan and Bill Blass love it.

> 3 cups sifted all-purpose flour
> 2 teaspoons baking powder
> ½ teaspoon salt
> ½ pound (2 sticks) butter
> 2 cups sugar
> 4 eggs
> 1 cup milk
> Finely grated rind of 2 large and firm lemons

Adjust rack one-third up from bottom of oven. Preheat oven to 350 degrees. Butter a plain or fancy tube pan with an 11- to 12-cup capacity and dust it lightly with fine, dry bread crumbs.

Sift together flour, baking powder, and salt and set aside. In large bowl of electric mixer beat the butter to soften it a bit. Add the sugar and beat for 2 to

3 minutes. Beat in the eggs individually, scraping the bowl as necessary with a rubber spatula to keep mixture smooth. On lowest speed alternately add the dry ingredients in three additions and the milk in two additions, scraping the bowl with the rubber spatula as necessary and beating only until incorporated after each addition. Remove the bowl from the mixer. Stir in lemon rind. Turn the batter into prepared pan. Level top by rotating pan briskly back and forth.

Bake for 1 hour and 10 to 15 minutes until a cake tester comes out dry.

Let cake stand in the pan for about 5 minutes and then cover with a rack and invert. Remove pan, leaving the cake upside down. Place over a large piece of aluminum foil or wax paper and prepare glaze.

GLAZE
⅓ cup lemon juice
⅔ cup sugar

The glaze should be used immediately after it is mixed.

Stir the lemon juice and sugar and brush all over the hot cake until absorbed.

Let cake cool completely. Use two wide metal pancake turners or a cookie sheet to transfer it to a cake plate.

Do not cut for at least several hours.

Note: I have a Key Lime tree. I have made this with ½ cup Key Lime juice in the glaze in place of the ⅓ cup lemon juice and it is divine. (But you should continue to use the lemon rind in the cake itself.)

Caraway Seed Cake

An Irish recipe for an old-fashioned favorite.

3 cups sifted all-purpose flour
2 teaspoons baking powder
½ teaspoon salt
¾ teaspoon nutmeg
½ pound (2 sticks) butter
1 teaspoon vanilla extract
2 tablespoons caraway seeds
2½ cups confectioners sugar
2 eggs plus 3 egg yolks
1 cup milk
Finely grated rind of 2 large lemons

Adjust rack one-third up from bottom of oven. Preheat oven to 350 degrees. Butter a 9 x 3½-inch tube pan and dust it lightly with fine, dry bread crumbs.

Sift together the flour, baking powder, salt, and nutmeg and set aside. In large bowl of electric mixer beat the butter to soften it a bit. Add the vanilla, caraway seeds, and sugar and beat well. Beat in the 2 eggs and then the yolks one at a time. On lowest speed alternately add the sifted dry ingredients in three additions and the milk in two additions, scraping the bowl with a rubber spatula as necessary and beating only until smooth. Stir in the lemon rind.

Turn into prepared pan. Level top by rotating pan briskly back and forth. Bake for 1 hour and 5 to 10 minutes until a cake tester comes out dry.

Remove from oven and let cake stand in pan for 10 minutes. Then cover with a rack and invert. Remove pan. Cover with another rack. Invert again over a large piece of wax paper. Prepare glaze immediately.

GLAZE

1¼ cups strained confectioners sugar
1 tablespoon lemon juice
1 tablespoon boiling water

Place all ingredients in a small mixing bowl. Stir with a rubber spatula until smooth. Pour over top of hot cake, letting some run down unevenly on the sides.

Note: This is best served in thin slices.

Orange Cake
(Texan)

Made with yogurt.

3½ ounces (¾ cup) raisins
2½ cups sifted all-purpose flour
1 teaspoon baking soda
¼ teaspoon salt
¼ pound (1 stick) butter
1 teaspoon vanilla extract
2 cups firmly packed light brown sugar
3 eggs
1 cup unflavored yogurt
Finely grated rind of 2 large oranges

Adjust rack one-third up from bottom of oven. Preheat oven to 350 degrees. Butter a 9 x 3½-inch tube pan and dust it lightly with fine, dry bread crumbs.

Chop the raisins coarse on a board, using a long, heavy knife. Place them in a small bowl and toss with about 1 tablespoon of the flour. Use your fingers to separate and thoroughly flour each piece. Set aside.

Sift together the remaining flour with the baking soda and salt and set aside. In the large bowl of an electric mixer beat the butter to soften it a bit. Add vanilla and sugar and beat for 1 to 2 minutes. Add eggs one at a time, beating until thoroughly incorporated after each. On lowest speed alternately add sifted dry ingredients in three additions and yogurt in two additions, scraping the bowl as necessary with a rubber spatula and beating only until smooth after each addition. Remove from mixer. Stir in orange rind and raisins.

Turn the batter into the prepared pan. Rotate pan briskly back and forth several times to level the batter.

Bake 1 hour and 5 minutes or until top springs back when lightly pressed and cake tester comes out dry. Remove from oven and let stand for 5 minutes.

Place a rack over the cake and invert. Remove pan. Cover with another rack and invert again. Place over a large piece of aluminum foil or wax paper. Prepare glaze.

GLAZE
½ cup sugar
½ cup orange juice, or ¼ cup orange juice and ¼ cup light rum or bourbon

Mix sugar with orange juice, or orange juice and rum or bourbon, and immediately brush all over top and sides of warm cake. Let stand for at least 2 to 3 hours.

Using a flat-sided cookie sheet as a spatula, transfer cake to a cake plate.

Spanish Orange Cake
(Valencian)
10 PORTIONS

> 2½ cups sifted all-purpose flour
> 1 tablespoon plus 1 teaspoon baking powder
> ¼ teaspoon salt
> ½ pound (2 sticks) butter
> 1½ cups sugar
> 2 eggs, separated, plus 3 egg yolks
> ⅔ cup orange juice (before squeezing juice, grate and reserve rind of 2
>   oranges to use below)
> Finely grated rind of 2 oranges

Adjust rack one-third up from the bottom of the oven. Preheat oven to 350 degrees. Butter a 9 x 3½-inch tube pan and dust it with fine, dry bread crumbs.

Sift together flour, baking powder, and salt. Set aside. In large bowl of electric mixer beat the butter to soften it a bit. Remove and reserve a few tablespoons of the sugar. Add the remaining sugar to the butter and beat for 2 to 3 minutes. One at a time, beat in the five egg yolks, beating well after each, and scraping the bowl with a rubber spatula as necessary to keep mixture smooth. On lowest speed alternately add sifted dry ingredients in three additions and the orange juice in two additions, continuing to scrape the bowl with a rubber spatula as necessary and beating only until smooth after each addition. Remove from mixer. Stir in orange rind. Beat the 2 egg whites until they hold a soft shape. Add the reserved sugar and beat until the whites hold a firm shape and fold them into the batter. Turn the batter into cake pan and level top by turning pan briskly back and forth.

Bake 1 hour or until cake tester comes out dry. Cool cake in pan for about 20 minutes. Cover with a rack and invert. Remove pan, leaving cake upside down. Place over wax paper or aluminum foil.

Prepare the following glaze:

GLAZE
½ cup orange marmalade
2 tablespoons water

Mix marmalade and water in a small saucepan. Bring to a boil. Brush over top and sides of cake. Let stand several hours before transferring to a cake plate, using a flat-sided cookie sheet as a spatula.

Indian River Sweet Orange Bread

2 LOAVES

Serve as a plain cake or, even better, toast it and serve with butter, cream cheese, or Honey Butter (page 509). This Florida specialty is unusually quick and easy—and delicious.

> 4 cups sifted all-purpose flour
> 1 tablespoon plus 1 teaspoon baking powder
> ½ teaspoon baking soda
> 1 teaspoon salt
> 3 large oranges, (to yield 1⅓ cups juice)
> 1½ cups sugar
> ⅓ cup water
> 3 tablespoons butter
> 3 eggs
> Optional: Walnuts or pecans and/or currants or raisins (see Note)

Adjust rack one-third up from bottom of oven and preheat oven to 350 degrees. Butter two loaf pans, 8½ x 4½ x 2½ inches, and coat them all over lightly with fine, dry bread crumbs.

Sift together flour, baking powder, baking soda, and salt into a large mixing bowl and set aside.

With a vegetable peeler, remove the very thin, bright-colored, outer rind of about 2½ oranges and reserve it. Squeeze the oranges. You will need 1⅓ cups of juice. Set it aside. Cut the rind into slivers.

Place the rind, sugar, and water into a large, heavy saucepan. Stir over high heat until sugar is dissolved and mixture comes to a boil. Reduce heat to moderate and let mixture boil gently without stirring for 5 minutes.

Remove from heat. Add butter and stir to melt. Stir in the 1⅓ cups of orange juice. Beat the eggs lightly just to mix and stir them in. Pour this over the sifted dry ingredients and stir until dry ingredients are thoroughly moistened.

Turn into prepared pans. Shake gently to level batter. Bake 55 minutes to 1 hour or until a cake tester comes out dry.

Cool in pans for about 10 minutes before removing to racks to finish cooling.

Note: The batter may be divided in half and ½ cup chopped walnuts or pecans may be stirred into one half and ½ cup currants or raisins into the other half to make one nut and one raisin loaf.

Honey Cake

1 9-INCH LOAF

2¼ cups sifted all-purpose flour

¾ teaspoon baking powder

¾ teaspoon baking soda

½ teaspoon salt

2 teaspoons cinnamon

3½ ounces (1 cup) walnuts, cut into medium-size pieces

Optional: 2 to 3 tablespoons candied orange peel and/or 2 to 3 tablespoons
    candied ginger, cut fine

3 eggs

¾ cup firmly packed dark brown sugar

3 tablespoons melted butter

¾ cup honey

¾ cup cold, very strong coffee (2 tablespoons instant coffee dissolved in
    ¾ cup hot water)

Finely grated rind of 2 large oranges

Adjust rack one-third up from the bottom of the oven. Preheat oven to 350 degrees. Butter a 9 x 5 x 3-inch loaf pan and dust it very lightly with fine, dry bread crumbs.

Sift together flour, baking powder, baking soda, salt, and cinnamon. In a small bowl toss a spoonful of the sifted dry ingredients with the walnuts and optional candied orange peel and/or candied ginger. Set aside remainder of dry ingredients and floured nuts.

In large bowl of electric mixer beat the eggs and sugar slightly only to mix. Add the butter and honey and beat only to mix. On lowest speed add half of the sifted dry ingredients, then gradually add all the coffee, and finally the remaining dry ingredients, scraping the bowl as necessary with a rubber spatula and beating only until smooth after each addition. Remove from mixer and stir in the grated orange rind, the floured walnuts, and the optional candied orange peel and/or ginger.

Pour the batter into the prepared pan. Pan will be filled almost to the top. Bake 1 hour and 20 to 30 minutes until the top springs back firmly when lightly touched. About 20 minutes before the baking time is up, check to see if the top is becoming too brown. If so, cover loosely with aluminum foil.

Cool in pan on a rack for 5 to 10 minutes before removing to a rack to cool completely. Let stand for several hours or overnight before slicing. This is best cut in very, very thin slices.

Note: The flavor of this cake depends on the honey—it will vary considerably with different honeys.

Marble Spice Cake

8 PORTIONS

An old-fashioned Southern loaf cake.

> 2 cups sifted cake flour
> 2 teaspoons baking powder
> ¼ teaspoon salt
> ¼ pound (1 stick) butter
> 1 cup sugar
> 2 eggs
> ⅔ cup milk
> 1 teaspoon powdered, unsweetened cocoa
> 1 teaspoon instant coffee
> 1 teaspoon cinnamon
> ½ teaspoon nutmeg
> ½ teaspoon powdered cloves
> 2 tablespoons molasses, light or dark

Adjust rack one-third up from bottom of oven. Preheat oven to 375 degrees. Butter a 9 x 5 x 3-inch loaf pan and dust it all lightly with fine, dry bread crumbs.

Sift together the flour, baking powder, and salt and set aside.

In small bowl of electric mixer, beat the butter to soften it a bit. Add the sugar and beat for a minute or two. Add eggs one at a time. Increase speed to high and beat for 1 to 2 minutes.

On lowest speed alternately add sifted dry ingredients in three additions and milk in two additions, scraping the bowl with a rubber spatula and beating only until smooth after each addition.

Remove about half of the batter and set aside.

To the remainder, add cocoa, instant coffee, cinnamon, nutmeg, powdered cloves, and molasses and beat only until smooth.

Alternately spoon or pour large tablespoonfuls of both batters into prepared pan.

Bake 1 hour and 5 minutes or until a cake tester comes out dry.

Let stand in pan for about 10 minutes. Cover with a rack, invert, remove pan, cover with another rack, and invert again to cool completely, right side up.

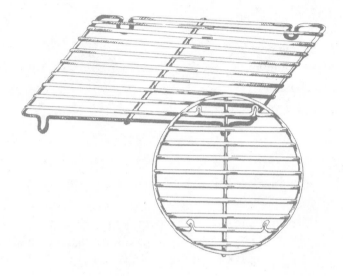

Marble Loaf Cake

1½ ounces unsweetened chocolate
2½ cups sifted cake flour
½ teaspoon salt
1 tablespoon baking powder
¼ pound (1 stick) butter
1 teaspoon vanilla extract
1 teaspoon almond extract
1½ cups sugar
3 eggs
¾ cup milk
1 tablespoon instant coffee

Adjust rack one-third up from bottom of oven and preheat to 375 degrees. Butter an 11 x 5 x 3-inch loaf pan (see Note) or similar shape with an 8- to 9-cup capacity. Dust all over lightly with fine, dry bread crumbs.

Melt the chocolate in a small, heatproof cup set in a pan of shallow hot water on moderately low heat. Set aside to cool.

Sift together the flour, salt, and baking powder and set aside. In large bowl of electric mixer beat the butter to soften it a bit. Add the vanilla and almond extracts and then the sugar. Beat for a minute or two. Add eggs one at a time and beat at high speed for 2 minutes, scraping the bowl occasionally with rubber spatula.

On lowest speed alternately add the sifted dry ingredients in three additions and the milk in two additions, scraping the bowl with the rubber spatula as necessary and beating only until smooth after each addition.

Remove from mixer. Transfer one-third of the batter to small bowl of electric mixer. Add the melted chocolate and instant coffee and, with the same beaters, on low speed, beat only until mixed. Remove from mixer.

Alternately place spoonfuls of both batters in the prepared pan. With a small metal spatula, or a knife, cut zigzag through the batter, cutting in one direction first and then the other—do not overdo it.

Bake 1 hour or until the top springs back when lightly touched and a cake tester comes out dry.

Cool in pan for 10 minutes. Cover with a rack, invert, and remove the pan. Cover with another rack and invert again to cool on the rack, right side up.

THICK CHOCOLATE GLAZE

    6 ounces semisweet chocolate
    1 tablespoon butter
    3 tablespoons light corn syrup
    2 tablespoons milk

In the top of a small double boiler over hot water on moderate heat, melt the chocolate and the butter. With a small wire whisk beat in the corn syrup and milk, beating until smooth.

Remove from heat. Cool slightly, stirring occasionally. Place a large piece of wax paper under the cake on the rack. While glaze is still warm, pour it thickly over the top of the cake. Smooth it over the top only. If a bit runs down the sides, just leave it. Transfer cake to a platter or cake board.

Let stand for a few hours to allow the glaze to set.

Note: This recipe may also be made in two smaller pans, each 8 x 4 x 2½ inches (1-quart capacity). The baking time will then be reduced to 50 minutes.

Cardamom Currant Cake

(Danish)

8 TO 10 PORTIONS

Raisins often have a tendency to sink to the bottom. Not so in this lovely recipe.

> 5 ounces (1 cup) currants, or coarsely chopped raisins
> 1½ cups sifted all-purpose flour
> 1 teaspoon baking powder
> 3 teaspoons ground cardamom (see Note)
> ½ pound (2 sticks) butter
> 1 teaspoon vanilla extract
> 5 eggs, separated
> ¼ teaspoon salt
> 1½ cups confectioners sugar
> Finely grated rind of 2 lemons

Adjust rack one-third up from bottom of oven. Preheat oven to 350 degrees. Butter a 9 x 5 x 3-inch loaf pan and dust it all over lightly with fine, dry bread crumbs.

Place the currants, or chopped raisins, in a small bowl with 1 tablespoon of the flour. Toss with your fingers until thoroughly coated. Set aside.

Sift the remaining flour with the baking powder and cardamom.

In large bowl of electric mixer beat the butter to soften it a bit. Beat in the vanilla. On low speed gradually add the sifted dry ingredients, scraping the bowl with a rubber spatula and beating only until thoroughly mixed. Remove from mixer.

In the small bowl of the mixer, with clean beaters, at medium speed beat the egg whites with the salt until they barely hold a soft shape. Then reduce the speed and still beating, gradually add ¾ cup of the sugar (reserve remaining ¾ cup). Increase speed to high and continue to beat until whites hold a definite shape, or are stiff but not dry—do not overbeat. Transfer beaten whites to a large bowl and set aside.

You may now use the egg white bowl and beaters without washing them to beat the yolks. Beat at high speed for a few minutes until they are pale lemon-colored. Gradually add the reserved ¾ cup sugar and continue to beat for about 3 minutes more until mixture is thick and very pale.

Return the butter mixture in a large bowl to the mixer. On low speed gradually beat in the egg yolk mixture, scraping the bowl with a rubber spatula and beating only until smooth. Remove from mixer and, with a rubber spatula, mix in the grated lemon rind and the floured currants or raisins. Fold in the beaten egg whites, one-fourth at a time, folding only until incorporated. Do not handle any more than necessary.

Turn the batter into the prepared pan—the pan will be almost full. Smooth the top and then spread the batter up on the sides a bit, leaving it slightly lower in the center.

Bake for 1 hour and 10 minutes or until a cake tester comes out dry.

Cool in the pan for 10 to 15 minutes. Place a folded towel or a pot holder over the cake and invert into the palm of your hand. Remove the pan, cover with a rack, and invert again to cool right side up.

Note: The cardamom may be omitted, or you may substitute 1 teaspoon cinnamon and ½ teaspoon nutmeg.

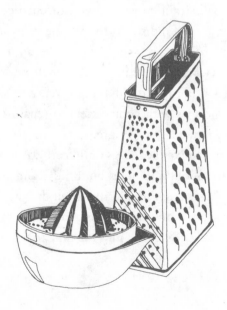

Rumanian Sour Cream–Raisin Loaf Cake

8 PORTIONS

This butterless cake has an unusual texture—moist, firm, not very sweet.

3 ounces (²/₃ cup) raisins, light, dark, or mixed
2 cups sifted all-purpose flour
1 teaspoon baking powder
1 teaspoon baking soda
¼ teaspoon salt
3 eggs
1 teaspoon vanilla extract
1 cup sugar
1 cup sour cream

Adjust rack one-third of the way up from the bottom of the oven. Preheat oven to 350 degrees. Butter a 9 x 5 x 3-inch loaf pan. Dust it lightly with fine, dry bread crumbs.

Place raisins in a small strainer over a deep saucepan containing a small amount of boiling water. Cover and steam for 5 minutes to soften the raisins. Remove from heat and dry on paper toweling. Place on a board and chop coarsely with a long, heavy knife. Place in a small bowl and set aside.

Sift together flour, baking powder, baking soda, and salt. Add a small spoonful to the raisins and toss with your fingers to separate and thoroughly coat each piece. Set aside remaining dry ingredients.

In large bowl of electric mixer beat eggs until frothy. Add vanilla and sugar and beat at high speed for about 3 minutes until fluffy and very light in color. Beat in the sour cream. On low speed add the sifted dry ingredients, scraping the bowl with a rubber spatula and beating only until smooth. Remove from mixer. Stir in the raisins. Turn the batter into the prepared pan.

Bake 1 hour and 10 to 15 minutes or until a cake tester comes out dry. Cool in pan for about 5 minutes. Cover with a rack and invert. Remove pan. Cover with another rack and invert again to finish cooling right side up.

Serve in thin slices, two or three to a portion.

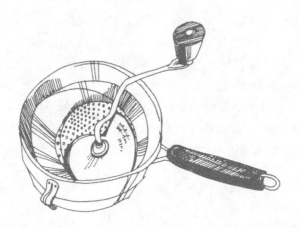

Moosehead Gingerbread

10 TO 12 PORTIONS

Moosehead Lake, which is up near the Canadian border, is the largest lake in Maine. Bill Merservey was the postmaster in Lily Bay, a town on the shore of Moosehead and the best fishing guide around, and a fabulous cook. He gave this recipe to my mother when we spent a summer there. After the first printing of this book I was flooded with mail about this recipe. People said it was the best gingerbread they ever ate. And then, pepper and mustard and coffee, which sounded shocking at first, became routine in gingerbread.

2½ cups sifted all-purpose flour
2 teaspoons baking soda
½ teaspoon salt
1 teaspoon cinnamon
1½ teaspoons powdered ginger
½ teaspoon powdered cloves
½ teaspoon dry mustard
½ teaspoon black pepper, ground fine
¼ pound (1 stick) butter
½ cup firmly packed dark brown sugar
2 eggs
1 cup molasses, dark or light
1 rounded tablespoon instant coffee
1 cup boiling water

Adjust rack to center of oven. Preheat oven to 375 degrees. Butter a 9-inch square pan. Dust it lightly with fine, dry bread crumbs.

Sift together the flour, baking soda, salt, cinnamon, ginger, cloves, mustard, and black pepper. Set aside.

In large bowl of electric mixer beat the butter to soften it a bit. Add the sugar and beat for 1 to 2 minutes. Beat in the eggs one at a time. Use a rubber spatula all through the beating to help mix ingredients. Add molasses. Beat until smooth. Dissolve the instant coffee in the boiling water. On low speed alternately add sifted dry ingredients in three additions and coffee, which will be hot, in two additions.

Beat only until smooth. Mixture will be very thin. Pour into prepared pan. Bake 35 minutes or until the top springs back when lightly touched. Cool in pan on a rack for about 10 minutes. Cover with a rack and invert. Remove pan and cover with another rack to invert again. Serve warm or let cool.

Java Cake

A plain loaf cake strongly flavored with coffee. Although I have given a recipe for Java Icing, this lovely plain cake may be served with no icing or it may be iced with Thick Chocolate Glaze (page 141).

½ cup milk
⅓ cup instant coffee
2 cups sifted all-purpose flour
2 teaspoons baking powder
¼ teaspoon salt
½ pound (2 sticks) butter
1 teaspoon vanilla extract
1½ cups sugar
4 eggs

Adjust rack one-third up from bottom of oven and preheat to 375 degrees. Butter a loaf pan (see Note) measuring 14 x 4½ x 3 inches (or similar shape with 2-quart capacity) and dust it lightly with fine, dry bread crumbs.

In a small saucepan, heat the milk and stir in the instant coffee to dissolve. Set aside to cool to room temperature.

Sift flour with baking powder and salt and set aside. In large bowl of electric mixer, beat the butter to soften it a bit. Add the vanilla and sugar and beat for 1 to 2 minutes. Add eggs one at a time, beating well after each and scraping the bowl with a rubber spatula to keep mixture smooth. Beat at high speed for 1 to 2 minutes after adding the last egg. The mixture may look curdled—O.K.

On low speed, alternately add the dry ingredients in three additions and the cooled coffee-milk in two additions, scraping the bowl with a rubber spatula as necessary and beating only until smooth.

Turn into prepared pan and, with the rubber spatula, spread level. Then run the batter up on the sides a bit, leaving it slightly lower in the center.

Bake 55 minutes or until a cake tester comes out dry and the top springs back firmly when lightly touched. Timing will depend on shape of pan—a long, narrow loaf pan will take less time than a short, wide one.

Cool in pan for about 10 to 15 minutes. Cover with a rack, invert, and remove pan. Let cake cool and ice it upside down.

Prepare following icing:

JAVA ICING

2 tablespoons butter, at room temperature
1½ cups confectioners sugar
1 tablespoon instant coffee
1 egg yolk
1½ to 2 tablespoons boiling water
Optional: Chocolate-candy coffee beans

Place butter, sugar, instant coffee, egg yolk, and 1½ tablespoons of boiling water in small bowl of electric mixer. Beat at high speed, scraping the bowl with a rubber spatula. Continue to beat for several minutes until the mixture forms a thick, marshmallow-like paste. If too thick, add a bit more water; if too thin, add more sugar.

As soon as mixture is smooth and thick, immediately spread it over the top of the cake. If a bit runs down the sides, just leave it—don't spread the sides.

Place optional chocolate coffee beans in a row down the center of the cake before the icing hardens.

Note: This recipe may also be made in two smaller pans, each 8 x 4 x 2½ inches (1-quart capacity). The baking time will then be reduced to about 40 minutes.

Copa Cake

8 TO 10 PORTIONS

Many years ago there was a night club called the Copa (or was it Copa City?) in Miami Beach. There was a wonderful Spanish pastry chef there, and he gave me this recipe. It is an exotic-looking and fancy "plain" cake.

2½ cups sifted all-purpose flour
1¼ teaspoons baking soda
¼ teaspoon salt
1 cup sugar
¼ pound (1 stick) butter
2 eggs
1 cup sour cream
1 teaspoon vanilla extract
Rind of 1 lemon, grated fine
1 cup thick fruit preserves (peach, pineapple, or apricot)
3½ ounces (1 cup) walnuts, in large pieces
3 tablespoons powdered, unsweetened cocoa
1 teaspoon instant coffee
½ teaspoon cinnamon
3 tablespoons boiling water

Adjust oven rack to the center of the oven. Preheat oven to 375 degrees. Butter a 13 x 9 x 2-inch pan. Coat it lightly with fine, dry bread crumbs and place it in the freezer or refrigerator.

Sift flour, 1 teaspoon baking soda (reserve remaining ¼ teaspoon baking soda), and salt into a large mixing bowl. Stir in sugar. With a pastry blender cut in the butter until mixture resembles coarse crumbs. Add unbeaten eggs, sour cream, and vanilla. Stir (or beat in the mixer at low speed, scraping bowl with a rubber spatula) until mixture is thoroughly mixed. Remove 1 cup of this batter and set aside. Stir lemon rind into remaining batter.

Remove the pan from the freezer or refrigerator and spread the batter with the lemon rind in a thin layer over the bottom of the pan. (The chilled pan will make it easier to do this.)

Stir the preserves briefly just to soften and then place them by small spoonfuls evenly over the batter. With the back of the spoon, spread preserves smooth, leaving a ½-inch border around the edges. Sprinkle the nuts evenly over all.

In a small bowl, mix the cocoa, instant coffee, cinnamon, reserved ¼ teaspoon baking soda, and boiling water to make a smooth paste. Add the cup of reserved batter and stir until smooth. Place this chocolate batter by teaspoonfuls all over the nuts, placing it in separate mounds so that the nuts and batter show through between the mounds. Do not flatten or smooth the chocolate mounds.

Bake for 35 to 40 minutes, or until the white batter has colored lightly and the top feels firm to the touch. Cool in pan on rack for 10 to 15 minutes.

To remove cake from pan: If the preserves ran out to the edge of the pan anywhere, run a knife around that part of the pan to release. Place a cookie sheet (not a rack) over the cake pan. Holding the cookie sheet firmly against the pan, invert it. Remove the cake pan. Cover with a rack or another cookie sheet. Invert again, leaving the cake right side up to finish cooling.

Transfer to a board and use a long, thin, sharp knife to cut.

Pound Cakes

Pound cakes should be served in thin slices, two or three slices to a portion. It is best to let pound cakes stand overnight before slicing. When completely cool, wrap in plastic wrap or aluminum foil and let stand at room temperature.

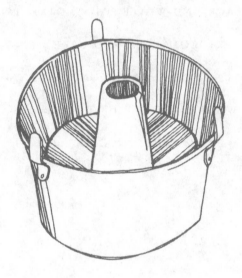

The King's Pound Cake

2 10-INCH LOAF CAKES

This is a new recipe. It is not in any of the previous printings of this book or in any of my other books. It is adapted from a recipe that was printed in *TV Guide* on August 16, 1997, with the title "Elvis Presley's Favorite Pound Cake." They say he often ate a whole one (or two) all by himself.

It is simply—and unequivocally—the best! Moist, tender, juicy, irresistible. With a smooth, fine, silky texture. And it is easy to make and it keeps well.

> ½ pound (2 sticks) unsalted butter
> ⅛ teaspoon mace (see Note 1)
> ½ teaspoon salt
> 1 teaspoon baking powder
> 2 teaspoons vanilla extract
> 3 cups sugar
> 7 eggs
> 3 cups sifted cake flour (this must be sifted or strained through a fine strainer before it is measured—see Note 2)
> 8 ounces (1 cup) heavy cream

Adjust an oven rack one-third up from the bottom of the oven and preheat the oven to 350 degrees. You need two loaf pans that should not be dark metal, which makes this cake too dark. They should each have at least a 7-cup capacity and should measure about 10 x 3¾ x 3¼ inches. Butter the pans and dust them all over with fine dry bread crumbs. Invert over paper to allow excess crumbs to fall out.

In the large bowl of an electric mixer beat the butter with the mace, salt, baking powder, and vanilla until mixed. Gradually add the sugar and beat for about 5 minutes. Then beat in the eggs one or two at a time, scraping the bowl with a rubber spatula and beating only until incorporated after each addition.

Then add half of the flour and stir/fold it in with a large rubber spatula (to prevent splashing) or beat on low speed to incorporate. Gradually add the cream and stir or beat to incorporate. Add the remaining flour and stir or beat to incorporate. Finally, beat only until smooth.

Then divide the batter among the two pans. Jiggle the pans just a little to slightly level the tops. (The cakes will really level themselves during baking.)

Bake for 1 hour and 15 or 20 minutes until the loaves begin to come away from the ends of the pans.

Let the loaves cool in the pans for about 25 to 30 minutes. Then cover a pan with a cake rack. Turn pan and rack upside down. Remove pan. With your hands very gently and carefully turn the loaf right side up. Remove the second loaf from the pan the same way. Let the loaves cool on racks.

Notes:

1. A little too much mace can be—a little too much mace. To measure it correctly, measure a level ¼ teaspoon. Then with a knife, cut straight down in the middle and return one-half to the jar.

2. Just for your interest and so you can see what a difference it makes to sift: 3 cups of unsifted cake flour equals 12 ounces. . . . 3 cups of sifted cake flour equals 9 ounces.

Toni's Pound Cake

16 PORTIONS

Thi his is named after my daughter because it's her favorite cake of all.

    Rind of 2 lemons, grated fine
    3 tablespoons lemon juice
    1 pound (4 sticks) butter
    1 tablespoon vanilla extract
    3⅓ cups sugar
    ½ teaspoon mace
    10 eggs
    4 cups sifted all-purpose flour

Adjust rack one-third up from the bottom of the oven. Preheat oven to 350 degrees. Butter a 10 x 4-inch tube pan, line the bottom with paper cut to fit, butter the paper, and dust it all lightly with fine, dry bread crumbs.

Mix lemon rind with juice and set aside. In large bowl of electric mixer beat the butter to soften it a bit. Add vanilla. Gradually add the sugar and mace. Beat at moderately high speed for two to three minutes, scraping the bowl with a rubber spatula as necessary to keep ingredients well mixed. Add eggs, two at a time, beating until thoroughly incorporated after each addition. On lowest speed gradually add the flour, scraping the bowl with the rubber spatula and beating only until smooth.

Remove from mixer. Stir in the lemon rind and juice.

Turn the batter into prepared pan. Turn pan briskly back and forth to level top. Cover the top of the pan with a piece of aluminum foil large enough to fold down loosely around the sides of the pan.

Bake for 30 minutes. Open oven door just enough to reach in and remove the aluminum foil. Continue baking for an additional 1¼ hours. (Total baking time is 1¾ hours.) Cake is done when a cake tester comes out dry.

Cool in pan on a rack for 10 to 15 minutes. Cover with a rack and invert. Remove pan and paper. Cover with a rack and carefully invert again to finish cooling right side up.

Kentucky Pound Cake (with Bourbon)

12 GENEROUS PORTIONS

3½ cups sifted all-purpose flour
1½ teaspoons baking powder
¾ pound (3 sticks) butter
1 tablespoon vanilla extract
½ teaspoon mace
1 pound plus 1 cup light brown sugar (this will be 3¼ cups total, firmly
    packed)
5 eggs
¾ cup milk
¼ cup bourbon (milk and bourbon may be measured into 1 cup)

Adjust rack one-third up from bottom of oven. Preheat oven to 350 degrees. Butter a 10 x 4-inch tube pan, line the bottom with paper, butter the paper, and dust it all lightly with fine, dry bread crumbs.

Sift flour with baking powder and set aside. In large bowl of electric mixer beat the butter to soften it a bit. Beat in vanilla and mace. On low speed gradually add the sugar. Increase speed to moderately high and beat for a few minutes, scraping the bowl as necessary with a rubber spatula. Add eggs one at a time, beating until thoroughly incorporated after each addition.

On lowest speed, alternately add the sifted dry ingredients in three additions and the milk and bourbon mixture in two additions, scraping the bowl with the rubber spatula and beating only until smooth after each addition.

Turn the batter into the prepared pan. Rotate pan briskly several times to level batter.

Bake 1 hour and 25 minutes or until a cake tester comes out dry and top springs back firmly when lightly touched. Remove from oven. Cool in pan for 10 to 15 minutes. Cover with a rack and invert. Remove pan and paper, leaving the cake upside down. Place cake on rack over a large piece of wax paper or aluminum foil. Prepare glaze.

GLAZE

⅓ cup granulated sugar
¼ cup bourbon

In a small saucepan stir the sugar and bourbon over heat only long enough to dissolve the sugar. Brush the warm glaze all over the warm cake. Let stand for several hours or overnight.

Black-and-White Pound Cake

16 PORTIONS

I have made this cake many times. And always—I can hardly wait to cut into it, because the design inside is different every time. It is a white cake with a big dark chocolate tunnel. The tunnel is never the same twice. But it is always spectacular—and delicious.

> 1 pound (4 sticks) butter
> 1 tablespoon vanilla extract
> 3⅓ cups sugar
> 10 eggs
> 4 cups sifted all-purpose flour
> ½ teaspoon almond extract
> ¼ teaspoon baking soda
> 2 tablespoons instant coffee
> ¾ cup Hershey's chocolate-flavored syrup (see Note 1)

Adjust rack one-third up from bottom of oven. Preheat oven to 350 degrees. Butter a 10 x 4-inch tube pan, line the bottom with paper, butter the paper, and dust it all lightly with fine, dry bread crumbs.

In large bowl of electric mixer beat the butter to soften it a bit. Beat in vanilla and gradually add the sugar. Beat on moderate speed for 2 to 3 minutes, scraping the bowl with a rubber spatula as necessary.

Add the eggs, two at a time, beating after each addition until thoroughly incorporated. On lowest speed very gradually add the flour, continuing to scrape the bowl with the rubber spatula and beating only until the flour is incorporated.

Remove half (or about 5 cups) of the batter and set aside. Mix the almond extract into the remainder and turn it into the prepared pan. Level the top by rotating pan briskly back and forth.

Return the other half of the batter to the mixer bowl and add the baking soda, instant coffee, and chocolate syrup. Beat on low speed, scraping the bowl with a rubber spatula and beating only until smooth.

Pour evenly over top of white batter. Level by rotating pan briskly back and forth.

Cover the top of the pan with a piece of aluminum foil large enough to turn down loosely around the sides of the pan.

Bake for 30 minutes. Open oven door just enough to reach in and remove the aluminum foil. Continue baking for an additional 1 hour and 20 minutes. (Total baking time 1 hour and 50 minutes.) Cake is done when cake tester comes out dry. Remove from oven. Cool in pan for 10 to 15 minutes.

Cover with a rack and invert. Remove pan and paper. Cover with another rack and carefully invert again to finish cooling right side up.

Notes:

1. Stir the syrup before using—the heavy part settles to the bottom if it has been standing for a while.
2. Some pound cakes form a too-heavy top crust; covering the cake with foil for the first half-hour helps prevent this.

Chocolate Pound Cake

12 TO 16 (OR MORE) PORTIONS

I f they had a chocolate pound cake Olympics this would win a gold medal. It is almost five pounds of dense, dark, delicious chocolate pound cake. And the chocolate icing is as smooth and shiny as a mirror.

3 cups sifted all-purpose flour
1 tablespoon baking powder
½ teaspoon salt
½ pound (2 sticks) butter
1 tablespoon vanilla extract
½ teaspoon almond extract
2 tablespoons plus 1 teaspoon instant coffee
3 cups sugar
3 eggs
1 cup strained, powdered, unsweetened cocoa (preferably Dutch process)
1¾ cups milk

Adjust oven rack one-third up from the bottom of the oven. Preheat oven to 350 degrees.

Butter a 10 x 4-inch tube pan, line the bottom with baking parchment cut to fit, butter the paper, and coat lightly with fine, dry bread crumbs.

Sift together flour, baking powder, and salt. Set aside.

In large bowl of electric mixer, beat the butter to soften it a bit. Add the vanilla and almond extracts, the instant coffee, and gradually add the sugar. Scrape sides and bottom of bowl with a rubber spatula as necessary all during mixing. Beat in the eggs one at a time, beating after each until it is incorporated. On lowest speed gradually add cocoa. Alternately add milk and sifted dry ingredients each in three additions; in this case, start with the milk since the batter is rather heavy at this stage. Beat only until smooth after each addition. Finish as usual with dry ingredients. Turn into pan. Jiggle the pan briskly several times to level top.

Bake 1½ hours or until the top springs back when lightly touched and the cake comes away slightly from the sides of the pan. Let the cake cool in the pan on a rack for 10 to 15 minutes. Cover with a rack and invert. Remove pan and paper. Let cool upside down. When completely cool, prepare the following:

ICING

9 ounces sweet or semisweet chocolate
4½ ounces (1 stick plus 1 tablespoon) butter, at room temperature

Break up the chocolate and place it in the top of a small double boiler over hot water on medium heat. When it is almost completely melted, remove the top of the double boiler and stir with a small wire whisk until smooth. Add the butter, about 1 to 2 tablespoons at a time, stirring with the whisk until smooth after each addition. The icing might thicken with the first few additions of butter, but then it will thin out as the remainder is added.

Place four strips of wax paper or baking parchment around the outer edges of a cake plate. Place the cake on it, upside down.

Pour the icing over the top, letting some run down on the sides. With a long, narrow metal spatula, quickly spread over the sides first, and then the top.

Remove wax paper strips by pulling each one out by a narrow end (see page xxxi).

Walnut or Pecan Pound Cake

16 PORTIONS

1 pound (4 sticks) butter
2 teaspoons vanilla extract
½ teaspoon almond extract
3⅓ cups sugar
10 eggs
4 cups sifted all-purpose flour
1 pound (4½ cups) walnuts or pecans, chopped medium fine

Using above ingredients, follow directions for Toni's Pound Cake (see page 157) through the addition of the eggs.

In a very large bowl stir the flour and nuts to mix thoroughly. Add the batter and, with a large wooden spatula, fold and stir only the flour is all moistened.

Turn into pan and follow remaining directions for Toni's Pound Cake.

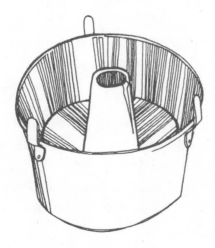

Whole-Wheat Pound Cake

10 TO 12 PORTIONS

½ pound (2 sticks) butter
1 teaspoon powdered ginger
1½ tablespoons instant coffee (I use Medaglia d'Oro espresso)
¼ teaspoon salt
1 teaspoon vanilla extract
2 cups firmly packed dark brown sugar
6 eggs
2 cups strained, all-purpose whole-wheat flour (see Note)
¼ cup milk

Adjust rack one-third up from bottom of oven. Preheat oven to 350 degrees. Butter a 9 x 3½-inch tube pan. Line the bottom with paper. Butter the paper and dust all over, including the center tube, with fine, dry bread crumbs. Or use a 9-inch Bundt pan buttered and crumbed.

In large bowl of electric mixer beat the butter to soften it a bit. Add the ginger, instant coffee, salt, vanilla, and brown sugar. Beat for 2 to 3 minutes. Add the eggs, one at a time, beating well after each. Mixture will look curdled—O.K.

On low speed, while scraping the bowl with a rubber spatula, mix in about half of the flour, then all the milk, and finally the remaining flour, beating only until smooth after each addition. It might *still* look curdled. Don't worry.

Turn the batter into the prepared pan. Rotate pan briskly to level batter. Bake 1 hour and 10 minutes or until a cake tester comes out dry and top springs back when lightly touched.

Cool in pan for 10 to 15 minutes. Cover with a rack and invert. Remove pan and paper if it was used. Cover with another rack and invert again to cool right side up.

Note: Flour packs down when it is left standing. It should be aerated in order to measure correctly. Most all-purpose whole-wheat flour is too coarse to go through a sifter; it is generally easier to strain it. Any coarse parts that don't go through the strainer may then be turned back into the strained flour and stirred in just a bit to mix.

Pepper Pound Cake

12 TO 16 PORTIONS

A fine-grained Jamaican pound cake made with cream cheese and butter.

3 ounces cream cheese
$\frac{1}{2}$ pound (2 sticks) butter
$\frac{1}{4}$ teaspoon salt
$\frac{1}{2}$ teaspoon allspice
$\frac{3}{4}$ teaspoon black pepper, ground fine (freshly ground is best)
1 tablespoon vanilla extract
1 cup dark brown sugar, firmly packed
1 cup granulated white sugar
7 eggs
3 cups sifted cake flour

Adjust rack one-third up from bottom of oven. Preheat oven to 350 degrees. Butter a 9 x 3½-inch tube pan. Line the bottom with paper cut to fit. Butter the paper and dust it all lightly with fine, dry bread crumbs. Or use a 9-inch Bundt pan buttered and crumbed.

In large bowl of electric mixer beat the cream cheese and butter with the salt, allspice, pepper, and vanilla. Add both sugars and beat for 2 to 3 minutes, scraping the bowl occasionally with a rubber spatula.

Increase speed to high and add the eggs one at a time, scraping the bowl with the spatula and beating until each is thoroughly incorporated. The mixture will look curdled. Reduce the speed to low and gradually add the flour, continuing to scrape the bowl with the spatula and beating only until smooth.

Turn batter into the prepared pan. Level batter by briskly rotating pan in opposite directions. Let stand for 10 minutes before baking.

Bake for 1 hour and 20 to 25 minutes or until a cake tester comes out dry. (The top of this cake frequently cracks deeply. It is to be expected and doesn't matter.) Remove from oven and let stand on a rack for 10 to 15 minutes. Cover with a rack or a cookie sheet. Invert. Remove pan and paper if it was used, cover with a rack, and invert again to cool right side up. Let stand 8 to 10 hours or overnight before serving.

Cookie-Jar Cookies

The rule is TLC—tender loving care. Try to make cookies all the same size. Practice. If they are not even, redo them. Use a ruler for icebox cookies and cookies cut into bars. Do not just put cookies in the oven, set the timer, and walk away until the bell rings. You must watch them . . . and baby them. If they are not browning evenly, reverse the pan front to back. If the bottoms are burning (check one to see), be prepared to slide an extra cookie sheet underneath. If the tops are burning, check the oven temperature—it might be too hot. Or lower the rack a bit. If you bake more than one cookie sheet at a time, rotate position of cookie sheets so that each one spends some time in each position.

When baking cookies on baking pan liner paper (baking parchment) or aluminum foil, you may shape the whole batch on pieces of paper or foil. They may then be baked by just sliding the cookie sheet under the paper. When recipes call for lining the cookie sheets with paper or foil, it is necessary to do so in order to keep the cookies from sticking.

Be sure to have plenty of racks handy for cooling the cookies, or the bottoms will get soggy and the cookies will be limp instead of crisp.

If cookies are large and thick (such as Aspen Rocks, New Orleans Oatmeal Cookies, Health-Food Cookies, etc.), it is advisable to raise the rack to make more room for air to circulate underneath. Just place the rack on a cake pan or any right side up bowl or baking dish. Otherwise the heat of the cookies causes steam to form on the counter or tabletop, and as the steam rises it makes the bottoms of the cookies moist. Incidentally, this holds true even if the rack has feet. They just don't leave enough room for large cookies.

Cookies must be completely cool before you store them—airtight. If you do not have enough airtight containers, use freezer bags, but wrap and handle gently in order not to crack the cookies. Or pack them in boxes and wrap the boxes in freezer paper or aluminum foil. Of course cookies freeze beautifully. Thaw before unwrapping.

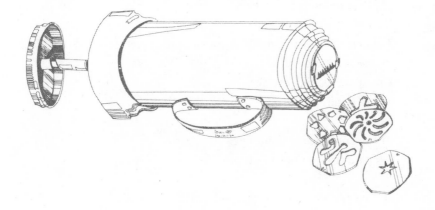

Cornmeal Cat's Tongues

ABOUT 110 SMALL COOKIES

This is a new recipe. It was not in any of the previous printings of this book or in any of my other books. It is a new version of a very old Italian recipe called Krumari, or Crumari. These are tiny, dainty, delicate . . . crisp, crunchy, wonderful. Although these are quite plain, they are addictive and totally irresistible. In other words, these are the cat's meow.

You will use a pastry bag to make them. And they will keep very well in an airtight container.

> 7 ounces (1¾ sticks) unsalted butter, at room temperature (see Note 1)
> ½ teaspoon salt
> 1 teaspoon vanilla extract
> ¾ cup sugar
> 2 eggs
> ⅔ cup cornmeal, ground fine
> 1¾ cups triple-sifted all-purpose flour (see Note 2)

Adjust two racks to divide the oven into thirds and preheat to 350 degrees. Line cookie sheets with baking parchment and prepare each parchment as follows with guide lines for three rows of 3-inch cookies.

Use a ruler and a pencil. Mark a 1-inch border along each long side. From these marks measure 3 inches toward the middle and make a mark. And then center a 3-inch strip in the middle. Draw connecting lines.

In the large bowl of an electric mixer beat the butter with the salt, vanilla, and sugar until well mixed. Then add the eggs one at a time, scraping the bowl with a rubber spatula and beating until well mixed after each. Stop the beater. Add the cornmeal and flour. Beat on low speed, scraping the bowl with the rubber spatula, and beating only until incorporated.

Fit a 16-inch pastry bag with a plain round tube #3 that has a ⁵⁄₁₆-inch opening. Fold down a deep cuff on the outside of the bag.

Work with only about a third of the dough at a time: Place about a third of the dough in the pastry bag. Unfold the cuff and close the top of the bag by twisting it together. Squeeze the top of the bag to force the dough down to the tip of the bag.

Using the guide lines, press out little sticks of the dough about as thick as a pencil and only 3 inches long, leaving almost an inch of space between the cookies.

To cut off the dough at the end of a cookie it is usually enough to just twist the bag a bit and pull it away from the cookie. But sometimes that doesn't do it. Then press the point of the tube flat against the cookie sheet. That will do it.

If the paper slips out of place while you are shaping the cookies, place a weight on one corner.

Bake two sheets at a time for 15 to 20 minutes. The success of these depends on careful timing. Please don't set a timer and walk away. Please watch them frequently. Reverse the sheets top to bottom and front to back once or twice during baking. Bake until the cookies are golden-colored (they might be darker on the edges).

Remove the cookies one at a time as they finish. Transfer baked cookies to racks or to a large brown paper bag to cool and then store airtight.

If you bake one sheet alone bake it on the higher of the two racks. One sheet alone will bake in less time.

Notes:

1. The butter must be at room temperature. If it is too cold it will make the batter too stiff.
2. The flour must be sifted before it is measured or you might be using too much and that would make the batter too stiff. I use a triple sifter. If you use a single sifter or a strainer, sift or strain the flour three times before measuring.

P.S. *Because I make these often, I reuse the same paper that has the drawn guidelines many times. I don't actually shape the cookies on that paper. I place another blank sheet of parchment on top and shape the cookies on that. The guidelines on the bottom paper show through the top sheet.*

Aspen Rocks

40 LARGE COOKIES

I learned these delicious cookies from The Swiss Bakery in Aspen, Colorado. The owner of the bakery was a great pastry chef from Switzerland. When I asked him how to make these he invited me to come in the next day and help him make them. What fun! I had a great time and I ate a lot of cookies. And I've made these ever since. They are loaded with raisins, dates, and nuts, and tantalizing spices.

3¾ cups sifted all-purpose flour
1 teaspoon baking soda
½ teaspoon salt
½ pound (2 sticks) butter
1 teaspoon each: cinnamon, mace, allspice, dry mustard
1 teaspoon vanilla extract
1 tablespoon instant coffee dissolved in 2 tablespoons boiling water
1¾ cups firmly packed light brown sugar
3 eggs
5 ounces (1 cup) raisins
12 ounces (1½ generous cups, packed) pitted dates, cut in quarters (see page xxv)
8 ounces (2 generous cups) walnuts, in large pieces

Adjust two racks to divide the oven into thirds. Preheat oven to 350 degrees. Line cookie sheets with parchment or foil.

Sift together flour, baking soda, and salt. Set aside. In large bowl of electric mixer beat the butter to soften it a bit. Beat in the cinnamon, mace, allspice, dry mustard, vanilla, and coffee. Gradually add the sugar and beat well. Beat in the eggs one at a time. Scrape the bowl frequently with a rubber spatula. On lowest speed gradually add the sifted flour mixture, scraping the bowl with the rubber spatula and beating only until blended. Remove from mixer. Stir in raisins, dates, and nuts.

Drop by heaping tablespoonfuls (make these large) about 2 inches apart on a lined cookie sheet. Dip a table fork into cold water and with the bottom of the wet prongs flatten a cookie to ½-inch to ¾-inch thickness. Repeat to flatten all the cookies. Put the sheet on the lower rack in the oven.

Put only one sheet of cookies in the oven at the beginning. Start them on the lower rack, finish them on the upper rack. When they are about half baked, a second sheet may go in. In this way you will be able to glaze all the cookies while they are still hot.

Bake 15 to 18 minutes until cookies are well browned and tops feel firm and spring back when lightly touched. Reverse position of pan during baking to insure even browning.

While the first sheet of cookies is baking, prepare the following glaze:

GLAZE
¾ cup confectioners sugar
1 tablespoon soft butter
1½ tablespoons light or heavy cream
1 teaspoon vanilla extract
Pinch of salt

In a small bowl beat above ingredients until smooth. If necessary add a bit more cream or sugar—mixture should be the consistency of mayonnaise. Cover it when not in use.

Slide the parchment or foil off the cookie sheet. Immediately, with a pastry brush, brush a thin coating of the glaze on the hot cookies. The heat of the cookies will melt it to a shiny, creamy coating, which will be dry to the touch in just a few minutes. With a wide metal spatula transfer cookies to racks to cool.

Oatmeal Cookies

These delicious cookies are large, thick, semisoft, moist, chewy, and loaded with raisins, nuts, and chocolate morsels. Yum!

It is best to bake these on double cookie sheets to protect the bottoms from burning.

> 7½ ounces (1½ cups) raisins
> 1 cup water
> 2 cups sifted all-purpose flour
> ¾ teaspoon baking soda
> 1 teaspoon salt
> 1½ teaspoons cinnamon
> ½ pound (2 sticks) butter
> 1 teaspoon vanilla extract
> 1 cup firmly packed light or dark brown sugar
> 2 eggs
> 1½ cups old-fashioned or quick-cooking (not instant) oatmeal
> 8 ounces (2¼ cups) walnuts, broken into large pieces
> 6 ounces (1 cup) semisweet chocolate morsels

Adjust oven rack one-third down from top of oven and preheat oven to 375 degrees. Line a cookie sheet with baking parchment.

In a small, heavy saucepan over high heat, boil the raisins and water for about 5 minutes until there is ¼ cup plus 1 tablespoon of water remaining. Drain the raisins in a strainer, reserving the water. If there is not enough water left, add water or coffee to make the required ¼ cup plus 1 tablespoon. Set aside.

Sift together the flour, baking soda, salt, and cinnamon. Set aside.

In the large bowl of an electric mixer beat the butter to soften it a bit. Add the vanilla and sugar and beat to mix. Add the eggs and beat, scraping the bowl with a rubber spatula, until mixed. Beat in the raisin liquid.

On low speed gradually add the sifted dry ingredients, continuing to scrape the bowl with a rubber spatula. Then mix in the oatmeal, raisins, nuts, and chocolate morsels.

Form drop cookies using a well-rounded tablespoon of the dough for each cookie and placing them about 2 inches apart on the lined sheet.

Flatten the tops a bit with a wet fork (dipped in water). Now place the filled cookie sheet on top of another cookie sheet to prevent the bottoms from becoming too dark.

Bake for about 15 minutes, reversing the sheet front to back once during baking. Bake until the cookies feel semifirm to the touch.

With a wide metal spatula transfer the cookies to racks to cool.

Repeat directions to bake the balance of the cookies.

Note: To store these cookies in a cookie jar or freezer box it is best to place them two together, bottoms together.

New Orleans Oatmeal Cookies

2¼ cups sifted all-purpose flour
1 teaspoon baking soda
1 teaspoon baking powder
1 teaspoon salt
1 tablespoon cinnamon
½ teaspoon nutmeg
½ teaspoon allspice
½ teaspoon powdered cloves
6 ounces (1½ sticks) butter
½ cup apricot preserves
2 teaspoons instant coffee
1½ cups firmly packed dark brown sugar
2 eggs
¾ cup milk
2¼ cups old-fashioned or quick-cooking (not instant) oatmeal
8 ounces (1½ generous cups) raisins
8 ounces (2 cups) whole salted peanuts (preferably the dry-roasted type)

Adjust rack to top position in oven. Preheat oven to 375 degrees. Line cookie sheets with baking parchment.

Sift flour with baking soda, baking powder, salt, cinnamon, nutmeg, allspice, and cloves. Set aside. In large bowl of electric mixer, beat the butter and apricot preserves. Add the instant coffee and sugar and beat until well mixed. Beat in the eggs one at a time, scraping the bowl with a rubber spatula as necessary to keep the mixture smooth. On lowest speed, alternately add the sifted dry ingredients in three additions and the milk in two additions. Beat only until smooth after each addition. Beat in the oatmeal. Remove from mixer. Stir in the raisins and peanuts.

Using a heaping tablespoonful of batter for each cookie, drop 2 inches apart on the lined cookie sheets. Bake for 20 minutes or until lightly browned and semifirm to the touch. Reverse sheet during baking to insure even browning.

With a wide metal spatula remove cookies to a rack to cool.

Note: These have a tendency to burn on the bottoms; if you bake more than one sheet at a time be sure to use double cookie sheets under the lower ones.

Health-Food Cookies

36 COOKIES, 4 INCHES IN DIAMETER

I created this recipe for a health-food store in Miami Beach, and then baked them for the store until the demand became more than I could handle.

1 cup unsifted all-purpose whole-wheat flour
1 teaspoon baking powder
¾ teaspoon salt
1 tablespoon cinnamon
¼ teaspoon powdered ginger
7½ ounces (1½ cups) raisins (see page xxv)
4 ounces (1 generous cup) walnuts, coarsely broken or cut
4 ounces (1 generous cup) pecans, coarsely broken or cut
3 ounces (½ generous cup) pignolias (pine nuts)
4 ounces (1 cup) peanuts, may be salted or not
2½ ounces (½ cup) sunflower seeds
2½ ounces (½ cup) sesame seeds
½ cup wheat germ
1 cup rolled oats or quick-cooking (not instant) oatmeal
½ pound (2 sticks) butter
½ cup peanut butter (see Note 1)
1¼ cups firmly packed dark brown sugar
2 eggs
¼ cup milk

Adjust rack to top position in the oven. Preheat oven to 350 degrees. Line cookie sheets with baking parchment.

Use a strainer and strain the flour, baking powder, salt, cinnamon, and ginger into a very large bowl. Add the raisins and, with your fingers, toss until they are separated and coated with the dry ingredients. Add the walnuts, pecans, pignolias, peanuts, sunflower seeds, sesame seeds, wheat germ, and rolled oats or oatmeal. Mix together and set aside.

Beat together the butter and peanut butter. Add the sugar and beat well. Beat in the eggs and the milk, scraping the bowl with a rubber spatula as necessary.

Pour over the flour-nut mixture. Stir with a heavy wooden spoon or spatula, until the dry ingredients are completely absorbed.

Make these large. Place by heaping tablespoonfuls 2½ to 3 inches apart on the cookie sheets. With the back of a spoon flatten the cookies to about ¾-inch thickness.

Bake 18 minutes or until cookies are lightly browned and semifirm to the touch. If necessary, reverse position of cookie sheet during baking to insure even browning.

Use a wide metal spatula to transfer cookies to racks to cool.

Notes:

1. Any other nut butter—cashew, almond, etc.—may be substituted for peanut butter.
2. It is best to bake these one sheet at a time. If you bake more than one at a time, use double cookie sheets under the lower ones to keep the bottoms from burning.

Tea Cakes

36 VERY LARGE COOKIES

The absence of salt and flavoring is typical of early American cookies, often called tea cakes. This dough should be refrigerated overnight before it is rolled out with a rolling pin.

> ½ teaspoon baking soda
> 5¼ cups sifted all-purpose flour
> ½ pound (2 sticks) butter
> 3 cups sugar
> 3 eggs
> 1 cup heavy cream

Sift the baking soda with 1 cup of the flour (reserve remaining 4¼ cups) and set aside.

In the large bowl of an electric mixer, beat the butter until soft. On low speed, gradually add the sugar and beat for 1 to 2 minutes. Scrape the bowl with a rubber spatula as necessary all during the mixing. Add the eggs one at a time, beating after each until it is thoroughly incorporated.

On lowest speed beat in 1 cup flour sifted with the baking soda. Then add the reserved flour in five additions, alternating with the cream in four additions. Beat only until smooth after each addition.

Divide the dough roughly in quarters. Wrap each airtight and refrigerate overnight.

Adjust rack to the top position in the oven and preheat oven to 400 degrees. Line cookie sheets with baking parchment.

Work with one quarter of the dough at a time, keeping the rest refrigerated. On a floured pastry cloth with a floured rolling pin, roll the dough ¼ to ⅓ inch thick. Work quickly before the dough softens.

Cut out the cookies with a 3½-inch round cookie cutter, dipping the cutter in flour as needed. Transfer the cookies onto the cookie sheets with a metal spatula, placing them 2 inches apart.

Bake 13 to 15 minutes until cookies are very lightly colored. Reverse position of cookie sheet during baking to insure even browning. With a wide metal spatula, transfer cookies to racks to cool.

Repeat rolling, cutting, baking with remaining dough. Leftover pieces should be pressed together and rechilled before rolling.

Note: Unrolled dough may be kept in the refrigerator for several days or it may be frozen. If it is frozen, it should be refrigerated for several hours or overnight before rolling.

Hungarian Butter Biscuits

(Vajas Pogácsa)

18 COOKIES

A rich butter cookie, somewhat like shortbread. This recipe is from Paprikas Weiss, the Hungarian food shop in New York City, where Mrs. Renée Weiss, the mother of the proprietor, prepares them. Mr. Weiss says, "This biscuit is direct from the folk culture of Hungary. So much so that my pastry chef friends tell me it is not taught in the culinary schools of Hungary. You can sense some social class distinctions in this food—remember Hungary was a feudal society until the end of World War II—but everyone in Hungary eats *Pogácsa* in its several variations."

> 3 cups sifted all-purpose flour
> ½ pound (2 sticks) butter
> 4 egg yolks
> 1 cup confectioners sugar
> ¼ teaspoon salt
> 1 egg (for egg glaze)

Place flour in a large bowl. With a pastry blender cut in the butter until the particles are the size of peas. Add the egg yolks, sugar, and salt. Stir briefly. Turn out onto a board or smooth surface and work the dough with your hands, squeezing it through your fingers and kneading it slightly only until the dough holds together and is smooth. Work quickly and do not handle any more than necessary. Form into a ball, flatten slightly. Wrap airtight and refrigerate for an hour or so until firm enough to be rolled.

Adjust rack to the top position in the oven. Preheat oven to 350 degrees.

Roll the dough between two pieces of wax paper until it is ½ inch thick (no thinner!). Remove top sheet of paper.

Score the top of the dough with a long, sharp knife, making shallow lines about ¼ to ½ inch apart first in one direction and then in the opposite direction (use the full length of the blade, not just the tip). Cut the scored dough with a round 2¼- to 2½-inch cutter. With a metal spatula transfer the cookies to an unbuttered cookie sheet, placing them about 1 inch apart. If the cookies are too sticky to be transferred, slide a cookie sheet under the wax paper and transfer to the freezer or refrigerator until firm. (Rechilled cookies may have to be cut again with the cookie cutter.)

Stir the egg lightly with a fork just to mix and, with a soft brush, brush it carefully over the top of each cookie. Bake about 30 minutes, reversing position of cookie sheet if necessary during baking to insure even browning.

Bake until cookies are a rich golden brown all over. Transfer with a metal spatula to cool on a rack.

Note: Mrs. Weiss rolls the dough 1 inch thick. I prefer ½ inch. In any event, cookies must be baked until dry and crisp all the way through. Do not underbake.

Currant Cookies

42 COOKIES

½ pound (2 sticks) butter
½ teaspoon mace
1 teaspoon vanilla extract
1 cup sugar, plus additional for dipping
1 egg
2⅓ cups sifted all-purpose flour
3½ ounces (¾ cup) raisins or currants
Finely grated rind of 1 large lemon (or 2 small)

In small bowl of electric mixer beat the butter to soften it a bit. Add mace, vanilla, and sugar, and beat for a minute or two. Beat in the egg. On lowest speed gradually add the flour, scraping the bowl with a rubber spatula and beating only until smooth. Remove from mixer, stir in raisins or currants and lemon rind.

Wrap airtight and refrigerate for about 1 hour. Or place in freezer until firm enough to handle.

Adjust rack to top position in the oven. Preheat oven to 375 degrees. Line cookie sheets with baking parchment.

Using 1 rounded teaspoonful of dough for each cookie, roll between your hands into 1-inch balls. Place 2 inches apart on lined cookie sheets.

Flatten tops with the back of a fork continually dipped in sugar. It is most efficient to press all the cookies first in one direction, and then cross-hatch them in the opposite direction, flattening the cookies to ⅓- to ½-inch thickness.

Bake one sheet at a time about 15 minutes until lightly colored, reversing position of cookie sheet if necessary during baking to insure even browning. Remove with a wide metal spatula to cool on a rack.

Black Pepper Cookies

50 TO 60 COOKIES

Especially crisp-crunchy and deliciously flavored. These are a treat. They are tantalizing.

 3 cups sifted all-purpose flour
 2 teaspoons baking powder
 ½ pound (2 sticks) butter
 ½ teaspoon salt
 ¾ teaspoon black pepper, ground fine (preferably fresh ground)
 Generous pinch of cayenne pepper
 ½ teaspoon powdered cloves
 2 teaspoons cinnamon
 1 tablespoon powdered ginger
 1½ cups sugar
 1 egg

Adjust rack high in the oven. Preheat oven to 400 degrees. Line cookie sheets with baking parchment.

Sift together flour and baking powder. Set aside. In large bowl of electric mixer beat the butter to soften it a bit. Beat in the salt, the black pepper, cayenne pepper, cloves, cinnamon, and ginger. Scrape the bowl with a rubber spatula as necessary to keep mixture smooth while beating in the sugar, the egg, and, on lowest speed, the sifted dry ingredients. When completely blended, remove from mixer to a board or smooth surface. Knead lightly. Divide the dough into three pieces. Work with one piece at a time. Do not chill the dough before rolling.

On a lightly floured pastry cloth, with a lightly floured rolling pin, roll to ⅛- to ¼-inch thickness. Cut with a 2¾-inch round cutter. Scraps may be rerolled and cut. Transfer cookies with a metal spatula to an unbuttered cookie sheet, placing them about ¾ inch apart.

Reverse the position of the sheet during baking to insure even browning and bake 12 minutes or until cookies are only lightly browned (not dark).

If you bake more than one sheet at a time, change positions of sheets during baking. With more than one cookie sheet in the oven at a time, they will take a bit longer to bake.

As cookies are done, transfer them with a wide metal spatula to cool on racks. Store airtight.

Sesame Pennies

36 COOKIES, 2½ INCHES IN DIAMETER

These are small (not as small as pennies), round, hard, crisp, and candy-like. They are an old Southern tradition.

2½ ounces (½ cup) benne (sesame) seeds
3 tablespoons butter
1 cup firmly packed light brown sugar
2 egg yolks
2 teaspoons vanilla extract
½ teaspoon salt
¼ cup plus 2 tablespoons sifted all-purpose flour

Adjust rack to top position in oven. Preheat oven to 350 degrees. Line two or more large cookie sheets with aluminum foil.

In a heavy 8- to 10-inch frying pan, stir the seeds over moderate heat with a wooden spatula to toast to a golden brown. Watch them constantly—they burn quickly. Remove from heat and set aside.

In a medium-size saucepan over low heat, melt the butter. Remove from heat and, with a wooden spatula, stir in the brown sugar, then the yolks, vanilla, and salt. Stir in the toasted seeds and then the flour.

Spread out a large piece of wax paper. Divide dough into thirty-six mounds, using 1 teaspoonful of dough for each and placing them on the wax paper.

Between your hands roll each cookie into a small ball and place the balls at least 2 inches apart on the lined cookie sheets and place in oven to bake 12 minutes or until lightly browned (see Note). Slide foil off cookie sheet and repeat baking process, baking only one sheet at a time.

Let cool completely and then peel foil away from cookies. Store airtight. Serve bottom or shiny side up.

Note: If the cookies have not browned enough they will not be as crisp as they should be—and they will not have the caramelized sugar flavor they should have.

Caraway Cookies
(English)

36 TO 42 COOKIES

> ¼ pound (1 stick) butter
> ½ cup sugar
> 2 egg yolks
> 2 cups sifted all-purpose flour
> ½ teaspoon baking soda
> ⅓ cup sour cream
> Caraway seeds

Adjust rack high in the oven. Preheat oven to 375 degrees.

In small bowl of electric mixer beat the butter to soften it a bit. Add sugar and beat for a minute or two. Beat in the egg yolks. On lowest speed, add half of the flour. Stir baking soda into sour cream and add that to the dough. Add remaining flour. Scrape the bowl with a rubber spatula as necessary to keep ingredients blended and beat only until smooth.

With a rolling pin, roll the dough between two sheets of wax paper until it is about ¼ inch thick. Place it, still between the sheets of wax paper, on a cookie sheet in the freezer for about 15 to 20 minutes, or longer in the refrigerator, until the wax paper can be pulled off neatly without pulling away any of the dough.

Remove top sheet of wax paper, just to release it, and then replace it. Invert dough and remove other sheet of wax paper. Do not replace it.

Cut cookies with a floured, 2-inch round cutter. If at any time dough sticks to bottom wax paper, simply invert it onto another piece of paper. If dough softens, rechill it.

Place cookies 1 inch apart (these spread only very slightly) on unbuttered cookie sheet. Sprinkle a pinch of caraway seeds over each cookie. With your fingertips, gently push seeds lightly into the dough.

Bake 15 minutes or until light golden brown. With metal spatula transfer to a rack to cool.

Caraway Seed Wafers

(Irish)

30 TO 36 COOKIES

2 cups sifted all-purpose flour
1 teaspoon baking powder
¼ teaspoon baking soda
¼ teaspoon salt
¼ pound (1 stick) butter
1 cup sugar
1 egg
1 tablespoon caraway seeds

Sift together flour, baking powder, baking soda, and salt. Set aside. In small bowl of electric mixer beat the butter to soften it a bit. Add the sugar and beat well. Beat in the egg. On lowest speed gradually add the sifted dry ingredients. Turn out onto a board or smooth surface. Add the caraway seeds and knead lightly only until seeds are evenly distributed.

Wrap airtight. Freeze for about 15 minutes and then refrigerate for 1 hour or until the dough is firm enough to be rolled out.

Adjust rack to center of oven. Preheat oven to 375 degrees.

Work with about one-third of the dough at a time. On a lightly floured pastry cloth with a lightly floured rolling pin, roll to ¹⁄₁₆- to ⅛-inch thickness. Cut with a round cookie cutter about 3¼ inches in diameter. (Scraps may be rerolled and cut.) With a metal spatula transfer to unbuttered cookie sheets, placing cookies about ½ inch apart.

Bake 13 to 15 minutes or until lightly browned all over, reversing position of cookie sheet during baking. With a wide metal spatula, transfer individually as they brown to a rack to cool. Store airtight.

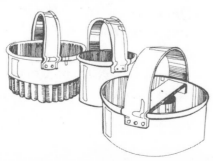

Italian Pine Nut Macaroons

22 COOKIES

These are especially yummy—chewy almond meringue macaroons coated with a generous amount of crisp-toasted pine nuts. They are wonderful. I can't resist them. They are a luxury—pine nuts are expensive but they add a delicious and exotic flavor.

5 ounces (1 cup) blanched almonds
1 cup sugar
2 egg whites
Pinch of salt
⅛ teaspoon cream of tartar
¼ teaspoon vanilla extract
¼ teaspoon almond extract
12 ounces (2½ cups) pignolias (pine nuts)

Adjust two racks to divide the oven into thirds and preheat the oven to 400 degrees. Line cookie sheets with baking parchment or foil and set aside (see Note).

Place the almonds in the bowl of a food processor fitted with the metal chopping blade. Add ¼ cup of the sugar (reserve remaining ¾ cup). Process for about half a minute until the nuts are fine.

Transfer the processed almonds to a large bowl. Add ½ cup of the sugar (reserve remaining ¼ cup) and stir to mix. Let stand.

In the small bowl of an electric mixer beat the egg whites with the salt and cream of tartar until they increase in volume and barely hold a soft shape. On low speed gradually add the remaining ¼ cup of sugar. Then beat on high speed again. During beating add the vanilla and almond extracts, and beat until the whites hold a firm, straight point and are quite stiff—beat this a little longer than you normally do.

Add the beaten whites all at once to the ground almonds. With a large rubber spatula fold the whites and almonds together until they are incorporated.

Now, it is best if the pine nuts are in a shallow bowl (like a wide and shallow soup plate). Use two teaspoons to form the cookies, one to pick up the dough and one to push it off. Use a heaping teaspoonful (really heaping) of dough for each cookie. Drop the cookies, a few at a time, into the pine nuts. Then, using the fingers of both hands, gently turn the cookies to coat them thoroughly with the pine nuts, pressing gently so that the nuts are imbedded in the dough.

Place them about 1½ inches apart on the lined cookie sheets.

Bake two sheets at a time for about 15 minutes, reversing the sheets top to bottom and from to back once during baking. (If you bake one sheet alone, place it on another cookie sheet to prevent the bottoms from burning, and bake it in the center of the oven.) When done, the pine nuts should be nicely toasted and the meringue should be only lightly colored. Do not overbake or the cookies will be crisp instead of chewy.

With a metal spatula transfer the baked cookies to racks to cool.

Note: If possible, use large-size cookie sheets (17 x 14) so that you can bake these all at one time, and the meringue doesn't have to stand around and wait. Meringue is not good at waiting.

Old-Fashioned Peanut Butter Cookies

48 COOKIES

1½ cups sifted all-purpose flour
¾ teaspoon baking soda
¼ pound (1 stick) butter
½ teaspoon vanilla extract
½ cup granulated sugar
½ cup firmly packed light brown sugar
1 egg
½ cup smooth peanut butter
3 ounces (¾ cup) salted peanuts, chopped fine, not ground (must be very
   fine)

Adjust rack to top position in oven. Preheat oven to 375 degrees.

Sift together flour and baking soda. Set aside. In small bowl of electric mixer beat the butter to soften it a bit. Add vanilla and both sugars and beat for about 1 or 2 minutes. Beat in the egg. On lowest speed add about half of the sifted flour mixture, scraping bowl as necessary with a rubber spatula. Add peanut butter and beat until smooth. Beat in remaining flour mixture and then the peanuts.

The mixture will be very stiff. Remove it from the mixer. Turn it out onto a board and knead it slightly only until everything is blended.

On a large piece of wax paper divide the dough into forty-eight mounds, using a rounded teaspoonful for each. Between your hands roll them into balls about 1 inch in diameter. Place 2 inches apart on unbuttered cookie sheets. Press the tops with the back of a fork. It is most efficient to press the cookies first all in one direction and then crosshatch them in the opposite direction, flattening the cookies to about ½-inch thickness. It is best to bake only one sheet at a time.

Bake about 12 minutes or until cookies are lightly browned, reversing position of cookie sheet as necessary to insure even browning. Watch carefully—they burn easily. These will harden and crisp as they cool. Cool on racks.

Craters

36 COOKIES

Wonderful! These have unusual ingredients (only 2 tablespoons of flour), an unusual technique (you can't shape them right away), and they are unusually good. Dark, semifirm, moist, chewy, and not too sweet.

    3 ounces unsweetened chocolate
    8 ounces (2¼ cups) walnuts
    ¼ cup fine, dry bread crumbs
    2 tablespoons sifted all-purpose flour
    2 eggs
    1 cup granulated sugar
    1 to 2 cups strained confectioners sugar

Chop the chocolate rather fine and place it in the bowl of a food processor fitted with the metal chopping blade. Process for 20 to 25 seconds until the chocolate is chopped fine. Add the walnuts, bread crumbs, and flour and process for 20 to 25 seconds until everything is fine. Transfer to a large mixing bowl.

In a small bowl beat the eggs and granulated sugar to mix.

Pour the egg mixture over the nut mixture and stir to mix thoroughly.

On a large piece of baking parchment or wax paper drop the dough by rounded teaspoonfuls making thirty-six mounds. (The dough will be very soft and wet now.) Let the mounds stand for an hour or more, turning them upside down occasionally, until they are just barely firm enough to be handled. Use two metal spatulas for turning them. After an hour or so the dough will still be soft and moist but will not still be sticky.

Adjust an oven rack one-third down from the top and preheat the oven to 350 degrees. Line cookie sheets with baking parchment.

Strain a mound of confectioners sugar onto another length of baking parchment.

Transfer a few of the mounds of dough to the mound of confectioners sugar. With your fingers turn them around to coat them with the sugar and then roll between your palms into balls. Handle gently.

Place the sugared mounds 1½ to 2 inches apart on a lined cookie sheet.

Bake for about 13 minutes until the tops feel semifirm to the touch. The centers should still be soft. Do not overbake.

With a wide metal spatula transfer to racks to cool.

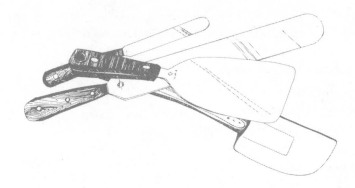

Mulattoes

18 VERY LARGE COOKIES

Soon after the first printing of this book, we had dinner at the Soho Charcuterie in Manhattan. They brought us a dish of huge, gorgeous, dark chocolate cookies that we had not ordered. They smiled secretively and knowingly and watched me. I tasted one. It was wonderful. I was about to ask for the recipe when they said, "These are yours." I soon learned that they meant it both ways: The cookies were mine to eat or take with me—and also, it was my recipe (it was this recipe). They had used 3 ounces of butter (instead of 1 ounce). I think it is an improvement and so I changed the recipe.

And at Sonrisa Bakery in beautiful Rancho Santa Fe in Southern California they baked these every day. They called them Charlie's Cookies in memory of a friend of ours who was a World War II naval pilot and a top ace. He shot down seventeen Japanese planes. After the war, when he came home to Rancho Santa Fe, he played golf almost every day—always with a few of these in his pocket. These were his favorites.

Other bakeries that make these call them Chocolate Dreams, Chocolate Whoppers, and other names indicating extreme chocolate. They all write to me to let me know how popular they are.

2 ounces unsweetened chocolate
6 ounces semisweet chocolate
3 ounces (¾ stick) butter
¼ cup sifted all-purpose flour
1 teaspoon baking powder
⅛ teaspoon salt
2 eggs
¾ cup sugar
2 teaspoons instant coffee (I use Medaglia d'Oro espresso)
½ teaspoon vanilla extract
6 ounces (1 cup) semisweet chocolate morsels or 6 ounces semisweet chocolate cut into ½-inch pieces
8 ounces (2¼ cups) walnuts or pecans, broken into medium pieces

Adjust two racks to divide the oven into thirds. Preheat oven to 350 degrees. Line cookie sheets with baking parchment.

In the top of a small double boiler over hot water on moderate heat, melt the unsweetened and semisweet chocolates and the butter. Stir until smooth. Remove top of double boiler and set aside.

Sift together the flour, baking powder, and salt. Set aside. In small bowl of electric mixer beat the eggs, sugar, coffee, and vanilla at high speed for a minute or two. On low speed add the chocolate mixture, and finally the sifted dry ingredients, scraping bowl with a rubber spatula as necessary and beating only until blended. Transfer to a large bowl.

Stir in the chocolate morsels or cut-up chocolate and nuts.

Drop by heaping tablespoonfuls 2 inches apart on the lined sheets. Bake immediately.

Bake two sheets together for 12 to 14 minutes reversing the sheets top to bottom and front to back once during baking. Tops will be dry. Centers should remain moist and chewy. Do not overbake. Let stand on cooke sheets until firm enough to be moved. Then, with a wide metal spatula remove cookies to a rack.

Note: Timing is everything in this recipe. Be careful.

French Chocolate Wafers

36 COOKIES

T hin and deliciously crisp/crunchy.

1½ cups sifted all-purpose flour
1¼ teaspoons baking powder
⅛ teaspoon salt
6 ounces (1½ sticks) butter
1¼ cups sugar
1 egg
1 tablespoon dark rum or ½ teaspoon vanilla extract
¾ cup strained, powdered, unsweetened cocoa (preferably Dutch process)
Milk

Sift together flour, baking powder, and salt. Set aside. In large bowl of electric mixer beat the butter to soften it a bit. Gradually add the sugar and beat for 1 to 2 minutes. Beat in the egg and rum or vanilla. On lowest speed gradually add the cocoa, scraping bowl with a rubber spatula. Beat in the sifted flour mixture, continuing to scrape bowl with spatula and beating only until smooth.

Remove from mixer and wrap airtight. Flatten lightly. Refrigerate for at least 1 hour or until firm enough to roll.

Adjust rack high in the oven. Preheat oven to 400 degrees. Line cookie sheets with baking parchment.

Work with about one-third of the dough at a time. Keep the rest refrigerated. Work quickly before the dough softens. Lightly flour a pastry cloth and rolling pin. Roll the dough to ⅛-inch thickness, turning it a few times to keep it from sticking, but don't use any more flour than necessary. Cut with a round 3¼-inch cookie cutter. Place 1 inch apart on a cookie sheet. With a soft brush, brush the tops lightly with milk.

Bake 8 to 10 minutes, reversing position of cookie sheet during baking to insure even baking. Watch carefully. Do not let the edges burn. If you cut these smaller they will bake in less time. With a wide metal spatula transfer cookies to a rack to cool. They will crisp as they cool. Store airtight.

Save all the scraps. Rechill, roll, and cut them all at once in order not to incorporate any more flour than necessary.

Note: I have a 5-inch round cookie cutter and I have used it for these—they are gorgeous.

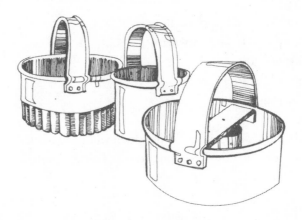

Chocolate Cracks

48 COOKIES

> 3 cups sifted all-purpose flour
> 1¼ teaspoons baking soda
> ½ teaspoon salt
> 1½ cups firmly packed dark brown sugar
> 6 ounces (1½ sticks) butter
> 2 tablespoons water
> 12 ounces semisweet chocolate, chopped coarse
> 2 eggs

Sift together flour, baking soda, and salt. Set aside. In a large, heavy saucepan over moderate heat, cook the sugar, butter, and water, stirring until the butter is melted. Add the chocolate and continue to stir over heat until partially melted. Remove from heat and stir until chocolate is completely melted. Transfer to large bowl of electric mixer and let stand for about 5 minutes to cool slightly.

On high speed, beat in the eggs one at a time. Reduce speed to low and gradually add the sifted dry ingredients, scraping bowl with a rubber spatula and beating only until dry ingredients are absorbed. Let dough stand for about 10 minutes or longer until it can be handled easily.

Adjust rack high in the oven. Preheat oven to 350 degrees. Line cookie sheets with baking parchment.

Using a heaping teaspoonful of dough for each cookie, roll between your hands into shiny and moist-looking balls. Place 2 inches apart on the cookie sheet.

Bake 12 to 13 minutes, reversing position of pan during baking to insure even baking. Tops will feel dry but not firm. Do not overbake. Cookies will crisp as they cool. With a wide metal spatula transfer to racks to cool.

Bar Cookies and Rusks

Brownies

These are the Brownies with which I started my reputation as a pastry chef when I was about ten years old. The recipe has been changed and revised continuously over the years. I will probably continue to change it.

> 5 ounces unsweetened chocolate
> 6 ounces (1½ sticks) butter
> 1 tablespoon instant coffee
> 4 eggs
> ½ teaspoon salt
> 2 cups sugar
> 1 teaspoon vanilla extract
> ¼ teaspoon almond extract
> 1 cup sifted all-purpose flour
> 10 ounces (2½ generous cups) walnut halves or pieces

Adjust rack one-third up from bottom of oven and preheat to 450 degrees. Butter a 15½ x 10½ x 1-inch jelly-roll pan and then line it with aluminum foil as follows. Turn the pan upside down. Center a piece of foil 18 to 19 inches long (12 inches wide) over the pan, shiny side down. Fold down the sides and corners to shape the foil. Remove the foil, turn the pan right side up, place the shaped foil in the pan, and press it carefully into place. Brush the foil all over with melted butter.

Melt chocolate and butter in a heavy saucepan over low heat or in the top of a large double boiler over hot water on moderate heat. Stir with a small wire whisk to blend. When melted and smooth, add instant coffee and stir to dissolve. Remove from the heat and set aside to cool.

Meanwhile, in small bowl of electric mixer beat eggs and salt until slightly fluffy. Gradually add sugar and continue to beat at medium-high speed for 15 minutes until the mixture forms a ribbon when the beaters are raised. Transfer to large mixer bowl.

Add vanilla and almond extracts to cooled chocolate mixture. On lowest speed add the chocolate to the eggs, scraping bowl with a rubber spatula and beating only enough to blend. Still using lowest speed and rubber spatula, add the flour, beating only enough to blend. Fold in the nuts, handling the mixture as little as possible.

Pour into prepared pan and spread smooth. Place in oven. Immediately reduce oven temperature to 400 degrees. Bake 21 to 22 minutes. Test with a toothpick. It should just barely come out dry. Do not overbake. Brownies should be slightly moist inside.

Remove from oven. Immediately cover with a large rack or cookie sheet and invert. Remove pan and foil. Cover with a large rack and invert again. After 10 or 15 minutes invert once again only for a moment to make sure that the Brownies are not sticking to the rack.

Cool completely and then chill for about 30 minutes in the freezer or a bit longer or overnight in the refrigerator. Transfer to a large cutting board.

To mark portions evenly, measure with a ruler and mark with toothpicks. Use a long, thin, very sharp knife, or one with serrated edge. Cut with a sawing motion into squares. I wrap these individually in clear cellophane.

Brownie Crisps

16 LARGE OR 32 SMALL COOKIES

Similar to Brownies in taste, but thin and crisp. Made without a mixer.

¼ pound (1 stick) butter
1 ounce unsweetened chocolate
1 teaspoon instant coffee
½ cup sugar
1 egg
¼ teaspoon vanilla extract
¼ teaspoon salt
¼ cup sifted all-purpose flour
½ cup walnuts (1⅓ oz.), cut in medium-size pieces

Adjust one rack one-third up from bottom. Preheat oven to 375 degrees. Butter a 15½ x 10½ x 1-inch jelly-roll pan.

Melt the butter and chocolate over the lowest heat in a 1½- to 2-quart heavy saucepan. Stir with a rubber spatula until smooth. Add the instant coffee and stir to dissolve. Remove from heat and stir in the sugar, and then the egg and vanilla. Mix thoroughly. Add the salt and flour and mix until smooth.

Pour batter into the prepared pan and spread smooth. Sprinkle with the walnuts.

Bake exactly 15 minutes, reversing position of pan once during baking to insure even browning.

Remove from oven and, without waiting, cut carefully with a small, sharp knife. Immediately, before cookies cool and harden, remove them with a wide, metal spatula. Cool on a rack. Store airtight.

Pecan Squares Americana

32 TO 48 (OR MORE) COOKIES

Many years ago a Miami newspaper published a letter to the food editor from the wife of Governor Collins of Florida. She raved about the pecan cookies she had eaten at the Americana Hotel in Miami Beach. She went on to say that she had requested the recipe from the hotel, that they had given it to her, but it did not work for her. The letter included the recipe as she had received it. I ran to the kitchen to try it. The recipe did not work for me either. I called the hotel and asked to speak to the pastry chef. His name was Jacques Kranzlin; he could not have been more gracious or charming, and he invited me to his kitchen to watch him work. It was a treat.

When I got home I was able to make the Pecan Squares. I made them again and again and again. I wrote the recipe. I taught it in my classes. It was unanimously *the best*! And when I taught classes around the country, it was one of my favorite recipes to teach because I knew how people would rave about them.

PASTRY SHELL
 8 ounces (2 sticks) unsalted butter
 ½ cup sugar
 1 egg
 ¼ teaspoon salt
 Finely grated rind of 1 large lemon
 3 cups sifted all-purpose flour

Butter a 15½ x 10½ x 1-inch jelly-roll pan and then line it with aluminum foil as follows: Turn the pan upside down. Center a piece of foil 18 to 19 inches long (12 inches wide) shiny side down over the pan; check the long sides to be sure there is the same amount of overhang on each side. Fold down the sides and the corners to shape the foil. Remove the foil, turn the pan right side up, place the shaped foil in the pan, and press it carefully into place. Do not butter the foil. Place the prepared pan in the freezer (it is easier to spread this dough on a cold pan—the coldness will make the dough cling to the pan).

In the large bowl of an electric mixer, beat the butter until it is softened, add the sugar, and beat to mix well. Beat in the egg, salt, and lemon rind. Gradually add the flour and beat, scraping the bowl with a rubber spatula, until the mixture holds together.

Now you are going to line the pan with the dough; it is important that you have enough dough on the sides of the pan to reach generously to the top of the pan. It will work best and be easiest if you place the dough, one rounded teaspoonful at a time, around the sides of the pan—that is, just touching the raised sides. (I don't actually use teaspoons for this. It is easiest to lift a generous mound of the dough, hold it in your left hand, and use the fingers of your right hand to break off teaspoon-size pieces.) Place the pieces about ½ to 1 inch apart. Then place the remaining dough the same way all over the rest of the bottom of the pan. Flour your fingertips (if necessary) and start to press the mounds of dough, working up on the sides first and then the bottom, until you have formed a smooth layer all over the sides and bottom. There must not be any thin spots on the bottom or any low spots on the sides (it is best if it comes slightly above the top). Take your time; it is important for this shell to be right.

With a fork, carefully prick the bottom at about ½-inch intervals. Chill in the freezer or refrigerator for about 15 minutes. (Do not freeze.)

Adjust a rack one-third up from the bottom of the oven and preheat oven to 375 degrees.

Bake for 20 minutes. Watch it constantly. If the dough on the sides starts to slip down a bit, reach into the oven and press it with your fingertips or the back of a spoon to put it back into place. If the dough starts to puff up, prick it gently with a cake tester to release trapped air and flatten the dough. (There have been times when it insisted on puffing up, and it was a question of which one of us would win. I did. Here's how: Place one or more pot holders on the puffed-up part for a few minutes. The puffed-up dough will get the message and will know you mean business, and it will lie down flat.) After 20 minutes, the edges of the dough will be lightly colored; the bottom will be pale but dry. Remove from the oven but do not turn off the heat. Prepare the topping.

PECAN TOPPING

8 ounces (2 sticks) unsalted butter
1/2 cup honey
1/4 cup granulated sugar
1 cup plus 2 tablespoons firmly packed dark brown sugar
1/4 cup heavy cream
20 ounces (5 cups) pecan halves or large pieces

In a heavy, 3-quart saucepan over moderately high heat, cook the butter and honey, stirring occasionally, until the butter is melted. Add both sugars, stir to dissolve, bring to a boil, and let boil without stirring for exactly 2 minutes.

Without waiting, remove from the heat, stir in the heavy cream and then the pecans. (Although the original recipe says to do the next step immediately, I have recently decided it is better to wait a bit.) Wait 5 minutes. Then, with a large slotted spoon, place most of the pecans evenly over the crust. Then drizzle the remaining mixture over the pecans so it is distributed evenly—watch the corners. Use your fingers or the back of a spoon to move around any nuts that are piled too high and place them in any empty or thin spots. (It will look as if there is not enough of the thin syrupy mixture, but there is.)

Bake at 375 degrees with the rack one-third up from the bottom for 25 minutes. (Now you will see that the syrupy mixture has spread out and boiled up and filled in any hollows.)

Cool in the pan on a rack.

Cover with a large rack or a cookie sheet, hold them firmly together, and turn the pan and rack or sheet over and remove the pan and the foil. If the bottom of the dough looks very buttery you may pat it with a paper towel if you wish, but it is not really necessary, the dough absorbs it as it stands. Cover with a rack or sheet and turn over again, leaving the cake right side up. It is easiest to cut the cake into neat pieces if it is well chilled first; chill it in the refrigerator or the freezer. Then transfer it to a large cutting board. Use a ruler and toothpicks to mark the cake into quarters. Use a long and heavy, sharp knife, and cut straight down (not back and forth). These are very rich, and although most people like them cut into forty-eight bars, I know several cateresses who make them almost as small as lump sugar. And I have made them larger because I wrap them individually in clear cellophane and it is more fun to wrap cookies that are not too small.

Pecan-Coconut Bars

24 BARS

CRUST
¼ pound (1 stick) butter
½ cup sugar
1 cup sifted all-purpose flour

Adjust rack one-third up from bottom of oven. Preheat oven to 400 degrees. Butter a shallow 9 x 13-inch pan and line only the bottom with aluminum foil.

In small bowl of electric mixer beat the butter to soften it a bit. Beat in the sugar and on low speed add the flour. Beat only until dough holds together. Transfer dough to prepared baking pan. With fingertips press it to cover the bottom of the pan evenly—not the sides.

Bake 12 to 15 minutes until the crust is lightly colored. While the crust is baking, prepare the topping.

TOPPING
2 tablespoons sifted all-purpose flour
½ teaspoon baking powder
⅛ teaspoon salt
2 eggs
1 teaspoon vanilla extract
1½ cups firmly packed dark brown sugar
3½ ounces (1⅓ cups) shredded coconut
3½ ounces (1 cup) pecans, broken into large pieces

Sift together flour, baking powder, and salt. Set aside. In small bowl of electric mixer, beat eggs slightly just to mix. Beat in vanilla and sugar. On low speed beat in sifted dry ingredients. Remove from mixer and stir in coconut and pecans.

When bottom crust is baked to a light golden color, remove it from the oven. Reduce oven temperature to 350 degrees and raise the rack to the center of the oven. Pour topping mixture over the hot crust. Spread evenly. Return to oven.

Bake 25 minutes. Remove from oven. Let cool in pan on a rack.

When completely cool, cut around edges to release. Cover with a cookie sheet and invert. Remove pan and aluminum foil. Cover with a rack and invert again. Prepare following icing:

ICING

1½ cups confectioners sugar
2½ tablespoons lemon juice

Mix sugar and lemon juice until very smooth. The icing should be quite thick, about the consistency of a heavy cream sauce. Adjust the consistency by adding more sugar or lemon juice as needed. Pour it over the cake and spread with a narrow metal spatula. Let cake stand for a few hours until icing is dry. Transfer cake to a board. Use a ruler and toothpicks to mark even pieces. Cut with a long, heavy knife, cutting down firmly with the full length of the blade.

Date-Nut Bars

1 cup sifted all-purpose flour
¼ teaspoon baking powder
⅛ teaspoon salt
¼ pound (1 stick) butter, melted
1 cup granulated sugar
2 eggs
16 ounces (2 cups) pitted dates, cut into large pieces
7 ounces (2 cups) walnut halves or large pieces
Confectioners sugar

Adjust rack to center of oven. Preheat oven to 350 degrees. Line a shallow 9 x 13-inch pan with one piece of aluminum foil long enough to cover bottom and sides. Press the foil with a pot holder or small towel to mold it into place without tearing it. Brush the bottom and sides with very soft or melted butter. Set aside.

Sift together flour, baking powder, and salt. Set aside. In large bowl of electric mixer beat the melted butter and sugar. Add the eggs and beat for a minute. On lowest speed add the sifted dry ingredients, beating only until incorporated. Mix in the dates and nuts.

Spread this thick batter as smooth as possible in the prepared pan, pressing it into place with the back of a large spoon.

Bake 35 minutes or until the top is a light golden brown. Remove from oven. Let cool in cake pan on a rack for about 10 minutes. Place a cookie sheet over the top. Invert. Remove pan and foil. Cover with another cookie sheet or a rack and invert again to cool completely.

Transfer to a cutting board. Use a ruler and toothpicks to mark even pieces. Cut with a long, thin, very sharp or finely serrated knife into twenty-four bars. Strain confectioners sugar generously over the tops.

Note: We were in a log cabin in the woods in Colorado. We had electricity and we had an oven, but not much else. This is what I made. Nothing ever tasted better. To make this without a mixer, melt the butter in a 2½- to 3-quart saucepan, remove from heat, and stir in the sugar. Beat the eggs and stir them in. Then add the sifted, dry ingredients and mix until smooth. With a heavy, wooden spoon or spatula, mix in the dates and then the nuts.

Soya Date Bars

12 LARGE BARS, 16 SQUARES, OR 24 SLICES

2 eggs, separated
1 cup firmly packed dark brown sugar
¼ cup plus 1 tablespoon boiling water
1 teaspoon vanilla extract
1 cup sifted whole-wheat pastry flour (see Note 1)
½ cup sifted soya flour (see Note 2)
¼ teaspoon salt
8 ounces (1 cup) pitted dates, cut into large pieces
4 ounces (1 generous cup) walnuts, broken or cut into large pieces

Adjust rack to center of oven. Preheat oven to 375 degrees. Butter a 9-inch square cake pan and dust it with fine, dry bread crumbs.

In small bowl of electric mixer beat the egg yolks, sugar, and boiling water at moderately high speed for 3 to 5 minutes until the mixture becomes very light in color. Beat in the vanilla and then, on lowest speed, add both flours and salt, beating only until blended. Add the dates and beat briefly. Remove from mixer. Stir in the nuts.

Beat the egg whites until they hold a point, or are stiff but not dry. With a wooden spatula stir about one-quarter of the whites into the batter and then fold in the balance.

Turn the batter into prepared pan. Smooth the top. Bake 30 to 35 minutes or until top springs back when lightly touched.

Remove from oven. Let stand for about 10 minutes. Cover with a rack and invert. Remove pan and cover with another rack. Invert again to cool right side up.

When completely cool, transfer to a board and cut with a long, thin, very sharp knife.

Notes:

1. Both whole-wheat pastry flour and soya flour are available at health-food stores.
2. Any particles of flour too coarse to go through the sifter should be added to the sifted flour.

African Date Bars

16 TO 24 SQUARES OR BARS

¾ cup sifted all-purpose flour
1 teaspoon baking powder
1 teaspoon cinnamon
Pinch of salt
1 cup sugar
8 ounces (1 cup) pitted dates, cut into large pieces
4 ounces (1 generous cup) walnuts, cut or broken into large pieces
2 eggs
1 teaspoon vanilla extract

Adjust rack one-third up from bottom of oven and preheat oven to 375 degrees. Butter a 9-inch square cake pan and line it with aluminum foil as follows: Turn pan upside down. Place a 12-inch square of foil shiny side down on the pan and fold down the sides. Remove foil and turn pan right side up. Place the foil in the pan and press gently into place, pressing with a pot holder or folded towel in order not to tear the foil. Brush or spread soft butter all over the foil and dust with flour. Shake out excess. Set pan aside.

Sift together flour, baking powder, cinnamon, salt, and sugar into a mixing bowl.

Add the dates and toss with your fingers to separate and thoroughly coat each piece. Add the nuts and toss again.

Beat the eggs and vanilla until very light and stir them in. Turn the dough into the prepared pan and spread even.

Bake for 30 minutes. Remove from oven and let stand for about 10 minutes. Cover with a rack or small cookie sheet and invert. Remove pan and aluminum foil. Cover with a rack, invert, and let cool right side up.

When completely cool, remove to a board and, with a long, heavy knife, cut into squares or bars.

Peanut Bars

32 COOKIES

Thin caramel cookie bars topped with peanuts. As irresistible as peanuts. Easily mixed in a saucepan.

> ¾ cup sifted all-purpose flour
> 1 teaspoon cinnamon
> ½ teaspoon powdered ginger
> ¼ pound (1 stick) butter
> 6 ounces (1 cup) butterscotch morsels
> 1½ teaspoons instant coffee
> ¼ cup sugar
> 1 egg
> 3 ounces (¾ cup) salted peanuts, chopped coarse (preferably the
>   dry-roasted type)

Adjust rack to center of oven. Preheat oven to 325 degrees. Line a 10½ x 15½ x 1-inch jelly-roll pan with aluminum foil as follows: Turn the pan upside down. Cover with a piece of foil large enough to fold down on all four sides and fold the edges just to shape them. Remove the foil. Invert the pan. Sprinkle a few drops of water in the pan to keep the foil in place. Place the foil in the pan. Use a folded towel or a pot holder to press the foil firmly against the pan. Brush the foil with soft or melted butter. Place in freezer or refrigerator. (Chilling the pan makes it easier to spread the thin layer of dough.)

Sift together the flour, cinnamon, and ginger and set aside.

Place the butter and butterscotch morsels in a 2½- to 3-quart saucepan over moderate heat. Stir occasionally until melted. Stir in the instant coffee. Remove from heat and stir with a wire whisk until smooth. With a rubber or wooden spatula stir in the sugar and sifted dry ingredients.

In a small bowl stir the egg briefly with a fork just to mix and add it to the batter. Stir until smooth.

Turn the batter into the chilled pan and, with the back of a large spoon, spread as level as possible. It will make a very thin layer. Sprinkle with the peanuts.

Bake for 25 minutes until top is golden-colored and springs back when lightly touched. Remove from oven and cool in pan for only 3 minutes. Cover with a large cookie sheet. Invert and remove pan and foil. Cover cake with another large cookie sheet and invert again. With a long, sharp knife, cut the warm cake into bars, cutting down firmly with the full length of the blade. With a wide metal spatula, transfer bars to a rack to cool.

Pecan Buttercrunch

16 LARGE BARS OR 32 SMALL SQUARES

These are the easiest (no mixing bowls). You simply collect the ingredients, open the containers or packaging, layer the ingredients in the pan, and bake. *Voilá!*

> ¼ pound (1 stick) butter
> 1¼ cups graham cracker crumbs
> 3½ ounces (1 to 1⅓ cups) shredded coconut
> 6 ounces (1 cup) semisweet chocolate morsels
> 6 ounces (1 cup) butterscotch morsels
> 1 15-ounce can (1⅛ to 1¼ cups) sweetened condensed milk (see Note)
> 7 ounces (2 cups) pecan halves

Adjust rack to center of oven and preheat to 350 degrees. Butter a 9 x 13 x 2-inch pan and then line it with aluminum foil as follows: Turn the pan upside down. Center a piece of foil 17 inches long over the pan, shiny side down. Fold down the sides and corners to shape the foil. Remove the foil, turn the pan right side up, place the shaped foil in the pan, and press it carefully into place. But if you are using a pan that has square (not rounded) corners and straight (not flared) sides use heavy-duty foil or the sharp corners will tear the foil.

If the foil doesn't reach to the top of the pan don't worry. These cookies are only ¾ inch high.

Put butter in lined pan and place it in oven until melted. Tilt pan to spread butter all over the bottom and about halfway up on the sides. Sprinkle crumbs evenly over butter in the bottom of the pan. Sprinkle coconut evenly over crumbs. Sprinkle chocolate and butterscotch morsels evenly over coconut. Slowly drizzle the condensed milk evenly over top. Cover with pecan halves placed rounded side up and quite close to each other.

Bake for 5 to 10 minutes, then reach into oven with a wide metal spatula and press gently on the nuts so that they become firmly imbedded and won't fall off later on.

Bake 35 to 40 minutes altogether, or until the condensed milk that shows between the nuts has turned a caramel color all over. Remove from oven.

Cool to room temperature. Place a cookie sheet on top and invert. Remove the pan and peel off the foil. Place a rack on top and invert again so that cake is now right side up. Let stand overnight or freeze about 1 hour (or refrigerate a bit longer) before transferring to a board and cutting with a long, sharp knife.

Note: Condensed milk should not be stored for more than 6 months. It darkens and thickens if it has been standing on the shelf for a long time, and becomes too thick to pour easily or to run over the top of the cake. Use fresh condensed milk, which is about the consistency of heavy cream and almost white in color.

Rusks, Italian Style
(Biscotti all'anice)
48 RUSKS

4 eggs, separated, plus 1 egg yolk
1 cup sugar
½ teaspoon vanilla extract
1 tablespoon whole anise seeds
1 cup sifted cake flour
Finely grated rind of 1 large orange
⅛ teaspoon salt

Adjust rack to center of oven and preheat to 375 degrees. Line the bottom only of a shallow 9 x 13-inch baking pan with unbuttered wax paper or baking parchment. (Do not line the sides.) Set aside.

In small bowl of electric mixer, beat the five yolks and ¾ cup of the sugar (reserve remaining ¼ cup sugar) at high speed for 5 minutes until very thick. Beat in the vanilla and anise seeds. On lowest speed gradually add the flour, scraping the bowl as necessary with a rubber spatula and beating only until incorporated. Remove from mixer and stir in the orange rind.

Beat the four egg whites with the salt until they hold a soft shape. Add the reserved sugar and continue to beat until the whites hold a straight point. The egg yolk mixture will be *very* stiff. With a large rubber or wooden spatula, stir about one quarter of the whites into the yolk mixture. In about three additions fold in the balance.

Turn into prepared pan and spread level. Bake 25 to 30 minutes until top is well browned and cake springs back firmly when lightly touched.

Cool for 5 minutes. With a small, sharp knife cut around sides to release. Invert onto a rack. Remove pan and peel off paper. Let stand until cool.

Preheat the oven to 250 degrees.

On a board, with a long, thin, sharp knife, cut the cooled cake down the center, the long way. Then cut each half into narrow slices, about ½ inch thick.

Place the slices, top side up with a bit of space between them, on a large cookie sheet.

Bake 45 minutes to 1 hour or longer, until very lightly colored around the edges. Cookies will be soft when removed from oven but will become crisp when cool. (If not, they need more baking.) The cookies on the outer edges of the cookie sheet will begin to color sooner than those in the center. Remove them individually when done.

Cool completely before storing.

...elnut Rusks

...ose flour

...owder

...er

...act

...tract

...blanched almonds or blanched hazelnuts (filberts)
(see page xxiii)

Adjust rack one-third down from top of oven. Preheat oven to 400 degrees. Line a 14 x 16-inch cookie sheet with baking parchment.

Sift together the flour and baking powder. Set aside. In small bowl of electric mixer beat the butter to soften it a bit. Add vanilla and almond extracts, and sugar. Beat for a minute or two. Beat in the eggs one at a time. On lowest speed gradually add sifted dry ingredients, scraping the bowl as necessary with a rubber spatula and beating only until smooth. Remove from mixer and stir in the nuts.

Using two teaspoons, place the batter, one teaspoonful at a time, to form three long, narrow strips across the width of the prepared cookie sheet. Each strip should be about 12 inches long and 1½ inches wide. Leave about 3 inches of space between the strips. It is not necessary to smooth the tops or sides, as the batter will run slightly in baking.

Bake 15 minutes or until strips are golden-colored and tops spring back when lightly touched. Remove from oven. Reduce oven temperature to 300 degrees. Using a flat-sided cookie sheet as a spatula, transfer baked strips to a large rack to cool.

Transfer cooled cakes to a cutting board. Use a finely serrated knife or a long, very sharp, thin knife to slice cakes on an angle into cookies about ¾ inch wide. Replace cut strips on cookie sheet, top side up, with a bit of space between them.

Bake at 300 degrees for 25 minutes. Turn off heat. Open oven door slightly. Let cookies dry in oven for about 10 minutes before removing. Cool on racks.

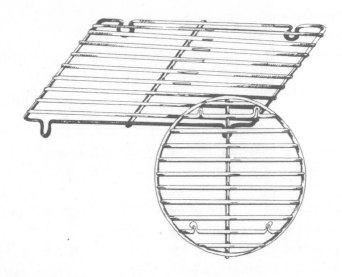

Icebox and Shortbread Cookies

I have made all of the cookies in this section (and many others) without a mixer. Beat the butter by hand in a bowl, add extracts if called for, and the sugar. Work them together by hand and then, in the bowl or on a board or smooth surface, work in the remaining ingredients. Knead until smooth by following directions for "breaking" the dough, page 276.

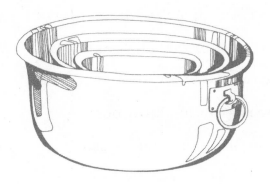

Swedish Icebox Cookies

Spicy almond-ginger cookies.

$3\frac{1}{2}$ cups sifted all-purpose flour
1 teaspoon baking soda
$\frac{1}{4}$ teaspoon salt
1 tablespoon powdered ginger
$\frac{1}{4}$ teaspoon nutmeg
1 teaspoon powdered cloves
2 teaspoons cinnamon
$\frac{1}{2}$ pound (2 sticks) butter
1 cup sugar
$\frac{1}{2}$ cup molasses, light or dark
5 ounces (1 cup) whole, blanched almonds

Sift together flour, baking soda, salt, ginger, nutmeg, cloves, and cinnamon. Set aside. In large bowl of electric mixer beat the butter to soften it a bit. Gradually add the sugar and beat well. Add the molasses and beat, scraping the bowl with a rubber spatula, until smooth. On lowest speed, very gradually add the sifted dry ingredients, continuing to use the rubber spatula as necessary.

Turn out onto a board or smooth surface. Knead slightly only until smooth. Add the almonds and knead until they are evenly distributed. Divide the dough in half and shape each half into an oblong. Place each half on a piece of wax paper about 15 inches long.

Holding the paper against the dough, smooth each oblong into an even shape about 3 inches by 1 inch and 10 inches long. Wrap in the wax paper. Slide a flat-sided cookie sheet under the two oblongs. Freeze for 30 to 45 minutes or refrigerate overnight, or until firm enough to slice.

Adjust rack high in the oven. Preheat oven to 325 degrees.

Using a very sharp, thin knife, slice cookies ⅛ to a scant ¼ inch thick. Place on unbuttered cookie sheets 1 inch apart. Bake about 10 minutes, reversing position of cookie sheet as necessary to insure even browning. Bake until cookies color very slightly and tops are semifirm to the touch. Do not overbake. These will crisp as they cool. With a metal spatula, transfer to a rack to cool.

Note: These cookies are best if they are sliced very thin. It is easiest to get them thin if the dough is frozen before it is cut.

French Icebox Cookies

60 COOKIES

½ pound (2 sticks) butter
1½ teaspoons vanilla extract
¼ teaspoon almond extract
¼ teaspoon salt
1 cup sugar
2½ cups sifted all-purpose flour
1 tablespoon water

In large bowl of electric mixer cream the butter. Mix in the vanilla and almond extracts, salt, and sugar. Beat until thoroughly mixed. On lowest speed gradually add about half of the flour. Then add the 1 tablespoon water. Add remaining flour, scraping bowl with a rubber spatula and beating only until flour is incorporated and mixture holds together.

Turn the dough onto a piece of wax paper about 20 inches long. Holding the paper against the dough, shape it into a roll about 2 inches in diameter and 15 inches long, or into an oblong about 3 inches x ¾ inch and 15 inches long. Enclose it in the wax paper. Slide a cookie sheet under the roll and place it in the freezer for about ½ hour, or refrigerate it overnight, until the dough is firm enough to be sliced.

Adjust rack high in the oven. Preheat oven to 400 degrees.

Use a very thin, sharp knife to slice the cookies ⅛ to ¼ inch thick.

Place 1 inch apart on unbuttered cookie sheets. Bake 10 minutes, or until cookies are sandy-colored and lightly browned around the edges. Reverse position of pan during baking to insure an even color. Do not let them get too brown. With a wide metal spatula, transfer to racks to cool.

Old-Fashioned Walnut Icebox Cookies

48 COOKIES

1¾ cups sifted all-purpose flour
2 teaspoons baking powder
⅛ teaspoon salt
½ teaspoon cinnamon
¼ pound (1 stick) butter
1 teaspoon vanilla extract
1 cup sugar, granulated, light brown, or dark brown (see Note)
1 egg, extra-large or jumbo
2½ ounces (¾ cup) walnuts, cut or broken into small pieces

Sift together flour, baking powder, salt, and cinnamon. Set aside. In small bowl of electric mixer, beat the butter to soften it a bit. Add vanilla and sugar, and beat for about a minute. Beat in the egg and then the walnuts. On lowest speed gradually add sifted dry ingredients, scraping the bowl with a rubber spatula as necessary and beating only until the flour is incorporated and the mixture holds together.

Turn out onto a piece of wax paper 15 to 20 inches long. Holding the paper against the dough, shape it into a roll about 2 inches in diameter and 12 inches long; or shape it as an oblong about 1 x 3 inches and 14 inches long. Enclose in the wax paper.

Slide a flat-sided cookie sheet under the roll. Place in the freezer for about ½ hour, or refrigerate overnight, until firm enough to slice evenly.

Adjust rack near the top of the oven. Preheat oven to 400 degrees.

Use a thin, sharp knife to slice the dough ¼ to ⅓ inch thick. Place on unbuttered cookie sheets 1 inch apart.

Bake 10 minutes or until cookies are lightly colored, reversing position of cookie sheet if necessary during baking to insure even browning. With a wide metal spatula transfer to racks to cool.

Note: The flavor of the cookies will vary considerably depending on the sugar used. Brown sugar should be firmly packed when measuring it.

Montego Bay Icebox Cookies

2 cups sifted all-purpose flour
¼ teaspoon salt
2 teaspoons baking powder
1 teaspoon mace
½ pound (2 sticks) butter
2 teaspoons vanilla extract
½ cup sugar
1 egg

Sift together flour, salt, baking powder, and mace. Set aside. In large bowl of electric mixer, beat the butter to soften it a bit. Add vanilla and sugar and beat until thoroughly mixed. Beat in the egg. On lowest speed gradually add the sifted dry ingredients, scraping the bowl with a rubber spatula and beating only until dry ingredients are thoroughly incorporated.

Turn out onto a piece of wax paper about 15 inches long. Holding the paper against the dough, shape it into a roll about 10 to 12 inches long. The roll may be either round and 2 inches in diameter, or oblong, about 1 x 3 inches. Enclose it in the wax paper. Slide a flat-sided cookie sheet under the roll and place in the freezer for 20 to 30 minutes, or refrigerate for several hours until firm enough to slice.

Adjust the rack high in the oven. Preheat oven to 400 degrees.

With a very sharp, thin knife, slice the dough about ¼ inch thick. Place cookies on unbuttered cookie sheets 1 inch apart.

Bake 10 minutes or until cookies are sandy-colored and light brown around the edges, reversing position of cookie sheet during baking to insure even browning.

With a wide metal spatula, gently transfer these very fragile cookies to racks to cool.

Scotch Shortbread Cookies

When a Scotch friend of mine went to visit her family in Scotland she returned with this recipe for me from her grandmother. She said that this is the real thing. It is easy and fun to make. The texture of the shortbread is light and sandy. Yummy!

½ pound (2 sticks) butter
1 cup strained confectioners sugar
1½ cups sifted all-purpose flour
1½ cups strained cornstarch

Adjust rack to center of oven. Preheat oven to 350 degrees.

In large bowl of electric mixer beat the butter until soft. Add sugar and beat for a few minutes. On lowest speed gradually add flour and cornstarch, scraping the bowl with a rubber spatula and beating until the ingredients hold together.

Turn mixture onto a board or smooth surface and knead lightly. Use about half of the dough at a time. Wrap the balance airtight.

On a very lightly floured pastry cloth with a lightly floured rolling pin, roll the dough to ¼- to ⅓-inch thickness. Cut with a floured 1½-inch round cutter. Save scraps, knead them together briefly, and reroll them all together. Place cookies ½ inch apart on an unbuttered cookie sheet.

Pierce each cookie three times with a fork, going all the way through to the cookie sheet. If this is a sticky job, first chill the cookies briefly in the freezer or refrigerator. Bake about 22 minutes, reversing position of cookie sheet during baking, until cookies have barely colored. Do not overbake. Shortbread should not brown—it should just barely turn a pale sandy color around the edges and on the bottoms.

Transfer with a metal spatula to a rack to cool.

Scotch Walnut Shortbread

54 COOKIES

> 2 cups sifted all-purpose flour
> ⅓ cup strained cornstarch
> ½ cup sugar
> ½ pound (2 sticks) butter
> ½ teaspoon vanilla extract
> 3½ ounces (½ cup) walnuts, chopped very fine (they must be fine, but not
>   ground)

Adjust rack to center of oven. Preheat oven to 375 degrees.

Strain together flour, cornstarch, and sugar into a bowl. With a pastry blender cut in the butter and vanilla until mixture forms crumbs. Stir in the nuts. Turn out onto a board or smooth surface. Squeeze the mixture together between both hands several times. Form it into a ball. Work quickly and, with the heel of your hand, push off small amounts at a time, pressing the dough firmly against the board and working away from you. Form it into a ball again and push it off two or three times until it holds together and leaves the board clean.

Roll about half of the dough at a time on a lightly floured pastry cloth with a lightly floured rolling pin, to a ⅓-inch thickness. Cut with a floured 1½-inch round cutter. Save scraps and reroll them all together.

Place ¾ inch apart on unbuttered cookie sheet. Pierce each cookie three times with a fork, going all the way through to the cookie sheet. If the dough is sticky, first chill the cookies briefly in the freezer or refrigerator.

Bake about 20 minutes until cookies are lightly colored, reversing position of cookie sheet during baking. Do not overbake. Cool on racks.

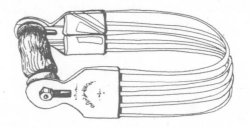

Shortbread Doughnut Cookies

24 LARGE COOKIES

½ pound (2 sticks) butter
1 cup confectioners sugar
2 cups sifted all-purpose flour

Adjust rack to center of oven. Preheat oven to 375 degrees.

In large bowl of electric mixer beat the butter a bit to soften. Add sugar and beat until blended. On lowest speed gradually add the flour, scraping bowl with a rubber spatula as necessary to keep mixture smooth.

(If necessary, chill the dough slightly only until it can be rolled. Do not let it get too firm. If it does, let it soften slightly at room temperature and then beat again.)

On a lightly floured cloth with a floured rolling pin, roll the dough to ¼-inch thickness. Cut with a floured 3-inch doughnut cutter (see Note). Save all the scraps and reroll and cut them together. Place ¾ inch apart on unbuttered cookie sheets.

Bake 13 minutes, reversing position of cookie sheet during baking, or until cookies are lightly colored on the edges and barely sandy-colored on top. These should not brown. Do not overbake.

Remove from oven and let cool briefly on cookie sheets. Transfer with wide metal spatula to cool on a rack.

Note: If you don't have a doughnut cutter, you can use two round cutters, one larger than the other, to cut doughnut shapes.

Short'nin' Bread

20 COOKIES

The kind mammy's little baby loves.

> 2 cups sifted all-purpose flour
> Generous pinch of salt
> ½ cup firmly packed dark brown sugar
> ½ pound (2 sticks) butter

Adjust rack one-third down from top of oven. Preheat oven to 375 degrees.

Place flour, salt, and sugar in a bowl. With a pastry blender cut in the butter until the mixture resembles coarse crumbs. Turn out onto a board or smooth surface. Briefly squeeze the mixture between your hands and then knead slightly only until the dough holds together smoothly. Do not handle any more than necessary. (If you handle the dough too much it must be chilled before rolling.)

On a lightly floured cloth with a lightly floured rolling pin, roll all of the dough at one time to ½-inch thickness. Cut with a floured 2-inch round cookie cutter. Reroll and cut scraps. Place cookies 1 inch apart on an unbuttered cookie sheet.

Pierce each cookie three times with a fork, going all the way through to the cookie sheet. If cookies are sticky, first chill them briefly in the freezer or refrigerator.

Bake 20 to 22 minutes, reversing position of cookie sheet during baking, until cookies are lightly colored. Do not overbake.

Remove with wide metal spatula to cool on rack.

Dainty Cookies

Hungarian Hazelnut Crescents

42 COOKIES

These are elegant and classic and very special. They are also very fragile; do not stack in a cookie jar or they will break. However, they may be frozen in a single layer on a tray and then stacked, or packed on top of each other, in a freezer container.

> 5 ounces (1 generous cup) hazelnuts, blanched (see page xxiv)
> 2¼ cups sifted all-purpose flour
> ½ pound (2 sticks) butter
> ⅓ cup sugar
> 1 teaspoon vanilla extract
> ¼ teaspoon almond extract
> Optional: Confectioners sugar or vanilla confectioners sugar

Adjust rack one-third down from top of oven. Preheat oven to 350 degrees.

Place the nuts in the bowl of a food processor fitted with the metal chopping blade. Add ¼ cup of the flour (reserve remaining 2 cups flour) and process for about 15 seconds or until fine. Set aside.

In large bowl of electric mixer beat the butter a bit to soften. Add sugar and vanilla and almond extracts and beat for a minute or two. Mix in the nuts and, on lowest speed, gradually add the reserved flour, scraping the bowl with a rubber spatula as necessary, and beating only until the flour is completely incorporated.

Place dough on a large piece of wax paper. Then, using approximately 1 slightly rounded tablespoonful of dough for each piece, divide into forty-two pieces.

Between your hands roll each piece into an elongated oval, about 3½ inches long, with tapered ends. Place cookies 1 inch apart on unbuttered cookie sheet, turning the ends down to form crescents.

Bake 18 minutes, reversing position of pan during baking to insure even browning, until cookies are lightly colored.

Very carefully, with a wide metal spatula, remove to a rack to cool.

Crescents may be served as they are, but I think they're better with a sprinkling of confectioners sugar or vanilla confectioners sugar (see Note) sprinkled on through a fine strainer.

Carefully, with a spatula, transfer cookies to serving platter.

Note: For sprinkling over cakes or cookies, vanilla sugar (page xxiii) is preferable to plain sugar because of its flavor.

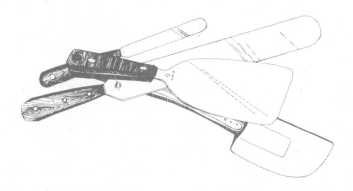

Mexican Wedding Cakes

24 SMALL COOKIES

¼ pound (1 stick) butter
2 tablespoons confectioners sugar (plus additional for sprinkling over the
  tops after baking)
½ teaspoon vanilla extract
1 cup sifted all-purpose flour
2½ ounces (¾ cup) walnuts, chopped very fine (they must be chopped fine,
  but not ground)

Adjust rack one-third down from top of the oven. Preheat oven to 375 degrees.

In small bowl of electric mixer beat the butter until softened a bit. Add sugar and vanilla and beat for 1 to 2 minutes. On lowest speed add the flour and then the walnuts, beating until the dough holds together.

Remove from mixer. Use a scant tablespoon of dough for each cookie. Roll into 1-inch balls. Place 1 inch apart on unbuttered cookie sheet. Bake about 15 minutes, reversing position of sheet during baking, until lightly colored.

With a metal spatula, transfer to a rack to cool. When completely cool, strain confectioners sugar generously over the tops.

Viennese Almond Crescents

2 ounces (scant ½ cup) almonds, blanched
1½ cups sifted all-purpose flour
5 ounces (1¼ sticks) butter
½ teaspoon almond extract
⅓ cup granulated sugar
Confectioners sugar

Adjust rack high in the oven. Preheat oven to 350 degrees.

Place the nuts in the bowl of a food processor fitted with the metal chopping blade. Add about ¼ cup of the flour (reserve remaining 1¼ cups flour) and process briefly until the nuts are ground. Set aside.

In small bowl of electric mixer beat the butter a bit to soften. Add almond extract and granulated sugar and beat for 1 minute. Beat in ground almonds and then, on lowest speed, add the reserved flour and beat until incorporated. Turn mixture onto a board or smooth surface and knead lightly just until smooth.

Break off small pieces of dough, each a well-rounded teaspoonful. Roll between your hands into small cigar shapes, each about 3½ inches long, with tapered ends. Place 1½ inches apart on unbuttered cookie sheet, turning down both ends to form a crescent.

Bake 15 minutes or until the cookies turn a very light golden color. Reverse position of cookie sheet during baking and, if you bake two sheets at the same time, exchange their positions during baking.

Use a wide metal spatula to transfer these delicate cookies gently to a rack to cool.

When completely cool, strain confectioners sugar generously over the tops.

Plantation Pecan Cookies

22 COOKIES

4 ounces (1 generous cup) pecans
1 cup sifted all-purpose flour
¼ pound (1 stick) butter
½ teaspoon vanilla extract
¼ teaspoon salt
¼ cup sugar
1½ teaspoons prepared coffee, water, or brandy
22 pecan halves

Place the 4 ounces of pecans in the bowl of a food processor fitted with the metal chopping blade. Add ¼ cup of the flour (reserve remaining ¾ cup flour) and process for about 15 seconds until ground. Set aside.

In small bowl of electric mixer beat the butter a bit to soften. Beat in the vanilla, salt, and sugar. Continue to beat for a minute or two. Beat in the coffee, water, or brandy. On lowest speed gradually add the reserved flour. Scrape the bowl with a rubber spatula and beat until smooth. Add the ground pecans and beat until incorporated.

Remove from mixer and place on aluminum foil, parchment, or wax paper. Flatten slightly, wrap, and refrigerate or freeze briefly until firm enough to handle.

Adjust rack one-third down from top of oven. Preheat oven to 375 degrees.

Remove chilled dough from refrigerator or freezer and cut into twenty-two equal pieces.

Roll each piece between your palms into a ball. Place 1½ inches apart on an ungreased cookie sheet. Press a pecan half firmly into the top of each cookie, flattening the cookie slightly as you do so.

Bake in preheated oven for 18 to 20 minutes until golden, reversing position of cookie sheet if necessary to insure even browning.

With a spatula, transfer cookies to a rack to cool thoroughly.

Swedish Jelly Slices

42 TO 48 BARS

2¼ cups sifted all-purpose flour
½ teaspoon baking powder
¼ teaspoon salt
6 ounces (1½ sticks) butter
2 teaspoons vanilla extract
⅔ cup sugar
1 egg
¾ to 1 cup apricot preserves (or any thick, tart jam or jelly)
2½ ounces (¾ cup) almonds, blanched and sliced thin

Adjust rack one-third down from top of oven. Preheat oven to 375 degrees.

Sift together flour, baking powder, and salt. Set aside. In large bowl of an electric mixer, beat the butter to soften a bit. Add vanilla and sugar and beat well. Beat in the egg. On lowest speed add the sifted dry ingredients, scraping the bowl with a rubber spatula and beating until the dry ingredients are thoroughly incorporated. Turn out onto a lightly floured board. Shape into a ball. Cut into four equal parts.

Working on the board, with your fingers (flour them if dough sticks) work each piece into a roll about 12 inches long and 1 inch in diameter.

Place the rolls crossways on a large, unbuttered cookie sheet, about 14 x 16 inches, leaving 2 to 3 inches of space between them. The rolls will spread a bit as they bake.

Make a narrow, shallow trench down the length of each roll by pressing gently with a fingertip. Leaving a little space at the ends, work the full length in one direction, and then work in the opposite direction. The ends and the sides should be higher. Do not make the trench too deep or the cookies will not hold together after they are baked and sliced.

To fill the trench with the preserves, use a pastry bag without a tube; or, if the opening of the bag is too large, use a plain, round tube about ½ inch in diameter. Or use a very small spoon. The filling should be level with the sides or very slightly higher. If it is thick enough it will not run over the sides. With your fingertips, generously sprinkle the sliced almonds over the preserves.

Bake about 25 minutes until the cookies are sandy-colored on top and golden brown around the edges, reversing position of pan during baking to insure an even color.

Shortly before removing cookies from oven, mix the following glaze.

GLAZE
  1¼ cups confectioners sugar
  2 tablespoons boiling water (approximately)

Mix sugar and water until smooth, using enough water to make the consistency similar to heavy cream. Cover airtight when not in use.

Remove cookie sheet from oven and apply the glaze by pouring it or spooning it down the length of each roll, over the preserves and nuts.

Using a flat-sided cookie sheet as a spatula, carefully slide the rolls onto a large rack to cool for about 5 minutes. Then carefully transfer them to a cutting board. With a very sharp, heavy knife, cut each warm roll on an angle into slices about 1 to 1¼ inches wide. Replace cookies on the rack to finish cooling.

Swedish Jelly Cookies

42 TO 48 COOKIES

½ pound (2 sticks) butter
⅛ teaspoon salt
¼ teaspoon almond extract
½ cup sugar
1 egg yolk
2¾ cups sifted all-purpose flour
Thick apricot preserves, or currant jelly

Adjust oven rack to top position. Preheat oven to 375 degrees.

In large bowl of electric mixer beat the butter, salt, and almond extract. Beat in the sugar and then the egg yolk. On lowest speed gradually add the flour, scraping the bowl with a rubber spatula, and beating only until mixture holds together.

Using about 1 tablespoon of dough for each cookie (or a bit less for daintier cookies), roll into even balls 1 inch or less in diameter. Place the cookies 1 inch apart on ungreased cookie sheets. After shaping the dough balls, make a shallow depression in the top of each, using a blunt instrument about ½ inch in diameter, e.g., the end of the handle of a wooden spoon or spatula. Form the depressions quickly before the cookies dry out, or they will crack.

After shaping and denting all the cookies, fill the hollows with preserves or jelly. This is best done with a small paper cone, in which case the preserves should be strained first. For making a paper cone see directions on page 513, but start with a 12-inch square of wax paper or baking parchment. Alternatively, the preserves or jelly may be applied with the tip of a small knife, in which case they would not have to be strained. Either way, fill the hollows level.

Bake only one sheet of cookies at a time, reversing position of pan during baking to insure even browning. Bake for 15 to 17 minutes until cookies are golden-colored.

While cookies are baking, prepare the following glaze:

GLAZE

> 1 cup confectioners sugar
> 2 tablespoons boiling water (approximately)

Mix sugar and water until smooth, using enough water to make the consistency similar to heavy cream. The glaze should not be too thick; it should be thin enough to flow easily when brushed on. Cover airtight when not in use.

When cookie sheet is removed from the oven, immediately brush the glaze over each cookie, using a soft brush and brushing over both jelly and cookie. Glaze will set immediately and then cookies may be transferred with a metal spatula to a rack to cool.

Note: To make these fancier, sprinkle a very little bit of coarsely chopped green pistachio nuts or chopped toasted almonds on cookies before glaze dries. It would be best if someone could help with this, since glaze must be applied while cookies are hot.

Spritz Cookies or Pretzels

48 SMALL COOKIES, OR 8 TO 10 LARGE PRETZELS (5 INCHES IN DIAMETER, MADE WITH ½-INCH ROUND TUBE)

These are the same but Spritz Cookies are shaped with a cookie press and Pretzels are shaped with a pastry bag.

½ pound (2 sticks) butter
1½ teaspoons vanilla extract
½ cup sugar
1 egg, extra-large or jumbo
2½ cups sifted all-purpose flour
Optional Toppings: Nuts, glacéed fruit, chocolate morsels

Adjust rack to the center of the oven. Preheat oven to 400 degrees.

In large bowl of electric mixer beat the butter to soften it a bit. Add vanilla and sugar and beat well. Beat in the egg. On lowest speed gradually add the flour, scraping the bowl with a rubber spatula and beating until smooth.

Press the dough through a cookie press onto unbuttered cookie sheets, placing the cookies 1 inch apart. Do not attempt to shape cookies through a press onto warm cookie sheets—they will pull away from the sheets. If necessary, chill the sheets in the freezer. Decorate cookies with optional toppings, pressing them in gently.

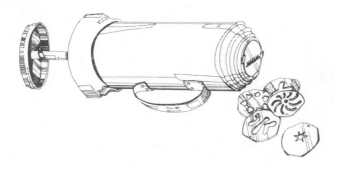

PRETZELS

Fit a large pastry bag with a plain, round tube ¼ to ½ inch in diameter. The dough will be stiff and it will take strength to force it through the pastry bag, but it will be easier if the bag is not too full. Use about one-third to half of the dough at a time in a 12- to 15-inch pastry bag. Until you become experienced at shaping pretzels, you may draw the shape roughly with a pencil directly on the cookie sheet and then just follow the lines.

GLAZE
1 egg yolk
1 teaspoon water
Pearl sugar

Make a glaze by stirring 1 egg yolk with 1 teaspoon water. With a small, soft brush, brush it over the tops of the pretzels. With your fingertips, sprinkle pearl sugar (see Note page 254) generously over the tops.

Bake 10 minutes, more or less, depending on the size of the cookies, until lightly colored. During baking reverse position of cookie sheet if necessary to insure even browning. With a metal spatula transfer to racks to cool.

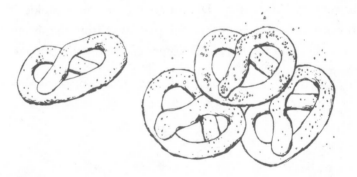

Chocolate Ribbons

60 4-INCH COOKIES

A chocolate variation on Spritz Cookies.

2 ounces unsweetened chocolate
¼ pound (1 stick) butter
1 teaspoon vanilla extract
¼ teaspoon salt
Optional: 1 tablespoon powdered instant coffee (see Note 1)
1 cup sugar
1 egg
2 tablespoons milk
2 cups sifted all-purpose flour

Adjust rack to center of oven. Preheat oven to 350 degrees.

Melt the chocolate in the top of a small double boiler over hot water on moderate heat. Set aside to cool.

In the large bowl of an electric mixer beat the butter to soften it a bit. Add vanilla, salt, optional powdered instant coffee, and the sugar. Beat until well mixed and then mix in the egg and the milk. Mix in the chocolate. On lowest speed gradually add the flour, scraping the bowl with a rubber spatula and beating only until smooth.

Fit a cookie press with the saw-toothed ribbon plate. Transfer some of the dough to the press. Use unbuttered cookie sheets. Hold the press at an angle, not upright, and press the dough into ribbons the full length of the cookie sheet, releasing the pressure as you near the end of each strip in order to stop the flow of dough. The ribbons may be placed close to each other—¼ to ½ inch apart.

Bake one sheet at a time for about 10 minutes. Reverse the position of the cookie sheet during baking to insure even baking.

Remove from oven and immediately, with a long, heavy knife, cutting across all the ribbons at once, cut into desired lengths—about 3 to 4 inches. Cut down firmly, using the full length of the blade. Immediately, before the cookies become crisp, loosen them from the sheet, using a wide metal spatula, a long, narrow one, or try using a flat-sided cookie sheet as a spatula. If you use a cookie sheet as a spatula, press down very firmly against the sheet that the cookies were baked on—you will be able to release them all and transfer them to a rack at the same time. Cool on racks.

Notes:

1. The coffee must be powdered instant, not the granules or chunks, which would clog the opening in the cookie press. If you only have granules or chunks, grind in a blender and strain.
2. When cool, these should be completely crisp. It is a good idea to bake a sample strip and adjust the timing accordingly.

Swedish Dream Cookies

36 COOKIES

This classic Swedish recipe calls for ammonium carbonate (see Note), a leavening agent that gives the cookies a specific texture—light, crisp, flaky. Ammonium carbonate is available in different forms. Buy the minimum amount available. If possible, buy it powdered; if you buy the granular, chip, or lump form, powder it using a mortar and pestle. It must be stored airtight in a dark place. Don't be concerned by the ammonia odor while cookies are baking—that will disappear completely.

> 2 cups sifted all-purpose flour
> 1 teaspoon powdered ammonium carbonate (see Note)
> ½ pound (2 sticks) butter
> ½ teaspoon vanilla extract
> ½ cup sugar
> 36 whole, blanched almonds
> 1 egg white
> Pearl sugar (see Note)

Sift flour with ammonium carbonate and set aside. In small bowl of electric mixer beat the butter to soften a bit. Add the vanilla and sugar and beat for a minute or two. On lowest speed gradually add the flour mixture, scraping the bowl as necessary with a rubber spatula and beating only until smooth.

Remove from mixer. Wrap airtight and chill in refrigerator or freezer only until dough is no longer sticky—do not chill it long enough for it to harden.

Meanwhile, adjust rack one-third down from top of oven. Preheat oven to 350 degrees.

Using a rounded teaspoonful of dough for each cookie, roll each between your palms into balls and place the balls about 2 inches apart on unbuttered cookie sheets.

Press an almond into the top of each, flattening the cookie very slightly as you do so.

Beat the egg white slightly only until foamy and, with a soft brush, brush it over each cookie.

Sprinkle cookies with the pearl sugar. Bake 20 to 23 minutes, reversing cookie sheet front to back once during baking to insure even browning.

When cookies are light golden brown, remove them with a wide metal spatula to cool on a rack.

Note: Ammonium carbonate (also called baker's ammonia) and pearl sugar (also called crystal sugar) are available from Sweet Celebrations in Minneapolis, Minnesota ([800] 328-6722). And also from The House-on-the-Hill, P.O. Box 7003, Villa Park, IL 60181 ([630] 969-2624).

Ladyfingers

ABOUT 30 4-INCH LADYFINGERS

Making ladyfingers is great fun. It's quick—but you have to beat egg whites correctly, fold them in correctly, and use a pastry bag correctly. Then, the satisfaction is tremendous. And the ladyfingers are delicious.

If you have extra-large cookie sheets (17 x 14 inches) use them for this recipe. And you will need a 15-inch pastry bag and a plain tube with a ⅝-inch opening (Number 8).

> **1 cup sifted unbleached flour**
> **4 eggs, separated**
> **1 teaspoon vanilla extract**
> **¼ teaspoon salt**
> **⅛ teaspoon cream of tartar**
> **½ cup plus 3 tablespoons superfine sugar (see Note)**
> **Confectioners sugar (for sifting over the tops before baking)**

Adjust two racks to divide the oven into thirds and preheat the oven to 325 degrees. Lightly butter two cookie sheets (see above), dust them with flour through a sifter, and over the sink shake off excess. Set aside.

Have ready a 15-inch pastry bag fitted with a plain round tube that has a ⅝-inch opening (Number 8). Fold down a cuff about 2 inches wide on the outside of the bag. Twist the tube end of the bag and push it up a bit into the bag to prevent the batter from leaking out. Place the bag in a tall glass or jar to support it while you fill it. Set aside.

Resift the flour two or three times and set it aside in the sifter on a piece of paper.

In a small bowl beat the yolks and vanilla with an eggbeater to mix well. Set aside.

Place the egg whites and salt in a clean small bowl of an electric mixer and, with clean beaters, beat on medium speed until foamy. Add the cream of tartar and beat on high speed until the whites hold a soft point when the beaters are raised. On moderate speed add the superfine sugar 1 rounded teaspoonful at a time. Then beat on high speed again until the whites are stiff but not dry. Remove the bowl from the mixer.

Add the beaten yolks all at once to the whites and fold together without being thorough about it. Turn into a large mixing bowl. In three additions, sift the flour over the top, folding it in with a rubber spatula. At first do not be completely thorough with the folding, and even at the end, fold only until you do not see any dry ingredients. Even if the mixture looks lumpy and not smooth, do not fold anymore.

Turn the mixture into the pastry bag. Unfold the cuff, gather the top of the bag closed, untwist the tube end, and press out ladyfingers onto the prepared sheets. Form the ladyfingers 4 inches long. Allow ½ to ¾ inch of space between ladyfingers.

At the end of each ladyfinger lift the pastry bag slowly toward the other end of the ladyfinger to prevent leaving a tail of the batter.

Through a fine strainer, quickly strain confectioners sugar generously onto the ladyfingers and bake immediately.

Bake for 15 to 18 minutes, reversing the sheets once, top to bottom and front to back, to insure even baking. Bake until the ladyfingers are lightly colored and feel dry and springy when gently pressed with a fingertip.

Then remove them with a wide metal spatula.

Ladyfingers are best when they are very fresh (the day they are made)—but they are also very good when they have been only loosely covered for a day or two and have become dry and almost crisp. But for lining a container (as for an icebox cake) they should be very fresh.

Note: If you do not have superfine sugar, place plain granulated sugar in the bowl of a food processor fitted with the metal chopping blade and process for 30 seconds.

Madeleines

12 MADELEINES, 3 INCHES LONG

Plain, buttery, and spongy—traditionally baked in shell-shaped forms, which are generally available in kitchen equipment shops. This recipe is for one pan with twelve forms for cookies 3 inches long.

Madeleines became famous in French literature because it was the taste of a madeleine dipped in a cup of tea which Marcel Proust used as the starting point of his literary journey into the past. They are delicious when just baked, but Proust's might well have been stale—when dry and stale they are great for dunking.

> 2 ounces (½ stick) butter
> 1 egg plus 2 egg yolks, at room temperature
> ¼ cup sugar
> ½ teaspoon vanilla extract
> ½ cup sifted all-purpose flour
> Finely grated rind of 1 large lemon

Adjust rack one-third up from bottom of oven. Preheat oven to 375 degrees. To prepare the pan: Bring about 1½ tablespoons of butter (this is in addition to that called for in recipe) to room temperature to soften. Do not use melted butter. With a pastry brush, brush the butter on the forms, brushing from the top to the bottom the long way and then reversing and brushing from the bottom to the top. Examine the forms carefully to make sure that you haven't missed any spots and also that the butter is not too thick anywhere. Now, over paper, sprinkle the forms with fine, dry bread crumbs. Tilt and shake the pan to coat the forms thoroughly. Invert the pan and tap it firmly, leaving a very light coating of crumbs.

Cut up the 2 ounces of butter and, in a small pan over low heat, melt it, stirring occasionally. Set aside to cool but do not let it harden.

In small bowl of an electric mixer beat the egg, egg yolks, sugar, and vanilla at high speed for about 15 minutes until mixture barely flows when beaters are lifted. On lowest speed gradually add the flour, scraping the bowl with a rubber spatula as necessary and beating only until the flour is incorporated—do not overbeat. Remove from mixer. (Use your fingertips to remove the batter from the beaters.)

Fold in the lemon rind and then, in four or five additions, the cooled butter, folding only until no butter shows. Bake immediately—do not let the batter stand.

Spoon the batter into the prepared forms. The batter will be mounded slightly above the tops of the forms. Do not smooth; the batter will level itself.

Bake 18 minutes or until the tops are golden brown and spring back firmly when lightly touched. If necessary, reverse the position of the pan for the last few minutes of baking to insure even browning.

Madeleines must be removed from the pan immediately. Quickly cover the pan with a rack or a cookie sheet and invert. Remove the pan. Cool the madeleines on a rack.

Notes:

1. Never clean madeleine pans with anything rough or anything other than soap and water—it might make the cookies stick.
2. This recipe may be doubled for two madeleine pans if they will both fit on the same oven rack. The madeleines must not be baked on two racks at one time or they will not brown properly. Therefore, to make a large number repeat the directions—the prepared batter should not stand.

Rolled Wafers and Paper-Thin Cookies

French Almond Wafers

Crisp, extremely delicate, and fragile lace wafers.

4 ounces (slightly generous ¾ cup) blanched almonds
1 tablespoon (must be exactly level) sifted all-purpose flour
½ cup sugar
¼ pound (1 stick) butter, at room temperature
2 tablespoons milk

Adjust rack one-third down from top of oven. Preheat oven to 350 degrees. Butter and lightly flour cookie sheets (see Note 1).

Place the almonds, flour, and sugar in the bowl of a food processor fitted with the metal chopping blade and process for about 30 seconds until fine and powdery.

Place all ingredients in a 10- to 12-inch heavy frying pan. Using a wooden spatula, stir over low heat until butter melts and ingredients are thoroughly mixed. Remove from heat.

Drop by slightly rounded teaspoonfuls about 4 inches apart on prepared cookie sheets, placing only four or five cookies on a large sheet. Bake one sheet at a time for 8 to 10 minutes, reversing position of sheet if cookies are not browning evenly, until well browned with no light spots left in the centers.

Remove sheet from oven and let cookies stand for a few seconds only, until they can be easily removed with a wide metal spatula.

Work quickly now—as you remove a cookie, immediately place it over a rolling pin (see Note 2) to shape (see Note 3). In a few minutes, as soon as they have set to hold their shape, they may be removed to make room for the remaining cookies.

Bake and shape remaining cookies.

As soon as cookies are thoroughly cool, place them in airtight containers.

They will become limp if exposed to the air too long. Store in a single layer in an airtight box (I use a Rubbermaid freezer box). They may be frozen.

Notes:

1. Baking pan liner paper may be used for these cookies (instead of buttering and flouring the sheets), but if so, do not remove the paper from the cookie sheet until cookies have been removed, or they will cool too quickly to be shaped over the rolling pin.
2. If you do not have two rolling pins to work with, use anything else of a similar shape—wine bottles, straight glasses, broom handles, etc.
3. If the cookies cool too quickly to shape, reheat in the oven long enough to soften.
4. Having said all of the above about shaping these cookies to curve them in the traditional manner, let me add that they are equally fine if left flat, and are much less fragile and therefore easier to wrap and store. If they are to be left flat, they may be baked on baking pan liner paper or unbuttered aluminum foil. When done, slide the paper or foil off the cookie sheet and let stand until cookies cool. Then just lift them off the paper or, very gently, peel the foil away.

Oatmeal Wafers

30 COOKIES

Spicy, crisp, extremely fragile.

- ¼ cup sifted all-purpose flour
- ½ teaspoon salt
- ⅛ teaspoon baking soda
- ½ teaspoon cinnamon
- ¼ teaspoon powdered cloves
- ¼ teaspoon allspice
- ½ teaspoon powdered ginger
- ¼ teaspoon nutmeg
- ¼ pound (1 stick) butter
- 1 teaspoon vanilla extract
- ¼ cup granulated sugar
- ½ cup firmly packed light brown sugar
- 1 egg
- 1 cup old-fashioned or quick-cooking (not instant) oatmeal
- ½ cup walnuts, thinly sliced or chopped medium-fine

Adjust rack one-third down from top of oven and preheat to 350 degrees. Line cookie sheets with aluminum foil shiny side up.

Sift flour with salt, baking soda, cinnamon, cloves, allspice, ginger, and nutmeg. Set aside.

In small bowl of electric mixer beat the butter to soften it a bit. Add vanilla and both sugars and beat for a minute or two. Beat in the egg and then the oatmeal. On lowest speed add the sifted dry ingredients and then the nuts, scraping the bowl with a rubber spatula and beating until well mixed.

Drop the batter on the aluminum foil by slightly rounded teaspoonfuls, placing them far apart—about 3 inches—as they spread a lot. With the back of a teaspoon dipped repeatedly in cold water, spread each cookie to flatten it to about 2 inches in diameter. Make it thin, but don't worry about keeping the shape round.

Bake about 15 minutes until completely browned, reversing position of cookie sheet during baking to insure even browning.

Slide the aluminum foil off the cookie sheet. Allow cookies to cool completely on the foil and then peel the foil away from the backs of the cookies.

Handle with care! These are not cookie-jar cookies—they are too fragile. Store in an airtight box (I use a Rubbermaid freezer box).

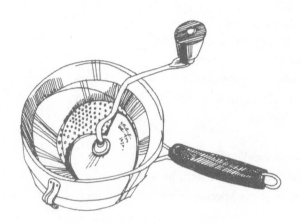

Benne Seed Wafers

25 WAFERS, 5 INCHES IN DIAMETER

Dramatic wafers about 5 inches in diameter. Benne seed is the old Southern name for sesame seeds, and there is a legend that eating them brings good luck. This is an old plantation recipe from Charleston, South Carolina, for cookies that taste like candy with a great flavor and an incredibly crisp texture.

> 1 cup sesame seeds (benne seeds)
> 6 ounces (1½ sticks) butter
> ½ cup sifted all-purpose flour
> ¼ teaspoon baking powder
> ¼ teaspoon salt
> 1 egg
> 1 teaspoon vanilla extract
> 1½ cups firmly packed light brown sugar
> 3½ ounces (1 cup) pecans, chopped medium

Adjust rack to center of oven. Preheat oven to 350 degrees. Place sesame seeds in a shallow pan and bake for 15 to 20 minutes, shaking the pan frequently to toast the seeds an even, light brown color. (Toasting brings out the nutlike flavor.) Remove from oven to cool slightly.

Raise oven temperature to 400 degrees. Cut baking parchment to fit cookie sheets.

Place the butter in a small pan over low heat to melt. Set aside to cool slightly.

Sift together flour, baking powder, and salt. In small bowl of electric mixer beat egg and vanilla just to mix. Beat in the sugar, sifted mixture, melted butter, toasted sesame seeds, and pecans, scraping bowl with a rubber spatula as necessary and beating until thoroughly mixed.

Drop by generous tablespoonfuls about 4 inches apart—they need a lot of room—on the paper. These need so much room that you will only be able to bake two or three cookies at a time on a standard cookie sheet. Slide a cookie sheet under the paper. Bake only one sheet at a time. Reverse position of pan during baking to insure even browning. Bake about 7 minutes or until evenly browned.

Slide paper off cookie sheet and let stand until cookies are cool. Then just lift them off the paper.

Store in an airtight container—a Rubbermaid freezer box works very well. A plastic bag does not.

Moravian Ginger Thins
(Pennsylvania Dutch)

48 COOKIES

These are paper-thin—dry, hard, crisp, brittle, and hot, sharp, spicy.

Originally this was a Pennsylvania Dutch recipe. But I doubt that they made them as peppery as these are. I need a new word to describe these. Maybe it is FIRECRACKERSINYOURMOUTH. If you don't want them this hot omit the cayenne. Or make it a tiny pinch (maybe I pinch a lot).

The dough should be refrigerated for 4 or 5 hours or longer before baking.

> 1¼ cups sifted all-purpose flour
> ¼ teaspoon salt
> ¼ teaspoon nutmeg
> ¼ teaspoon allspice
> ¼ teaspoon powdered cloves
> ¾ teaspoon cinnamon
> ½ teaspoon powdered ginger
> ½ teaspoon finely ground black or white pepper
> Pinch of cayenne pepper
> 3 tablespoons butter
> 2 tablespoons firmly packed dark brown sugar
> ⅓ cup molasses, dark or light

Sift together flour, salt, nutmeg, allspice, cloves, cinnamon, ginger, black or white pepper, and cayenne pepper. Set aside. In small bowl of electric mixer, beat the butter to soften it a bit. Beat in the sugar and then the molasses. On lowest speed add the sifted dry ingredients, scraping the bowl with a rubber spatula as necessary to keep mixture smooth. Beat only until smooth.

Transfer to a piece of plastic wrap or wax paper. Flatten the dough to about an inch thickness. Wrap airtight and refrigerate for 4 to 5 hours. (May be refrigerated for several days, if you wish.)

Adjust rack one-third down from top of oven. Preheat oven to 350 degrees. Line a cookie sheet with aluminum foil.

Work with one-quarter of the dough at a time. Keep the rest refrigerated. On a well-floured pastry cloth with a well-floured rolling pin, roll the dough very slightly. Turn it over, roll slightly, and turn again to thoroughly flour both sides. Work quickly before the dough softens and becomes sticky. Roll it paper-thin ($\frac{1}{16}$ inch thick). Cut with a $2\frac{3}{4}$-inch round cookie cutter. With a wide metal spatula transfer cookies to lined cookie sheet, placing them close together.

When there is a piece of rolled-out dough not quite large enough for a round cookie, use the same cutter and cut a crescent.

Bake 8 minutes, or until cookies darken slightly. If necessary, reverse cookie sheet front to back to insure even browning. With a wide metal spatula transfer to a rack to cool.

Repeat with remaining portions of dough. Reserve scraps, wrap, chill, and reroll.

These cookies must be stored airtight in order to remain crisp for any length of time. I use a Rubbermaid freezer box. They may be frozen.

Rolled Cigarettes

24 COOKIES

Crisp, fragile, rolled wafers.

2 ounces (½ stick) butter
2 egg whites
Pinch of salt
½ cup sugar
½ teaspoon vanilla extract
1 tablespoon plus 2 teaspoons sifted all-purpose flour

Adjust rack to center of oven. Preheat oven to 350 degrees. Butter several cookie sheets (or only one, if you prefer, since these will be baked one sheet at a time) and dust them lightly with flour. Shake off excess and set aside.

Melt the butter and set aside to cool.

In a small bowl beat the whites and the salt with a small wire whisk or a fork, beating only until foamy. Add the sugar and beat until mixed. Add the vanilla, flour, and melted butter, beating or stirring only until mixed smooth.

Bake one sample cookie. If you wish, this may be done on an inverted layer-cake pan, buttered and floured.

Drop about 1 tablespoonful of the batter onto the sheet, and with the back of the spoon spread it as smooth as possible into an oval about 4 to 4½ inches long. It will be very thin—almost sheer.

Bake 6 to 8 minutes until golden brown with barely any light spots remaining. Remove from oven and wait for just a second or two before removing cookie with a wide metal spatula. Working quickly, immediately place cookie upside down on smooth surface and immediately roll rather tightly on a pencil or the handle of a wooden spoon or spatula. (These are very hot. Some people wear gloves to roll them.) Slip cookie off and set aside to cool.

If sample cookie shows that batter needs adjusting, add 1 to 2 teaspoons of melted butter to make it more flexible; or if the cookie is sticky and difficult to remove from the cookie sheet, add about ½ teaspoon of flour to make it firmer.

Until you get the hang of baking and shaping these cookies, I suggest baking only two at a time. If necessary, reverse position of pan during baking to insure even browning. If one cookie browns sooner than the other, remove it when it is ready and then continue to bake the other until done. If cookies cool on cookie sheet too long and become brittle, replace in oven for a minute or so until soft. Or, if a cookie becomes crisp while you are rolling it, don't force it or it will break. Remove the pencil and replace the cookie, on the cookie sheet, in the oven to soften. Remove from oven and finish rolling without the pencil.

Each cookie sheet must be washed, dried, buttered, and floured before reusing. Stir batter occasionally to keep it mixed.

Making these cigarettes is slow work (I mean "play"). You may quit whenever you want and place any remaining batter in a covered container in the refrigerator.

As soon as the shaped cookies cool, place them carefully in a covered airtight container. Do not expose these fragile wafers to humidity for any length of time or they will become sticky, but they will keep well if airtight (I use a Rubbermaid freezer box). They may be frozen. If frozen, thaw covered.

Individual Pastries and Petits Fours

Mushroom Meringues

24 RATHER LARGE OR 26 MEDIUM MUSHROOMS

I did not want to include this recipe because I thought it would be too difficult for most people to make. I was stunned when soon after the original publication of this book readers started sending photos to me of their Mushroom Meringues. They were perfect! I received several letters from people who were making them from this recipe and selling them to department stores (Bloomingdale's, Henri Bendel, and others).

These call for patience, talent with a pastry bag, and a dry atmosphere. Making them is an art.

> ½ cup egg whites (about 4 whites), at room temperature
> Scant ¼ teaspoon salt
> ¼ teaspoon cream of tartar
> 1 cup sugar
> 1 teaspoon vanilla extract
> Powdered, unsweetened cocoa
> Chocolate (see Notes)

Adjust two racks to divide the oven into thirds. Preheat oven to 225 degrees. Cut baking parchment to fit two cookie sheets at least 12 x 15 inches.

In the small bowl of electric mixer at moderately slow speed, beat the whites for about half a minute or until they are just foamy. Add the salt and cream of tartar. Increase the speed to moderate and beat for almost a minute more until whites hold a soft shape. Continue to beat and start adding the sugar, 1 rounded tablespoonful at a time—beat about half a minute between additions. When half the sugar has been added, add the vanilla and then continue adding the sugar as before. When all of the sugar has been added, increase the speed to high and beat for 7 to 8 minutes more or until the meringue is very stiff and the sugar is dissolved—test it by rubbing a bit between your fingers. (Total beating time from start to finish is about 15 to 18 minutes, but it depends on the power of your mixer.)

To hold the parchment in place, put a dot of the meringue on each corner of the cookie sheets. Cover with the parchment and press firmly on the corners.

Do not let the meringue stand. Fit a large pastry bag (preferably at least 15 to 16 inches long) with a plain, round tube ½ to ¾ inches in diameter. (I like to use one that is ⅝ inch.) Fold down the top of the bag to form a deep cuff on the outside. Support the bag by holding it under the cuff with one hand (or place in a tall jar). Using a rubber spatula, with your other hand transfer all of the meringue into the bag. Lift the cuff up and twist the top closed.

On one piece of the parchment shape the mushroom stems first. Hold the bag at a right angle and close to the cookie sheet. Press the meringue out gently while slowly raising the bag straight up. The base of the stem should be a bit wider for support. Keep the stem as straight as possible. Hold the bag upright and steady with one hand while, with the other hand, use a small knife to cut the meringue away from the tube. Don't worry if a small point is left on top of the stem; it can be removed later on. The stems may be about 1 to 1¾ inches high (the taller they are, the more difficult), but they may vary as real mushroom stems do. They should be placed ½ to 1 inch apart. (Some of the stems may fall over the sides, so it is a good idea to make a few extras to be sure you wind up with a stem for each cap.)

Strain cocoa through a fine strainer lightly over the stems to imitate soil and natural mushroom coloring. Place in the oven on the higher rack.

On the other sheet shape the mushroom caps. Holding the bag straight up and close to the sheet, press out even rounds of the meringue. The caps should be placed about ½ inch apart. The caps may average about 1½ to 1¾ inches in width and ¾ inches in height, but they may also vary as real mushroom caps do. Sharply twist the bag away to avoid leaving a peak on the top. The top should be as smooth as possible.

Strain cocoa lightly over the caps. Bake on the lower rack.

The measurements I have given are approximate—don't worry about them. Smaller or larger mushrooms are equally attractive. Even mushroom meringues with crooked stems or a slight point on the cap will look great when finished.

Bake for 1 hour or longer depending on size, until meringues may be lifted easily from the sheet and the bottoms are firm to the touch. The longer they bake the drier they are—and the better—but they should not be allowed to color (it affects the taste). Turn the heat off, prop the oven door open a little, and let the meringues dry out even more in the turned-off oven until cool. (I have, at times, put the meringues back in a barely warm oven for the night.)

Remove meringues from the sheets. They may be placed on a clean piece of paper, or on a tray. Immediately, while the meringues are very crisp, using a finely serrated knife or a sharp paring knife, gently saw any points off the tops of the stems cutting parallel with the base.

Now, to glue the tops and stems together, it is best to use compound chocolate (see page xviii). Real chocolate will discolor (unless you temper it), but compound chocolate will not (see Note 1.)

One ounce of chocolate will be needed for five mushroom caps if they measure 1¾ to 2 inches in diameter. Using this formula, figure how much chocolate you will need and cut it coarsely and place in the top of a small double boiler over warm water to melt slowly over low heat. When almost melted, remove from the heat and stir until completely melted and smooth.

Hold a mushroom cap upside down. With a demitasse spoon spread a layer of chocolate over the bottom of the cap, spreading it just to the edge. It should be thin but not too thin. Place a stem upside down on the chocolate.

Now the mushroom must stand in that position, upside down, until the chocolate hardens. There are several ways to do this. The inverted mushrooms will rest securely in small cordial glasses, small brandy snifters, small egg cups, or in an empty egg carton—it will depend on their size.

Let stand until the chocolate is hard—and then, do not cover airtight.

Serve the mushrooms either standing upright on a platter, or tumbled in a basket like real mushrooms, which these will resemble to an unbelievable degree. (Try a napkin-lined basketful as a centerpiece—at dessert time pass it around.)

The number of mushrooms this recipe yields will depend on their size— approximately twenty-four rather large or thirty-six medium. If you want more, prepare and bake one batch, and then repeat; meringue should not stand any longer than necessary before baking.

Notes:

1. Compound chocolate (see page xviii) is the easiest to use for these mushrooms.

2. Years ago I entered an international cooking Olympics. (Incidentally, I

won first prize for originality.) A large basket of Mushroom Meringues was part of my entry. The display of food at the Olympics lasted three or four days. Then Burdine's, a department store here in Miami, asked if they could use my entry in a window display. And that lasted for two weeks with the sun beating down on the window most of the time. After Burdine's I took my entry home. The meringues were perfect. I put the basket of them on a table in the living room where it remained for many months. And after that the mushrooms looked the same as the day they were made.

Victorias

18 TARTLETS

These shells are made of classic French pastry dough called pâte brisée, which means "broken pastry." When you follow the directions for "pushing off" or "breaking off" the dough, you will understand its name. It is a joy—no problem to make and delicious. This dough may be baked in any size form and used with any filling.

When I discovered these divine chocolate tartlets at Angelina's (previously Rumpelmayer's) on the Rue de Rivoli in Paris, I fell madly in love with them. I tried desperately to get the recipe but it was impossible. The recipe was a secret. After returning home, I wrote to Angelina's requesting that they mail some Victorias to me. They answered saying that Victorias should be eaten while still fresh, and, therefore, they were enclosing the recipe so that I could make them myself and have them whenever I wanted them. I think there's a lesson somewhere in this but I don't know what it is.

PASTRY SHELLS

2½ cups sifted all-purpose flour
½ teaspoon salt
½ cup sugar
5 ounces (1¼ sticks) butter, cut in ½-inch pieces
1 egg plus 2 egg yolks

Place the flour on a large board, marble, or other smooth work surface. Make a large well in the center and add all the remaining ingredients. With your right-hand fingertips, work the center ingredients together. Gradually incorporate the flour, using a dough scraper or a wide spatula in your left hand to help move it in toward the center. When all the flour has been absorbed, knead briefly until the dough holds together and then finish by "breaking" the pastry as follows.

Form it into a ball. Start at the further side of the dough and, using the heel of your hand, push off small pieces (about 2 tablespoons), pushing against the work surface and away from you. Continue until all the dough has been pushed off. Re-form the dough and push it or "break" it off again. Re-form the dough. Do not chill the dough.

Adjust the rack one-third up from the bottom of oven. Preheat oven to 400 degrees.

Work with half or less of the dough at a time. On a floured pastry cloth, with a floured rolling pin, roll evenly to ⅛-inch thickness. Reverse the dough occasionally to keep both sides lightly floured. With a 4-inch round cookie cutter cut eighteen rounds. Scraps of dough may be reserved and then rerolled together. (You will have a bit more dough than you need—extra shells may be frozen before or after baking, or extra dough may be frozen unrolled.)

As the pastry circles are cut, transfer them with a metal spatula and fit them into tartlet pans (see Note; if you don't have enough tartlet pans to use the eighteen rounds all at once, place the extras on wax paper and cover them with wax paper or plastic wrap until you are ready for them). Do not stretch the dough. Press it gently into place. Place the lined pans on a jelly-roll pan or cookie sheet and freeze or refrigerate until firm.

Tear aluminum foil (against a ruler or table edge) into 4-inch squares. Line each frozen or refrigerated shell with foil, pressing it firmly against the bottom and sides. (Do not fold the foil down over the sides of the pastry.) Fill with small, dried beans or uncooked rice, to keep the pastry from puffing up. Replace on pan or cookie sheet and bake 10 minutes until pastry is set. Then remove from oven and remove the foil and beans or rice by carefully lifting opposite corners of the foil. Return to the oven to continue baking for a few minutes more until bottoms begin to color slightly and edges are golden.

As shells are baked, remove the pans from the oven individually with a wide metal spatula. With your fingertips, carefully remove the shells from the pans to cool on a rack. When cool, transfer to trays that will fit in the refrigerator. Prepare filling.

CHOCOLATE FILLING

8 ounces semisweet chocolate, broken into pieces
½ cup sugar
2 cups heavy cream, scalded

In the top of a large double boiler over hot water on moderate heat, melt the chocolate. Stir in the sugar. Add the boiling hot cream all at once and stir and stir and stir with a wire whisk until smooth.

Cook uncovered over moderate heat for 30 minutes, scraping sides and bottom frequently with a rubber spatula. (Replace water in bottom of double boiler as necessary.) Remove from heat and place top of double boiler in ice water. Stir continuously and gently with a rubber spatula, scraping the sides and bottom in order not to let the chocolate start to set. Test the temperature frequently (I use the fingertip test). As soon as it is cold, pour it into a pitcher.

Pour into pastry shells, pouring carefully just to the tops of the shells. They should be as full as possible, but be very careful not to let any run over in spots where the shells are lower. Carefully transfer to refrigerator. Refrigerate for a few hours.

Victorias may be served very simply as they are at Angelina's, with just a light sprinkle of chopped green pistachio nuts right in the center, put on while the chocolate is still soft. Or they may be very elaborate, with whipped cream swirled on through a pastry bag and a star tube after the chocolate has become firm and then topped with candied roses or violet petals, or coarsely grated chocolate.

Serve these chilled.

Note:

You will need individual tartlet pans 3½ inches in diameter and ½ inch in depth, and a 4-inch round cookie cutter. (I have also made tiny Victorias only 2¼ inches in diameter. They take time but are fabulous.)

French Almond Macaroon Crescents

12 LARGE CRESCENTS

These are large and truly beautiful. They are seriously delicious—both chewy and crunchy and they have some kind of magic that will make you very happy. These are totally French. Vive les macaroons!

These take time and patience, but what a way to spend your time.

You will need both whole blanched almonds, and sliced (very thin slices) or slivered (fatter, julienne, oblongs) blanched almonds. But if you have the time, slice your own. Cut them one at a time, on a board. Don't try to cut them too thin. The uneven slices you get when you cut your own are more charming than those that have been cut by machine.

7½ ounces (1½ cups) blanched almonds
1½ cups confectioners sugar
1 tablespoon strained apricot preserves
½ teaspoon vanilla extract
1 egg white plus 1 egg (used separately)
8 to 10 ounces (2½ cups) sliced or slivered blanched almonds (see above)

Adjust a rack to the center of the oven. Preheat the oven to 350 degrees. Place one cookie sheet on top of another (these want to burn on the bottoms—the double sheet will prevent that). Place baking parchment on top of the top sheet, and set aside.

Place the 7½ ounces of almonds and the confectioners sugar in the bowl of a food processor fitted with the metal chopping blade. Process for about 30 seconds until the nuts are ground fine. Transfer to a mixing bowl and set aside.

Place the apricot preserves, vanilla extract, and the 1 egg white (reserve the whole egg) in a small bowl and whisk just a bit to mix. Add this mixture to the ground nuts and sugar and stir with a large rubber spatula until the dry ingredients are all moistened. It will be a very thick mixture but if necessary you can add a bit more of the preserves, but no more than is really necessary.

Turn the dough out onto a very lightly floured surface. With lightly floured hands roll the dough into a 12-inch roll. Cut into twelve equal pieces.

Beat the egg lightly just to mix and place it in a flat-bottomed dish. Place the cut-up almonds on a large piece of aluminum foil.

Lightly flour your hands and roll the pieces of dough into cylinders about 6 inches long with slightly tapered ends.

Roll each cookie, first in the egg to coat thoroughly, and then in the almonds, pressing on as many almonds as possible. Place on the prepared cookie sheet curving the ends to form crescents.

Bake one sheet (that is, double sheet) at a time for about 20 minutes until the crescents are golden-colored. Reverse the sheet front to back as necessary during baking. Do not overbake—these must remain chewy, at least in the middle.

Slide the parchment off the sheet and let stand for a minute or two. Then use a wide metal spatula to carefully transfer the crescents to a rack to cool.

Irish Almond Cakes

8 PORTIONS (16 LITTLE CAKES)

These look like elegant French pastry. Each one has a ball of marzipan (almond paste, which you make yourself), wrapped in a thin layer of delicious flaky pastry, topped with chopped almonds, and baked to a gorgeous pale gold color.

PASTRY

1½ cups sifted all-purpose flour
½ teaspoon baking powder
Generous pinch of salt
3 ounces (¾ stick) butter
¼ cup plus 1 tablespoon sugar
1 egg

Sift together flour, baking powder, and salt into a bowl. With a pastry blender cut in the butter until the mixture resembles coarse crumbs. Stir in the sugar. Beat the egg lightly just to mix and add it to the mixture. Stir together a bit and then turn out onto a board or smooth surface. Squeeze the dough between your hands to work it together, and then knead it until it is smooth and the board is clean. On a lightly floured surface roll into a strip about 8 inches long. Wrap airtight. Set aside at room temperature.

ALMOND PASTE

2½ ounces (½ cup) blanched almonds
2 tablespoons superfine or granulated sugar
3 tablespoons confectioners sugar
1 egg
¼ teaspoon almond extract
Optional: 2 drops green food coloring

Place the almonds and both sugars in the bowl of a food processor fitted with the metal chopping blade. Process for 30 seconds until the nuts are ground fine. Transfer to a small mixing bowl.

Place the egg in a small mixing bowl. Beat it lightly with a small wire whisk or a fork just to mix. Remove and reserve half of it (2 to 3 tablespoons) to use later. To the remaining half mix in the almond extract and the optional food coloring.

Add this egg mixture to the almond mixture. Stir well with a rubber spatula, pressing against the sides and bottom of the bowl, until completely mixed. Now, on a lightly floured surface form this almond mixture into a roll 8 inches long. I do it in a piece of plastic wrap like icebox cookies. Cut the roll into eight slices and cut each slice in half crossways.

Adjust a rack to the center of the oven and preheat to 400 degrees. If possible, use a large cookie sheet (17 x 14 inches). Place the sheet on top of another sheet (to prevent the bottoms of the cookies from burning) and cover the top sheet with baking parchment. Set aside.

TOPPING

> Sugar
> Reserved ½ egg
> 2½ ounces (½ cup) blanched almonds, chopped medium-fine
> Confectioners sugar

Place some sugar in a shallow bowl. Roll each piece of the almond paste in the sugar and then roll between your hands into a small ball. Set aside.

Cut the reserved pastry in half the long way and then across into eighths, forming sixteen even pieces. Working with one piece at a time, flatten it quite thin between your hands, pressing with your fingers against the pastry in the palm of your other hand—if the pastry is sticky, flour your hands lightly (very lightly).

Enclose a ball of the almond paste in a piece of the flattened pastry. Bring up the edges of the pastry and pinch to seal. The almond paste should be completely enclosed. Roll into a smooth ball. Place 1 inch apart on the prepared cookie sheet (all sixteen will fit on one 17 x 14-inch sheet).

Brush the tops and sides of the cakes with the reserved half egg. Sprinkle generously with the chopped almonds.

Bake for about 20 minutes until the cakes are golden colored, reversing the sheet front to back once during baking to insure even browning.

With a metal spatula transfer the cakes to a rack to cool.

When completely cool strain confectioners sugar generously over the tops.

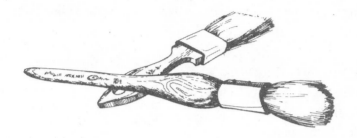

Capri Pastries

This is a gorgeous sponge roll flavored with rum, filled with rum-chocolate filling, topped with whipped cream and a chocolate glaze. It is something special!

ALMOND SPONGE ROLL

4 ounces (generous ¾ cup) blanched almonds
7 eggs, separated
¼ cup plus 2 tablespoons sugar
½ teaspoon vanilla extract
¼ teaspoon almond extract
¼ teaspoon salt

Adjust a rack one-third up in the oven and preheat the oven to 350 degrees. Turn a 15½ x 10½ x 1-inch jelly-roll pan upside down. Cover it with a length of regular weight aluminum foil, shiny side down. Press all four sides down to shape the foil to the pan. Remove the foil. Turn the pan right side up. Place the foil in the pan and press it into place. Put a piece of butter (1 generous tablespoon) in the pan and place it in the oven just to melt the butter. Then, with a pastry brush, carefully spread the butter all over the bottom and sides of the lined pan. Set aside.

Place the almonds in the bowl of a food processor fitted with the metal chopping blade. Pulse the machine a few times and then process for about 30 seconds until the nuts are fine but no longer (or they will become oily). Transfer to a small bowl and set aside.

In the small bowl of an electric mixer beat the egg yolks at high speed for 3 minutes. Add 2 tablespoons of the sugar (reserve remaining ¼ cup sugar) and the vanilla and almond extracts. Continue to beat at high speed for 5 minutes more until the mixture is thick, pale, and has increased in volume. Remove from the mixer.

(If you do not have an extra set of beaters for your mixer, wash and dry them thoroughly.)

In the large bowl of electric mixer beat the egg whites with the salt until they hold a very soft shape. Reduce the speed to low and gradually add the reserved ¼ cup sugar. Continue to beat at high speed until the whites hold a straight point.

Fold one-fourth of the whites into the yolks, but do not be thorough about it.

Now, add the yolks to the remaining whites and carefully fold together, while gradually adding the ground nuts. Do not handle even a bit more than necessary. Without waiting, spray the buttered pan generously with non-stick cooking spray, and turn the batter into the pan. Spread it level, preferably with an off-set spatula, and place in the oven.

Bake for 40 minutes until the top springs back when gently pressed with a fingertip.

While the cake is baking, wet and wring out a kitchen towel (preferably smooth cotton or linen).

As soon as the cake is removed from the oven cover it with the damp towel, and cover the whole thing with a length of aluminum foil large enough to fold down around the sides. (I use heavy-duty foil because it is wider.) Press down around the sides to make the cake airtight. Set aside until cool.

Prepare the syrup and filling.

RUM SYRUP
  2 tablespoons sugar
  2 tablespoons boiling water
  3 tablespoons dark rum

In a small pan stir the sugar into the boiling water and boil for half a minute. Remove from the heat. Cool slightly and stir in the rum. Set aside.

RUM CHOCOLATE FILLING

4 ounces semisweet chocolate

2 ounces unsweetened chocolate

5 ounces (1¼ sticks) butter

⅔ cup confectioners sugar

4 egg yolks

3 tablespoons dark rum

In the top of a small double boiler over hot water on moderate heat, melt both chocolates. Remove from the heat and set aside to cool.

In small bowl of electric mixer beat butter until softened a bit. Add sugar and beat until smooth. Then add the egg yolks, chocolate, and the rum and beat only until smooth—no longer. Remover from the mixer and let stand.

Now, remove the foil from the top of the sponge roll. Cover the cake with a length of wax paper. Place a cookie sheet on top. Turn the cookie sheet and cake pan upside down, and remove the cake pan and the foil lining.

Brush the cake generously with the Rum Syrup. Spread the Rum Chocolate Filling over the cake. Use the wax paper to help you start to roll the cake, rolling it from one long side to the other long side. Leave the wax paper on the outside of the cake, and transfer it to a chocolate roll board (see Note, page 344) or a tray, seam side down, and refrigerate.

You have now made a Rum Chocolate Almond Roll. It may be served as is with confectioners sugar strained over the top. However, to make these individual pastries, continue.

When the filling is firm enough cut the cake into eight to ten (or more) slices. If necessary, wipe the blade and hold under hot water before making each cut. Place the slices cut side up on a board or tray (they will be transferred for serving).

Prepare Whipped Cream Topping.

WHIPPED CREAM TOPPING

1 teaspoon unflavored gelatin
2 tablespoons cold water
2 cups heavy whipping cream
½ cup confectioners sugar
2 teaspoons vanilla extract

Sprinkle the gelatin over the cold water in a small heatproof cup. Let stand for a few minutes and then place the cup in a small pan of shallow hot water on low heat and stir occasionally until the gelatin is dissolved. Remove from heat.

Chill the small bowl and beaters of an electric mixer. In the chilled bowl, mix all but 1 to 2 large spoonfuls of the cream with the confectioners sugar and vanilla, and beat until the cream barely begins to thicken. Stir the reserved one to two spoonfuls of cream into the dissolved gelatin and beat into the cream. Beat until the mixture just holds a shape, but is not really stiff.

Fit a large pastry bag with a large star tube. Place the whipped cream in the bag, and form a large, high, pointed rosette on each slice of cake. The rosette should be wide enough to cover the chocolate filling and part of the cake roll; there should be only a small border of cake showing on the sides of the whipped cream.

Refrigerate for an hour or more until completely set.

Prepare the Chocolate Glaze.

CHOCOLATE GLAZE

1 teaspoon instant coffee
½ boiling water
1 tablespoon vegetable shortening or butter
⅓ cup sugar
1 ounce unsweetened chocolate
4½ ounces semisweet chocolate

In a small saucepan on high heat, stir the coffee into the boiling water. Add vegetable shortening or butter and sugar and stir to dissolve the sugar. Reduce the heat to moderate. Add both chocolates. Stir occasionally until melted.

Transfer to the small bowl of an electric mixer and stir or beat occasionally until cooled to room temperature.

When cool, beat 2 or 3 minutes until smooth and barely thickened. Place the cake slices on a rack over wax paper.

Transfer the chocolate glaze to a small pitcher and pour it over each slice, pouring unevenly so that a bit of the whipped cream shows through in places and the chocolate runs down unevenly in just a few places on the sides of the cake.

As soon as the chocolate has set enough, use a wide metal spatula to transfer to a serving tray and refrigerate.

Chocolate Cupcakes

24 CUPCAKES

2 cups sifted all-purpose flour
1 teaspoon baking soda
¼ teaspoon salt
½ cup powdered, unsweetened cocoa (preferably Dutch process)
5⅓ ounces (1¼ sticks plus 2 teaspoons) butter
1 teaspoon vanilla extract
1½ cups sugar
3 eggs
1 cup milk

Adjust two racks to divide oven into thirds. Preheat oven to 350 degrees. Butter two pans of cupcake forms, each pan with twelve forms and each form measuring about 2¾ inches in diameter. Sift a bit of flour or cocoa over them and shake out the excess. Or line twenty-four forms with cupcake liner papers (see Note 2). Set aside.

Sift together flour, baking soda, salt, and cocoa. Set aside. In large bowl of electric mixer beat the butter to soften a bit. Beat in the vanilla and sugar. Add eggs one at a time, beating until smooth after each and scraping the bowl with a rubber spatula as necessary to keep mixture smooth. On lowest speed alternately add sifted dry ingredients in three additions and milk in two additions. Continue to scrape the bowl with the rubber spatula and beat only until smooth. Do not overbeat.

Spoon the batter into the prepared pans, filling the cups only two-thirds to three-quarters full. There is no need to smooth the tops—the batter will level itself.

Bake for 25 minutes or until tops spring back when lightly touched. Do not overbake. Cool in the pans for 2 to 3 minutes before removing to a rack to finish cooling. Ice with the following Chocolate Cupcake Icing:

CHOCOLATE CUPCAKE ICING

6 ounces semisweet chocolate
⅓ cup heavy cream
1 tablespoon sugar
1½ tablespoons butter

Place all ingredients in a small, heavy saucepan over moderate heat. Cook, stirring occasionally, until the chocolate is almost melted. Remove from heat. Continue to stir until the chocolate is completely melted and the mixture is smooth. Transfer to a very small, shallow bowl. Let stand, stirring occasionally, until icing reaches room temperature.

Hold cupcakes upside down and dip the tops into the icing. Twirl slightly and then hold upside down for a few seconds for excess to drip off. Then, use a teaspoon and place a rather generous mound of the icing on each cake—do not spread it.

Let stand for a few hours, or overnight if you wish, for the icing to set.

Notes:
1. When baking cupcakes, if you have only one pan with twelve cups, reserve the remaining batter and bake additional cakes after the first panful. If baking only one pan at a time, bake in the center of the oven.
2. Lining the pans with papers is a convenience and a time saver. The cakes take on a better shape and rise higher, and they stay fresh longer.
3. To freeze frosted cupcakes, let them stand until the icing is no longer sticky. Place them on a pan or tray in the freezer until frozen firm. Then place over them a large piece of plastic wrap, turning it down securely on the sides and under the bottom. Return to freezer. To thaw, remove from freezer, but do not remove plastic wrap until cupcakes have thawed.

Ethiopian Truffles

20 COOKIES

This is a dark, moist, chocolate macaroon mixture that is wrapped in a thin layer of light, flaky, tender pastry.

PASTRY

4 ounces (1 stick) butter
¼ teaspoon vanilla extract
¼ cup confectioners sugar
Pinch of salt
1 cup sifted all-purpose flour

Adjust rack one-third down from top of oven. Place one cookie sheet on top of another (to prevent the bottoms from burning) and cover the top sheet with baking parchment. Set aside.

In a small bowl of an electric mixer beat the butter a bit to soften. Add the vanilla, sugar, and salt and beat to mix. Then add the flour and beat until it is all incorporated.

Transfer the dough to a piece of plastic wrap, form it into an oblong or a tube shape, wrap, and refrigerate briefly while you prepare the following:

BLACK TRUFFLES

4 ounces (¾ cup) blanched almonds
4 ounces semisweet chocolate
3 tablespoons sugar
½ teaspoon vanilla extract
¼ teaspoon almond extract
1 egg white

Place the almonds in the bowl of a food processor fitted with the metal chopping blade. Cut the chocolate into small pieces and add to the almonds. Add the sugar and process for about a minute until the ingredients are fine. Then, with the motor running, add the vanilla and almond extracts and the egg white through the feed tube and continue to process until well mixed.

Turn the mixture out onto a work surface, and form it into an oblong or tube shape.

Cut the truffles mixture into twenty pieces. Roll each piece between your hands into a ball shape, and set aside.

Now cut the pastry into twenty pieces.

Flatten one piece of the pastry between your fingers until very thin. Place a truffle ball on the pastry and with your fingers bring the pastry up and around the truffle. It probably will cover only part of the truffle—that's right. Now roll it around and around your palms to make a smooth ball (part dark and part light). Place it on the prepared cookie sheet.

Continue to shape them all, and place them about 1 inch apart on the sheet.

Refrigerate the sheet of cookies for 15 to 20 minutes before baking.

Bake for about 20 minutes, reversing the sheet front to back once during baking. Bake until the light dough is lightly colored.

With a wide spatula transfer the baked cookies to a rack to cool.

Optional: Top the cookies with a generous sprinkling of confectioners sugar, strained over the cookies through a fine strainer.

French Sandwich Cookies with Chocolate Filling

12 TO 14 LARGE SANDWICH COOKIES

Classy, classic, and delicious.

> 7 ounces (1¾ sticks) butter
> ¼ teaspoon salt
> 1 teaspoon vanilla extract
> ⅓ cup sugar
> 3 egg yolks
> 2 cups sifted all-purpose flour
> Confectioners sugar for dusting cookies

In large bowl of electric mixer beat the butter to soften it a bit. Add the salt, vanilla, and sugar, beating well. Add the egg yolks and beat until smooth. Gradually, on lowest speed, add the flour, scraping the bowl as necessary with a rubber spatula and beating until the mixture holds together. Remove from mixer. Wrap airtight and refrigerate for about ½ hour.

Adjust rack to the center of the oven. Preheat oven to 350 degrees. Line cookie sheets with baking parchment.

Work with half of the dough at a time. On a lightly floured pastry cloth, with a floured rolling pin, roll the dough ⅛ to ¼ inch thick. Cut with a floured 2¾-inch cookie cutter, and place cookies 1 inch apart on the lined sheet. Save the scraps and reroll them all together in order not to incorporate any more flour than necessary.

Bake 15 to 17 minutes until lightly browned, reversing position of cookie sheet during baking to insure even browning. Transfer with a wide metal spatula to racks to cool. Prepare following filling:

CHOCOLATE GANACHE FILLING

6 ounces semisweet chocolate
2 ounces (½ stick) butter
¼ cup plus 1 tablespoon heavy cream

In top of a small double boiler over hot water on moderate heat, melt the chocolate and butter. When partially melted, stir with a small wire whisk until completely melted. Remove top of double boiler from heat. Gradually add the cream, stirring with the whisk. Let stand at room temperature, stirring occasionally, for ½ hour or longer until barely thickened. Do not let it begin to harden.

Place half the cookies on a large piece of parchment or wax paper, upside down. Divide the filling among the inverted cookies, placing about a tablespoonful on each. Quickly cover with the remaining cookies, right sides up, and, very gently, press down to spread the filling just to the edges.

Let stand at room temperature or chill briefly until filling is set.

Arrange the sandwiched cookies in straight rows on parchment or wax paper. Place a long strip of parchment or wax paper, ½ inch wide, on each row covering the center strip of each cookie. Sprinkle generously with confectioners sugar through a fine strainer. Remove paper carefully, leaving an unsugared strip through the center of each cookie.

Fried Cookies and Pastries

Squid

4 SQUID, SERVE 1 TO A PERSON

To make these exotic, crisp, fried cookies, it will be necessary to have an empty tin can, measuring about 4 x 4 inches (i.e., a 1-pound Crisco can or one approximately the same size). Remove both the top and bottom of the can.

> Oil or shortening for deep frying
> ⅓ cup sifted all-purpose flour
> 1 cup sifted cake flour
> Pinch of salt
> ¼ teaspoon baking powder
> 1 egg
> 3 tablespoons granulated sugar
> 1 tablespoon melted butter
> 1 tablespoon dark rum
> Confectioners sugar for dusting

Put the oil or shortening at least 3 inches deep in a deep, narrow saucepan. Insert a frying thermometer. Slowly bring it to 370 degrees while preparing the dough.

Sift together the all-purpose flour, cake flour, salt, and baking powder and set aside. In the small bowl of an electric mixer, beat egg at high speed until it is light lemon-colored. Gradually add granulated sugar and continue to beat for about 5 minutes until mixture flows very slowly when beaters are lifted. On low speed, add the butter, rum, and then the sifted dry ingredients, scraping the bowl with a rubber spatula and beating only until mixture is smooth.

Turn out onto a well-floured board. Turn the dough to coat with flour. Cut into four pieces, turning each piece to flour all sides.

With a floured rolling pin, roll one piece of the dough, turning it over occasionally to keep it from sticking. Roll into an oblong, a scant ⅛ inch thick. With a pastry wheel or a small sharp knife, starting ½ inch from the edge, cut slits ½ inch apart—do not cut through outer edge; leave a ½-inch border on two sides.

With tongs, place the empty can upright in the oil or shortening, which should be kept at a temperature of 370 degrees. Gather the cut pastry together loosely and casually place it in the can, letting it fold over on itself. Fry for 1 minute until the squid holds its shape and is golden brown on the bottom. With tongs, remove the can. With two slotted metal spoons or flat wire whisks, turn the pastry over and fry for another ½ minute or until evenly and lightly colored. Remove from saucepan to drain and cool on absorbent paper.

Repeat with three remaining pieces of dough. Strain confectioners sugar generously over the tops.

Note: Squid should be served on individual plates. They are eaten with the fingers, by breaking off the crisp tentacles of pastry.

French-Fried Wafers

16 LARGE WAFERS

Dramatic, gargantuan, paper-thin, and as crisp as potato chips. To fry these pastries it will be necessary to have a very wide, shallow saucepan or frying pan, 11 to 12 inches wide and 2½ to 3 inches deep. A large electric frying pan, although not quite this deep, may be used.

> 4 cups sifted all-purpose flour
> 1 teaspoon baking powder
> 1 teaspoon salt
> ½ teaspoon mace
> 2 tablespoons granulated sugar
> 2 eggs
> ¾ cup milk
> 2 ounces (½ stick) butter, melted
> Large quantity of oil or shortening for deep frying
> Confectioners sugar

Sift together flour, baking powder, salt, mace, and sugar into large bowl of electric mixer. In a small bowl, beat the eggs. Add milk and butter and beat to mix. On low speed gradually add the egg mixture to the sifted dry ingredients, scraping the bowl with a rubber spatula. The mixture will be too stiff to blend it all in the bowl. Turn it out onto a lightly floured board and knead just until it is smooth.

With your hands, roll it into an even roll 2 to 3 inches thick. Cut into eight even slices. Cut each slice in half across the diameter. Place the sixteen pieces on a tray, cover airtight with plastic wrap, and let stand at room temperature for about 30 minutes, or longer, if you wish. Standing makes the dough easier to roll and helps it hold its shape better.

Meanwhile, heat the oil or shortening in a wide frying pan or saucepan until it reaches 370 degrees. Adjust the heat to maintain that temperature.

On a lightly floured pastry cloth, with a lightly floured rolling pin, roll one piece of the dough until it is paper-thin, turning it over frequently. Don't worry about what shape the edges takes. When it is evenly rolled to 10 inches or more in diameter, lift it gently and carefully lower it into the hot oil. (If you wish to roll out several at a time you may, but stack with wax paper between them.)

With two flat wire whisks or two slotted metal spatulas, immediately straighten any edges that have folded over. Fry for about 1½ minutes until the bottom is golden. Using the two whisks or spatulas, turn to brown the other side, pressing down lightly on any white spots, until it is all evenly browned and there are no white spots remaining. With the two whisks or spatulas, raise it vertically over the saucepan for a few seconds to drain.

Place on crumpled paper toweling to continue to drain and to cool. Repeat with remaining pieces of dough. Strain confectioners sugar generously over the tops.

Pile them on a very large tray. Serve individually on dinner plates.

Note: This recipe may easily be divided in half.

Churros

These Cuban doughnuts are similar to French crullers. *Delicioso!*

Oil or shortening for deep frying
²⁄₃ cup water
1½ tablespoons granulated sugar
⅛ teaspoon salt
2 ounces (½ stick) butter, cut in small pieces
1 cup minus 2 tablespoons sifted all-purpose flour
2 eggs, extra-large or jumbo
1 tablespoon dark rum
⅛ teaspoon mace
Confectioners sugar

Place oil or shortening 1½ to 2 inches deep in a wide, shallow saucepan, a wide, deep frying pan, or an electric frying pan. Slowly bring it to a temperature of 370 degrees while preparing batter.

Place water, sugar, salt, and butter in a 1½- to 2-quart heavy saucepan over high heat. Stir with a wooden spatula until butter is melted and mixture boils rapidly. Remove from heat and immediately add flour all at once. Stir vigorously with wooden spatula until mixture is smooth and comes away from sides of pan to form a ball.

Transfer to small bowl of electric mixer and beat in eggs, one at a time. Add rum and mace and beat at high speed until smooth and shiny. Transfer to a large pastry bag fitted with a large star tube (about ¾-inch opening).

Tear or cut six squares of wax paper about 6 inches in diameter. Lightly brush them with salad oil.

Press the Churros onto the oiled paper squares in thick rings like doughnuts, about 3½ to 4 inches in diameter, cutting them away from the star tube with a small knife.

Holding the edges of the paper with both hands, invert the Churros, only one or two at a time, over the hot oil or shortening. They will easily slide off the paper. Fry until richly browned on one side. Turn with flat wire whisk or slotted metal spoon to brown the other side. Do not undercook.

Drain on absorbent paper. Cool. Strain confectioners sugar generously over the tops. These are at their best when very fresh.

Note: During frying maintain the temperature at 370 degrees and fry Churros about 3 minutes on each side.

P.S. *In Little Havana in Miami, I often see these shaped in a straight line about 6 inches long, instead of the round doughnut shapes.*

Beignets Soufflés

Oil or shortening for deep frying
Pâte à Choux, see Cream Puffs (page 314)
Confectioners sugar

In a wide, shallow saucepan, heat oil or shortening about 2 inches deep for deep frying. The fat should be maintained at a temperature of 370 degrees. Meanwhile, prepare Pâte à Choux as in Cream Puff recipe.

Dip two teaspoons into the preheated oil or shortening. On one, scoop up a well-rounded teaspoon of the paste, and with the other push it off into the oil. Continue forming more and putting them into the oil, but do not crowd them. They need room to swim around in the oil, and adding too many at once lowers the temperature. Continue to dip the spoons in the oil occasionally to keep the paste from sticking to them.

As the Beignets fry, they will turn over by themselves, but they might need a nudge or a bit of help occasionally. (There are very few cooking experiences more fun than watching the Beignets roll around from one side to another as they puff up in size.) Fry for about 10 minutes until they are an even golden brown with no light spots left. Do not remove from the oil too soon or they will collapse.

Remove with a slotted spoon or a flat wire whisk. Drain on absorbent paper. Generously sprinkle through a strainer on all sides with confectioners sugar.

Beignets may be served immediately while still warm or after standing several hours at room temperature. Pile them on a platter in a pyramid. Serve as is, to be eaten with the fingers, or on dessert plates with cold Custard Sauce (page 492) or warm Apricot Sauce (page 493).

Crêpes, Blintzes, Popovers, Cream Puffs, Puff Pastry, and Chocolate Soufflé

Crêpes, blintzes, cream puffs, and popovers are all variations of the same recipe; they have almost the same ingredients.

Crêpes

24 TO 30 5-INCH CRÊPES

3 eggs
1 cup milk
½ cup sifted all-purpose flour

Beat the eggs lightly just to mix. Gradually add the milk and mix together. Place the flour in a small bowl. With an electric mixer or an eggbeater, gradually mix the egg-milk mixture into the flour, beating only until smooth. Cover and refrigerate for at least 2 hours (or overnight if you wish).

A standard crêpe pan is made of black iron, and has widely flared, shallow sides. An average small size will have a 5-inch bottom. A new iron pan should be seasoned before using. Fill it with vegetable oil; over very low heat, heat it slowly until very hot. Remove from heat and let stand until the oil is cold. Then pour the oil out and wipe the pan with paper towels. It should be used only for making crêpes and it should never be washed. Just wipe it with oil and dry it with paper towels after every use. In place of a crêpe pan, use a small non-stick frying pan (see Note 1), or any other small heavy frying pan with about a 5-inch base. With a crêpe pan, it will probably only be necessary to butter the pan once, before making the first crepe. With other pans, butter as necessary. If you have clarified butter, use it. If not, use regular unsalted butter.

Heat the pan over moderately high heat. Spread very lightly with butter, spreading it with crumpled wax paper. Stir the batter briefly and continue to stir occasionally as the heavy part settles to the bottom. For a 5-inch pan, turn 1 generous tablespoon of batter into the hot pan and quickly tilt and rotate the pan in all directions to spread the batter thinly and evenly. (I use a kitchen tablespoon, which holds a little more than a measured tablespoon.) Continue tilting and rotating the pan until the batter stops running.

If the temperature is correct, it should take about ½ minute for the bottom to brown lightly and for the top to dry. With a small metal spatula, loosen the edges and then, with your fingers, turn the crêpe over (see Note 1). Cook for 15 seconds more. The other side should not brown—it should only dry and have a few brown spots. (Do not be disappointed if the first few crepes do not come out perfectly; they seldom do. But don't be discouraged, they always behave better as you go along.)

Remove the finished crêpe by inverting the pan and letting the crêpe fall out upside down on a plate. If necessary, straighten the crêpe with your fingers.

Continue making crepes, stirring the batter occasionally, and stacking them on top of each other.

Crepes may be made ahead of time, and may be reserved piled on top of each other. They should be wrapped airtight for the refrigerator or freezer. If you freeze them and think you might want to use a few at a time, pack with plastic wrap between them in order to remove them individually.

Notes:

1. Non-stick pans are wonderful. The good ones are expensive. but it's such a joy to use one. Get the best you can. There *is* a difference.
2. To warm crêpes: Remove plastic wrap if you used it. Stack crêpes on top of each other. Wrap airtight in aluminum foil. Place in a moderate oven for 10 to 15 minutes until warm.
3. Serve 3 to 4 crêpes to a portion.

English Crêpes, LONDON STYLE

Warm crêpes and fold them in quarters, browned side out. Place them overlapping on warm dessert plates. Through a fine strainer, coat generously with confectioners sugar. Serve with lemon wedges and warm Apricot Sauce (page 493).

English Crêpes, BUCKINGHAM PALACE

Spread the browned side of the crêpes with slightly warmed Apricot Sauce (page 493). Roll them loosely. Place them seam down in a lightly buttered, shallow, ovenproof serving dish. Sprinkle generously with granulated sugar. Place in a moderate oven for 5 to 10 minutes to warm—do not leave them in the oven longer than necessary or the edges will become dry. In a small, heatproof container, warm about ¼ to ⅓ cup Grand Marnier. At the table, pour the warm Grand Marnier over the warm crêpes and touch with a match to flambé.

The Grand Marnier and the crêpes must both be warm in order to flame. After the flame dies down, serve with generous lemon wedges on warm plates.

Crêpes Suzette

Suzette Sauce (page 496)
Crêpes (page 305)
¼ to ⅓ cup brandy or cognac

In a large chafing dish, at the table (or in a large, shallow frying pan, in the kitchen), heat the sauce. Fold the crêpes in quarters and place them in the sauce to warm, gently turning them as necessary.

Immediately before serving, warm the brandy or cognac in a small heat-proof container. Pour it over the crêpes and quickly and carefully touch with a match to flambé. Spoon the flaming sauce over the crêpes. Serve when flame has died down.

Serve on warm plates, serving three or four crepes to a portion and topping each with some of the julienne of orange rind and some of the sauce.

Note: The sauce, crêpes, and brandy or cognac must all be hot in order to flambé. But watch the brandy or cognac—do not overheat or it will quickly boil away.

Saidie Heatter's Blintzes

I can't tell you at how many important occasions I served these blintzes—to important people—always to raves. Most often as an entrée at lunch. They freeze perfectly. It is great to have them in the freezer. (Let them thaw covered at room temperature before frying.)

I have a large oblong non-stick pan that covers two burners. I can fry most of a double batch of blintzes at once (that is, the final frying).

PANCAKES

3 eggs
1½ cups skimmed milk
1 cup minus 2 tablespoons sifted all-purpose flour
¼ teaspoon salt
3 tablespoons melted butter

In a small bowl, beat the eggs lightly just to mix. Gradually add the milk and mix together. Place the flour and salt in small bowl of electric mixer. On low speed, gradually add egg-milk mixture, scraping the bowl with a rubber spatula, and beating only until smooth. Beat in the melted butter. Cover and refrigerate for 2 hours or more. (This may be refrigerated overnight if you wish.)

Cook the pancakes in a frying pan (preferably non-stick) with about a 6-inch base. Use a large mixing spoon, one that holds a generous two tablespoonfuls, or one of the scoops that comes in some cans of coffee, to measure the batter.

Heat the pan over moderately high heat. With crumpled wax paper, spread unsalted or clarified butter generously on the bottom and sides of the pan (or spray with non-stick cooking spray). The heat should not be so high that the butter burns. The heavy part of the batter will settle in the bowl, so stir it occasionally and always spoon from bottom. Place 1 large measure (2 generous tablespoonfuls) of batter in the hot, buttered pan. Quickly tilt and rotate the pan in all directions to spread the batter even. Continue tilting and rotating the pan until the batter stops running.

Cook until top is dry. Bottom of pancake might not have browned, or it might be very lightly browned. If the heat is correct, it should take about 45 seconds to cook each pancake. Fry it on one side only. When top is completely dry and pancake is set, either jerk it to one side to slide it out onto a plate, or, if jerking the pan tears the pancake, release and remove it with a rubber or metal spatula instead. (If pancakes have holes in them, the filling will run out, see Note.) Continue with the remaining batter, sliding each pancake out on top of the others. Rebutter the pan (or respray) before making each pancake. This batter makes about twenty 6-inch pancakes.

FILLING
1 pound farmer cheese
3 tablespoons sugar
2 eggs
Finely grated rind of 1 large bright-colored orange

In large bowl of electric mixer, beat the cheese just to soften it. Add sugar and eggs. Scrape the bowl with a rubber spatula and beat for a minute or two. Remove from mixer and stir in orange rind. (Mixture will not be smooth.) Transfer to a small bowl for ease in handling.

Spread out several long pieces of wax paper. Gently, in order not to tear them, lift off the pancakes and place them browned side (underside) up on the paper.

Divide the filling evenly over the pancakes. If you have made twenty pancakes, you will have enough filling for a heaping teaspoonful on each. Place it in the center of the pancake. Fold the edge of the side nearest you over the filling and roll the pancake loosely. Loosely turn under both ends to make an oblong package with the seam on the bottom. Place prepared blintzes on a tray covered with wax paper. Cover airtight with plastic wrap. Refrigerate for at least a few hours. (May be refrigerated overnight, or may be frozen.)

FINAL FRYING
In a large, heavy frying pan, over moderately low heat, melt enough unsalted or clarified butter to coat the bottom generously. Do not fry too many

blintzes at once or it will be hard to turn them. They are delicate; handle with care. Fry them, seam down, until bottoms are lightly browned. Very carefully, with two metal or rubber spatulas, turn to brown the tops. They should be golden brown. (Two panfuls may be fried at one time if you watch them both and do not let them burn.) To keep the blintzes from sticking, shake the pan occasionally, or move them gently with a spatula. The heat must not be so high that the blintzes become too brown before they heat all the way through. But cooking them too slowly or too long will make the filling dry and heavy. At the correct temperature, the frying should take about 8 to 10 minutes.

Serve immediately on warm plates, three or four to a portion.

Serve with apricot preserves, which have been stirred well to soften, and cold sour cream. It is best to pass the preserves and cream separately.

Note: Small holes or tears in the pancakes may be patched. Cut the one with the worst holes into large pieces and use the pieces as patches. Just place a piece over a small hole or tear before filling the pancake.

Saidie Heatter's Popovers

My mother was called the Popover Queen—she was also the Blintz Queen, the Blueberry Pie Queen, the Queen of the Barbecue, etcetera. My father bestowed a title on her at almost every meal. Her popovers were incredible. They are gorgeous. They are amazing. This is truly an heirloom recipe.

Making these is really simple and easy and I don't see how anything can go wrong. But plan ahead. Plan to make the batter a day ahead and refrigerate it overnight. And plan the timing so that the popovers will be served immediately after they come out of the oven.

These are baked in individual china or pottery custard cups that are deep and narrow; do not use cups that are wide and shallow and flare at the tops. They have a 4- or 6-ounce capacity. Bridge Kitchenware ([800] 274-3435 or, in New York City, [212] 838-1901) has a 7-ounce porcelain cup that they say everyone loves and that *Good Housekeeping* magazine has been recommending for popovers for the last twenty years.

But I have a friend who bakes them in 1-cup ovenproof glass measuring cups and they are quite possibly the most dramatic of all. She uses ½ cup of batter in each cup. She says use cooking spray, not butter, to prepare the cups. She checks on them after 50 minutes of baking, and she uses words like, "Fabulous! Divine! So exciting!" (And the handles make it so easy to handle.)

> 2 cups sifted all-purpose flour
> 1 teaspoon salt
> 6 eggs
> 2 cups milk
> 3 ounces (¾ stick) butter, melted and cooled

You may use an electric mixer, an eggbeater, or a wire whisk. Whichever you use, beat as little as possible to blend the ingredients. (An electric mixer must be used at low speed.)

Place the flour and salt in a large bowl. Beat the eggs lightly only to mix. Mix in the milk and butter. Very gradually beat the liquids into the dry ingredients. Do not overbeat; the batter should not be foamy. If it is lumpy, strain it. If necessary, strain it again. Do not worry about little bits of butter you see. Cover and refrigerate overnight.

The next day, before baking, adjust rack one-third up from the bottom of the oven and preheat the oven to 375 degrees. Butter the cups generously. Use eight 6-ounce cups or ten 4-ounce cups. Arrange them on a jelly-roll pan for ease in handling, spacing them as far apart as possible. Stir the batter well without beating to make it smooth without incorporating any air. Pour into a pitcher and pour into the prepared cups, filling them to about ½ inch from the tops.

Place in preheated oven. Bake 6-ounce cups for 1 hour; 4-ounce cups for 50 minutes. Do not open the oven door until the baking time is almost up. However, ovens vary, so check the popovers about 10 minutes before the time is up. They should bake until they are really well browned. Unless they are dark enough they will be soggy and limp instead of crisp and crunchy. When done, without removing them from the oven, reach in and with a small sharp knife quickly cut two or three slits in each popover to release steam. Continue to bake 5 minutes more.

Remove from oven and take the popovers out of the cups immediately. If necessary, use a small, sharp knife to release them from the cups.

Serve immediately in a napkin-lined basket, but do not cover with the napkin or they will steam and soften. Serve with butter or Honey Butter (page 509) and, if you wish, jam, jelly, or marmalade, and cottage cheese.

Cream Puffs

10 CREAM PUFFS

Ｍy ovens have clear glass doors. Watching these rise into high, billowy, cloud-like shapes, and turn to a gorgeous honey color is a thrill. Serving them is a joy. Eating them is a delicious treat. (And making them is easy.)

CREAM PUFF PASTRY (PÂTE À CHOUX)

¼ pound (1 stick) butter, at room temperature
1 cup boiling water
Generous pinch of salt
1 cup sifted all-purpose flour
4 eggs
Confectioners sugar

Adjust oven rack to center of oven. Preheat oven to 425 degrees. Place a 14 x 17-inch cookie sheet on top of another to prevent bottoms from burning. Cover top sheet with baking parchment and set aside.

In a heavy 2- to 3-quart saucepan over high heat, stir the butter, boiling water, and salt with a wooden spatula. As you stir, also cut the butter into pieces. When the butter is melted and the mixture boils hard, remove the pan from the heat and immediately add the flour all at once, stirring vigorously until the mixture forms a ball and leaves the sides of the pan clean. If necessary, replace briefly over low heat.

Turn mixture into small or large bowl of electric mixer. On medium speed, beat in one egg at a time, beating only until incorporated before adding the next. After adding the final egg, beat for an additional 1 minute, scraping the bowl occasionally with a rubber spatula.

Drop on the prepared cookie sheet by rounded tablespoonfuls into ten mounds, shaping them high and placing them 2 to 3 inches apart. Try to avoid leaving sharp, uneven peaks. Peaks may be flattened with a wet fingertip.

Bake for 15 minutes. Reduce the oven temperature to 350 degrees and bake for an additional 35 minutes (total baking time 50 minutes). Do not open oven door during first ½ hour of baking. Five minutes before the baking time is up, without removing puffs from the oven, reach in and, with a small, sharp knife, cut two or three slits in the tops and sides of each puff in order to let the steam escape. Do not underbake puffs or they will collapse. It will not hurt to bake them longer—but do not let them burn. Remove from oven and cool on a rack.

(When completely cool, puffs may be frozen in a freezer box [I use Rubbermaid] for future use. To serve, thaw and then place on a cookie sheet in a 325 degree oven for about 5 minutes to regain crispness. Cool on a rack and then fill.)

Either immediately before serving, or 1 to 2 hours before, cut the upper third off each puff. Remove any soft dough from the centers.

Prepare either plain whipped cream or Rum-Mocha Whipped Cream, using 2½ cups of heavy cream.

Plain whipped cream: To the unwhipped cream add ⅔ cup confectioners sugar, 2 teaspoons vanilla, and an optional few drops of almond extract. (In place of the vanilla and almond extracts, you might use 3 tablespoons of Grand Marnier or rum.)

Rum-Mocha Whipped Cream: To the unwhipped cream add ⅔ cup confectioners sugar, 2 tablespoons instant coffee, 3 tablespoons unsweetened cocoa, and 2 tablespoons dark rum.

In a chilled bowl with chilled beaters, whip the cream mixture until it holds a shape.

Spoon generously into the bottom halves of the puffs, mounding it very high. Place the top halves of the puffs on the cream, letting a bit of cream show on the sides.

Strain confectioners sugar generously over the tops. Place on a platter and refrigerate.

Serve with Old-Fashioned Walnut-Chocolate Sauce (page 500), at room temperature. Serve with a knife and fork.

Note: Puffs may be baked on a smaller cookie sheet in two separate batches, baking only one sheet at a time. Reserve the remaining batter covered, at room temperature.

Profiteroles

8 PORTIONS OF 3 PROFITEROLES EACH

Adjust rack to center of oven and preheat oven to 425 degrees. Follow the recipe and directions for Cream Puffs (page 314), dropping the paste by the heaping teaspoonfuls about 2 inches apart to make twenty-four small puffs.

Bake 15 minutes. Reduce oven temperature to 350 degrees and bake 30 minutes longer (total baking time 45 minutes), cutting one or two small slits in each puff 5 minutes before the baking time is up.

When cool, with a serrated knife cut off upper third of each puff, remove soft dough from centers, fill generously with ice cream and replace top.

As soon as each one is filled, immediately place it in freezer. When all are filled, wrap or package airtight.

To serve, pile on a platter in a pyramid and sprinkle with confectioners sugar. Serve with Old-Fashioned Walnut-Chocolate Sauce (page 500), first pouring a bit over the pyramid and passing the rest separately.

Note: If you wish, serve with Hot Fudge Sauce (page 503) in place of Old-Fashioned Walnut-Chocolate Sauce, but if so, do not pour any of it over the pyramid. The ice cream might harden the sauce and make serving difficult. Pass the sauce separately.

Counterfeit Puff Paste

This incredibly delicious product has the crisp, flaky, buttery qualities of classic puff paste, but it's child play to put it together. When used in the following recipes, it is almost indiscernible from that made by the classic method. Puff paste items are best when very fresh. If they are not be served soon, freeze them.

PASTRY
$1\frac{1}{2}$ cups unsifted all-purpose flour
$\frac{1}{2}$ pound (2 sticks) butter, cold and firm, cut into small pieces
$\frac{1}{2}$ cup sour cream

Place the unsifted flour in a bowl. Add the cut butter. With a pastry blender, cut the butter into the flour until the mixture resembles coarse crumbs. Stir in the sour cream. Turn out onto a board or smooth surface and knead briefly only until the mixture holds together. Pieces of butter should still show. Form into a ball, flatten into an oblong shape about 3 x 6 or 4 x 8 inches, place on wax paper, and wrap airtight. Refrigerate for at least 2 hours, or overnight or longer. Or if you wish, freeze it.

Voilá! Puff paste! That's it. The directions for using it from this stage on are classic.

If the dough has been frozen, allow it to thaw in the refrigerator for 12 to 24 hours, or at room temperature for a few hours.

Cut the dough into two equal squares. Work with half of the dough at a time. Refrigerate the other half until you are ready to use it.

On a board, with a heavy rolling pin, pound the unfrozen but still firm dough to make it workable.

Petits Palmiers

48 SMALL PALMIERS

Cover a section of a large board or smooth work surface generously with granulated sugar. Place the dough on the sugar, turning it to coat the top and bottom. Keeping the dough well sugared, roll it into a square about ⅛ inch thick and 11 to 12 inches square. Trim the edges. (Scraps may be rolled and cut to make Shoe Soles; see page 320.)

Sprinkle top of dough generously with additional sugar. Determine the center of the dough. Mark it lightly with a ruler or the back of a knife. Fold each side in thirds toward the center, folding so that, rather than meeting in the center, there is a ½-inch space between the edges. Then close it along that space like a book, making a compact roll about 2 inches wide, ¾ to 1 inch thick, and 12 inches long. Wrap airtight. Refrigerate for 1 hour or more, or freeze for about ½ hour, until dough is firm enough to be sliced evenly.

Adjust rack to center of oven. Preheat oven to 400 degrees. Line a cookie sheet with one large piece of aluminum foil or baking parchment.

With a very sharp, thin knife, slice the dough ½ inch thick. Dip both cut sides into sugar. Place cookies on a cut side at least 2½ inches apart (they will spread considerably). Bake only one sheet at a time.

Bake 12 minutes or until the sugar on the bottom has melted and is well caramelized. (During baking reverse position of pan if necessary to insure even

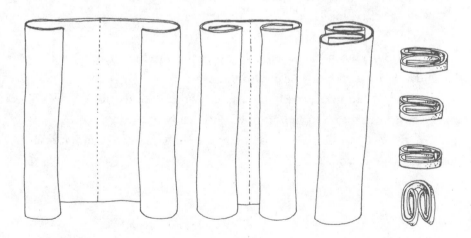

browning.) With two metal spatulas turn Palmiers over and continue to bake about 3 minutes longer until the sugar is lightly browned on the second side. Do not underbake; if Palmiers are underdone they will not be crisp as they should be.

Slide the foil or parchment off the cookie sheet. Let stand until Palmiers may be easily lifted off. Finish cooling on a rack.

Repeat with remaining half of dough. Store airtight. If the Palmiers are not to be served rather soon, they should be frozen.

Almond Twists
24 TO 48 TWISTS

Adjust rack one-third down from the top of oven. Preheat oven to 400 degrees. Line a large cookie sheet with aluminum foil or parchment. You may have to use two cookie sheets, but bake only one sheet at a time.

Prepare a glaze by mixing 1 egg with 1 teaspoon of water and set it aside. Prepare topping: Mix 5 ounces (1 cup) of very finely chopped almonds with ⅓ cup sugar and set aside.

Roll the dough out on a well-sugared board, turning it frequently to sugar both sides. Roll ⅛ inch thick to a rectangle 8 x 12 inches. Trim the edges.

Brush the top heavily with some of the egg glaze. Sprinkle generously with half of the almond-sugar mixture. With the rolling pin gently press the almond-sugar into the dough.

Cut the dough into strips 8 inches long—they may be from ½ to 1 inch wide but they must all be the same size; use a ruler. With a long, heavy knife cut down firmly, using the full length of the blade.

Using both hands, pick up each strip by the ends and twist each end two or three times in opposite directions to make a corkscrew twist. Then place the strips on the cookie sheet with both ends sugar-nut side down. Place them 1 inch apart. After they are all in place, press down gently near the ends to keep the spirals from unwinding. Do not press directly on the ends. (It would flatten the ends and they would burn before the rest of the spiral had baked.)

Bake only one sheet at a time for 15 to 18 minutes, depending on the width of the strips. If necessary, reverse position of pan during baking to insure even browning. Do not overbake. These must be thoroughly dry and crisp but do not overbake.

Slide the foil or parchment off the cookie sheet and let stand briefly until the twists can be lifted off easily. Transfer to racks to finish cooling.

Excess sugar that runs out on the sides of the twists may be removed when twists are completely cool.

Repeat with the other half of the dough and remaining almond-sugar mixture.

These are best when very fresh. Store airtight. These may be frozen.

Shoe Soles
20 LARGE WAFERS

Adjust rack one-third down from top of oven, so that the bottoms of the cookies will not burn before the tops are brown. Preheat oven to 400 degrees. Line a cookie sheet with one large piece of aluminum foil or parchment.

Roll the dough out on a generously sugared board, turning often to coat both sides heavily with sugar. Also sprinkle the top frequently with additional sugar. Roll to ¼-inch thickness. Cut with a 3-inch round cutter. (Remaining scraps may be pressed together and rerolled.)

Sprinkle the tops with additional sugar and roll each round into an oval about 5 inches long, continuing to keep both sides heavily sugared. With a small, sharp knife cut a slit about 3 inches long along the length of each cookie. Do not cut all the way to the ends. (This cut is not traditional, but it will help the bottoms brown evenly.)

Place the cookies on the foil or parchment 1 inch apart. Bake only one sheet at a time. Bake about 14 minutes until tops are golden brown and the sugar on the bottoms has caramelized. Do not underbake—these must be crisp and the bottoms must be well caramelized. Slide the foil or parchment off the sheet and let stand until completely cool.

Repeat with remaining half of the dough. Store airtight. These may be frozen.

Chocolate Soufflé

4 PORTIONS

Marilyn (Mrs. David) Evins is a fabulous hostess. A meal at her table is memorable. She claims that the secret of her super soufflés is that she uses a bit of cornstarch in the mixture. This is Marilyn's recipe.

- 1 tablespoon cornstarch
- 5 tablespoons sugar
- Salt
- ⅔ cup milk
- 2 teaspoons instant coffee
- 1 tablespoon butter
- 4 ounces semisweet chocolate, chopped coarse
- 1 tablespoon Grand Marnier, or other orange liqueur
- ½ teaspoon vanilla extract
- 5 eggs, separated, plus 1 egg white

Adjust rack to the lowest position in the oven. Preheat oven to 400 degrees. Butter a 2-quart soufflé dish. Prepare a collar. Tear off a length of aluminum foil long enough to wrap around the dish and overlap slightly and fold it in half the long way. Butter the top half of one side of the folded length. Wrap it around the dish, buttered side up and facing in. Tie with string or fasten it with straight pins to make a tight fit. Place a few large spoonfuls of sugar in the dish. Tilt, tap, and turn to coat the dish and the foil completely with sugar. Shake out excess.

In the top of a small double boiler off the heat, mix the cornstarch, 3 tablespoons of the sugar (reserve remaining 2 tablespoons), and a pinch of salt. Gradually at first, mix in the milk to make a smooth mixture.

Place over hot water on moderate heat. Cook, stirring very gently with a rubber spatula (do not beat), for about 6 minutes until the mixture thickens. Continue to cook, stirring gently for 1 minute more.

Remove top of double boiler from heat. Immediately add coffee, butter, and chocolate, continuing to stir gently until smooth. Mix in the Grand Marnier or other liqueur and the vanilla. Set aside to cool briefly for 5 minutes.

Meanwhile, in the small bowl of an electric mixer, beat the egg yolks at high speed for 4 to 5 minutes until pale lemon-colored. On low speed gradually beat in the chocolate mixture, scraping the bowl with the rubber spatula and beating only until smooth.

The soufflé may be completed now or the chocolate mixture may be covered and set aside at room temperature to be completed a few hours later.

If you have a large copper bowl and a large balloon-type whisk for beating egg whites, this is the time you should use it. If not, use any large bowl of an electric mixer. Add a pinch of salt to the six egg whites and beat at high speed until they increase in volume and hold a soft shape. While beating, gradually add remaining 2 tablespoons of sugar and continue to beat until whites barely hold a firm shape or are stiff but not dry.

Add one third of the whites to the chocolate and fold together just a bit. Repeat with another one third of the whites. Then add the chocolate to the whites and fold gently only until blended. Do not handle any more than necessary.

Gently turn the batter into the soufflé dish. Immediately place it in the oven, being careful not to hold the oven door open longer than necessary. Bake for 2 to 3 minutes and then reduce oven temperature to 375 degrees. Total baking time is 40 minutes.

Ovens vary, so test the soufflé about 5 minutes before the time is up. (Do not open the oven door before then.) Open the door only enough to be able to reach in and gently touch the top. Wiggle it a bit. It should move slightly, indicating that it is firm enough to hold its shape for a few minutes but still very light and only barely set.

Remove from oven. Quickly remove foil collar and serve immediately— I mean now!—on slightly warm dessert plates. Serve with any one of the custard sauces (pages 490-492), or with the following:

WHIPPED CREAM

1 cup heavy cream

¼ cup confectioners sugar

1 scant teaspoon vanilla extract, or 1 to 2 tablespoons Grand Marnier or other orange liqueur

In a chilled bowl with chilled beaters, whip above ingredients only until the cream thickens slightly and barely holds a soft shape. Do not whip until firm; this is a sauce.

If the cream is prepared ahead of time, refrigerate it and, immediately before serving, stir briefly to mix. Serve cold.

Icebox Cakes and Cake Rolls

Lemon Chiffon Icebox Cake

ICEBOX CAKE, PIE, OR COLD SOUFFLÉ—EACH SERVES 6 TO 8

48 single ladyfingers or a jelly roll cut in thin slices
1 tablespoon (1 envelope) unflavored gelatin
¼ cup cold water
4 eggs, jumbo or extra-large (or 5 smaller), separated
Finely grated rind of 1 large lemon
½ cup lemon juice
1 cup sugar
1 cup heavy cream
Generous pinch of salt

Prepare a loaf pan with 2½- to 3-quart capacity. Cut two strips of aluminum foil to line the pan, one for the length and one for the width. Put them into place carefully. Place ladyfingers, curved side against the pan, close together on bottom and sides (see Note). Or line pan with thin slices of jelly roll—push the slices together to fill in empty spaces.

Sprinkle gelatin over cold water and set aside. Place egg yolks in top of small double boiler off the heat, and stir lightly just to mix. Add the grated lemon rind and then gradually stir in the lemon juice and ½ cup of the sugar (reserve remaining ½ cup sugar). Place over hot water on moderate heat and cook, scraping the sides and bottom continuously with a rubber spatula until mixture thickens slightly "to coat a metal spoon"—about 180 degrees on a candy thermometer. Remove top from heat. Add gelatin and stir to dissolve. Let stand, stirring occasionally, until completely cool.

When lemon mixture is cool, in a chilled bowl with chilled beaters whip the cream until it holds a soft shape.

In small bowl of electric mixer beat the salt and the egg whites until whites have increased in volume and have started to thicken. While beating, gradually add reserved ½ cup sugar and continue to beat at moderately high speed until whites stand in peaks—do not overbeat; meringue must not be dry.

Gradually, in several additions, fold the lemon mixture into the whites and then, in a large bowl, fold together the lemon mixture and the whipped cream.

Turn into pan lined with ladyfingers or sliced jelly roll. Cover the top with a layer of ladyfingers or slices of jelly roll. Refrigerate for 5 to 6 hours.

To serve, cover with a serving dish and invert. Remove pan and aluminum foil.

TOPPING

Optional: 2 to 3 tablespoons tart jam or preserves (sour cherry, currant, raspberry, apricot)

1 cup heavy cream

¼ cup confectioners sugar

1 scant teaspoon vanilla extract

Optional: Green pistachio nuts, chopped, or semisweet chocolate, coarsely grated

Stir the preserves, if used, to soften and then spread over the top of the cake, or just place on at random by small spoonfuls.

In a chilled bowl with chilled beaters, whip the cream with the sugar and vanilla until it holds a definite shape. Either smooth it over the top, or apply it with a pastry bag and a large star tube, making heavy, rippled lines.

If you wish, sprinkle with chopped pistachio nuts or grated chocolate. Refrigerate for several hours.

Note: When lining the pan with ladyfingers, cut them as necessary to fit into place. If they won't stand up on the sides, dot the aluminum foil lightly with a bit of soft butter wherever necessary to hold them up. If the ladyfingers are too long for the sides of the pan, cut one end and place them cut side up.

Lemon Chiffon Pie

Use the same lemon chiffon mixture to fill a 9-inch graham cracker crust (page 352), or Chocolate Cookie Crust (page 357). Refrigerate several hours until set. Cover with above topping drizzling the optional preserves over the filling and spreading the whipped cream on top.

Cold Lemon Soufflé

The same lemon chiffon mixture may be used for a cold soufflé. Prepare a 3-inch collar for a 5- to 6-cup soufflé dish. Use a piece of aluminum foil long enough to wrap around the dish and overlap a few inches. Fold it in half lengthwise. Brush tasteless salad oil on the top half of one side or spray it with cooking spray. Wrap it around the dish, oiled side up and facing in. Fasten tightly with string or straight pins. Pour in the lemon chiffon mixture. Refrigerate 5 to 6 hours. Remove collar and cover with above topping (page 327).

Kentucky Chocolate Icebox Cake with Bourbon

6 TO 8 PORTIONS

1 ounce unsweetened chocolate
3 ounces semisweet chocolate
¼ pound (1 stick) butter
1 cup sugar
2 egg yolks
½ cup light cream
1 teaspoon vanilla extract
36 double or 72 single ladyfingers
¼ to ⅓ cup bourbon (see Note)

In the top of a large double boiler over hot water, melt both chocolates and butter. Stir in the sugar. Mix the yolks, cream, and vanilla and, with a wire whisk, stir them into the chocolate. Cook over moderate heat, stirring occasionally, for about 15 minutes.

Remove top of double boiler and set aside to cool slightly, stirring occasionally; or stir very briefly over ice water.

Meanwhile, line a 9 x 5 x 3-inch loaf pan. Cut two strips of aluminum foil to line the pan, one for the length and two small (end) sides and one for the width and two larger sides. Put them into place carefully.

Line the bottom of the pan (not the sides) with a solid layer of single ladyfingers, placing the curved side against the pan and cutting them as necessary for a snug fit. Brush or sprinkle lightly with 1 tablespoon of the bourbon. Cover with one third of the chocolate in a thin layer. Tilt pan to level chocolate. Continue making layers; four of ladyfingers and bourbon, three of chocolate.

After brushing or sprinkling the bourbon on the top layer of ladyfingers, cover that with another layer of ladyfingers without bourbon. Cover airtight and refrigerate 5 to 6 hours, or for a day or two, or freeze it. Although this is an icebox cake generally served from the refrigerator, I think it is also delicious served frozen.

To serve if you have frozen the cake, unmold it and either decorate with whipped cream immediately before serving, or serve the whipped cream separately.

To serve if you have refrigerated the cake, unmold and decorate with whipped cream whenever convenient before serving.

WHIPPED CREAM
1 cup heavy cream
¼ cup confectioners sugar
1 scant teaspoon vanilla extract

Whip above ingredients in a chilled bowl with chilled beaters until barely stiff.

Spread over cake (top only), or apply over top using a pastry bag with a medium star tube to form three heavy rippled lines down the length of the top—first one on each side and then one in the center. Use the remaining cream to form two more long lines between the first three—or form six to eight heavy rippled lines going across the width of the cake.

Note: The bourbon may be increased or decreased according to taste, or it may be eliminated entirely, or you may substitute light rum or brandy.

Chocolate Rum Icebox Cake

8 PORTIONS

2 ounces unsweetened chocolate
2 ounces semisweet chocolate
½ cup light rum
2½ to 3 dozen double ladyfingers (see Note)
½ pound (2 sticks) butter
¼ cup strong prepared coffee (you can use 1 tablespoon instant coffee
    dissolved in ¼ cup water)
1½ cups confectioners sugar
5 eggs, separated
⅛ teaspoon salt

Use a loaf pan that has a 10-cup capacity, preferably long and narrow instead of short and wide (about 14 x 4½ x 3 inches). Cut two strips of aluminum foil to line the pan, one for the length and two small (end) sides and one for the width and two larger sides. Put them into place carefully.

Melt both chocolates in the top of a small double boiler over hot water on moderate heat. Stir until smooth. Set aside to cool.

Brush or sprinkle some of the rum on the flat side of the ladyfingers and line the pan with them, placing them with the curved sides against the pan. Line the bottom of the pan first and then the sides.

In the small bowl of an electric mixer beat the butter to soften it a bit. Gradually beat in the prepared coffee and then the sugar. Beat until smooth. Add the yolks one at a time, beating well after each, and continue to beat for 2 to 3 minutes until very creamy. Beat in the chocolate, scraping the bowl with a rubber spatula as necessary to keep mixture smooth. Transfer to a large mixing bowl.

Add the salt to the egg whites and beat until they hold a point and are stiff but not dry. Fold about half of the whites into the chocolate. Then fold the chocolate into the remaining whites. Pour about half of the chocolate filling into the ladyfinger-lined pan. Cover with a layer of ladyfingers, brushing or sprinkling them with some of the rum.

Cover the ladyfingers with balance of chocolate filling. Spread the filling smooth. Again, make a layer of ladyfingers with rum. Any remaining rum may be sprinkled over the top. If you wish, cover with another layer of ladyfingers without rum.

If the ladyfingers on the sides of the pan extend too high, they should be cut level with scissors. Cover tightly with plastic wrap or aluminum foil. Press down very gently to make a compact loaf. Refrigerate overnight. (This may be frozen.)

Remove plastic wrap or foil topping. Place a serving plate on top and invert pan and plate. Remove pan and foil lining.

Cover with the following:

TOPPING

    1 cup heavy cream
    ¼ cup strained confectioners sugar
    1 teaspoon vanilla extract
    Optional: Chocolate, grated; pistachio nuts, chopped; or almonds, toasted
        and sliced

In a chilled bowl with chilled beaters, beat cream, sugar, and vanilla until cream holds a shape. Spread thickly over top of cake or apply with pastry bag and large star tube. (If you use the pastry bag, make three long, rippled lines going down the length, first on one edge, then the other, and finally in the center. They should be heavy enough so that they touch each other and completely cover the top of the cake.) Do not put whipped cream on the sides.

Cake may be left as is or dusted lightly with grated chocolate, chopped pistachio nuts, or toasted, sliced almonds. Refrigerate.

Note: The ladyfingers should be separated so that they are not double; however, they may be left in one piece, side by side, and cut to length as needed.

Chocolate Icebox Cake, Country Style

8 PORTIONS

T his one must be made 12 to 24 hours ahead.

1 cup sugar
1 tablespoon (1 envelope) unflavored gelatin
1⅓ cups milk
5 ounces unsweetened chocolate, chopped
5 eggs, separated
Ladyfingers
Pinch of salt
1 cup heavy cream
1½ teaspoons vanilla extract
⅓ cup walnuts, broken or cut coarse

Reserve 3 tablespoons of the sugar. In an 8- to 10-cup heavy saucepan, mix the remaining sugar and gelatin. Stir in the milk and then add the chocolate. Cook over moderate heat, stirring constantly, until the mixture is smooth and comes to a boil. Simmer for 1 minute. Beat with a wire whisk until smooth. Remove from heat.

In a bowl stir the egg yolks briefly just to mix. Gradually stir in a few spoonfuls of the chocolate mixture and then, stirring constantly, add the egg yolks to the remaining chocolate mixture.

Stir over low heat for a minute or two until mixture thickens slightly. Remove from heat. Transfer to a large mixing bowl and stir occasionally until cool.

Meanwhile, prepare a 10-cup serving bowl. This is most attractive in a straight-sided glass bowl or soufflé dish. Line the bottom and sides with ladyfingers. (For the sides, separate the double strips of ladyfingers, but do not separate each individual finger. Stand whole strips of them upright on the sides of the bowl, curved sides against the bowl.)

When the chocolate mixture has cooled, add the salt to the egg whites in the small bowl of an electric mixer. Beat until mixture has increased in volume and thickened slightly. While beating, gradually add the reserved 3 tablespoons of sugar and beat until mixture has the consistency of thick marshmallow sauce and holds its shape, but do not overbeat. It must not be dry.

In a chilled bowl with chilled beaters, whip the cream until it just holds a shape—not too stiff.

Stir the vanilla into the chocolate mixture.

Gradually fold a cup of the chocolate mixture into the whipped cream, and then fold the whites into the remaining chocolate mixture.

Now gradually fold a cup of the chocolate mixture into the whipped cream, and then fold the whipped cream into the remaining chocolate mixture. Handle lightly. If necessary, pour gently from one bowl to another to insure thorough blending.

Pour into ladyfinger-lined bowl. If the tops of the ladyfingers do not reach the top of the bowl, after pouring in most of the chocolate mixture, use a fork to gently raise the ladyfingers and then pour in the remaining chocolate.

Refrigerate for 10 minutes and then sprinkle top with walnuts. Return to refrigerator. When the top is firm enough, cover airtight with plastic wrap and refrigerate for 12 to 24 hours before serving.

Serve with a side dish of Soft Whipped Cream.

SOFT WHIPPED CREAM
1 cup heavy cream
¼ cup confectioners sugar
1 teaspoon vanilla extract

In a chilled bowl with chilled beaters, whip the above ingredients only until they thicken to the consistency of a sauce, semifirm.

Charlotte Russe

6 TO 7 PORTIONS

This brings back memories of days when charlotte russes were sold from pushcarts on the streets of New York. (I was in about the fourth grade.) How did an elaborate and classic French dessert wind up on pushcarts on the Lower East Side? And how did they make them so good?

18 double ladyfingers
Optional: Light rum, framboise, or kirsch

This is beautiful if prepared individually in 8-ounce old-fashioned cocktail glasses, or other straight-sided glasses no deeper than the length of the ladyfingers.

Separate ladyfingers and cut them into individual fingers.

Pour 3 or 4 tablespoons of optional rum, or framboise or kirsch, into a small dish. With a pastry brush, brush the flat side of each ladyfinger very briefly with a bit of the rum and place fingers touching each other, rounded side against the glass, around the sides of six or seven straight-sided wide and shallow glasses.

FILLING

Prepare Vanilla Filling (see Vanilla Cream Pie, page 357), adding a scant 1/4 teaspoon of almond extract along with the vanilla.

Spoon the filling (or pour from a wide pitcher) into the prepared glasses, mounding them high. Refrigerate 2 to 3 hours.

TOPPING

Optional: Tart, dark red jam or jelly
1 cup heavy cream
1/4 cup confectioners sugar
1 teaspoon vanilla extract

Top each dessert with a small spoonful of the optional jam or jelly. In a chilled bowl with chilled beaters, whip the cream with the sugar and vanilla until it holds a shape. With a pastry bag and a large star tube, pipe a heavy ring of the cream around the other edge of each dessert letting the jam or jelly show through in the middle. Refrigerate.

Optional: Before serving decorate with candied violets or rose petals, a bit of grated chocolate, a piece of glacéed fruit, a few toasted, sliced almonds, and/or . . .

Black Velvet

16 TO 24 PORTIONS

This is a big job, but well worth it. The ultimate chocolate icebox cake, adapted from the famous Chocolate Velvet, one of the most popular desserts served at Restaurant Associates' grand and elegant Four Seasons restaurant in New York City. Dense and rich—portions should be small.

The dessert should be refrigerated for 5 hours or more before it is iced.

Prepare two sponge sheets from the following recipe, making one after the other instead of doubling the recipe.

SPONGE SHEET
(This classic recipe will make a thin, rather solid but flexible sheet.)

5 eggs, separated
¼ cup sugar
1 teaspoon vanilla extract
3 tablespoons sifted all-purpose flour
⅛ teaspoon salt

Adjust rack one-third up from the bottom of oven. Preheat oven to 375 degrees. Turn a 10½ x 15½ x 1-inch jelly-roll pan upside down. Cover it with a length of regular weight aluminum foil shiny side down. Press all four sides down to shape the foil to the pan. Remove foil. Turn pan right side up. Place foil in pan and press into place.

Put a piece of butter (a generous tablespoonful) in the pan and place the pan in the oven to melt the butter. Then with a pastry brush, brush the butter all over the bottom and sides of the pan. Set aside.

In small bowl of electric mixer, at high speed, beat the yolks for about 3 to 4 minutes until thick and light lemon-colored. Add 2 tablespoons of the sugar (reserve remaining 2 tablespoons sugar) and the vanilla. Continue to beat at high speed for 3 to 4 minutes more until mixture is very thick and falls very slowly from beaters when they are lifted.

Reduce speed to lowest and add the flour, scraping bowl with a rubber spatula and beating only until flour is incorporated.

In large bowl of electric mixer, with clean beaters, at high speed beat the whites with the salt until the mixture thickens enough to hold a very soft shape. Gradually add the reserved 2 tablespoons of sugar and continue to beat at high speed until mixture holds a firm shape and is stiff but not dry.

In three additions, fold one-half of the whites into the yolks—don't be too thorough—then fold the yolks back into the remaining whites only until no whites show. Handle as little as possible.

Spray the bottom and sides of the buttered pan generously with cooking spray and then turn the batter into the pan. Handle lightly and spread smooth (preferably with an off-set spatula). Place in the oven.

Bake for 15 to 18 minutes or until top is golden brown and springs back when lightly touched in the center, and cake comes away from sides of pan.

While cake is baking, spread out a dry kitchen towel (preferably smooth cotton, flour sacking, or linen).

Remove baked cake from oven. Invert immediately onto the towel. Remove pan and wax paper. Let cool on the towel.

Repeat to make second sponge sheet.

TO ASSEMBLE

Line the bottom of a 9 x 3–inch springform pan (sides must be 3 inches high) with wax paper or baking parchment, unbuttered.

At one end of a sponge sheet, right up against the end, touching the edge trace around the springform with a small, sharp knife just to indicate the circle. Remove springform and, with scissors, cut out the circle of cake. Repeat with second sponge sheet, making second circle of cake. Place one of the cake rounds in the pan.

With a ruler and toothpicks, carefully mark remaining pieces of cakes into even slices 2¾ inches wide (two from one cake and one from the other) marking from end of sponge sheet, so they are 9½ inches long. (Even though the pan is 10½ inches on its shorter side, the sponge sheets will shrink to about 9½ inches.) Cut with a small, sharp knife, cutting against the ruler. That will give you three slices, each one 2¾ x 9½ inches.

Cut 1 inch off one of the long strips, making it 8½ inches long. Place it and the other two longer strips standing up around the sides of the pan, the top side of the cake against the pan. Fit the strips together tightly, pushing them into each other to make a tight fit.

Reserve remaining round of cake. You will not need the cut ends and pieces.

Prepare following Chocolate Filling:

CHOCOLATE FILLING
1½ pounds semisweet chocolate
1½ tablespoons instant coffee
½ cup boiling water
½ cup Grand Marnier
3 egg yolks
1 cup egg whites (see page xxi)
¼ teaspoon salt
¼ cup sugar
1 cup heavy cream

Place chocolate in top of a large double boiler over hot water on moderate heat. Cover until partially melted, then uncover and stir occasionally until melted. Turn it into small bowl of electric mixer and let stand, stirring occasionally, until cooled to room temperature.

Meanwhile, dissolve instant coffee in boiling water and set aside.

When chocolate has completely cooled, on lowest speed very gradually beat in the prepared coffee and the Grand Marnier and then the egg yolks, scraping the bowl with a rubber spatula as necessary to keep mixture smooth. Beat only until smooth. Set aside.

In a large bowl of electric mixer at high speed, beat the egg whites with the salt until they hold a very soft shape. Gradually beat in the sugar and continue to beat until whites hold a definite point, or are stiff but not dry.

Fold one large spoonful of the beaten whites into the chocolate mixture. Fold in another large spoonful. Gradually, in several additions, fold in half of the remaining whites—don't be too thorough. Then fold the chocolate into the remaining whites, folding completely until no whites show.

In a chilled bowl with chilled beaters, whip the cream until it holds a soft shape but is not stiff. Fold the cream into the chocolate mixture.

Pour the filling into the cake-lined pan. If it reaches to the top of the cake on the sides, cover with remaining circle of cake.

If the filling does not quite reach the top of the cake (if it is ⅓ to ½ inch below), cut around the remaining circle of cake with scissors, cutting in ¼ inch from the edge to make the circle small enough to fit down inside the cake on the sides. Place it over the filling.

Cover with clear wrap or aluminum foil and a light weight. (I use a cake pan or a small cookie sheet with something not too heavy placed on the center of it.) Refrigerate for 5 hours or more.

Remove sides of springform. Place dessert platter over dessert. Very carefully invert. Remove bottom of pan and paper.

Cut six strips of wax paper or baking parchment, each 1½ to 2 inches wide and 6 to 8 inches long. With a wide metal spatula or pancake turner, very gently raise a small section of the cake and slide a strip of wax paper under it to protect the plate when icing the cake. Continue all around the cake.

Cover with the following icing:

ICING

    6 ounces semisweet or extra-bittersweet chocolate
    ½ cup boiling water

Break or cut chocolate into pieces and place them in a small, heavy-bottomed saucepan. Add boiling water and place over low heat. Stir with a small wire whisk until smooth. Remove from heat and let stand at room temperature to cool. Stir the icing well. Work quickly before the cold cake hardens the icing. Pour it over the cake, completely covering the top and letting very little run down on the sides. With a small, narrow metal spatula spread smooth on the sides.

Remove paper strips immediately before icing sets, pulling each piece out by a narrow end of the paper. (If the icing hardens before the paper is removed, cut around the base of the cake with a small knife to release the paper before pulling it away.) Refrigerate.

Notes:

1. Black Velvet may be refrigerated for a day or two, or it may be frozen before it is iced.

2. Dip the knife in hot water, or hold it under running hot water, before cutting each slice.

3. Black Velvet may be served as is or with Grand Marnier Custard Sauce (page 491) or with whipped cream sweetened with confectioners sugar and flavored with Grand Marnier.

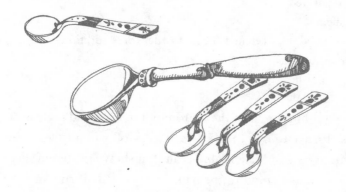

Chocolate Roll

8 PORTIONS

T his is really a flourless soufflé baked in a jelly-roll pan. The recipe is practically foolproof, and it is quite spectacular and absolutely delicious.

> 6 eggs, separated
> ¾ cup sugar
> ⅓ cup strained unsweetened cocoa powder (plus additional cocoa powder for sprinkling)
> ¼ teaspoon salt

Adjust rack one-third up from the bottom of the oven and preheat the oven to 375 degrees. Turn a 10½ x 15½ x 1-inch jelly-roll pan upside down. Cover it with a length of regular weight aluminum foil shiny side down. Press all four sides down to shape the foil to the pan. Remove foil. Turn pan right side up. Place foil in the pan and press into place.

Put a piece of butter (about 1 tablespoon) in pan and place pan in the oven just to melt the butter. Then with a pastry brush or crumbled plastic wrap spread the butter over the bottom and sides of pan. Set aside.

In small bowl of electric mixer at high speed beat yolks for about 4 minutes until light lemon-colored. Add half of the sugar (reserve remaining sugar) and continue to beat for 4 minutes more until very thick and pale. On lowest speed add the ⅓ cup cocoa and beat only until mixed. Set aside.

In large bowl of electric mixer, with clean beaters, beat the whites with the salt until they increase in volume and hold a soft shape. On low speed gradually add the reserved sugar. Then beat at high speed until the whites hold a straight point when the beaters are raised.

In a few additions fold half of the whites into the chocolate mixture and then fold the chocolate mixture into the remaining whites. Do not handle any more than necessary!

Spray the bottom and sides of the buttered pan with Pam and then turn the batter into the pan, pouring it all over the bottom of the pan. Handle lightly and spread smooth. Place in the oven.

Bake the cake for about 30 minutes until the top springs back when gently pressed with a fingertip.

While cake is baking, wet and wring out a kitchen towel (preferably smooth cotton or linen). Set aside.

When the cake is removed from the oven it should be covered with the damp towel. And to keep the steam and moisture in the cake, the towel should be covered with foil, which should be pressed down around the sides of the pan. Let stand until cool.

WHIPPED CREAM FILLING

To make the best whipped cream, the bowl and beaters should be chilled in the freezer for about ½ hour before you use them. The cream should be refrigerated until you are ready for it. If everything is cold enough you will be able to make beautiful whipped cream, with less chance of having it curdle or turn to butter.

1½ **cups heavy cream**
3 **tablespoons strained confectioners sugar**
1 **teaspoon vanilla extract**

Place the cream, sugar, and vanilla in the bowl. Beat until the cream is quite firm.

Uncover the cooled cake. Cover it with a length of wax paper. Place a flat cookie sheet or an inverted jelly-roll pan over it. Turn everything upside down. Remove the pan and foil lining. Sprinkle the cake generously with cocoa powder through a fine strainer. Cover again with a length of wax paper and another cookie sheet or inverted jelly-roll pan. Turn everything upside down again. Uncover cake.

Now place the whipped cream all over the cake and spread it smooth, but make it thinner on the farther long side and keep it about an inch away from the farther long edge of the cake.

Start to roll the cake by lifting the edge of the wax paper on the long side nearest you. Continue to use the paper to help roll the cake.

Now, this is tricky. Handle gently. As you finish rolling the cake, the final turn should deposit the cake seam down onto a chocolate roll board (see Note) or any long serving plate. Actually, to transfer the cake to the board I not only use my hands—I roll up my sleeves and support the roll with my arms.

Sprinkle the top with a bit more cocoa. Trim the edges of the cake. With a pastry brush, brush excess cocoa off the board or plate.

Refrigerate and serve cold. Serve with the following sauce.

CHOCOLATE SAUCE

½ cup whipping cream
1 teaspoon powdered instant espresso or coffee (I use Medaglia d'Oro espresso)
6 ounces semisweet chocolate, chopped fine
1 tablespoon unsalted butter

In a small saucepan over moderate heat, heat the cream until it just begins to bubble. Stir in the espresso or coffee, and then add the chocolate and butter and stir until thoroughly melted. Remove from the heat. Whisk or stir and then strain through a fine strainer.

Sauce should be at room temperature when you use it. If necessary, it may be reheated a bit.

Spoon or pour a generous amount of the sauce alongside each portion.

Note: A chocolate roll board is a long, narrow, wooden board with a handle. It is classic and traditional and beautiful—and a great thing to have. When I recently gave this recipe to *Ocean Drive*, a classy society and fashion publication, and they printed it, I bought a dozen chocolate roll boards for my friends. I knew that when they had this recipe—and saw the photo of the cake—they would all want to make it. And they did and they are all thrilled with their results. I bought the boards from Bridge Kitchenware ([800] 274-3435 or, in New York City, [212] 838-1901).

Cream Roll

8 PORTIONS

T his should be refrigerated at least 5 to 6 hours before serving.

SPONGE CAKE

  6 eggs, separated
  ¼ cup plus 2 tablespoons granulated sugar
  Finely grated rind of 1 large orange
  ¼ teaspoon salt
  ¼ cup plus 2 tablespoons sifted all-purpose flour
  Optional: Confectioners sugar for sprinkling

Adjust rack one-third up from the bottom of the oven and preheat the oven to 375 degrees. Turn a 10½ x 15½ x 1-inch jelly-roll pan upside down. Cover it with a length of regular weight aluminum foil shiny side down. Press all four sides down to shape the foil to the pan. Remove foil. Turn pan right side up. Place foil in pan and press into place.

Put a piece of butter (about 1 tablespoon) in pan and place pan in the oven just to melt the butter. Then with a pastry brush or crumbled plastic wrap spread the butter over the bottom and sides of pan. Set aside.

In small bowl of electric mixer at high speed, beat the egg yolks for 3 minutes until light lemon-colored. Gradually beat in 3 tablespoons of the sugar (reserve remaining sugar) and continue to beat at high speed for 5 minutes more, until the mixture is very thick. Remove from mixer. Fold in orange rind and transfer to a large bowl.

In a large bowl of electric mixer, with clean beaters, beat the egg whites and the salt until they hold a soft shape. Add the remaining sugar and beat until the whites hold a straight shape or are stiff but not dry. Place half of the whites on the yolks. Sift half of the flour on top. Gently fold together—do not be too thorough. Repeat with remaining whites and flour, folding gently only until completely blended.

Spray the bottom and sides of the buttered pan generously with Pam and then turn the batter into prepared pan and spread gently with a spatula to level.

Bake 20 to 25 minutes until top of cake springs back when lightly touched and sides come away from pan.

While the cake is baking, wet and thoroughly wring out a smooth towel (smooth cotton, flour sacking, or linen). When the cake is removed from the oven it should be covered with the damp towel. And to keep the moisture in the cake, the towel should be covered with foil, which should be pressed down around the sides of the pan. Let stand until cool.

CREAM FILLING
    2 teaspoons unflavored gelatin
    2 tablespoons water
    1½ cups heavy cream
    ¼ cup confectioners sugar
    ⅓ cup Cointreau
    ½ cup orange marmalade

Sprinkle the gelatin over the water in a small heatproof cup and let stand for about 5 minutes. Place cup in a small saucepan of hot water about a third of the way up the sides of the cup on moderate heat until gelatin is dissolved. Remove from heat and set aside.

In chilled bowl with chilled beaters, whip the cream, sugar, and ¼ cup Cointreau (reserve balance) until it starts to thicken. Quickly stir a large spoonful of the cream into the gelatin and immediately add the gelatin to the cream, continuing to beat until cream is firm and holds a definite shape. Fold in marmalade. Set bowl into a larger bowl of ice and water and fold cream occasionally, until it is firm enough not to run out of the cake when it is rolled. (This might take 20 to 30 minutes in a small, narrow mixer bowl—it will take less time if transferred to a wider bowl.)

Uncover the cooled cake. Cover it with a length of wax paper. Place a flat cookie sheet over it. Turn the cake pan and sheet upside down. Remove the pan the foil lining. Sprinkle or brush with reserved Cointreau. (Use a bit more than called for, if you wish.)

When whipped cream is firm enough to hold its shape, spread it on the cake, heavily along one long edge and stopping ½ to 1 inch from the opposite edge. With the help of the wax paper, roll the cake the long way so that the two long sides just meet in the middle and do not overlap. It will look like a tube.

(If the roll is too soft to be transferred, slide a cookie sheet under the wax paper and place it all in the freezer or refrigerator until it is firm enough to be handled.) Then, using a cookie sheet as a spatula, place the cake on a chocolate roll board or a long platter, seam side down. Refrigerate for 5 to 6 hours.

The top may be sprinkled with confectioners sugar through a fine strainer. If you wish to make a pattern on top, cut wax paper in strips ¼ inch wide (9 to 10 inches long). Place them diagonally over the top of the cake about 1 inch apart. Sprinkle generously with confectioners sugar through a fine strainer. Carefully remove wax paper strips. Brush excess sugar off board or platter.

Optional: Serve with a side dish of sliced and sweetened strawberries (page 380), to be spooned over or alongside each portion after it is placed on an individual dessert plate. And/or serve with Honey Chocolate Sauce, page 502.

Note: Cut with a sawing motion in order not to squash the cream.

Crumb Crust Pies

GENERAL DIRECTIONS FOR CRUMB CRUST

How to line a pie plate with aluminum foil, shape and bake the crust, and then how to remove the foil.

Although the crumb mixture may be pressed into place directly in the pie plate, I prefer to line the plate with foil first and then remove the foil before filling the crust. This guarantees easy serving—the crust can't stick to the plate. It's a bit more work (or play), but I think well worth it.

For a 9-inch pie plate, use a 12-inch square of foil. Place the pie plate upside down on the work surface. Center the foil evenly, shiny side down, over the plate. Fold down the foil all around the plate to shape it to the plate. Remove the foil. Turn the plate right side up. Place the shaped foil in the plate. Using a towel or pot holder to press with, press the foil firmly into place, making sure that it is touching all parts of the plate. Fold the edges of the foil down over the rim of the plate.

Turn the crumb crust mixture into the lined plate. Using your fingertips, distribute the mixture evenly and loosely over the sides first and then over the bottom. Then press the crust firmly and evenly over the sides, pushing it up from the bottom to form a rim slightly raised above the edge of the plate. Be careful that the top of the edge of the crust is not too thin. To shape a firm edge, use the fingertips of your right hand against the inside and press down against it with the thumb of your left hand. After firmly pressing the sides and the top edge, press the remaining crumbs evenly and firmly over the bottom. There should be no loose crumbs.

Bake in the center of a preheated 375 degree oven for 8 minutes, or until very lightly browned on the edges. Cool to room temperature.

Place in freezer for at least 1 hour, or more if possible. It must be frozen solid.

Remove from freezer. Raise edges of foil. Carefully lift foil (with crust) from plate. Gently peel away the foil by supporting the bottom of the crust with your left hand and peeling the foil, a bit at a time, with your right hand. As you do so, rotate the crust gently on your left hand.

Supporting the bottom of the crust with a small metal spatula or a knife, ease it back into the plate very gently so as not to crack it. It will not crack or break if it has been frozen sufficiently.

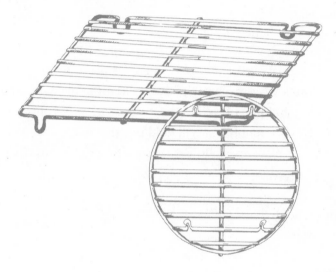

Rum Pie

This is no kidding—no holds barred—*rum*. Not for sissies. I use Myers's Dark Jamaican Rum. Yummy. *Wow!*

Refrigerate for at least 5 to 6 hours before serving.

CRUST

1¼ cups graham cracker crumbs
¼ cup sugar
2 ounces (½ stick) butter, melted

Adjust rack to center of oven. Preheat oven to 375 degrees.

Mix the crumbs with the sugar and then add the melted butter. With a rubber spatula, stir and press firmly against the bowl until completely mixed. The mixture will look crumbly but will hold together when pressed into place.

Use a 9-inch pie plate and follow directions for crumb crust (page 350).

FILLING

1 tablespoon (1 envelope) unflavored gelatin
¼ cup cold water
5 egg yolks
¾ cup sugar
¾ cup dark rum
1 cup heavy cream

Sprinkle gelatin over cold water in a heatproof glass measuring cup or a small heatproof bowl. Let stand.

In small bowl of electric mixer at high speed, beat the yolks. Gradually add the sugar and beat for 5 minutes.

Meanwhile, stir ¼ cup of the rum (reserve remaining ½ cup rum) into the gelatin. Place the cup or bowl in a small pan of shallow hot water on moderate heat until the gelatin is dissolved. (Stir with a metal spoon so that you can see when the granules have dissolved.)

Beating on low speed, slowly add the warm gelatin mixture to the egg yolks, scraping bowl with a rubber spatula to keep mixture smooth. Beat in the reserved ½ cup rum.

In a chilled bowl with chilled beaters, whip the cream until it holds a soft shape, not stiff. Set aside.

Place the bowl of egg yolk mixture into a larger bowl of ice and water. Stir and scrape the bowl occasionally until the mixture starts to thicken to the consistency of a medium cream sauce. This might take as long as 15 minutes in a small, narrow bowl. However if you transfer it to a large, wide bowl, it will probably thicken in 5 to 7 minutes. In a large, wide bowl, stir and scrape the bowl almost constantly. Once it has thickened, fold one quarter of the egg yolk mixture into the whipped cream. Fold in another quarter and then fold the cream into the remaining egg yolk mixture. If necessary, gently pour back and forth from one bowl to another to insure thorough blending.

Fill the shell as full as possible without letting it run over. There will be some leftover filling. Let it stand at room temperature while you chill the filled shell (only about 7 to 8 minutes in the freezer, or a bit longer in the refrigerator) until the filling is semiset. Then pour on the remaining filling, mounding it higher in the center.

Refrigerate at least 5 to 6 hours or more. Prepare following whipped cream topping:

WHIPPED CREAM
1½ cups heavy cream
⅓ cup confectioners sugar
1½ teaspoons vanilla extract

In a chilled bowl with chilled beaters, whip above ingredients until firm enough to hold a shape. Place a spoonful at a time first around outer edge of filling, and then continue toward the center. If the spoonfuls are even, leave the top as is. If not, it may be spread smooth or swirled with the back of a spoon.

Optional: Sprinkle the outer rim of the whipped cream with finely chopped green pistachios nuts and/or place coarsely grated chocolate in the center.

Note: A variation of this pie my be made by substituting for the rum ½ cup whiskey and 2 tablespoons instant coffee dissolved in ¼ cup hot water.

Coffee Buttercrunch Pie

8 PORTIONS

This rich creation is the famous Coffee-Toffee Pie from Blum's in San Francisco. I never know what to answer when people tell me, as they often do, that this is better than sex. (What would you say?)

This should be refrigerated for at least 5 to 6 hours before serving.

CRUST

(This may be doubled. The extra crust may be frozen.)

½ package pie crust mix (measure the contents of a package into a measuring cup and use half)

1 ounce unsweetened chocolate

¼ cup firmly packed light brown sugar

2½ ounces (¾ cup) walnuts, very finely chopped (must be finely chopped— not ground)

1 teaspoon vanilla extract

1 tablespoon water

Place the pie crust mix in a mixing bowl.

Cut the chocolate into small pieces and place it in the bowl of a food processor fitted with the metal chopping blade. Process for about half a minute until fine. Add the sugar and nuts. Pulse briefly and then transfer the mixture to a bowl. Mix the vanilla and water and gradually drizzle it over the mixture—don't pour it all in one place—while using a fork to stir and toss. The mixture will be lumpy and crumbly. Do not try to make it smooth, stir it very briefly. It will hold together when you press it into place.

Adjust rack to center of oven and preheat to 375 degrees.

Use a 9-inch pie plate and follow directions for crumb crust (page 350). However, for this recipe bake the crust for 15 minutes.

Meanwhile, prepare the following filling:

FILLING

(This may be doubled if you have made two crusts. The extra filled crust may be frozen.)

1 ounce unsweetened chocolate
¼ pound (1 stick) butter
¾ cup light firmly packed brown sugar
2 teaspoons instant coffee
2 eggs

Melt chocolate over hot water and set aside to cool. In small bowl of electric mixer beat the butter to soften a bit. Gradually add the sugar and beat at moderately high speed for 2 to 3 minutes. Mix in the cooled, melted chocolate and the instant coffee. Add the eggs individually, beating for 5 minutes after each, and scraping the bowl occasionally with a rubber spatula.

Pour the filling into the prepared crust. Refrigerate for 5 to 6 hours or overnight. (Pie may be frozen now or it may be refrigerated for a day or so. If you freeze it, freeze until filling is firm before wrapping airtight. Frozen pie should be uncovered and thawed overnight in the refrigerator.)

Either shortly before serving, or a few hours before, prepare the following:

TOPPING

2 cups heavy cream
2 tablespoons instant coffee
½ cup confectioners sugar
Optional: Coarsely grated semisweet chocolate

In a chilled bowl with chilled beaters, whip the cream with the coffee and sugar until firm. Do not overbeat, but it must be firm enough so that it holds its shape when pie is served.

Spread smooth over filling, or apply in fancy swirls with a pastry bag and a large star tube.

Sprinkle top with optional grated chocolate. Refrigerate.

Vanilla Cream Pie

6 TO 8 PORTIONS

$\mathbf{M}$ade with a chocolate cookie crumb crust.

CHOCOLATE COOKIE CRUST

1½ cups of crumbs made from 6 ounces of chocolate wafers (sometimes
   called icebox cookies; the crumbs may be made in a processor or by
   placing the cookies in a bag and crushing them with a rolling pin)
Optional: 1 teaspoon instant coffee
3 ounces (¾ stick) butter, melted

With a rubber spatula, mix the crumbs and optional instant coffee with the
butter, pressing against the sides of the bowl until completely mixed. Use a 9-
inch pie plate and follow directions for crumb crust, page 350.

VANILLA FILLING

3 eggs, separated
1¼ cups milk
1 tablespoon (1 envelope) unflavored gelatin
½ cup sugar
1 teaspoon vanilla extract
1 cup heavy cream
⅛ teaspoon salt

In the top of a small double boiler off the heat, stir the egg yolks just to mix.
Gradually mix in the milk and then the gelatin and ¼ cup sugar (reserve
remaining ¼ cup sugar).

Place over hot water on moderate heat and stir until custard thickens
enough to coat a spoon (175 to 180 degrees on a candy or sugar thermometer).
Remove from heat and stir in vanilla.

Place the top of the double boiler into a bowl of ice water and stir until
cool. Remove from ice water and set aside.

In a chilled bowl with chilled beaters, whip the cream until it holds a soft shape, not stiff. Set aside.

Add the salt to the egg whites and beat until they increase in volume and barely begin to thicken. Gradually add the reserved ¼ cup sugar and continue to beat only until whites hold a point, barely stiff. Set aside.

Replace the custard over the ice water and stir again until custard begins to thicken slightly. Gradually fold custard into whites and then gradually fold that into the cream.

Turn the filling into the prepared pie crust. There will probably be a little too much filling. Let the excess stand at room temperature while you chill the filled shell (about 10 minutes in the freezer or a bit longer in the refrigerator) until filling is almost set. Then pour on the remaining filling, mounding it higher in the center.

Refrigerate for a few hours. Prepare whipped cream topping.

WHIPPED CREAM

1 cup heavy cream
¼ cup confectioners sugar
1 teaspoon vanilla extract

In a chilled bowl with chilled beaters, whip above ingredients until firm enough to hold a shape.

Place the whipped cream by heaping teaspoonfuls in a ring around the outer edge of the pie, very close to the crust. Leave the center of the pie uncovered. With the back of the teaspoon pull the cream up in peaks. Refrigerate.

Black Bottom Pie

8 PORTIONS

Marjorie Kinnan Rawlings, the Pulitzer Prize–winning author of *The Yearling*, also wrote a delightful cookbook, *Cross Creek Cookery* (Charles Scribner's Sons, 1942), which is a mouthwatering account of the food served in her home in central Florida. In it, she says of her Black Bottom Pie, "I think this is the most delicious pie I have ever eaten . . . a pie so delicate, so luscious, that I hope to be propped up on my dying bed and fed a generous portion. Then I think that I should refuse outright to die, for life would be too good to relinquish."

My sentiments are the same. This is glorious.

CRUST

    1¼ cups graham cracker crumbs
    1 tablespoon sugar
    1 teaspoon powdered ginger
    1 teaspoon cinnamon
    2 ounces (½ stick) butter, melted

Adjust rack to center of oven. Preheat to 375 degrees.

In a bowl mix the crumbs with the sugar, ginger, and cinnamon, and then add the melted butter. Stir with a rubber spatula, pressing the mixture against the sides of the bowl until completely mixed. The mixture will look crumbly but will hold together when pressed into place.

Use a 9-inch pie plate and follow directions for crumb crust (page 350).

FILLING

2 ounces unsweetened chocolate

1 tablespoon (1 envelope) unflavored gelatin

¼ cup cold water

1 cup sugar

1 tablespoon cornstarch

Salt

4 eggs, separated

1¾ cups milk

2 tablespoons dark rum

1 teaspoon vanilla extract

⅛ teaspoon cream of tartar

Melt the chocolate in the top of a small double boiler over hot water on moderate heat. Remove from hot water and set aside.

Sprinkle the gelatin over the cold water and set aside.

In a small bowl mix ½ cup of the sugar (reserve remaining ½ cup sugar) with the cornstarch and a pinch of salt. Set aside.

In the top of a large double boiler, stir the yolks lightly with a small wire whisk or a fork just to mix.

Scald the milk uncovered in a small, heavy saucepan over moderate heat until you can see small bubbles on the surface. Stir in the sugar-cornstarch mixture and pour very slowly, in a thin stream, into the yolks—stirring constantly. Place over, but not touching, hot water in the bottom of the double boiler on moderate heat. Cook, stirring gently and scraping the pot with a rubber spatula, for about 12 to 15 minutes, until the custard thickens to the consistency of a medium cream sauce. Lift top of double boiler off the hot water.

Remove 1 cup of the custard and set aside to cool for about 5 to 10 minutes until tepid, stirring occasionally.

Meanwhile, to the remainder of the custard in the top of the double boiler, immediately add the softened gelatin and stir until thoroughly dissolved. Stir in the rum and set aside.

Gradually add the reserved cup of custard to the chocolate, stirring constantly with a small wire whisk. Mix thoroughly until smooth. Add the vanilla and turn the mixture into the prepared crust. Spread level and refrigerate.

In the small bowl of electric mixer at moderate high speed, beat the whites with a pinch of salt and the cream of tartar until the mixture increases in volume and starts to thicken. While beating, gradually add the reserved ½ cup sugar and continue to beat until mixture holds a shape and is the consistency of thick marshmallow sauce.

Gradually fold the rum custard (which may still be warm) into the beaten whites. Pour gently from one bowl to another to insure thorough blending.

Pour over the chocolate layer, mounding it high in the center. (If there is too much filling and it might run over, reserve some at room temperature. Chill the pie in the freezer for about 10 to 15 minutes, or in the refrigerator a bit longer, to partially set the filling. Then pour on the reserved portion and it will not run over.)

Refrigerate pie for 2 to 3 hours. Prepare whipped cream.

WHIPPED CREAM
    1 cup heavy cream
    ¼ cup confectioners sugar
    1 scant teaspoon vanilla extract

In a chilled bowl with chilled beaters, whip above ingredients until the cream holds a shape. Spread evenly over filling or use a pastry bag with a star tube and form a heavy, ruffled border of the cream.

Optional: If the cream was spread over the pie, sprinkle it with coarsely grated chocolate; if it was put on to form a border, fill the center with grated chocolate.

Black Bottom Pecan Cream Pie

6 TO 8 PORTIONS

CRUST

1¼ cups graham cracker crumbs
¼ cup sugar
2 ounces (½ stick) butter, melted
⅓ cup pecans, chopped or cut medium-fine

Adjust rack to center of oven and preheat oven to 375 degrees.

Mix the crumbs with sugar and then add the melted butter. Stir with a rubber spatula, pressing the mixture against the sides of the bowl until completely mixed. Stir in the nuts. The mixture will look crumbly but will hold together when pressed into place. Use a 9-inch pie plate and follow directions for crumb crust (page 350).

BLACK BOTTOM

1 cup light cream
8 ounces semisweet chocolate
1 tablespoon instant coffee
4 egg yolks

In a medium-size, heavy saucepan heat the cream. Break up the chocolate and add it, stirring frequently with a wire whisk until smooth. Add coffee and stir to dissolve. Remove from heat. With a wire whisk beat in the yolks one at a time. Let stand, stirring occasionally, until slightly cooled. Pour into shell and refrigerate for 2 to 3 hours until firm. Prepare topping.

CREAM TOPPING WITH NUTS

2 cups heavy cream
½ cup confectioners sugar
2 scant teaspoons vanilla extract
3½ ounces (1 cup) pecans, cut medium
Optional: 6 to 8 large pecan halves

In a chilled bowl with chilled beaters, whip the cream with the sugar and vanilla until firm. Fold in the cut nuts.

Place one spoonful at a time on top of the chocolate layer, starting at the outer edge and working toward the center. Leave uneven or smooth with a metal spatula.

Top with optional pecan halves. Refrigerate.

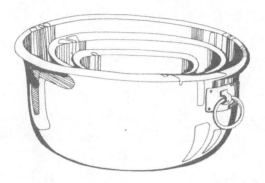

Peace and Plenty

6 TO 8 PORTIONS

From the Bahamas—cream cheese, sweet cream, sour cream, and fresh strawberries. A great combination.

Prepare Chocolate Cookie Crust as in recipe for Vanilla Cream Pie (page 357).

STRAWBERRIES FOR TOPPING

Use 1½ to 2 pints of berries. Rinse them briefly in a bowl of cold water, hull, and place on paper toweling to drain. Let stand until ready to use.

FILLING
    1 tablespoon (1 envelope) unflavored gelatin
    ½ cup cold water
    8 ounces cream cheese, at room temperature
    Pinch of salt
    1½ teaspoons vanilla extract
    Optional: 3 tablespoons curaçao, Cointreau, Grand Marnier, or kirsch
    ½ cup sugar
    ½ cup sour cream
    1 cup heavy cream

Sprinkle the gelatin over the water in a heatproof measuring cup. Let stand for a few minutes and then place cup in a small saucepan of shallow hot water over moderate heat until dissolved. Remove from heat and set aside.

In small bowl of electric mixer beat the cream cheese until soft and smooth. Beat in the salt, vanilla, optional liqueur, and sugar. Beat well, scraping the bowl with a rubber spatula. Beat in the sour cream. On low speed, very gradually beat in the dissolved gelatin (which may be slightly warm), continuing to scrape the bowl occasionally with a rubber spatula.

In a chilled bowl with chilled beaters, whip the heavy cream until it holds a soft shape, not stiff. In several additions fold the cheese mixture into the whipped cream and then gently pour from one bowl to another to insure thorough blending.

Pour into prepared crumb crust. Immediately, before filling has a chance to set, start at the outer edge and form a ring of strawberries, placing them upright and touching each other. Continue with additional berries, placing them in concentric rings working toward the center until the top is completely covered. Refrigerate and prepare glaze.

GLAZE

¼ cup red currant jelly (or any other seedless red jelly)
1 tablespoon sugar

In your smallest frying pan or saucepan, on moderate heat, stir the jelly and sugar until melted and smooth. Bring to a boil and let the glaze bubble gently, stirring constantly, for 3 minutes. Use glaze immediately while very hot. With a soft brush, brush over the strawberries. If glaze cools and thickens it may be remelted over low heat.

Refrigerate for several hours or more before serving.

Cheesecakes

I recommend Philadelphia Brand cream cheese for the following cheesecakes; other brands of cream cheese do not all work the same. (I learned this the hard way.)

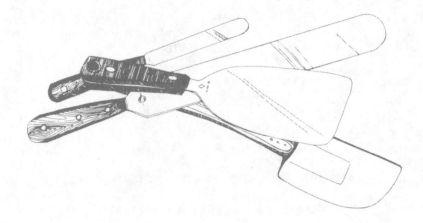

Craig Claiborne's Cheesecake

10 PORTIONS

This is the cheesecake that Craig Claiborne, dean of the food establishment, made famous when he printed the recipe in the *New York Times*. I made it daily for many years for my husband's restaurant—everyone loved it.

After ten years my husband sold the restaurant to Mr. and Mrs. Schwartz. Mr. Schwartz's mother was Mrs. Meyer Lansky. Then, for many years, Mrs. Lansky made the cheesecakes. She told me that her biggest thrill was sitting in the restaurant and watching customers order *her* cheesecake. I know what she meant.

Bull's Eye and Polka Dot and 3-layer (which is named "The Newest") and most of the other cheesecakes that I designed (these cakes are in my other books) are all variations of this one—this is the original.

This should be refrigerated for at least 5 to 6 hours before it is served.

> **Finely grated rind of 1 lemon**
> **3 tablespoons lemon juice**
> **2 pounds cream cheese, preferably at room temperature**
> **1 teaspoon vanilla extract**
> **1¾ cups sugar**
> **4 eggs**
> **⅓ cup graham cracker crumbs (to be used after cake is baked)**

Adjust rack to lowest position in the oven. Preheat oven to 350 degrees.

Cheesecake pans can be bought in restaurant or bakery supply stores (see Note 1). They are deep and do not have removable bottoms. Do not use a springform. Use a round, 8-inch cheesecake pan, 3 inches deep. Butter it lightly all the way up to the rim and inside of the rim itself, or the cake will stick to the rim and will not rise evenly. Any unbuttered spots will prevent the finished cake from sliding out of the pan easily.

Mix the lemon rind and juice and set aside. In the large bowl of an electric mixer at medium-high speed, beat the cheese until it is absolutely smooth. All during the mixing continue to scrape the sides and bottom of the bowl with a rubber spatula in order to keep everything evenly mixed. When the cheese is smooth, beat in the vanilla and sugar. Beat well and then add the eggs one at a time. After adding eggs, do not beat any more than is necessary to mix ingredients thoroughly. With rubber spatula stir in the lemon rind and juice.

Spray the buttered pan generously with Pam or some other non-stick spray. (Yes. Trust me. Butter and spray.)

Turn the batter into the prepared pan. Level top by briskly rotating pan a bit, first in one direction then in the other. Place the cheesecake pan inside a large pan. The larger pan must not touch the sides of the cake pan and must not be deeper than the cake pan. Pour hot water into the larger pan until it is about 1½ inches deep. (If the larger pan is aluminum, adding about ½ teaspoon of cream of tartar to each quart of water will keep the pan from discoloring.)

Bake for 1½ hours. The top of the cake should be a rich golden brown and feel dry to the touch, but cake will be soft inside (it will become firm when it has cooled and been refrigerated).

Lift the cheesecake pan out of the water and place it on a rack for 2½ to 3 hours until it is completely cool. Do not cool the cake in the refrigerator or the butter will harden and the cake will stick to the pan.

Cover the pan with plastic wrap (I use Saran Wrap; do not use one that claims to be cling wrap—it will pull the top of the cake off). Place a flat plate or a board on top and invert. Remove the cake pan. Sprinkle the bottom of the cake evenly with graham cracker crumbs. Gently place another flat plate or board on top of the crumbs. Very carefully and quickly invert so that the cake is right side up. Do this without pressing too hard or you will squash the cake, which will still be soft.

Refrigerate for at least 5 to 6 hours or overnight. Or freeze it—it freezes perfectly. Serve very cold.

When cutting the cake, always dip the knife into hot water, or hold it under running hot water, before each cut to prevent the cake somewhat from sticking to the knife. (It will stick a bit anyhow.)

Notes:

1. Cheesecake pans are available at Bridge Kitchenware, ([800] 274-3435 or, in New York City, [212] 838-1901).

2. The cheesecake will rise above the top of the pan while it is baking and will sink down below the top as it cools.

Nut Cheesecake

Craig created a marvelous Nut Cheesecake based on the previous recipe.

Prepare 7½ ounces (1½ cups) of blanched almonds or skinned hazelnuts as follows: Spread them in a shallow pan and bake in a 350 degree oven, stirring them occasionally, for about 15 minutes until lightly browned. Cool and then chop the nuts briefly in a blender or processor—it is all right if they are not evenly ground and if there are some pieces larger than others. They should not be ground to a powder.

Mix the batter as in the previous recipe but eliminate the lemon rind and juice, add a scant ½ teaspoon extract almond along with the vanilla, and add the ground nuts to the batter after adding the eggs. Beat until evenly mixed. Continue with remaining directions.

Serve this rich cake in small portions.

Black-and-White Cheesecake

In the top of a small double boiler over hot water, melt 2 ounces of unsweetened chocolate. Remove from heat and let cool.

Prepare oven, cake pan, and batter for cheesecake as in recipe, page 369, omitting lemon juice and rind and adding ¼ teaspoon almond flavoring with the vanilla.

Place one-third of the batter (2 cups) in the small bowl of an electric mixer. Add melted chocolate and mix until smooth.

Place alternate large spoonfuls of the white batter and small spoonfuls of the chocolate batter in the prepared pan, placing some of the chocolate directly against the rim of the pan so that it will show on the outside of the cake. Bake and finish as above.

Apricot Cheesecake Squares

16 PORTIONS

A large cake with a definite lemon flavor. Suitable for a buffet, since it is cut into portions ahead of time. Cake may be made a day ahead; topping should be put on the day it is to be served.

> Finely grated rind of 1 large lemon
> ¼ cup lemon juice
> 3½ pounds (7 8-ounce packages) cream cheese, preferably at room
>   temperature
> 1¼ cups sugar
> Pinch of salt
> 1 teaspoon vanilla extract
> 1 cup sour cream
> 6 eggs

Adjust rack to lowest position in oven. Preheat oven to 400 degrees. Butter a 13 x 9 x 2-inch pan.

Mix lemon rind and juice and set aside. In large bowl of electric mixer at low speed beat cream cheese until soft and smooth. All during beating scrape the bowl as necessary with a rubber spatula. Add sugar. Gradually increase speed to medium. Beat in salt, vanilla, and sour cream. Beat until smooth. Add the eggs one at a time and beat until smooth after each. Remove from mixer and stir in lemon rind and juice.

Spray the buttered pan with Pam or another non-stick spray. Turn the batter into the prepared pan. Shake gently to level or spread smooth with a rubber spatula. Place the cheesecake pan in a larger pan, which must not be deeper than the cake pan. Place pans in oven. Pour 1 inch of hot water into the larger pan. (If the larger pan is aluminum, adding ½ teaspoon of cream of tartar to each quart of water will keep the pan from discoloring.)

Bake about 45 minutes until top is golden. (During baking, if the back of the cake browns faster than the front, carefully reverse position of pan.) The sides will rise about ¾ inch above the pan. Remove the cheesecake pan from hot water and place cake pan on rack to cool until only slightly warm. Do not chill before removing from pan. (The butter would harden and the cake could not be removed easily.) During cooling, cake will sink to the level of the pan.

Place a large board over the cake. It may be a board to be used for serving or, if you wish, use any kitchen board or a cookie sheet and later transfer the finished individual portions to a serving tray. Carefully invert. Remove pan leaving cake upside down. Refrigerate for a few hours or overnight.

The cake is cut into portions before the topping is put on. With a ruler and toothpicks mark the cake into sixteen portions. Cut with a very long, sharp knife. Hold the knife under hot running water for a few seconds before each cut. Cut straight down with the full length of the blade. The portions must stay in place—do not move them. Prepare the topping.

TOPPING
  16 canned apricot halves
  1 cup apricot preserves
  ¼ cup sugar
  Optional: Green pistachio nuts, chopped

Drain the apricots and set them aside on toweling to dry.

Strain the preserves. In a saucepan mix the preserves and sugar. Stir over heat until the mixture comes to a boil. Let boil for 2 minutes.

Pour a little more than half the mixture over the cake and smooth with a brush. Place one apricot half, cut side down, on each portion. Brush remaining preserves over the apricots. If desired, top each apricot with a pinch of pistachio nuts. Refrigerate.

Before serving, hold the knife under hot water again and cut through the glaze.

Notes:

1. Canned cherry-pie filling may be used as a quick and easy alternate topping. Use 2 21-ounce cans. In a large strainer set over a bowl, drain most of the syrup. Arrange the cherries on the cake and then pour on part of the syrup—you will probably not need all of it. Or use blue-

berry pie filling. Either one of the pie fillings may be spooned generously over individual portions or passed separately.

2. The cake may also be served with no topping, with a help-yourself
   bowl of fresh strawberries, raspberries, blueberries, and/or sliced
   peaches.

Florida Chiffon Cheesecake

8 PORTIONS

This cake should be refrigerated for 7 to 8 hours or overnight before it is served.

PECAN CRUST
    4 ounces (1¼ cups) pecans
    2 tablespoons sugar
    2 ounces (½ stick) butter, melted

Adjust rack to center of oven. Preheat oven to 350 degrees. Remove sides of a 9 x 2½- or 3-inch springform pan and set aside.

Place the nuts and sugar in the bowl of a food processor fitted with the metal chopping blade. Process for about half a minute until fine. Add the butter and process until well mixed. Turn mixture out into the bottom of the springform. With your fingertips (floured if necessary), press the mixture to cover the bottom of the pan evenly.

Bake for 12 to 15 minutes until slightly colored. With a wide metal spatula, remove from oven very carefully. Immediately, while crust is hot, attach the sides of the pan. Set aside to cool completely.

FILLING
    1 tablespoon (1 envelope) unflavored gelatin
    1 cup cold water
    3 eggs, separated
    ¾ cup sugar
    16 ounces cream cheese, preferably at room temperature
    ¼ cup lemon juice
    Finely grated rind of 1 large orange
    1 cup heavy cream
    Pinch of salt

Sprinkle gelatin over ¼ cup of water (reserve remaining ¾ cup water). Set aside.

In a 1-quart, heavy saucepan stir the egg yolks lightly just to mix. Gradually mix in the reserved ¾ cup water and the sugar. Place over moderate heat and cook, stirring constantly, until mixture barely coats a spoon, or reaches 180 degrees on a candy thermometer. Add gelatin-water mixture and stir to dissolve. Remove from heat and set aside.

In large bowl of electric mixer beat the cream cheese very well until it is soft and completely smooth. Beat in the lemon juice and then, very gradually, beat in the warm egg yolk mixture, scraping the bowl with a rubber spatula to keep the mixture very smooth. Remove from mixer. Stir in the grated orange rind and set aside to cool completely.

In a chilled bowl with chilled beaters, whip the cream until it just holds a shape, but is not stiff, and set aside. Add the salt to the egg whites and beat until they just hold a shape, or are stiff but not dry.

Gradually fold part of the cheese mixture into the whites, then fold all of the whites into the rest of the cheese mixture. Now gradually fold a bit of this into the whipped cream and fold the whipped cream into the cheese mixture. If mixtures aren't completely blended, very gently pour from one bowl to another to insure thorough mixing.

Turn filling into springform pan over baked and cooled crust. Refrigerate for 7 to 8 hours or overnight.

Cut around sides of cake to release. Remove sides of pan. Do not remove cake from bottom of pan. Place on a folded napkin on a cake platter. (The napkin will keep the pan from sliding on the plate.)

Note: Make this early in the day for that night and serve it very cold.

Cream Cheese Pie

6 TO 8 PORTIONS

This one has a sour cream topping. It's a treat.

Refrigerate this pie for several hours or overnight before serving.

CRUST

1¼ cups graham cracker crumbs

1 tablespoon sugar

½ teaspoon cinnamon

¼ teaspoon powdered ginger

3 ounces (¾ stick) butter, melted

Butter a 9-inch pie plate and set aside.

In a bowl stir the crumbs, sugar, cinnamon, and ginger to mix. Add the melted butter and stir until thoroughly mixed.

Turn the mixture into the pie plate.

First, with your fingertips, distribute it loosely and evenly all over the sides and bottom, working enough up on the sides to form a ridge slightly above the top of the pie plate. Then, with your fingertips, press it firmly into place, first pressing the sides and then the bottom. Refrigerate while preparing filling:

FILLING

12 ounces cream cheese, preferably at room temperature

1 teaspoon vanilla extract

½ cup sugar

2 eggs

⅓ cup heavy cream

Adjust rack one-third up from bottom of the oven and preheat to 350 degrees.

In small bowl of electric mixer beat the cream cheese until completely smooth. Beat in the vanilla, sugar, and then the eggs one at a time. Beat at moderate speed, scraping the bowl with a rubber spatula, until smooth.

Add the heavy cream and beat only until smooth. Turn filling into chilled crust.

Bake for exactly 25 minutes. Remove from oven and let stand at room temperature for 20 minutes.

Adjust oven temperature to 300 degrees and, when the 20 minutes are up, prepare the topping:

TOPPING
2 cups sour cream
½ cup sugar

In a small bowl stir sour cream and sugar briefly just to mix. With a tablespoon, gently spoon it over the cheese filling, starting around the outer edge and then filling in toward the center. With a long, narrow metal spatula (an offset spatula is best), smooth over the cheese, being careful not to let the topping run over the crust.

Bake at 300 degrees for exactly 5 minutes. Remove from oven. Cool to room temperature. Refrigerate for several hours or overnight before serving.

Pineapple Cheese Pie

6 TO 8 PORTIONS

Refrigerate this pie for 5 to 6 hours or overnight before serving.

Prepare crust and filling as for above Cream Cheese Pie. Bake for 25 minutes. Remove from oven and cool completely. Meanwhile, prepare Pineapple Topping.

PINEAPPLE TOPPING

1 can (1 pound, 4 ounces) crushed pineapple
1 tablespoon cornstarch
1 tablespoon sugar
Optional: Yellow food coloring
½ teaspoon vanilla extract

In a large strainer set over a bowl, thoroughly drain the pineapple. Reserve pineapple and 1 cup of the juice. (If necessary add water to make 1 cup.)

In a 1-quart saucepan stir together the cornstarch and sugar to mix and then gradually stir in the pineapple juice.

Place over moderate heat and cook, stirring gently, until mixture barely begins to boil. Reduce heat and simmer gently for 1 minute.

Remove from heat. Stir in about 3 drops of optional yellow food coloring and the vanilla. Add the drained pineapple and stir gently to mix. Set aside to cool.

Gently spoon the cooled topping over the cooled pie. Spread level. Refrigerate for 5 to 6 hours or overnight. Serve very cold.

Cream Cheese and Yogurt Pie

8 PORTIONS

Must be made at least 24 hours ahead.

Prepare graham cracker crust as in recipe for Rum Pie (page 352).

FILLING:
>2 pounds cream cheese, preferably at room temperature
>1 teaspoon vanilla extract
>¼ cup honey
>1 pint unflavored yogurt

In small bowl of electric mixer, beat the cheese until soft and smooth. Beat in the vanilla and honey. On low speed gradually add the yogurt, scraping the bowl with a rubber spatula and beating only until smooth.

Pour as much of the mixture as you can into the prepared crust. There will be a bit too much filling. Chill the filled crust for about 20 to 30 minutes in the freezer or a bit longer in the refrigerator, until semifirm. (Do not freeze any longer or the filling will lose its super-creamy consistency.) Then you will be able to top it with the remaining filling without having it run over.

Refrigerate for at least 24 hours or more. Serve very cold.

Serve as is, or accompany each portion with a generous spoonful of the following strawberries:

STRAWBERRIES

Using 1 pint of berries, dip them briefly into a bowl of cold water to wash, then hull and drain. Cut in thick slices, lengthwise. Place in a bowl and sprinkle with 3 tablespoons of sugar. Let stand, stirring occasionally, for ½ hour or so. Cover and refrigerate.

Serve separately in a small bowl.

Chocolate Cream Cheese Pie

8 PORTIONS

Wowie! If you like chocolate—if you like cheesecake—you will be wild about this. You can make it a day ahead if you would like to, or just a few hours before serving. I think it is easy—and the best chocolate cheesecake I know.

CRUST
   1¼ cups graham crumbs
   1 tablespoon sugar
   3 ounces (¾ stick) butter, melted

Adjust rack to the center of the oven and preheat the oven to 350 degrees.

In a bowl mix the crumbs, sugar, and melted butter. Turn into a 9-inch pie plate. Using your fingertips distribute the mixture evenly and loosely over the sides first and then over the bottom. Then press the crust firmly and evenly over the sides, pushing it up from the bottom to form a ridge slightly raised above the edge of the pie plate. After pressing the sides—including the top edge—so that it is firm and compact, then press the bottom. There should be no loose crumbs.

Bake for 8 minutes. Remove from the oven and set aside to cool. Then chill the crust.

FILLING
   3 ounces semisweet chocolate
   2 ounces unsweetened chocolate
   12 ounces cream cheese
   Pinch of salt
   1 cup sugar
   ½ teaspoon vanilla extract
   3 eggs

Rack should still be in the center of the oven and oven temperature should be 350 degrees.

Place both chocolates in the top of a double boiler over warm water on moderate heat. Cover briefly until the chocolates start to melt. Then uncover and stir until all melted and smooth. Remove from the heat and set aside to cool.

Place the cream cheese in the bowl of an electric mixer and beat until soft and smooth. Add the salt, sugar, and vanilla, and beat to mix. Then beat in the eggs one at a time while scraping the sides of the bowl with a rubber spatula. Finally add the chocolate and beat to mix.

Turn into the prepared pie crust.

Bake for 30 minutes.

Remove from the oven and let stand until cool.

Then refrigerate for a few hours, or overnight.

This can be served as it is, or with the following topping:

TOPPING
  ½ cup heavy cream
  ½ teaspoon vanilla extract
  2 tablespoons confectioners sugar
  2 bananas

In a small, chilled bowl with chilled beaters whip the cream with the vanilla and sugar until the cream holds a shape. Place eight large spoonfuls of the cream around the edge of the pie.

Just before serving slice the bananas on a sharp angle forming eight long slices. Place one slice of banana standing on its edge in each mound of whipped cream.

Cottage Cheese and Pineapple Icebox Cake

10 PORTIONS

This should be refrigerated for at least 4 to 5 hours before serving.

CRUST

  1 cup graham cracker crumbs
  2 tablespoons sugar
  ½ teaspoon cinnamon
  2 ounces (½ stick) butter, melted

Stir the above ingredients until thoroughly mixed. Place in bottom of a 9 x 1-inch springform pan with sides attached. Press firmly and smoothly all over bottom of pan.

Bake in a preheated 375 degree oven for 8 minutes. Then set aside to cool completely.

FILLING

  2 tablespoons (2 envelopes) unflavored gelatin
  ¾ cup sugar
  ¼ teaspoon salt
  3 eggs, separated
  ¾ cup milk
  1 small can (8¼ ounces—about 1 cup) crushed pineapple with syrup
  3 cups (1½ pounds) regular or nonfat cottage cheese
  Finely grated rind of 1 large lemon
  3 tablespoons lemon juice
  1 cup heavy cream

In top of large double boiler mix gelatin with sugar and salt. In a small bowl stir three egg yolks just to mix and gradually stir in the milk. Stir into sugar mixture. Add the pineapple and mix well.

Place over boiling water on moderate heat and cook, stirring almost constantly for 10 minutes until mixture thickens slightly. Remove from heat and turn the mixture into a large bowl. Set aside until cool.

Meanwhile, place the cottage cheese in the bowl of a food processor fitted with the metal chopping blade and process for 1 full minute. Mix lemon rind and juice together. When pineapple mixture has cooled, stir in the processed cheese and lemon rind and juice.

In a chilled bowl with chilled beaters, whip the cream until it holds a soft shape. Beat the egg whites until they hold a soft point, not dry. Fold the whipped cream and beaten whites into the cheese mixture. Pour it over the crust in the springform pan. Rotate pan gently to level filling. Refrigerate for 4 to 5 hours or overnight. With a small, sharp knife, pressing firmly against the pan, cut around sides of pan to release and remove.

TOPPING

1 cup heavy sour cream
3 tablespoons toasted, sliced almonds (see Note)

In a small bowl stir the cream briefly only until it is soft enough to spread. With a long, narrow metal spatula spread it evenly over the top of the filling. Crumble the almonds coarse and sprinkle them over the sour cream. Refrigerate.

Note: To toast the nuts, place them in a shallow pan and bake in a moderate oven, shaking pan occasionally until nuts are a rich golden brown.

P.S. *When I process cottage cheese (nonfat or other) for 1 full minute something wonderful happens to it. Many days a bowl of cut-up fresh pineapple, or a peeled and cut-up mango, or just some strawberries, loaded with the processed cheese, becomes my lunch and I couldn't be happier. It is delicious!*

Cottage Cheese Kuchen

9 PORTIONS

A German recipe with a thin pastry crust; the German name for this type of pastry is *Mürbteig*.

PASTRY

1¼ cups sifted all-purpose flour
¼ teaspoon salt
¼ teaspoon baking powder
¼ cup sugar
2 ounces (½ stick) butter
1 egg

Sift together flour, salt, baking powder, and sugar into a bowl. With a pastry blender, cut in the butter until the mixture resembles fine meal. Add the unbeaten egg and stir thoroughly with a fork. Then work the dough very briefly with your hands until the mixture holds together and forms a ball.

Place in a 9 x 1¾-inch square cake pan. Dipping your fingers in flour as necessary, press the dough over the bottom and about three quarters of the way up on the sides. This will make a thin layer—patience. (Watch the corners—one has a tendency to make them too thick.) Trim the top edge even, using any trimmings to fill in empty or thin areas. Refrigerate the pastry shell while preparing the filling.

FILLING

Finely grated rind of 1 lemon

3 tablespoons lemon juice (see Note 1)

12 ounces (1½ cups) regular or nonfat cottage cheese

½ cup sugar

1 teaspoon vanilla extract

⅛ teaspoon salt

1 tablespoon melted butter

2 eggs

½ cup sour cream

½ cup apricot preserves

⅓ cup raisins, light or dark (see Note 2)

Adjust rack one-third up from bottom of oven and preheat to 450 degrees.

Mix lemon rind and juice and set aside. Place the cottage cheese in the bowl of a food processor fitted with the metal chopping blade. Process for 1 full minute. Add the sugar, vanilla, salt, melted butter, and the eggs. Process briefly until mixed. Add the sour cream and process again to mix. Finally add the lemon rind and juice and pulse just to mix.

Heat the apricot preserves to soften. Strain and then brush evenly over bottom and sides of pastry shell.

Pour the filling into the prepared shell. Spread the top smooth and shake pan gently to level. Sprinkle raisins evenly over the top, and with the back of a spoon tap them down gently into the filling so that they are just barely covered with filling.

Bake for 15 minutes. Reduce the oven temperature to 375 degrees and bake for an additional 15 minutes.

Remove the cake from the oven and turn off the heat but keep oven door closed. Prepare the topping.

TOPPING

2 cups sour cream

¼ cup sugar

1 or 2 drops almond extract

Stir the sour cream with the sugar and almond extract just to mix. Spoon the topping all over the filling and then spread smooth. Return to oven with the heat off for 5 minutes.

Remove from oven and cool to room temperature. Serve at room temperature or refrigerate and serve cold.

If necessary, cut around sides to release from pan. Cut into squares and, with a wide metal spatula, transfer to a serving plate.

Notes:
1. This filling will be tart—if you prefer it blander, adjust or eliminate the lemon juice.
2. If raisins are dry and hard they should be softened by steaming in a strainer, covered, over boiling water for a few minutes. Then drain and dry.

Pots de Crème, Custards, and Puddings

To test custard to see if it is cooked enough, gently insert a small, sharp knife into the top. As soon as the knife comes out clean, the custard is done. But the knife will leave a scar; do not test any more than is necessary.

With practice you can learn how to time a custard without having to use a knife and leave scars. When you first bake a custard, keep an exact record of just how long it took, then, all things being equal, the knife test won't be necessary the next time you prepare the same recipe.

Also, before the custard is done, reach into the oven and with a knife gently tap the edge of the custard cup and watch how the unbaked custard shakes. You will be able to see that it is still liquid. Continue to tap the edge of the cup occasionally during the end of the cooking and watch carefully as it becomes firm. You will be able to teach yourself to recognize when it is done without having to insert the knife. Or, until you are sure of yourself with this method, make as few knife tests as necessary.

Always be on guard not to overbake custard or it will separate.

Pots de Crème à la Vanille

12 POTS DE CRÈME POTS, OR 7 OR 8 CUSTARD CUPS

3 cups heavy cream
6 egg yolks
¼ cup sugar
⅛ teaspoon salt
1½ teaspoons vanilla extract

Adjust rack to the center of the oven. Preheat the oven to 350 degrees.

Scald the cream over hot water in the top of a large, uncovered double boiler on moderate heat until tiny bubbles begin around the edge or a slight wrinkled skin forms on top.

Meanwhile, stir egg yolks with a fork, or very briefly with a wire whisk just to mix them—do not beat any air into them.

When the cream is scalded, remove it from the heat, add the sugar and salt, and stir to dissolve. Stirring constantly, very gradually pour the hot cream into the yolks. Do not beat enough to make any foam. Stir in the vanilla and strain into a pitcher.

Pour into ovenproof cups, using either about a dozen pots de crème pots with lids, or seven or eight custard cups. Do not fill them too full. (If you use pots de crème pots, be sure to leave enough headroom so that the lids do not touch the custard.) With a small spoon remove any foam that might have formed.

Place in a baking pan, which must not be deeper than the cups. Pour hot water into the baking pan about halfway up the cups. Cover the crème pots with their covers; place a piece of aluminum foil or a cookie sheet over the tops of the custard cups.

Bake for 25 to 30 minutes or until a small, sharp knife inserted into the custard just barely comes out clean.

Optional: A spoonful of whipped cream on the top of these seems to cut their richness, unlikely as it sounds. (Either with or without the whipped cream, if you have candied violets or rose petals this is a good time to use them—just one on each.)

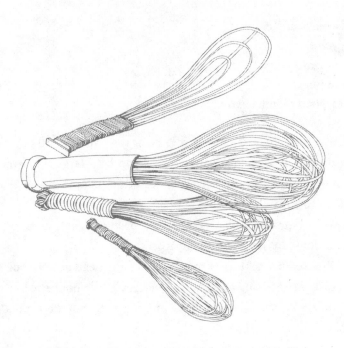

Pots de Crème au Café

6 TO 8 PORTIONS, DEPENDING ON SIZE OF CUPS

¼ cup dry instant coffee
¾ cup boiling water
7 egg yolks
1½ cups heavy cream
1½ cups light cream or coffee cream
¼ cup sugar
Pinch of salt
½ teaspoon vanilla extract

Adjust rack to the center of the oven and preheat to 350 degrees.

Dissolve the instant coffee in boiling water and set aside.

In a large mixing bowl stir the yolks just to mix.

Scald both creams over boiling water in the top of an uncovered double boiler, or in a heavy saucepan. When the cream forms a wrinkled skin on top or tiny bubbles around the edge, remove it from the heat. Add the sugar, salt, and prepared coffee and stir to dissolve sugar. Very gradually at first, and stirring constantly, add the cream mixture to the yolks. Just stir; do not beat or whip. Strain into a pitcher and stir in vanilla. Pour into six to eight custard cups, leaving a bit of headroom on each. With a small spoon remove any foam from the tops.

Place the cups in a baking pan, which must not be deeper than the cups. Pour hot water into the pan to about halfway up the sides of the custard cups. Cover cups with a cookie sheet or a large piece of aluminum foil.

Bake 30 minutes or until a small, sharp knife inserted into the custard comes out clean.

Remove from hot water. Cool uncovered to room temperature. Refrigerate covered.

Note: This recipe may be made in twelve small pots de crème pots, in which case the baking time will be reduced slightly. Bake the cups covered, but remove the covers while the desserts are cooling or moisture will form in the covers and drip back onto the custards. When cool, the covers may be replaced.

Pots de Crème au Chocolat

4 OR 5 PORTIONS

Nick Malgieri is a great pastry chef, teacher, and cookbook author, and a good friend of mine. He gave me this recipe. This is dark, shiny, smooth-smoother-smoothest. It is delicious and elegant in its simplicity and perfection. This is as good as it gets. *Merci beaucoup,* Nick.

Different chocolates work differently. Although I have used others with equally good results, the chocolate I am using now for this recipe is Lindt Excellence. It comes in 3-ounce bars and is made in Switzerland. Here in Miami it is available in supermarkets.

This recipe can be easily doubled.

> 6 ounces semisweet chocolate
> ½ cup heavy cream
> ½ cup milk
> 3 tablespoons sugar
> 1 vanilla bean (see Note)
> 3 egg yolks
> ¼ cup prepared strong coffee or espresso

Cut or break the chocolate into rather small pieces and place it in a medium-size mixing bowl and set aside.

Place the cream, milk, and sugar in a small saucepan. Slit the vanilla bean the long way and add it to the saucepan. Stir frequently over moderate heat until the mixture comes to a full boil.

Meantime, in a bowl, whisk or beat the yolks briefly only to mix.

When the cream and milk come to a boil, remove the vanilla bean and in a thin stream whisk or beat the hot mixture into the yolks.

Turn the mixture into the saucepan. Stir constantly with a rubber spatula over medium-low heat, scraping the bottom of the pan, until the mixture just barely begins to thicken. Nick said this would be a matter of seconds. I find that it actually takes minutes. It might depend on whether the saucepan is heavy or light weight. But watch it very carefully. If it cooks too long or too fast the mixture will not be smooth—as in scrambled eggs. If it does not cook long enough the mixture will remain too thin. They say that the correct stage is "when it will coat a wooden spoon" (but just barely).

Now quickly, without waiting, pour this hot mixture through a fine strainer over the chocolate. Let stand for a few minutes and then whisk gently until the chocolate is all melted and the mixture is smooth and shiny and gorgeous.

Whisk in the coffee or espresso.

(The mixture might be slightly thin now but it will become just perfect when it is chilled.) Pour into four 4-ounce individual soufflé dishes or custard cups, or five 3-ounce pots de crème pots or any other little bowls or glasses. If you use pots de creme pots with covers do not cover until cool.

Refrigerate for a few hours. Serve this very cold.

If you wish, top with a bit of whipped cream just before serving. But when I had this in some of the top restaurants in France it was plain—no topping.

Note: In place of the vanilla bean you can use 1 teaspoon vanilla extract. Stir it in along with the coffee or espresso. (I use 2 to 3 teaspoons Medaglia d'Oro instant espresso dissolved in ¼ cup hot water. I can really taste the espresso in the finished dessert. But you could use just plain water if you prefer.) I stir the vanilla extract into the espresso.

P.S. *Any thin, crisp cookies would go well with this, but I recently served Cornmeal Cat's Tongues (page 174) with it—to raves!*

Baked Vanilla Custard

5 OR 6 PORTIONS, DEPENDING ON SIZE OF CUPS

2¼ cups milk
1 vanilla bean, or 1 teaspoon vanilla extract
¼ cup sugar
Pinch of salt
4 egg yolks plus 1 egg

Adjust rack to the center of the oven and preheat to 325 degrees.

Place the milk in a heavy saucepan. If you are using the vanilla bean, split it, scrape the seeds into the milk, and add the bean also. (If you are using vanilla extract, add it later.)

Cook over moderate heat until milk is scalded or almost boiling. Stir in the sugar and salt and remove from heat.

In a bowl large enough to hold the milk also, beat the yolks and egg slightly, just to mix. Stirring constantly, very gradually add the hot milk mixture to the eggs. Just stir; do not beat any air into the mixture. Strain into a pitcher. If you are using vanilla extract, stir it in now.

Pour into five or six custard cups, leaving a bit of headroom on each. If you have used a vanilla bean, stir the mixture occasionally while pouring, so that the seeds of the vanilla bean do not all settle into the bottom of the pitcher.

If there is any foam on the tops of the custards, spoon it off.

Place cups in a shallow baking pan, which must not be deeper than the cups. Pour hot water into the pan to about one-half the depth of the cups. Cover with a cookie sheet or aluminum foil.

Bake for 1 hour, or a few minutes longer, until a small, sharp knife inserted into the custard comes out clean.

Remove from hot water. Cool uncovered on a rack and then refrigerate covered.

Note: Apricot Sauce (page 493) with vanilla custard is a natural.

Crème au Cacao

6 PORTIONS

> 1 cup milk
> 1 cup light cream or coffee cream
> ½ cup sugar
> Pinch of salt
> ¼ cup plus 1 tablespoon powdered, unsweetened cocoa
> 1 tablespoon instant coffee
> 2 eggs plus 4 egg yolks

Adjust rack to the center of the oven and preheat oven to 300 degrees.

In a heavy saucepan, stir the milk, cream, sugar, salt, cocoa, and coffee occasionally over moderate heat until the mixture comes to a boil. Reduce heat and simmer for about 3 minutes.

Stir eggs and yolks slightly just to mix. Gradually, in a slow thin stream, while stirring constantly, add the hot milk mixture to the eggs.

Strain into a pitcher and pour into six custard cups, leaving a little headroom on each.

Place the cups in a baking pan, which must not be deeper than the cups. Pour hot water into the pan to about halfway up the sides of the cups.

Place in oven and cover with a cookie sheet or a large piece of aluminum foil.

Bake 35 to 40 minutes or until a small, sharp knife inserted into the custard barely comes out clean.

Remove custards from hot water and cool uncovered to room temperature. Refrigerate covered.

Optional: Before serving, pour a thin layer of heavy cream (not whipped) over the tops.

Caramel Custard

4 OR 5 PORTIONS

Caramel all the way through.

1 cup milk
1 cup heavy cream
½ cup sugar
4 egg yolks
Pinch of salt
½ teaspoon vanilla extract

Adjust rack to the center of the oven. Preheat oven to 350 degrees.

In the top of a double boiler over hot water, or in a heavy saucepan over moderate heat, scald the milk and heavy cream until small bubbles appear around the edge or a wrinkled skin forms on top. Reduce heat to lowest and cover to keep warm.

Meanwhile, in a large, heavy frying pan (at least 12 inches in diameter) over moderate heat, melt the sugar. As soon as it starts to melt, stir constantly with a wooden spatula until it is smoothly melted and golden brown.

Very, very carefully, gradually pour the hot milk and cream, stirring continuously, into the caramelized sugar. It will bubble up furiously—that's why the pan must be large. Continue to cook and stir until the caramel has melted and the mixture is smooth. Remove from heat and pour into a pitcher.

In a bowl at least 6- to 8-cup size, stir the yolks gently only to mix them. Very gradually, just a bit at a time at first, stir in the hot milk mixture. Do not beat or whip—the mixture should not be foamy. Stir in the salt and vanilla and strain back into the pitcher.

Pour into four or five custard cups. Cups should not be too full—there should be at least ¼-inch headroom. If there is foam on top, spoon it off.

Place the cups in a baking pan, which must not be deeper than the cups. Pour hot water into the pan to about halfway up the sides of the cups.

Cover the cups with a cookie sheet or a large piece of aluminum foil. Bake 1 hour or until a small, sharp knife inserted into the custard comes out clean.

Remove from oven and place cups uncovered on a rack to cool to room temperature. Refrigerate loosely covered with a paper towel.

Note: If you wish, these custards may be topped with a spoonful or rosette of whipped cream.

Flan

8 TO 10 PORTIONS

This tropical custard, flavored with lime, is baked in one large caramelized dish. It has an exquisite flavor and texture. Must be made a day ahead.

Although Flan is traditionally served in Spanish-speaking countries, this recipe is from the Philippines (they speak Filipino and English).

> $1\frac{1}{3}$ cups sugar
> 4 cups light cream or coffee cream
> Finely grated rind of 1 large lime
> 3 tablespoons lime juice
> 12 egg yolks
> Optional: 2 to 3 cups of raspberries

Adjust rack to the center of the oven and preheat oven to 350 degrees.

Caramelize 1 cup of the sugar (reserve remaining $\frac{1}{3}$ cup sugar) by placing it in a heavy skillet over moderately high heat. Stir occasionally with a wooden spatula until the sugar starts to melt, and then stir constantly until it has all melted to a smooth caramel. It should be a rich brown but do not let it become too dark or it will have a bitter burnt taste. If it is not cooked long enough it will be tasteless.

Immediately pour the caramelized sugar into a 2-quart soufflé dish or other round ovenproof dish with a 2-quart capacity. Using pot holders, quickly tilt and turn the dish to coat the bottom and almost all the way up on the sides. Continue to tilt and turn the dish until the caramel stops running. Set aside.

Scald the cream uncovered in a heavy saucepan or in the top of a large double boiler over boiling water. Meanwhile, mix the lime rind and juice together and set aside. In a large mixing bowl stir the yolks just to mix. When the cream forms tiny bubbles around the edge, remove it from the heat. Add the remaining $\frac{1}{3}$ cup of sugar and stir to dissolve. Very gradually, just a bit at a time at first, add it to the yolks, stirring constantly. Strain and then gradually and gently stir in the lime rind and juice.

Pour into the caramelized dish. Place in a large pan, which must not touch the sides of the dish and must not be deeper than the dish. Pour hot water into the large pan to about two thirds of the way up the sides of the custard dish. Cover loosely with a cookie sheet or large piece of aluminum foil.

Bake for about 1¼ hours, or until a small sharp knife inserted into the center comes out clean. Do not make any more knife tests than necessary. Do not insert the knife all the way to the bottom of the custard or it will spoil the appearance when inverted. Remove from hot water and place on a rack. Cool uncovered to room temperature. Refrigerate for 18 to 24 hours. Do not stint on the chilling time (see Note).

If necessary, cut around the upper edge of the custard to release. Choose a dessert platter with a flat bottom and enough rim to hold the caramel, which will have melted to a sauce. Place the platter upside down over the custard. Carefully invert. Remove dish. Refrigerate. Serve very cold.

Optional: Serve with a side dish of fresh raspberries.

Note:

If Flan is underbaked or if it is not refrigerated long enough, it will collapse when cut. It is best not to invert it too long before serving. The beautiful shiny coating will become dull as it stands.

P.S. *This recipe is from a United Nations cookbook called* The World's Favorite Recipes, *which was published in 1951 by Harper & Brothers. The book has an introduction by Eleanor Roosevelt.*

Crème Brûlée

8 PORTIONS

A rich baked custard covered with a thin, crisp, caramelized sugar topping. The custard may be made a day ahead. The topping may be completed just before serving or up to 2 to 3 hours before serving. Crème Brûlée is generally considered a French recipe and it is occasionally referred to as English, but it is found in very few French or English recipe books. It is, however, in almost all old New Orleans publications.

4 cups heavy cream
8 egg yolks
¼ cup plus 1 tablespoon granulated sugar
2 teaspoons vanilla extract
Light brown sugar

Adjust rack to center of oven. Preheat oven to 325 degrees.

In the top of a large double boiler over hot water on moderate heat, or in a heavy saucepan, over low heat, scald the cream uncovered until it forms a thin wrinkled skin on top or tiny bubbles around the edge.

Meanwhile, in a large bowl stir the egg yolks briefly with a fork or a wire whisk just to mix.

When the cream is scalded, add the granulated sugar to it and stir to dissolve. Very gradually, just a spoonful at a time at first and then in a slow stream, stir the hot cream into the yolks. Do not beat—the mixture should not be foamy. Mix in the vanilla.

The custard should be baked in a wide, shallow, ovenproof casserole with a 6-cup capacity. An 11-inch Pyrex pie plate about 1 inch deep is very successful. Pour the custard into the casserole or pie plate and place it in a large, shallow baking pan. Pour hot water into the baking pan to halfway up the sides of the custard plate.

Bake for about 30 minutes in the pie plate, or longer if the custard is deeper, until a small, sharp knife inserted into the center comes out clean.

Remove from hot water and place on a rack. (If custard was baked in a shallow pie plate it might be difficult to remove from the hot water. If so, use a bulb baster to remove most of the hot water first.) Cool to room temperature. Refrigerate 6 to 8 hours or overnight.

Use a scant ¾ cup of light brown sugar for an 11-inch pie plate; less for one with a smaller diameter. With your fingertips force the sugar through a strainer held over the custard to make a very even layer about ⅛ to ¼ inch thick. There should not be thinner spots or thin edges—they will burn. Also, the sugar should not be too thick or the caramel will be coarse instead of delicate. Cover the sugar with a large piece of plastic wrap and, with your fingertips and the palm of your hand, pat gently to make a smooth, compact layer. Remove plastic wrap. Wipe the rim of the plate clean.

Preheat the broiler for a few minutes, then place the custard about 8 inches below the heat. Leave the door open slightly so that you can watch it. Do not take your eyes off the sugar. Broil until the sugar is completely melted. It will only take a few minutes. If a few spots start to burn, cover them with small pieces of aluminum foil. When completely melted remove from broiler immediately. Cool to room temperature and then refrigerate briefly or up to 2 to 3 hours. (Cooled any longer than this, the caramel will start to melt; although it will not be as crisp, it is still delicious.)

Crème Brûlée is best very cold. It should be placed in the freezer for a few minutes before serving on well-chilled plates. At the table tap the caramel with the edge of a serving spoon to crack it.

Note: Crème Brûlée is a magnificent dessert as is. However, in New Orleans it is frequently served with cold, drained, stewed pears. Or it may be served with one or more brandied fruits—black cherries, pears, peaches, greengage plums. You may make your own by draining the syrup from canned fruit and placing the fruit in a shallow bowl. Pour on some brandy or kirsch. Cover and refrigerate, turning the fruit occasionally, for 12 hours or more.

P.S. *At Le Cirque 2000 in New York City, Crème Brûlée is one of their most popular desserts, and has been for more than fifteen years. They make it in individual oval dishes that measure about 3 x 5 inches and are 1 inch high.*

At the Gotham Bar and Grill, also in New York City, they also make it in individual dishes, and they make a ginger version. They add ½ cup of chopped fresh ginger to the same volume as above. They add the ginger to the cream while it is heating, and then strain the cream.

John Ash, San Francisco chef and cookbook author, adds a bit (I would use more) of diced fresh mango to each dish of Crème Brûlée.

And one of the best Crème Brûlées I ever had was Nancy Silverton's in Los Angeles. (Nancy—of La Brea Bakery, Campanile Restaurant, and many wonderful cookbooks.) Nancy soaked several small pieces of sponge cake in brandy (maybe some were rum or something else) and put them in the bottoms of small cups before pouring in the crème mixture.

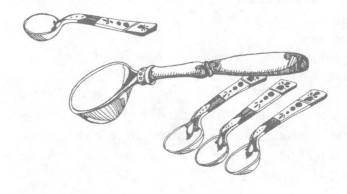

Pumpkin Custard

1½ cups light cream
⅛ teaspoon salt
1 teaspoon cinnamon
¼ teaspoon powdered ginger
Generous pinch of allspice
Generous pinch of powdered cloves
Generous pinch of nutmeg
2 tablespoons dark rum
3 eggs
½ cup sugar
1 cup canned solid-pack pumpkin (not pie filling)
Finely grated rind of 1 cold and firm orange

Adjust rack to the center of the oven and preheat to 325 degrees.

On moderate heat scald the cream uncovered in a heavy saucepan or in the top of a double boiler over hot water until it forms a wrinkled skin on top or small bubbles around the edge.

Meanwhile, in a small cup mix salt, cinnamon, ginger, allspice, cloves, nutmeg, and rum. Set aside.

With a wire whisk or a fork, stir the eggs lightly just to mix. Add the mixed spices and rum, sugar, pumpkin, and grated orange rind, stirring until smooth. Very gradually at first, stir in the hot scalded cream, mixing until smooth.

Transfer to a pitcher and pour into six to eight large custard cups, leaving about ⅓- to ½-inch headroom at the top of each.

Place the cups in a baking pan, which must not be deeper than the cups. Pour hot water into the pan to about halfway up the sides of the cups. Cover the cups with a cookie sheet or aluminum foil.

Bake for 40 to 45 minutes, or until a small, sharp knife inserted slightly into the top of custard comes out clean.

Remove cups from hot water. Place on a rack to cool uncovered to room temperature. Refrigerate loosely covered with a paper towel.

If you wish, top with Ginger Cream (page 499), or the following:

OPTIONAL WHIPPED CREAM
    ½ cup heavy cream
    2 tablespoons confectioners sugar
    ½ teaspoon vanilla extract

In a chilled bowl with chilled beaters, whip above ingredients until the cream holds a soft shape, and spoon a bit on top of each custard.

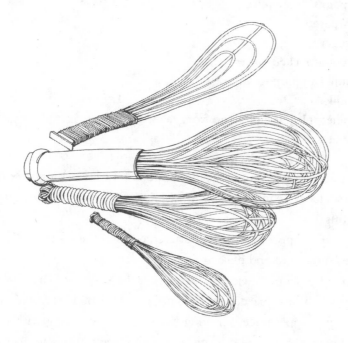

Pineapple Custard Pudding

6 TO 8 PORTIONS

Individual baked puddings with cake-like tops, creamy custard bottoms—
served upside down.

> 1 cup drained, diced, canned pineapple (if you use chunks, cut them
>   in quarters)
> Finely grated rind of 1 cold and firm lemon
> 2 tablespoons lemon juice
> 3 eggs, separated
> ½ cup sugar
> 2 tablespoons melted butter
> ¼ cup sifted all-purpose flour
> ¼ cup milk
> ⅔ cup pineapple juice, or syrup from canned pineapple
> Pinch of salt

Adjust rack to center of oven. Preheat oven to 350 degrees. Butter six or more
of your largest custard cups. The six-ounce cups (see popover recipe, page 312)
are best for this.

Divide the pineapple among the buttered cups and set aside.

Mix the lemon rind and juice and set aside.

In the small bowl of an electric mixer beat the yolks and sugar until light
lemon-colored. On low speed, add the butter and flour. Then, gradually add
the milk and pineapple juice, scraping the bowl as necessary with a rubber
spatula and beating only until smooth. Stir in the lemon rind and juice.

Beat the egg whites with the salt, only until the whites hold a definite
shape but not until they are dry. Gradually, just a bit at a time at first, fold the
yolk mixture into the whites. Pour into a pitcher and pour over the pineapple
in the prepared cups. (The cups will be full.)

Place cups in a baking pan, which must not be deeper than the cups. Pour
hot water into the pan to about halfway up the sides of the cups.

If you have made six custards in large cups, bake for 30 minutes; in smaller cups 3 or 4 minutes less. Puddings will brown on top and they will rise above the tops of the cups.

Remove from hot water, cool to room temperature, and then refrigerate. Puddings will sink back to level with the tops of the cups.

Just before serving, cut around sides to release and invert onto individual dessert plates or shallow bowls. With a rubber spatula scrape any remaining custard out of the cups.

French Custard Rice Pudding

4 cups milk
⅓ cup sugar
½ teaspoon salt
½ cup uncooked rice (not instant, and not washed—I use Uncle Ben's
   converted rice)
3½ ounces (¾ cup) raisins, light or dark
4 egg yolks
2 teaspoons vanilla extract
¼ teaspoon almond extract
1 teaspoon nutmeg (preferably freshly grated)

In the top of a large double boiler, mix 3 cups of the milk (reserve remaining 1 cup milk), sugar, salt, and rice. Cook over moderate direct heat, stirring occasionally until very hot. Place over hot water in bottom of double boiler. Cover. Cook over moderate heat, stirring occasionally, for 1¼ to 1½ hours, or until rice is very tender and milk is almost but not completely absorbed, replacing water in bottom of double boiler if necessary.

While the rice is cooking, pour boiling water over the raisins to cover. Let stand 5 minutes. Drain.

Adjust rack to center of oven. Preheat oven to 350 degrees. Butter a 6-cup shallow casserole or baking dish.

Stir yolks with a small wire whisk or fork just to mix them. Gradually stir in the remaining cup of milk and vanilla and almond extracts.

Gradually mix part of the cooked rice into the yolks, and then mix the yolks into the rest of the rice. Stir in the raisins. Turn into the prepared casserole. Sprinkle with nutmeg. Place in a larger pan, which must not be deeper than the casserole. Pour hot water into the larger pan to about halfway up the side of the casserole.

Bake 45 minutes or until a small, sharp knife inserted into the pudding comes out clean.

Remove pudding from hot water. Cool on a rack. Serve warm, at room temperature, or chilled.

Note: Serve as is, or with Apricot, Raspberry, or Custard Sauce (pages 493, 494, or 490).

Icebox Rice Pudding

8 PORTIONS

With gelatin.

> 3½ ounces (¾ cup) raisins, light or dark
> ⅓ cup light rum
> 4 cups milk
> ⅓ cup sugar
> ¼ teaspoon salt
> ¾ cup uncooked rice (not instant and not washed—I use Uncle Ben's converted rice)
> 1 tablespoon (1 envelope) unflavored gelatin
> 3 tablespoons cold water
> 2 teaspoons vanilla extract
> 1 cup heavy cream

In a small jar with a tight cover, soak the raisins in the rum for 1 hour, more or less, turning the jar occasionally.

In a heavy saucepan over moderate heat, cook the milk, sugar, salt, and rice, stirring occasionally until it comes to a boil.

Reduce heat to low, cover the saucepan, and let it simmer, stirring occasionally for about 45 minutes until the milk is almost, but not completely, absorbed. Watch it carefully toward the end of the cooking time. The mixture will thicken more as it cools and it should not be too dry.

About 5 minutes before the rice is done, sprinkle the gelatin over the cold water in a small cup. Let stand for a few minutes to soften and then stir into the hot rice to dissolve.

Remove rice from heat and turn into a large mixing bowl. Stirring occasionally and gently, let it cool. Stir in the vanilla, raisins, and rum.

When the rice is completely cool, whip the cream in a chilled bowl with chilled beaters until it holds a soft shape. Don't beat the cream stiff or the pudding will be heavy.

Fold into the rice. Turn the pudding into a dessert bowl (about 8-cup capacity, preferably glass and wide rather than deep). Smooth the top.

This should be served with Apricot Sauce (page 493). Pour the sauce over the pudding. Tilt dish very gently to run it all over the top.

Refrigerate for several hours.

Notes:

1. This may also be prepared individually; it is attractive in large wine-glasses or straight-sided glasses meant for old-fashioneds. Or it may be prepared in a 2-quart bowl or mold, chilled until firm, and then inverted and unmolded onto a dessert platter, in which case pour on the Apricot Sauce immediately before serving, or pass it separately.

2. If the pudding is unmolded as above, it may also be circled with fruit—either fresh, unhulled strawberries, or fresh stewed apricots, peaches, or pears, or a combination.

3. With a generous amount of fruit, the pudding will easily make twelve portions, in which case double the Apricot Sauce, pour a bit over the pudding just for looks, and serve the rest separately from a pitcher.

Pineapple Rice Pudding

6 TO 8 PORTIONS

1½ cups water
½ teaspoon salt
1 tablespoon butter
½ cup uncooked rice (not instant and not washed—I use Uncle Ben's converted rice)
2 8-ounce cans (or 1 20-ounce can) crushed pineapple
2 cups heavy cream
3 eggs
½ cup sugar
1½ teaspoons vanilla extract

In a 2½- to 3-quart heavy saucepan, bring the water to a boil. Stir in the salt, butter, and rice. Reduce the heat, cover, and let cook slowly for about 25 minutes or until the water is absorbed.

Meanwhile, drain the pineapple thoroughly in a strainer and set aside.

Adjust rack to center of oven. Preheat oven to 350 degrees. Butter a 6-cup shallow ovenproof casserole.

Add the cream to the rice. Stirring occasionally, bring to a boil. Remove from heat.

In a large bowl beat the eggs lightly just to mix. Very gradually stir in the hot rice and cream. Add the sugar, vanilla, and drained pineapple. Stir to mix thoroughly. Pour into prepared casserole.

Place casserole in a large pan, which should not be deeper than the casserole. Pour hot water into the large pan to one-half the depth of the casserole.

Bake for 40 to 45 minutes until a small, sharp knife inserted in the pudding barely comes out clean.

Remove pan and casserole from the oven, and take casserole out of the hot water. Cool to room temperature. Refrigerate for at least 2 to 3 hours. Serve very cold.

Note: This rich, custardy pudding may be served as is, but it's even better with a generous amount of Strawberry Topping (page 493).

Plain Old-Fashioned Rice Pudding

3 TO 4 PORTIONS

Takes just a minute or two to prepare and 3 hours to bake.

- 4 cups milk
- ¾ cup sugar
- Pinch of salt
- 2 tablespoons butter
- 3 tablespoons uncooked rice (not instant, and not washed—I use Uncle Ben's converted rice)
- ½ teaspoon vanilla extract
- ⅓ cup raisins or currants
- Cinnamon and/or nutmeg (preferably freshly grated)

Adjust rack to center of oven. Preheat oven to 300 degrees.

In a 5- to 6-cup ovenproof casserole, preferably shallow, mix milk, sugar, salt, butter, and the rice, which must be measured carefully. (Just a bit too much will make the pudding heavy.)

Bake uncovered for 2 hours, stirring occasionally—at least three or four times, or more, if you wish.

Add vanilla and raisins or currants. Stir well. Sprinkle a bit of cinnamon and/or nutmeg over the top. Bake 1 hour longer without stirring, in order to let a "skin" form on top.

Remove from oven. The pudding will sink slightly. Cut around the edge so that the "skin" will sink down with the pudding.

Serve while slightly warm, at room temperature, or chilled. Spoon into dessert bowls and pass a pitcher of very cold heavy cream.

Bread Pudding

10 TO 12 PORTIONS

2½ ounces (½ cup) raisins, light or dark
20 slices of firm white bread (1 1-pound thin-sliced sandwich loaf)
3 ounces (¾ stick) soft butter
1 cup sugar
4 cups milk
1 cup light cream or coffee cream
6 eggs
2 teaspoons vanilla extract
Scant ½ teaspoon almond extract
⅛ teaspoon salt

Steam the raisins in a small strainer, covered, over boiling water for 5 minutes. Set aside.

Lightly butter the bread on one side. Stack in piles of five slices each. Cut the crusts from each stack. Cut each stack in thirds to make fingers.

Butter a shallow, oblong, 3-quart baking dish. Place a layer of the bread in the dish, buttered side up, leaving spaces between the fingers of bread. Sprinkle with 2 tablespoons of the sugar and some of the raisins. Continue stacking the fingers into layers, alternating the direction of the fingers, using ½ cup of the sugar (reserve remaining ½ cup sugar) and all of the raisins. Do not use raisins over the top layer. There will probably be about four layers of bread, but that will depend on the size and shape of the baking dish.

In the top of a large double boiler over boiling water, or in a heavy saucepan over moderate heat, scald the milk and cream just until you see tiny bubbles around the edge or a wrinkled skin forming on top.

Meanwhile, in a large bowl mix the eggs lightly with a wire whisk or a fork. Do not beat them frothy. Continue to mix while gradually adding the hot milk, ¼ cup of the reserved sugar (reserve remaining ¼ cup sugar), vanilla and almond extracts, and salt.

Transfer the mixture to a pitcher, then carefully pour it around the bread in the baking dish, pouring into the corners and along the sides. Do not pour over the top layer of bread. Let stand for at least 1 hour, pressing down occasionally with a wide metal spatula to help bread absorb custard from the bottom.

Adjust rack one-third down from the top of the oven. Preheat oven to 350 degrees.

Sprinkle reserved remaining ¼ cup of sugar over the top of the pudding. Place baking dish in a large, shallow pan, which must not be deeper than the baking dish. Pour hot water into the large pan to a 1-inch depth. (If the large pan is aluminum, adding ½ teaspoon of cream of tartar to each quart of water will keep the pan from discoloring.)

Bake 40 to 45 minutes until a knife inserted near the center just barely comes out clean. The sugar on top should have caramelized lightly to a golden color. If not, place it under the broiler for a very few minutes. Watch it carefully!

Remove from water. Serve warm (delicious!), at room temperature, or refrigerated.

Note: Serve Bread Pudding as is, or with Custard, Apricot, or Raspberry Sauce (page 490, 493, or 494).

Apple Pudding

6 TO 8 PORTIONS

A shallow baking dish almost full of a delicious mixture of apples, almonds, and raisins topped with a bit of apricot preserves—covered with a wonderful crisp, crumbly, and crunchy crust.

And it is easy.

TOPPING
(in Germany this is called a Streusel—*pronounced "shtroyzel")*

    1 cup sifted all-purpose flour
    ½ cup firmly packed dark brown sugar
    1½ teaspoons cinnamon
    ¼ pound (1 stick) butter, cut up

Mix flour, sugar, and cinnamon in a bowl. With a pastry blender cut in the butter until mixture resembles coarse crumbs. Refrigerate.

APPLE MIXTURE

    2½ ounces (½ cup) almonds, blanched, and slivered or sliced
    3 pounds (6 to 8 medium) apples
    3 tablespoons sugar
    Grated rind and juice of 1 small lemon
    ¼ cup raisins
    ⅓ cup apricot preserves

Place the almonds in a shallow pan in a 350-degree oven. Stir them occasionally until golden. Remove and set aside to cool.

Adjust rack one-third up from bottom of oven. Preheat oven to 400 degrees. Butter a shallow, ovenproof baking dish with a 2-quart capacity (about 8 x 10 x 2 inches).

Peel, quarter, and core the apples. Cut each quarter the long way into three or four slices. Mix them in a large bowl with the sugar, rind, juice, raisins, and almonds. Turn it all into the baking dish, scraping the bowl clean with a rubber spatula. Dot with small spoonfuls of apricot preserves.

Crumble the refrigerated topping loosely over the apple mixture to cover the apples completely.

Do not pack it down. Wipe the edges of the dish. Bake 30 to 45 minutes until apples are tender and top is lightly browned.

Remove from oven to cool. Serve warm or at room temperature, as is—or even better, with vanilla ice cream or Old-Fashioned Lemon Sauce (page 498).

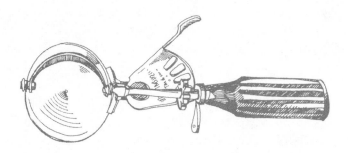

Mousses, Cold Soufflés, Bavarians, and Gelatin Desserts

Chocolate Mousse Heatter

6 PORTIONS

It has been said that chocolate is the sexiest of all flavors. If so, this is the sexiest of all desserts.

For all the years that I made desserts for my husband's restaurant there was never a day without this chocolate mousse. Customers would have objected. That was years ago; but I still meet people who rave about it and say it is the best. It sure is!

Over the years I made this with a variety of chocolates. I don't know of a time that it was less than wonderful. But somehow when I wrote the recipe to give out to customers (every customer who ordered a dessert got a copy of the recipe for their dessert with their order) I specified Tobler Tradition or Lindt Excellence.

½ pound semisweet or bittersweet chocolate
1 tablespoon instant coffee or espresso
⅓ cup boiling water
5 eggs, separated
Pinch of salt

Break up the chocolate into a small, heavy saucepan. Dissolve the coffee or espresso in the boiling water and pour it over the chocolate. Place over low heat and stir occasionally with a small wire whisk until mixture is smooth. Remove from heat and set aside to cool for about 5 minutes.

In the small bowl of an electric mixer at high speed, beat the egg yolks for 3 to 4 minutes until pale lemon-colored. Reduce the speed and gradually add the slightly warm chocolate mixture, scraping the bowl with a rubber spatula and beating only until smooth. Remove from mixer.

Add the salt to the whites and beat until they hold a definite shape but are not dry (see Note 1). Without being too thorough, gently fold about one-quarter of the beaten whites into the chocolate mixture, then fold in a second quarter, and finally fold the chocolate into the remaining whites, folding only until no whites show.

Gently transfer the mousse to a wide pitcher and pour it into six large dessert glasses or wineglasses, each with about a 9-ounce capacity. Do not fill the glasses too full; leave generous headroom on each.

Cover with plastic wrap or aluminum foil and refrigerate 3 to 6 hours. (The mousse may stand longer—12 to 24 hours, if you wish. The texture will become more spongy and less creamy. Delicious both ways.)

Prepare the following:

MOCHA CREAM
   1 cup heavy cream
   ¼ cup confectioners sugar
   1 tablespoon instant coffee or espresso (I use Medaglia d'Oro)

In a chilled bowl with chilled beaters, beat the heavy cream with the sugar and coffee or espresso only until thickened to the consistency of a heavy custard sauce, not stiff. Pour or spoon onto desserts to completely cover the tops.

Optional: Top with a light sprinkling of coarsely grated chocolate or place a few large Chocolate Slabs (page 516) standing upright in the cream.

Notes:
1. I beat the whites with the salt in the large bowl of the mixer, beating at high speed only until the whites thicken or hold a very soft shape. Then I finish the beating with a large wire whisk so that there is less chance of overbeating.
2. This recipe may easily be doubled, if you wish.

Mousse au Chocolat

As it is served at New York's Regency Hotel—a creamier and denser mousse than the previous.

6 ounces semisweet chocolate
4 eggs, separated
Pinch of salt
2 tablespoons confectioners sugar
½ cup heavy cream
½ teaspoon vanilla extract

Place chocolate in top of small double boiler over hot water on low heat. When it is partially melted, remove it from the heat and stir until completely melted and smooth. With a small wire whisk beat in the egg yolks, one at a time. Transfer to a larger bowl and set aside.

Beat whites with salt until foamy. Gradually add sugar and continue to beat until whites hold a shape. Set aside.

In a chilled bowl with chilled beaters, whip the cream with the vanilla until it holds a soft shape.

Stir one-quarter of the egg whites into the chocolate mixture. Then fold in remaining whites and whipped cream, handling lightly and folding only until mixture is smooth. Pour into a serving bowl or six individual dessert bowls or glasses. Cover and refrigerate for at least 2 to 3 hours, or longer if you wish. It may stand overnight.

Serve as is or with whipped cream.

WHIPPED CREAM

1 cup heavy cream
¼ cup confectioners sugar
½ teaspoon vanilla extract

In a chilled bowl with chilled beaters, whip above ingredients until they barely hold a shape, not stiff. Think "sauce" instead of "whipped cream" in order not to overbeat.

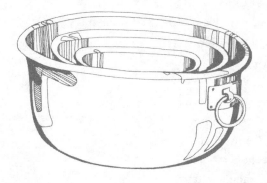

Turin Loaf

6 PORTIONS

This candy-like chestnut-fudge loaf, or Pavé aux Marrons, is a creation of Henri-Paul Pellaprat, at one time head chef of Le Cordon Bleu Cooking School in Paris. If this is not the richest of all desserts, you could have fooled me. A Hungarian pastry chef friend of mine insists on the addition of a few spoonfuls of dark rum. Note: This is a seasonal dessert and must be made with fresh chestnuts.

1 pound fresh chestnuts
¼ pound (1 stick) butter
5 ounces bittersweet chocolate
1 cup confectioners sugar
½ teaspoon vanilla extract

TO SHELL CHESTNUTS

With a strong, sharp, small knife, cut a cross in the flat end of the chestnuts, cutting through the hard outer shell. Don't worry if the cut goes down into the nut itself. In a large saucepan cover the chestnuts with boiling water and boil, covered, for about ½ hour until tender. Test one through the cut in the shell with a small, sharp knife or a cake tester. Replace water as necessary to keep chestnuts covered. Remove from hot water only one or two at a time—they peel more easily while still hot. Remove shells and as much of the inner skin as possible. While the chestnuts are still warm, work them through a food mill or a strainer. (Yes, it is a slow job.) Or puree them in a food processor.

Meanwhile, melt the butter and chocolate in the top of a small double boiler over hot water on moderate heat. Transfer to the small bowl of electric mixer. Add sugar and vanilla and beat only until smooth. Beat in the chestnuts.

Prepare a small loaf pan, 3- to 4-cup capacity, lining it with aluminum foil. Use one piece of foil cut to fit the length and two small sides and another for the width and two wider sides. Press the foil in place in the pan. Brush the foil lightly with tasteless salad oil or spray it with non-stick spray. Press the mixture firmly into the pan—pack it down. Smooth the top. Cover and refrigerate for 4 hours or longer. (Overnight is O.K.)

Cover with a small platter and invert. Remove pan and foil. Refrigerate.

Optional: Decorate with marrons glacés.

Note: This is traditionally served as is; however, it may be served with whipped cream: ⅓ cup heavy cream, 1 tablespoon confectioners sugar, and ¼ teaspoon vanilla. Apply with a pastry bag fitted with a star tube, or use more of each and whip only until thickened, not stiff, and serve separately as a sauce.

Dark Chocolate Sponge

6 TO 8 PORTIONS

> 1 tablespoon (1 envelope) unflavored gelatin
> ¼ cup cold water
> 1 cup heavy cream
> 8 ounces semisweet chocolate, cut or broken
> 2 teaspoons instant coffee
> 4 eggs
> ⅓ cup sugar
> 1 teaspoon vanilla extract

Sprinkle the gelatin over the cold water and set aside.

In a small, heavy saucepan over low heat cook the cream and chocolate, stirring occasionally until chocolate is melted. Stir with a small wire whisk until smooth. Stir in the coffee and the gelatin to dissolve. Remove from heat and set aside.

In the small bowl of an electric mixer beat the eggs and sugar at high speed for a few minutes. When eggs expand to reach top of bowl, transfer to large bowl of mixer and continue to beat for 5 minutes more.

Stir vanilla into chocolate mixture.

Fold a few spoonfuls of the eggs into the chocolate and then gently fold the chocolate into the remaining eggs, handling lightly. Pour gently from one bowl to another to insure thorough blending.

Rinse a 7- to 8-cup metal mold or loaf pan with ice water. Shake out but do not dry.

Turn chocolate cream into cold, wet mold. Refrigerate for 4 to 5 hours, depending on shape of mold, until thoroughly set. (As soon as the top of the chocolate is set, cover with plastic wrap or aluminum foil. If you wish, this may wait overnight before being unmolded.)

Very lightly brush dessert platter with a bit of tasteless salad oil or spray it with non-stick spray in order to be able to move the unmolded dessert if necessary. Dip the mold briefly in very hot water. Place on towel. Quickly cover with inverted dessert platter. Invert mold and platter to unmold dessert. If necessary, dip again very briefly into hot water and/or tap mold carefully against platter to unmold. Refrigerate. Prepare whipped cream.

WHIPPED CREAM

$1\frac{1}{2}$ cups heavy cream
1 teaspoon vanilla extract
$\frac{1}{3}$ cup confectioners sugar

In a chilled bowl with chilled beaters, whip above ingredients until the cream holds a shape. Spread it over the top of the unmolded dessert, or use a pastry bag and a star tube to decorate the dessert with the whipped cream.

Optional: If you wish, decorate with coarsely grated chocolate, or with finely chopped green pistachio nuts, or with chocolate cat's-tongue candies.

Chocolate-Mocha Mousse-Soufflé

6 PORTIONS

Refrigerate for 6 to 10 hours before serving.

2 ounces unsweetened chocolate
2 ounces semisweet chocolate
2 rounded tablespoons instant coffee or espresso
¼ cup boiling water
4 eggs plus 3 yolks
½ cup sugar
Pinch of salt
1 tablespoon (1 envelope) unflavored gelatin
¼ cup cold water
1 teaspoon vanilla extract
2 tablespoons dark rum
1 cup heavy cream

Prepare a 3-inch collar for a 5- to 6-cup soufflé dish (see Note). Use a piece of aluminum foil long enough to wrap around the dish and overlap a few inches. Fold it in half lengthwise. Brush tasteless salad oil on a long half of one long side or spray it with non-stick spray. Wrap it tightly around the dish, oiled side facing up and in. Fasten with string or straight pins and set aside.

In the top of a small double boiler over hot water on moderate heat, melt both chocolates. Stir until smooth and remove from heat to cool.

Dissolve the coffee or espresso in the boiling water and set aside to cool.

In large bowl of electric mixer, at high speed beat the eggs, yolks, sugar, and salt for 15 minutes until very thick, fluffy, and pale lemon-colored.

Meanwhile, sprinkle the gelatin over the cold water in a small heatproof cup. Let stand for about 5 minutes and then place cup in shallow hot water over moderate heat to dissolve. Remove from hot water and cool briefly.

Very gradually, mixing constantly with a small wire whisk, add the coffee to the chocolate. Mix until smooth, and then gradually stir in the gelatin, vanilla, and rum. Mix until smooth again.

Fold a few large spoonfuls of the beaten egg mixture into the chocolate, and then fold the chocolate into the remaining egg mixture.

In a chilled bowl with chilled beaters, whip the cream until it holds a soft shape. Gently fold the whipped cream into the chocolate.

Pour into prepared dish and smooth the top. Refrigerate for 6 to 10 hours.

Remove the foil collar and dry the outside of the soufflé dish. (Do not remove collar too far ahead of time—right before dinner is fine.)

Optional:
1. Before removing the foil collar, sprinkle the top generously with finely grated chocolate, which may be grated on a regular grater or in a Mouli grater.
2. This may be served as is but it is better with a sauce which may be passed separately—either sweetened and rum-flavored whipped cream, whipped only to the consistency of a sauce, Rum Cream Sauce (page 491), or Custard Sauce (page 490).

Note: This does not have to be prepared as a soufflé. It can be made in any serving bowl, individual glasses, or individual soufflé dishes.

Cold Walnut-Coffee Soufflé

8 PORTIONS

This should be prepared at least 5 or more hours before serving.

4 eggs, separated
2½ cups milk
¼ cup dry instant coffee or espresso
1 cup sugar
2 tablespoons (2 envelopes) unflavored gelatin
½ cup cold water
1½ teaspoons vanilla extract
1 tablespoon dark rum or cognac
1 cup heavy cream
Pinch of salt
½ cup walnuts, finely sliced

Prepare a 3-inch collar for a 5- to 6-cup soufflé dish: Use a piece of aluminum foil long enough to wrap around the dish and overlap a few inches. Fold it in half lengthwise. Brush tasteless salad oil on a long half of one long side. Wrap it tightly around the dish, oiled side facing up and in. Fasten with string or straight pins and set aside. (Or this may be prepared in a fancy mold that has been rinsed with cold water and not dried.)

In the top of a large double boiler off the heat, stir the yolks lightly just to mix. Gradually mix in the milk, instant coffee or espresso, and ½ cup of the sugar (reserve remaining ½ cup sugar). Place over hot water on moderate heat. Cook, stirring frequently and scraping the sides and the bottom of the pan with a rubber spatula, for about 15 minutes or more until the mixture thickens slightly (about 180 degrees on a candy thermometer).

Meanwhile, sprinkle the gelatin over the cold water and let stand for 5 minutes. When the coffee or espresso mixture is done, remove the top of the double boiler. Add the softened gelatin and stir to dissolve.

Place the top of the double boiler in a bowl of ice and water and stir occasionally until completely cool. Stir in the vanilla and rum or cognac. Remove from ice water temporarily and set aside.

In a chilled bowl with chilled beaters, whip the cream until it holds a soft shape. Set aside.

In the small bowl of an electric mixer, beat the whites with the salt until they barely hold a very soft shape. Gradually add the reserved ½ cup sugar and continue to beat only until whites achieve a thick marshmallow consistency that holds a shape but is not stiff or dry. Set aside.

Replace upper section of double boiler in the ice water, adding more ice if necessary. Stir gently until mixture begins to thicken and is about the consistency of a thin cream sauce. Remove from ice water. Stir in the nuts.

Gradually fold about half of the coffee mixture into the whites and then fold the whites into the remainder.

Fold 1 to 2 cups of the coffee mixture into the whipped cream. In a large bowl fold the remaining coffee mixture and the whipped cream together. If necessary, gently pour from one bowl to another to insure thorough blending.

Pour into prepared soufflé dish.

Refrigerate 5 to 8 hours. Remove the foil collar. Wipe the soufflé dish. Prepare whipped cream.

WHIPPED CREAM
1 cup heavy cream
¼ cup confectioners sugar
1 scant teaspoon vanilla extract

In a chilled bowl with chilled beaters, whip the above ingredients only until the cream has thickened to hold a soft shape. Serve separately as a sauce.

Note: If you wish, you may also serve Honey Chocolate Sauce (page 502). It goes beautifully with this soufflé.

Cold Apricot Soufflé

8 PORTIONS

This should be prepared 4 hours or longer before serving.

- 2 1-pound cans apricot halves
- 4 eggs plus 3 egg yolks
- 1/8 teaspoon salt
- 1/2 cup sugar
- 2 tablespoons (2 envelopes) unflavored gelatin
- 1/4 cup cold water
- 1/4 cup lemon juice
- 1/2 teaspoon vanilla extract
- 1/4 teaspoon almond extract
- 2 tablespoons cognac or rum
- 1 cup heavy cream

Prepare a 3-inch collar for a 5- to 6-cup soufflé dish: Use a piece of aluminum foil long enough to wrap around the dish and overlap a few inches. Fold it in half lengthwise. Brush tasteless salad oil on a long half of one long side or spray it with non-stick spray. Wrap it around the dish, oiled side facing up and in. Fasten tightly with string or straight pins and set aside (see Note).

Drain the juice from the apricots and puree the halves in a food processor. Set aside.

In the large bowl of an electric mixer, at high speed beat the eggs, yolks, salt, and sugar for about 15 minutes until mixture is as thick as soft whipped cream.

Meanwhile, sprinkle the gelatin over the cold water and lemon juice in a heatproof cup or bowl. Let stand for a few minutes to soften and then place the cup in a shallow pan of hot water on moderate heat to dissolve the gelatin. (Stir occasionally with a metal spoon to see when the gelatin is dissolved.) Remove from hot water and set aside.

When egg mixture has been sufficiently beaten, add vanilla and almond extracts and cognac or rum. Still beating at high speed, beat in the dissolved gelatin. Reduce speed to low and mix in the pureed apricots. Remove from mixer.

In a chilled bowl with chilled beaters, whip the cream until it holds a soft shape. Fold 1 to 2 cups of the apricot mixture into the cream. Fold the cream into the remaining apricot mixture.

Pour into prepared soufflé dish. Refrigerate 4 to 5 hours. Remove foil collar. Wipe sides of dish.

Prepare topping.

WHIPPED CREAM TOPPING
1 cup heavy cream
¼ cup confectioners sugar
1 teaspoon vanilla extract, or 1 tablespoon cognac or rum

In a chilled bowl with chilled beaters, whip the cream, sugar, vanilla, or cognac or rum until mixture holds a shape. With a pastry bag fitted with a star tube, form a lattice or rosettes over the top.

Note: This may also be prepared in a serving bowl or a ring mold (with 10-cup capacity) that has been rinsed with cold water but not dried. Or it may be poured into eight dessert bowls or wineglasses. In glasses, each portion may be topped with a drained apricot half, cut side down, and the whipped cream may be shaped in a ring around the apricot. Sprinkle with a bit of finely chopped green pistachio nuts or toasted, sliced almonds.

Strawberries and Cream

4 PORTIONS

CREAM
1½ teaspoons (½ envelope) unflavored gelatin
1 cup heavy cream
½ cup sugar
1 cup sour cream
1 teaspoon vanilla extract

Place the gelatin, heavy cream, and sugar in a small saucepan. Let stand for 2 to 3 minutes and then place over moderate heat. Stir with a metal spoon until the gelatin and sugar are dissolved.

Place sour cream in small bowl of electric mixer. On lowest speed gradually add the hot cream and the vanilla, scraping bowl with a rubber spatula and beating only until smooth.

Rinse a 2½-cup metal mold with cold water. (A small, shallow mixing bowl may be used, or a small loaf pan, or a saucepan.) Shake out, but do not dry. Transfer cream mixture to wet mold. Refrigerate 4 to 5 hours or longer.

STRAWBERRIES
Wash 1 pint of strawberries quickly by dipping them briefly in cold water. Hull and drain on a towel. Slice them, cutting each berry lengthwise in three or four slices. Sprinkle with a few spoonfuls of sugar and, if you wish, a bit of optional kirsch. Turn into a bowl and let stand for about ½ hour, turning occasionally. Then cover and refrigerate.

TO UNMOLD THE CREAM
Brush a serving platter very lightly with tasteless salad oil or spray it with non-stick spray in order to be able to move the unmolded dessert if necessary.

Cut around upper rim of mold to release it. Dip briefly in hot water. Place on a towel for just a second to dry. Cover with inverted serving platter and invert. If cream doesn't slip out easily, dip it again briefly in hot water.

Surround with the strawberries or pass them separately.

Serve a slice of the cream partially covered with a generous amount of the strawberries.

Notes:

1. This recipe may easily be doubled or tripled; however, the mold should not be too deep. For larger amounts, use a ring mold, a melon mold, a loaf pan, or a round cake pan.

2. This may be prepared a day ahead if you wish. If so, cover it airtight and leave it in the mold overnight.

Orange Cream

8 GENEROUS PORTIONS

2 tablespoons (2 envelopes) unflavored gelatin
⅔ cup cold water
1 cup plus 3 tablespoons sugar
Finely grated rind of 2 deep-colored cold and firm oranges
1 cup orange juice
¼ cup lemon juice
4 egg whites
Generous pinch of salt
1 cup heavy cream
Fresh oranges and strawberries

In the top of a large double boiler off the heat, sprinkle the gelatin over the cold water. Let stand for about 5 minutes. Place over boiling water to dissolve. Stir in 1 cup of the sugar (reserve remaining 3 tablespoons sugar). Stir to dissolve. Remove from heat and stir in the orange rind, orange juice, and lemon juice. Set aside to cool.

Meanwhile, in the small bowl of an electric mixer, beat the egg whites with the salt until foamy. Gradually add reserved 3 tablespoons of sugar and continue to beat until whites hold soft peaks, not stiff. Set aside.

In a chilled bowl with chilled beaters, whip the cream until it holds a soft shape, not stiff. Set aside.

Place the top of the double boiler into a bowl of ice water and stir continuously until the mixture barely begins to thicken to syrup consistency. (If it thickens a bit too much, whip briefly with a wire whisk; however, if it actually sets it will have to be melted again over hot water.) Gradually fold gelatin mixture into the beaten whites, and then gradually fold that into the whipped cream. Pour the mixture back and forth from one container to another to insure thorough blending. (If mixture separates, if the thinner part settles to the bottom, place over ice water and fold gently until it thickens enough so that it does not separate.)

Rinse a 6-cup ring mold or loaf pan with ice water. Shake it out but do not dry it. Pour in the Orange Cream and smooth the top.

Refrigerate until firm (about 2 to 3 hours in a ring mold).

Meanwhile, prepare fresh fruit. Peel oranges, removing every bit of white. Loosen sections by cutting down as close to the membrane as possible on both sides of each section. Rinse strawberries briefly, hull, and place on towel to drain.

To unmold the Orange Cream: Brush a serving platter lightly with tasteless salad oil or spray it with non-stick spray in order to be able to move the unmolded dessert if necessary. With a small, sharp knife cut around the upper rim of the mold to loosen. Dip mold briefly in very hot water. Place it for a moment on a towel and invert the serving platter over it. Quickly and carefully invert. If the cream does not slip out easily, dip it again briefly in hot water. Remove mold. Place in refrigerator.

Prepare whipped cream.

WHIPPED CREAM
  1 cup heavy cream
  3 tablespoons confectioners sugar
  1 teaspoon vanilla extract

In a chilled bowl with chilled beaters, whip the cream with the sugar and vanilla only until it holds a soft shape. Don't let it get stiff.

If dessert has been prepared in a ring mold, place the whipped cream in the center and the fruit around the outside. If it has been prepared in a loaf pan, the fruit may be placed around the outside but the cream should be served separately.

Note: If you wish, the Orange Cream may be flavored with 3 tablespoons of Grand Marnier or Cointreau in place of the lemon juice, and the sectioned oranges and strawberries may both be sprinkled with Grand Marnier or Cointreau and a bit of sugar. If so, prepare them a little ahead of time and let them stand, turning occasionally. The whipped cream may also be flavored with 1 to 2 tablespoons of Grand Marnier or Cointreau in place of vanilla.

Tropical Mango Cream

6 TO 8 PORTIONS

When mangoes are ripe enough they are a great treat. But not until they are ripe enough. You can't judge by their color. They must begin to feel soft to the touch. Like ready tomatoes.

> 1 tablespoon (1 envelope) unflavored gelatin
> 1/3 cup cold water
> 3 mangoes, ripe and ready to eat, or even a bit overripe (to make 2 cups of pulp) (see Note 1)
> 1/2 cup sugar
> 2 tablespoons lime juice
> 1 cup heavy cream
> Optional: Additional fresh fruit, including additional mangoes

Sprinkle the gelatin over the cold water in a small heatproof cup and set aside.

Peel the 3 mangoes. Cut the meat away from the pits, cutting away as much pulp from the pits as possible, and dice it coarsely. Place it in the bowl of a food processor fitted with the metal chopping blade and process briefly to puree. Measure 2 cups of the puree and transfer it to a bowl. Stir in the sugar and lime juice and set aside.

Place the cup of gelatin in a small pan of hot water to reach about halfway up the cup. Place over moderate heat until the gelatin is dissolved; stir it into the mango mixture.

In a chilled bowl with chilled beaters, whip the cream until it holds a soft shape, not stiff. Stir the mango mixture over ice until it barely begins to thicken. Gradually fold some of the mango mixture into the cream and then fold the cream into the remaining mango mixture. If necessary, pour back and forth from one container to another to insure complete blending.

Rinse a 5- to 6-cup metal ring mold with ice water (see Note 2). Shake it out; do not dry it. Pour the Mango Cream into the mold and chill for at least 3 to 4 hours until well set.

Brush a dessert platter very lightly with tasteless salad oil or spray it with non-stick spray so the unmolded dessert may be moved if necessary. Cut around the upper edges of the mold with a small, sharp knife to release. Dip mold very briefly in hot water. Place on towel for a second to dry. Cover with inverted dessert platter.

Carefully invert to release dessert. If dessert does not slip out easily, dip it again very briefly. If necessary, tap it firmly on dessert platter. Remove mold and refrigerate the cream.

Fill the center of the mold with additional fruit, peeled and cut into large dice.

Optional: If you wish, place a ring of additional fruit around the outer edge—strawberries go very well, as do peaches or orange sections.

Notes:

1. The number of mangoes needed will depend on their size, and how much additional mango is to be served with the finished dessert. (I say the more the better, if it is ripe enough and delicious.)

2. Instead of serving this as a molded dessert, it may be poured into a dessert bowl or individual glasses. Serve as above with diced mango and/or other fresh fruit, or top with whipped cream and sprinkle generously with toasted coconut.

3. This soft, creamy dessert may be served as is, or with soft whipped cream: 1 cup heavy cream, ¼ cup confectioners sugar, with 1 scant teaspoon vanilla or 1 tablespoon of dark rum, whipped together only until the cream holds a soft shape.

Raspberry-Strawberry Bavarian

9 PORTIONS ·

This is not an authentic Bavarian. It is, however, one of the most popular desserts I ever made. Many people have said that this is so delicious and so easy that they feel like they're cheating when they make it. There's not only no cooking involved, there's not even any preparation. Just some stirring. Honest.

> 6 ounces strawberry-flavored gelatin (Jell-O)
> 2 cups boiling water
> 1 cup sour cream
> 1 pint strawberry ice cream
> 1 tablespoon lemon juice
> 2 10-ounce packages frozen raspberries (whole berries packed in syrup)
> 1 10-ounce package frozen strawberries (halves, packed in syrup)

Place gelatin in large bowl. Add boiling water and stir to dissolve. Add sour cream and beat with wire whisk or eggbeater until smooth. Cut the frozen ice cream into the gelatin mixture, cutting it into about ten pieces. Stir until melted and smooth. Add lemon juice and frozen fruit. Use a fork to break up the frozen fruit a bit, then use your bare hands until there are no pieces larger than a single piece of fruit. It feels cold, but it does the best job. (Adding the fruit while it is frozen helps to set the gelatin mixture, so that by the time the fruit is broken up and separated, the Bavarian is firm enough to keep the fruit from sinking.)

Quickly pour mixture into a pitcher and pour into nine large glasses, each with about a 9-ounce capacity (see Note 1). Leave a generous amount of headroom on each. Refrigerate. Do not freeze. This will be ready to serve in an hour or two, or it may stand overnight.

Top with the following:

WHIPPED CREAM

2 cups heavy cream
1½ teaspoons vanilla extract
½ cup confectioners sugar

In a chilled bowl with chilled beaters, whip above ingredients until cream holds a shape. Place a large spoonful on each dessert. Decorate, if and as you wish. I use chopped green pistachio nuts, glacéed cherries, and Chocolate Leaves (page 515) or Slabs (page 516).

Notes:

1. I prepare this in heavy, stemmed beer glasses. This must be prepared for individual servings—it is too delicate to serve from one large bowl.
2. About ½ teaspoon each of strawberry and raspberry flavorings, added with the lemon juice, emphasize the flavor and are a welcome addition.
3. If either frozen raspberries or frozen strawberries are not available, use three packages of whichever one you can get.

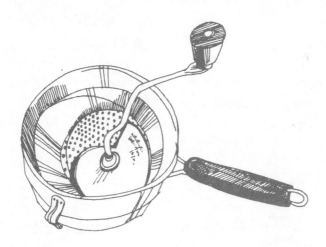

Irish Coffee Jelly

4 PORTIONS

Clear coffee aspic which may take the place of both dessert and coffee for a light summer meal.

1 tablespoon (1 envelope) plus 1 teaspoon unflavored gelatin
½ cup cold water
2 tablespoons instant coffee or espresso
2½ cups boiling water
½ cup sugar
⅓ cup Irish whiskey or brandy
¾ cup heavy cream

Sprinkle the gelatin over the cold water and let stand. Dissolve the instant coffee in the boiling water.

In a saucepan, mix the coffee, sugar, and softened gelatin. Place over high heat and cook, stirring with a metal spoon, until sugar and gelatin are dissolved. Remove from heat and set aside to cool.

Stir in the whiskey or brandy, and pour into four wineglasses, coffee cups, brandy snifters, or straight-sided old-fashioned cocktail glasses, leaving generous headroom. Refrigerate a few hours until set.

Top with a generous layer of unwhipped heavy cream.

Ice Creams and Frozen Desserts

These ice creams and frozen desserts are all frozen in a home freezer or in the freezer section of a refrigerator without an ice-cream churn.

Before starting any of the following recipes, make room in the freezer, preferably on the bottom of the freezing compartment or on a shelf with a freezing coil, and adjust the control to coldest. When dessert is frozen, return the control to normal.

If ice cream has been frozen in an ice-cube tray or other shallow pan, it may be transferred after freezing. Pack it firmly in a deep, covered container.

For ease in serving, ice cream can be scooped ahead of time; place the scoops in a single layer in a shallow pan, cover, and store in the freezer.

One note of caution: In recipes in this section that call for whipped cream, be sure not to whip the cream stiff or the finished product will be heavy and buttery. Whip only until the cream holds a soft shape. Test it often. And it is best to whip the cream in a chilled bowl with chilled beaters. It's a good idea to put the bowl of cream into a larger bowl of ice—and use a balloon whip.

Jean Hewitt's Old-Fashioned Lemon Ice Cream

ABOUT 3 CUPS

This was Jean Hewitt's recipe when she was the home economist of the *New York Times*. This started me on a beautiful binge of ice creams and other frozen desserts made without an ice-cream churn. Mrs. Hewitt's recipes are infallible—this one is also miraculously easy and delicious.

Finely grated rind of 1 large lemon (or 2 small)
3 tablespoons lemon juice
1 cup sugar
2 cups light cream or coffee cream
1/8 teaspoon salt

Combine lemon rind, juice, and sugar and stir to mix. Gradually stir in the cream and salt, mixing well. Pour into an ice-cube tray and freeze until solid around the outside and mushy in the middle. Stir well with a wooden spoon. Cover and continue to freeze until firm.

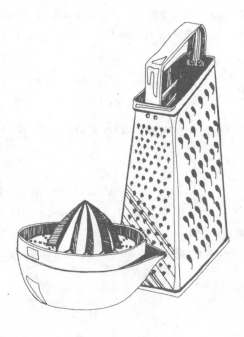

Honey Parfait

1 QUART

2 egg whites
Pinch of salt
⅓ cup honey
1 cup heavy cream
¼ teaspoon almond extract

In the small bowl of an electric mixer beat the whites and the salt until whites hold a soft shape. White beating, gradually add the honey, pouring it slowly in a thin stream. Continue beating until meringue holds a point.

In a chilled bowl with chilled beaters, whip the cream and almond extract until it holds a soft shape.

Fold cream into beaten whites and turn into a large ice-cube tray, or a serving bowl, or, if you wish, freeze individually in large wineglasses, leaving a bit of headroom. Cover and freeze for about 4 to 5 hours (or longer) until firm.

Note: Serve as is, or with a sprinkling of toasted, sliced almonds, and, if you wish, Honey Chocolate Sauce (page 502) may be passed separately.

Almond Parfait

1 QUART

In a moderate oven, toast ½ cup coarsely chopped blanched almonds until golden brown.

Cool completely.

Prepare Honey Parfait. Reserve 2 tablespoons of the toasted almonds. Fold the remainder into the parfait along with 2 or 3 tablespoons of cognac or rum. Spoon into about 6 glasses or individual soufflé dishes. Sprinkle with reserved almonds. Freeze for about 4 hours until firm, or longer, if you wish.

Crème Courvoisier

2 QUARTS

I am indebted to Arno B. Schmidt, executive chef of New York's Waldorf Astoria, for this great recipe. It is heavenly.

This should be frozen for 8 hours or more before serving.

¾ cup water
1 cup sugar
8 egg yolks
⅓ cup Courvoisier
1 cup heavy cream

In a small saucepan (5- to 6-cup size) over high heat, stir the water and sugar to dissolve. Boil without stirring for 5 minutes. Meanwhile, in large bowl of electric mixer at high speed beat the yolks. Very gradually, still beating at high speed, add the hot syrup. Continue to beat until thick and completely cool. Gradually fold in the Courvoisier.

In a chilled bowl with chilled beaters, whip the cream only until it holds a soft shape, not stiff.

Lightly fold about half of the egg yolk mixture into the cream and then fold the cream into the remaining egg yolk mixture.

Pour into an icebox container or, if you wish, leave it in the bowl. Or pour into brandy snifters. Cover and freeze until firm (8 hours or more).

Note: If you wish, you may make almost any substitution for the cognac—rum, kirsch, Cointreau, bourbon, etc.—but I don't know if anything else can be as good; surely nothing can be better.

Grand Marnier Parfait

2 GENEROUS QUARTS

6 egg yolks
⅓ cup water
1 cup sugar
Finely grated rind of 2 cold and firm oranges
⅓ cup Grand Marnier
2 cups heavy cream

In the small bowl of an electric mixer beat the yolks on high speed until very thick and light lemon-colored.

Meanwhile, in a small saucepan over moderate heat cook the water, sugar, and orange rind, stirring continuously until the sugar dissolves. Raise the heat to high and let boil for a minute or two without stirring until the temperature reaches 220 degrees on a candy thermometer.

Pour the hot syrup in a thin stream onto the egg yolks, beating constantly. Continue to beat until completely cool. (If the mixture splashes, reduce the speed as necessary.) When cool, mix in the Grand Marnier and remove from mixer.

In a chilled bowl with chilled beaters, whip the cream only until it holds a soft shape, not stiff.

Gradually fold about half of the yolk mixture into the cream and then, in a larger bowl, fold the cream into the remaining yolk mixture.

Pour into any container, cover, and freeze until firm. (If you're in a hurry, freeze in a shallow metal pan or ice-cube trays—a deep container takes longer.)

Maple-Pecan Parfait

2 QUARTS

1½ teaspoons (½ envelope) unflavored gelatin
¼ cup cold water
4 eggs, separated
1 cup maple syrup
2 cups heavy cream
Pinch of salt
2 ounces (generous ½ cup) pecans, coarsely broken or cut

Sprinkle gelatin over cold water and let stand. Stir egg yolks slightly, just to mix, in top of small double boiler. Gradually mix in the maple syrup and place over boiling water on moderate heat. Cook, stirring constantly, until mixture thickens very slightly (about 180 degrees on a candy thermometer). Remove from heat. Stir in gelatin to dissolve. Transfer to a large bowl and set aside to cool completely. (May be stirred briefly over ice and water to hurry cooling.)

In a chilled bowl with chilled beaters, whip the cream until it holds a soft shape, not stiff. Beat the whites with the salt until they hold a soft shape, not stiff.

When maple syrup mixture is completely cool, very gradually fold it into the whites and then, gradually, fold that into the whipped cream.

Fold in the nuts and turn into any 2- to 2½-quart container or serving dish. Cover and freeze for several hours until firm.

About ½ hour before serving take this out of the freezer and put it in the refrigerator so it will be soft enough to serve.

Frozen Honey Mousse

This is elegant and posh and, to me, completely irresistible. In spite of its "haute," the recipe, surprisingly, comes from a little roadside bee-raiser in Kansas.

> 4 eggs, separated, plus 2 egg yolks
> 1 pound (1⅓ to 1½ cups) honey
> 2 cups heavy cream
> Pinch of salt

In the top of a double boiler, off the heat, beat the six egg yolks briefly (reserve the four egg whites) with a small wire whisk or an eggbeater. Beat in the honey.

Cook over simmering water on moderate heat, stirring constantly with a rubber or wooden spatula for about 10 minutes, or until mixture reaches about 185 degrees on a candy thermometer.

Remove from heat and place top of double boiler into a bowl of ice and water. Keep stirring until it is cool. (Test on the inside of your wrist.) Remove from ice water and set aside.

In a chilled bowl with chilled beaters, whip the cream until it holds a soft shape.

Beat the four egg whites with a pinch of salt until they hold a definite shape, but are not dry.

Gradually fold about half of the honey mixture into the whites and then gradually fold the other half into the whipped cream. In a large bowl gently fold the two together.

Turn into any covered icebox container, or a 10- to 12-cup serving bowl, or 8 to 10 large wineglasses, leaving a bit of headroom. Cover with plastic wrap or aluminum foil and freeze until firm. (Freeze large container or bowlful for at least 12 hours; individual glasses for at least 4 to 6 hours.)

Optional: The bee-raising gentleman responsible for this recipe folds some chopped pecans in. I've made it both ways, and I serve Honey Chocolate Sauce (page 502) with it.

Deep South Chocolate Ice Cream

2 QUARTS

This recipe was given to me after I could not stop eating this extraordinary ice cream at a New Year's Eve buffet in a traditional Mississippi plantation mansion, where a bottle of Grand Marnier was passed around for pouring over the ice cream.

I have often made this with Grand Marnier, and espresso (Medaglia d'Oro), and Lindt Excellence bittersweet chocolate. The flavor is beautiful—the smooth texture is beautiful. And although I originally made this the way the recipe is written—without a churn—now I use an electric churn. To use a churn: Do not whip the heavy cream. Instead, mix it (unwhipped) with the chocolate mixture. Make sure it is all very cold. Freeze.

> 2 tablespoons instant coffee or espresso
> ½ cup boiling water
> 6 ounces semisweet chocolate
> 5 egg yolks
> ¼ cup water
> ½ cup sugar
> ¼ teaspoon cream of tartar
> ⅓ cup crème de cacao or Grand Marnier
> 3 cups heavy cream

Dissolve the coffee or espresso in the ½ cup boiling water. Place it with the chocolate in a small, heavy saucepan, or in the top of a small double boiler over hot water on moderate heat. Stir occasionally to melt the chocolate. Remove from heat and set aside to cool.

Beat the yolks in the small bowl of an electric mixer at high speed for several minutes until thick and light lemon-colored.

Meanwhile, in a small saucepan mix the ¼ cup water with the sugar and cream of tartar. With a small wooden spatula, stir over high heat until the sugar is dissolved and the mixture comes to a boil. Let boil without stirring for about

3 minutes until the syrup reaches 230 degrees on a candy thermometer (light-thread stage).

Gradually, in a thin stream, add the hot syrup to the egg yolks, still beating at high speed. Continue to beat for about 5 minutes more until the mixture is cool.

Stir the crème de cacao or Grand Marnier into the cooled chocolate mixture, and add that to the cooled egg yolk mixture, beating only until blended. Remove from mixer.

In the chilled large bowl of the electric mixer, with chilled beaters, beat the cream only until it holds a very soft shape. Fold 1 cup of the cream into the chocolate mixture and then fold the chocolate mixture into the remaining cream.

Pour into a shallow metal pan, measuring 13 x 9 x 2 inches (or several ice-cube trays) and freeze until firm around the edges (1½ to 2 hours in one large pan). Meanwhile, place large bowl and beaters of electric mixer in the freezer.

Beat the partially frozen cream in the chilled bowl until smooth. Return to pan or trays or any icebox container. Cover and freeze until firm (about 1½ hours in the one large pan).

P.S. *People often ask me what my favorite dessert is. My answer is that it's like a line in a wonderful Broadway show some time ago, "When I'm not near the girl I love, I love the girl I'm near." That's how I feel about desserts. But frankly, just between you and me, my favorite dessert is chocolate ice cream. Preferably in a cone.*

Walnut Ice Cream

2 QUARTS

⅔ cup sugar
¼ cup plus 2 tablespoons water
6 egg yolks
2 cups heavy cream
2 tablespoons dark rum
2 teaspoons vanilla extract
2 teaspoons instant coffee or espresso
Generous pinch of salt
7 ounces (2 cups) walnuts, finely ground (see page xxiv)
3½ ounces (1 cup) walnuts, coarsely cut

In a small saucepan over high heat, cook the sugar and water, stirring until the sugar dissolves. Bring to a boil and let boil without stirring for 2 minutes.

Meanwhile, in the small bowl of an electric mixer at high speed, beat the yolks. Very gradually, in a thin stream, add the hot sugar syrup to the yolks, beating constantly. Continue to beat at high speed until mixture is as thick as whipped cream and completely cool. (Test it on the inside of your wrist.)

Meanwhile, in a chilled bowl with chilled beaters, beat the cream, rum, vanilla, instant coffee or espresso, and salt until the cream barely holds a soft shape, but is not stiff.

Fold the cooled egg yolk mixture into the whipped cream mixture until completely blended and then fold in the ground nuts and the cut nuts.

Pour into 2 large ice-cube trays or any shallow container, cover, and freeze until firm.

Note: This is great with any chocolate sauce.

Gin Ice Cream

7 CUPS

If you taste the gin at all in this rich, vanilla ice cream, you will barely recognize it. But the ice cream has a lovely flavor and the alcohol keeps it from freezing too hard.

> 1½ cups light cream or coffee cream
> ½ cup sugar
> ¼ teaspoon salt
> 4 egg yolks
> 2 teaspoons vanilla extract
> ½ cup plus 2 tablespoons 90- to 94-proof gin
> 2 cups heavy cream

See Note 2.

Scald the light cream in the top of a double boiler, uncovered, over hot water on moderate heat. When tiny bubbles begin to appear around the edge, or a slight skin forms on top, add the sugar and salt and stir to dissolve.

In a small bowl stir the egg yolks lightly with a fork just to mix. Very gradually, stirring with the fork, add about half of the hot cream to the yolks, and then add the yolks to the remaining cream in the top of the double boiler.

Replace over hot water on moderate heat and cook, stirring gently and scraping the pot with the rubber spatula, until custard thickens enough to coat a spoon (a scant 175 degrees on a candy thermometer).

Immediately transfer custard to a mixing bowl, or place top of double boiler in a bowl of ice and water to stop the cooking. Stir occasionally until custard is completely cool. Mix in the vanilla and gin.

In a chilled bowl with chilled beaters, whip the heavy cream only until it holds a soft shape, not stiff. Gradually, in several small additions, fold the cooled custard into the whipped cream. Gently pour back and forth from one bowl to another to insure thorough blending.

Pour into freezer trays, cover airtight, and freeze without stirring until it is firm.

Notes:

1. Serve as you would vanilla ice cream. It is delicious as is, or with sliced and sugared fresh strawberries, or with any one of the chocolate sauces (pages 500–503).
2. Both Gin Ice Cream and Rum Raisin Ice Cream, which is a variation on it, are best made 6 to 12 hours before serving. If they stand longer than that there is a chance they might become granular and crystallized.

Rum Raisin Ice Cream

See Note 2 above.

Soak ⅔ cup (3 ounces) dark raisins in ½ cup dark rum (80 proof) in a small, covered jar for several hours or overnight.

Follow above directions for Gin Ice Cream, omitting the gin. Substitute the raisins and rum and stir them into the cooled custard.

You will need three average-size, or one average and one extra-large size ice-cube trays. When turning the mixture into the trays, spoon from the bottom to make sure that the raisins are equally distributed.

When the ice cream is slightly frozen—before it is actually firm—stir once gently, right in the tray, to keep the raisins evenly distributed.

Lime Sherbet

1 GENEROUS QUART

This recipe may be used for lemon sherbet, substituting lemon juice for the lime juice.

To make this in a churn, see Note.

3 cups water
1¼ cups sugar
¾ cup light corn syrup
⅔ cup lime juice
2 egg whites
Pinch of salt

Combine water, 1 cup of sugar (reserve remaining ¼ cup sugar), and corn syrup in a saucepan. Stir over high heat to dissolve the sugar. Bring to a boil, reduce the heat to moderate, and let boil for 5 minutes without stirring. Remove from heat and let cool to room temperature. (May be hurried by setting saucepan in a bowl of ice and water.) Stir in lime juice.

Pour into ice-cube trays or any shallow metal pan about 9 inches square. Place in freezer and freeze until firm throughout. Also freeze large bowl and beaters from electric mixer.

Remove lime mixture from freezer. Break up with a wooden spoon or spatula, and turn into frozen mixer bowl. With frozen beaters beat on low speed scraping bowl with a rubber spatula and beating only until free from lumps.

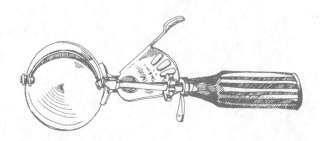

Work quickly and do not let the mixture start to melt. Immediately return to freezer right in the mixing bowl and refreeze until firm again. You may leave the beaters in the bowl, as they should be chilled, too, for the next beating.

When mixture is refrozen, beat the egg whites with the salt until slightly thickened. Gradually beat in reserved ¼ cup sugar and beat only until whites hold a definite shape, firm but not dry.

Remove lime mixture from freezer. Repeat breaking up and beating only until smoothly free from lumps. On lowest speed beat in beaten egg whites, beating very briefly only until whites are incorporated.

Immediately replace bowl of sherbet in the freezer, or return sherbet to ice-cube trays. Refreeze, folding gently two or three times during freezing, and folding all the way from the bottom up.

Serve when firm, or transfer to a deep covered container to store.

Note: Something wonderful happens when you make this in a churn. Something deeelicious! It will look and taste almost creamy. Ice creamy.

Prepare the water, sugar, and corn syrup mixture. Cook it and cool it. Add the lime juice. Now chill it, get it very cold. Either put it in the freezer until very cold or in the refrigerator for several hours or overnight. Then freeze it in the churn until it is almost but not completely frozen.

At this point prepare the egg white and sugar mixture. The egg white mixture (meringue) should be beaten until it holds a straight shape when you remove the beaters (it will look something like marshmallow whip).

Add the egg white mixture to the almost frozen mixture in the churn and continue to churn.

Churn only until thickened and almost semifirm—do not overchurn. Then transfer to the freezer.

And also put the serving dishes in the freezer.

Apricot Sherbet

2 QUARTS

2 cans (each 1 pound, 14 ounces), or 4 smaller cans (each 1 pound, 1 ounce), apricot halves
¼ cup lemon juice
Scant ¼ teaspoon almond extract
1 cup sugar
4 egg whites
Pinch of salt

Drain apricots, reserving the juice, and puree them in a food mill or press them through a strainer. Add enough of the juice to make 4 cups. Turn into a large bowl. Stir in the lemon juice, almond extract, and sugar.

Beat the whites with the salt until they hold a definite peak, but are not dry. Stir 1 cup of the apricot mixture into the whites and then stir and fold the whites into the remaining apricots.

Turn the sherbet into a large, shallow metal pan, or several ice-cube trays, and place in freezer. Also place large bowl of electric mixer and beaters in the freezer (or in the refrigerator, if there isn't room in the freezer).

When the sherbet has frozen solid around the edges and is mushy in the center, turn it into the cold bowl and beat it with the cold beaters until smooth and fluffy. Either return it to its original container or leave it in the mixing bowl. Freeze again until partly frozen. Beat again at high speed for 2 minutes. Turn it into a container or leave it in the bowl, cover, and freeze until firm.

Note: About ½ hour before serving remove the sherbet from the freezer and place it in the refrigerator so it can thaw a bit to the right consistency to serve.

Spanish Lime Pie

8 PORTIONS

The his is served frozen. If you wish, it may be made a few days ahead.

CRUST

1¼ cups graham cracker crumbs
1 tablespoon sugar
1 teaspoon cinnamon
3 ounces (¾ stick) melted butter

Adjust rack to center of oven and preheat to 375 degrees. Mix the graham cracker crumbs with the sugar and cinnamon. Add the melted butter. Stir with a rubber spatula, pressing the mixture against the sides of the bowl, until completely mixed. It will look crumbly but will hold together when pressed into place.

Use a 9-inch pie plate and follow crumb crust directions, page 350.

FILLING

Finely grated rind of 2 cold and firm limes
1 cup lime juice
4 eggs, separated
2 15-ounce cans sweetened condensed milk
Pinch of salt

Mix the lime rind and juice. In a large mixing bowl, stir the yolks lightly with a small wire whisk or a fork just to mix. Gradually mix in the condensed milk. Very gradually add the rind and juice, stirring until smooth.

Add the salt to the whites and beat until they hold a point, or are stiff but not dry. In two or three additions, fold the whites into the yolk mixture.

The crust will not hold all of the filling. Pour in as much as the crust will hold without any running over. Reserve the balance at room temperature.

Freeze the filled crust for about 20 minutes until semifirm. Then pour the balance of the filling on the top, mounding it high in the center. Return to freezer immediately. Freeze for 4 to 5 hours until firm. (May be frozen overnight or longer.) Let stand at room temperature 5 to 10 minutes before serving.

Note: If this is to be kept frozen for any length of time: After it is frozen very firm, it may be covered with clear plastic wrap, but it must be completely firm or the wrapping will stick and will spoil the looks. If that should happen, the top may be dusted lightly with a camouflage—grated chocolate, chopped nuts, cookie crumbs, or whipped cream.

French Ice-Cream Cake

8 PORTIONS

I n France, this is Biscuit Glacé au Grand Marnier. It may be made with
bought ice cream, and is quite easy for such a fancy dessert. Must be made
a day ahead.

> ¾ cup candied orange peel, finely chopped
> 1 cup Grand Marnier
> Ladyfingers, or sponge cake baked in a loaf pan
> ½ cup heavy cream
> 1 quart vanilla ice cream

In a small covered jar, marinate the orange peel in ½ cup Grand Marnier.
(Reserve remaining ½ cup Grand Marnier.) Let stand for an hour or so, or as
much longer as you wish. Place large bowl and beaters from electric mixer in
the freezer (or in the refrigerator if there isn't room in the freezer).

Line a loaf pan with a 2-quart capacity (11 x 5 x 3 inches) with one long
piece of wax paper or aluminum foil to cover both long sides and the bottom
and extend several inches above the top of the pan. It is not necessary to line
the two short ends.

Line the long sides only with the ladyfingers (round sides against the pan)
or with ½-inch-thick slices of sponge cake, brushing both sides of each one
with some of the reserved Grand Marnier before putting it in place. (Reserve
some Grand Marnier for final layer of cake on top.) Do not place the cake or
ladyfingers against the bottom or on the short ends of the pan.

In a chilled bowl with chilled beaters (not the ones in the freezer) whip the
cream until it holds a soft shape.

Now, in the large chilled bowl with the chilled beaters, beat the ice cream
briefly to soften slightly, beating only until smooth but not melted. Quickly, on
lowest speed, mix in the orange peel with its Grand Marnier marinade.
Remove from the mixer and fold in the whipped cream. Immediately pour into
prepared pan and place in freezer.

Freeze for a few hours until slightly firm, and then cover top with a double or triple layer of ladyfingers, or sponge cake cut thicker than for the sides. Brush each layer generously with remaining Grand Marnier; use extra if you wish. Cover airtight and freeze overnight or longer.

To serve, cut the two short ends to release, invert onto a chilled serving platter, remove pan and wax paper or aluminum foil, and replace in freezer.

Optional: Shortly before serving, decorate the top with sweetened and flavored whipped cream, using a pastry bag and a star tube, or pass a bowl of whipped cream separately. Also, if you wish, serve with Honey Chocolate Sauce (page 502).

Fresh Fruit, and Fruit and Ice-Cream Desserts

Preparing Oranges

Use large "in-season" oranges, preferably seedless—California navels or Florida temples.

To pare the rind: Use deep-colored oranges. Wash the fruit well. Use a vegetable peeler with a swivel blade to remove the colored, thin, outer rind. Do not press too hard or you will also be removing the white underskin, which is bitter. Try to make the pieces long instead of short.

To cut the rind in slivers: Use a long, heavy, sharp knife. Pile two or three long pieces of the rind on top of each other on a board. Hold the pieces in place with your left hand while cutting down firmly and sharply with your right, cutting into the thinnest and longest slivers possible. These are referred to as julienne.

To peel an orange (or grapefruit): Place it on a board on its side. With a very sharp, long knife, cut off the top and the bottom. Turn the orange upright, resting on a flat end. Hold the orange with your left hand as you cut down toward the board with your right hand, curving around the orange and cutting away a strip of the peel—cut right to the orange itself in order not to leave any of the white underskin. Turn the orange a bit and cut away the next strip of peel. Continue all the way around the orange. After cutting all the way around, lift the orange and, holding it in the palm of your left hand, cut away any remaining white parts.

To section the orange (or grapefruit): Work over a bowl to catch the juice. With a thin, sharp knife, cut down against the inside of the membrane of one section on both sides, releasing the section and leaving the membrane.

After removing one or two sections, continue as follows: Cut against the membrane on one side of a section and then, without removing the knife, turn it up against the membrane on the other side of the section. The section will fall out clean. After removing all the sections, squeeze the leftover membrane in your hand for any juice. Carefully pick out any seeds in the sections; even seedless oranges frequently have them.

Fresh Fruit

 As prepared at Le Cordon Bleu Cooking School in Paris.

Use only ripe, in-season fruit—oranges, grapefruit, melons, apricots, peaches, pineapples, mangoes, berries, grapes, bananas—whichever are available.

Prepare the oranges and grapefruit according to the directions for sectioning oranges (page 468). Peel the peaches by dropping them very briefly in boiling water only until the skins can be peeled off with your fingers. Fifteen seconds is enough if the fruit is ripe. Cut up the fruit in rather large pieces, but still only one bite—do not dice too small. Wash, hull if necessary, and drain the berries. If you are using bananas, don't peel or cut them until the last minute or they will darken. If the grapes have seeds, cut them in half the long way and pick out the seeds. Place all the fruit in a large bowl.

Prepare the following syrup:

SYRUP
(This is enough syrup for fruit to serve 6 to 8 portions)

    1½ cups sugar
    1 cup water
    2 to 3 tablespoons kirsch

Stir the sugar and water in a small saucepan on moderate heat until it boils. Let it boil for 5 minutes. Remove from heat and cool slightly for just a few minutes. Stir the kirsch into the warm syrup. Pour the warm syrup over the fruit and stir gently to mix. Stir very carefully in order not to break up the fruit. Cover and refrigerate 1 to 2 hours or all day if you wish, stirring occasionally. Serve cold in chilled bowls or glasses.

At Le Cordon Bleu, this fruit is served in scooped-out melon shells (from which the fruit has been spooned out, cut up, and added to the other fruits). In Paris, very small melons are available so that each portion is served in an individual melon shell. Use chilled melons, cut off about one third from the top. Discard seeds. Remove fruit. Place the prepared fruit mixture in the shell and replace the top. Refrigerate. Serve with the melon tops on, on individual dessert plates, preferably placing the melons on large, flat, fresh green leaves.

The same procedure may be followed with larger melons (especially watermelon), serving the fruit at the table in chilled bowls or glasses.

If using watermelon, first find the flattest side for the bottom. Make sure it will stand firmly. Mark the upper third with a soft pencil and, with a very long, heavy, sharp knife, cut it off. Scoop out the fruit. If you wish, with a very sharp small knife cut the top edge in scallops or zigzag, first marking the pattern with a soft pencil. Cover the shell with a damp towel and then with plastic wrap. Refrigerate until serving time. Fill with chilled prepared fruit immediately before serving. Place on a large platter and circle with fresh green leaves.

Applesauce

6 CUPS APPLESAUCE

"Select fine-flavored apples" is a safe and common direction. The best way to accomplish this is to use apples when they are in season.

> 3 pounds apples (about 8 medium-large)
> Optional: 1 vanilla bean, 6 to 8 inches long
> Optional: 2 cinnamon sticks
> Water
> Sugar

Peel, quarter, and core the apples. Place them in a large heavy saucepan. Slit the optional vanilla bean, scrape the seeds into the apples, and add the pod also. Add optional cinnamon sticks. Add about 2 cups of water, but the amount needed will depend on the applies. Additional water may be added later if needed, or excess water may be boiled down. Keep in mind that the applesauce thickens as it stands and is best if not too dry.

Cover and cook over moderate heat for 5 to 10 minutes until the apples begin to soften. Uncover and, with a heavy wooden spatula, stir and break up the apples. Leave some small chunky pieces. Continue to stir and mash, cooking only until tender but not completely mushy.

The amount of sugar needed will depend on the apples. Start with ¼ to ⅓ cup. Stir to dissolve. Taste and add more if necessary.

If you have not used the vanilla bean and cinnamon sticks, flavor with vanilla, powdered cinnamon, and/or nutmeg or mace, but with good apples go easy on the seasoning or you will hide the natural flavor.

If you have used vanilla bean and cinnamon sticks, do not remove them until serving time (they continue to give flavor), or, if the applesauce is being served from a glass bowl, they may be left in just for looks.

Stewed Peaches

When peaches are wonderful and full of flavor this is super-delicious—and beautiful. By the way, these stewed peaches freeze perfectly.

6 large freestone peaches, ripe but firm
1½ cups water
1 cup sugar
1 vanilla bean, 6 to 8 inches long

To peel the peaches: Have ready a large bowl of ice-cold water, a slotted spoon, and a saucepan of boiling water deep enough to cover the peaches.

With the slotted spoon, place the peaches in the boiling water, two or three at a time. If the peaches are fully ripe they will need only about 15 seconds in the boiling water; if not quite ripe they will need more. With the slotted spoon, raise a peach from the boiling water and move your thumb firmly over the skin. If the skin has loosened enough it will wrinkle and feel loose from the fruit. At that point transfer to the ice water.

Peel with your fingers, starting at the stem end, and return the peeled fruit to the ice water. Partially peeled peaches may be returned to the boiling water for additional boiling if necessary. Continue blanching and peeling the remaining peaches.

In a saucepan large enough to hold the peaches in a single layer, place the water and sugar. Slit the vanilla bean and scrape the seeds into the water; add the pod also. Bring to a boil, stirring, and let boil about 5 minutes to make a syrup. With the slotted spoon, add the peaches and adjust the heat so that the syrup simmers gently. Cook covered, turning the peaches a few times with two rubber spatulas in order not to mar them. Baste occasionally with the syrup.

Test for doneness with a cake tester. Do not overcook. When just barely tender, transfer peaches gently with the slotted spoon to a large wide bowl or casserole.

Raise the heat and boil the syrup rapidly for a few minutes to reduce slightly. Taste the syrup, and continue to boil until it tastes right—sweet enough and not watery. Pour the hot syrup over the peaches. Do not remove the vanilla bean. Set aside to cool, basting occasionally with the syrup.

Cover with plastic wrap or transfer to a covered icebox container. Refrigerate and serve very cold.

Serve in dessert bowls with a generous amount of the syrup.

The classiest way to serve these is to serve one whole peach that still has the pit for each portion. Serve with a fork and a spoon, or a knife, fork, and spoon. However, if that does not fit your plans, cut each peach in half and remove the pits and serve either one or two halves per portion.

Stewed Pears

Peel the pears as for Poires au Vin Rouge (page 476). Prepare the same syrup as for Stewed Peaches (page 472). Poach the pears covered until tender. Remove from syrup. Reduce the syrup as in the recipe for Stewed Peaches and pour over the pears. Cool and then chill, occasionally spooning the syrup over the pears.

Poires Hélène

On each chilled dessert plate, place a scoop of vanilla ice cream and a drained Stewed Pear. Separately, pass Plain Old-Fashioned Chocolate Sauce (see Note, page 500), or any other chocolate sauce, either slightly warm or at room temperature.

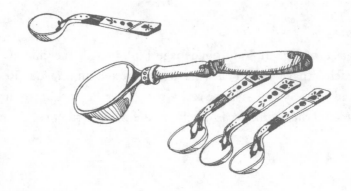

Pêches Melba (Maxim's)

"Melba" was a great Australian opera star named Dame Nellie Melba. Escoffier was the chef at the Savoy Hotel in London. The year was 1892, when Escoffier created this famous dessert in Dame Melba's honor. (Melba toast was also named in honor of this same lady.)

In the original version a swan carved of ice (symbolic of the swan in the opera *Lohengrin*) was in the center of a platter and the peaches and ice cream were arranged around it.

> Stewed Peaches (page 472)
> Vanilla ice cream
> Fresh Raspberry Sauce, Raspberry Sauce, or Sauce Melba (pages 495,
>   494, 495)
> Toasted, sliced almonds

The peaches should be stewed only until barely tender; they should remain slightly firm.

For each portion: On a chilled, flat dessert plate, place a scoop of vanilla ice cream and a drained, whole, stewed peach. Top with either Fresh Raspberry Sauce, Raspberry Sauce, or Sauce Melba, and sprinkle lightly with toasted, sliced almonds.

At Maxim's in Paris, this is served with whole, fresh raspberries, not a sauce.

Serve with a dessert spoon and a fork.

Poires au Vin Rouge

6 PEARS

3 cups cold water
Juice of 1 large lemon
6 large pears, firm but ripe
2 cups dry red wine
1 cup sugar
1 vanilla bean, 6 to 8 inches long

In a bowl large enough to hold the pears, place 3 cups of cold water and half of the lemon juice (reserve remaining lemon juice).

Use a vegetable peeler with a swivel blade to peel the pears, leaving the stems on. If necessary, slice a little off the bottoms so they can stand upright. As you peel them, place them in the cold, acidulated water.

In a saucepan large enough to hold the pears in a single layer, mix the wine, sugar, and remaining lemon juice. Slit the vanilla bean, scrape the seeds into the wine, and add the pod also. Bring to a boil and boil for about 5 minutes to make a syrup. Transfer pears from acidulated water to the syrup. Adjust the heat for the syrup just to simmer. Cook covered, occasionally turning the pears gently from side to side with two rubber spatulas in order not to bruise the pears. Baste occasionally with the syrup.

Test for doneness with a cake tester. They should be tender all the way to the core, but do not overcook. When done, with a slotted spoon carefully transfer the pears to a large, wide bowl or casserole, standing them upright.

Raise the heat and boil the syrup rapidly for a few minutes to reduce slightly. Pour the hot syrup over the pears. Do not remove the vanilla bean, as it continues to flavor the syrup—and it looks great. Set aside to cool, occasionally spooning the syrup over the pears. Cover with plastic wrap or gently transfer to a covered icebox container. Refrigerate and serve very cold. Serve individually in dessert bowls with a generous amount of the syrup.

Optional: If you wish, 2 to 3 tablespoons of cognac or kirsch may be stirred into the cooled syrup.

Bananas Niçoise

This lovely, simple dessert must be prepared immediately before serving, but it takes only a few minutes.

Use bananas that are fully ripe, but not overripe or mushy. Refrigerate the bananas for an hour or two before using. Peel and slice into ½-inch-thick rounds. Place the slices in a wide, shallow bowl. For each small banana sprinkle on 2 teaspoons kirsch and 2 tablespoons heavy sweet cream. If bananas are large, use a bit more kirsch and cream. Stir briefly and gently with a rubber spatula, coating each slice with the sauce. Let stand for just a few minutes and the cream will thicken slightly.

Serve immediately in shallow dessert bowls or flared glasses (champagne or double-martini glasses).

Plan on 1 to 1½ bananas per person.

Bananas Cubaine

Follow above directions, substituting dark rum for the kirsch. Fill an ice-cream scoop half full with coffee ice cream and the other half chocolate ice cream. (May be prepared ahead of time and frozen.) Place ice cream in chilled dessert bowls or large, wide glasses and cover generously with prepared bananas. Yummy!

Baked Bananas

6 PORTIONS

> 6 large, ripe but firm bananas
> 3 to 4 tablespoons lime juice
> ½ cup dark rum
> ½ cup brown sugar, strained if lumpy
> 2 tablespoons butter

Adjust oven rack high in the oven. Preheat oven to 400 degrees. Butter a shallow baking dish just large enough to hold the bananas; it should not be larger.

Peel the bananas. Cut each one into three pieces, cutting on a sharp angle. Arrange the pieces in the baking dish. Sprinkle with lime juice and ¼ cup rum (reserve remaining ¼ cup rum). Sprinkle with sugar and dot with butter (most easily done with frozen butter).

Bake for 10 to 15 minutes, gently turning the bananas and basting them once or twice.

Heat the reserved rum in a small metal cup. Bring to the table immediately and bring the bananas also in their hot baking dish. Pour the rum over the bananas and immediately touch with a match to flambé.

As soon as the flame goes out, serve on warm dessert plates. Or serve on chilled plates with ice cream.

Glacéed Strawberries

The first time I saw these was at The Four Seasons restaurant in New York City. The maître d' brought them—with great fanfare—to the Duke and Duchess of Windsor, who were dining at a table near ours. I wanted some. We asked our waiter if we could order them and were told no—they were not on the menu. Chef Albert Stockli had made them especially for the Duke and Duchess.

Now that I know how to make them I can have them whenever I want them. So can you.

At the Four Seasons these are not served as a dessert, but they come with after-dinner coffee on silver pedestal platters. Although they represent the height of elegance, they are quite quick and easy to make. (I do serve them as dessert, along with some cookies.)

The berries are coated with a paper-thin layer of clear, shiny glaze, as crisp and brittle as glass. They are eaten with the fingers, and biting through the thin, crisp coating and the soft sweet berry together is an exquisite experience. And they are so beautiful that even just looking at them is a thrill for me.

Make them only at the height of the strawberry season, when giant berries are available. They must be perfect berries with no soft spots. Ideally, the strawberries should have long stems, but since I am never able to get berries with long stems, and only occasionally with short stems, I use stemless berries.

Glacéed Strawberries must be made as close to serving time as possible. The sooner you serve these, the better. They can not wait for more than 1 hour or the glazed coating will start to melt. Actually it is great if your guests stand around you at the stove and eat them as they are made. They should, if possible, be made on a dry day. You must use a candy thermometer.

1 to 2 dozen large strawberries
2 cups sugar
½ cup plus 1 teaspoon water
1 tablespoon light corn syrup
⅛ teaspoon cream of tartar
1 teaspoon water

Do not wash the berries but instead brush them gently with a soft, dry pastry brush. Pat and wipe them lightly with a soft towel. Place them on paper toweling on a tray in the refrigerator.

Also prepare another tray, this one for the berries after they have been glazed. Either cover the tray with baking parchment or with foil and spray the foil lightly with non-stick spray.

In a heavy 1½- or 2-quart saucepan mix the sugar, ½ cup water (reserve remaining 1 teaspoon water), and corn syrup. Bring to a boil over moderate heat, stirring occasionally. Mix cream of tartar with remaining 1 teaspoon water and stir into syrup. Raise the heat to high. Cover the pan for 1 minute and then uncover. Place a candy thermometer in the saucepan and let the syrup boil without stirring until the temperature reaches 300 degrees (the hard-crack stage). Immediately remove from heat. Work quickly. Holding a cold strawberry by the stem, or raising the leaves enough so that you can hold them, carefully dip the strawberry into the syrup to coat it thoroughly except for the stem and leaves. Remove quickly and brush the berry lightly against the rim of the pan to remove excess syrup. Then place the berry on its side on the lined tray. The glaze will harden almost immediately and the berries are ready to serve. Repeat with remaining berries, refrigerating the glazed berries as quickly as possible.

Leave the thermometer in the saucepan while you are working. Reheat the syrup if necessary to maintain a temperature of 290 to 300 degrees. Work quickly before the syrup becomes dark—it affects the taste.

Keep the berries refrigerated until serving time, which should be just as soon as possible.

If you can do it, serve two or three berries per person. But these are such a rare treat that even one or two will make an event.

P.S. *Try this. Insert toothpicks into dried apricots, pitted prunes, pitted dates, even dried apple rings, and dip into the glaze. These will all be gorgeous! (Do not remore the toothpicks.) And they can wait a bit longer than the strawberries before serving, but the sooner they are served the better.*

Brookfield Center Strawberries

Brookfield Center is a beautiful small town in Connecticut where my parents had a dairy farm. My mother grew many fruits and vegetables there. Her strawberries were fabulous. This is one of the ways she served them.

Quickly wash fresh strawberries in cold water. Remove the green leaves, drain thoroughly, and slice each berry lengthwise into three or four slices. Refrigerate and serve very cold in individual bowls with a generous topping of very cold Custard Sauce (page 490), or any of the custard sauces in the next section except chocolate. Pass the sauce separately. For more than three or four people, double the sauce recipe.

When strawberries are really good, this is one of the finest of all desserts.

Coupe Longchamps

This may be made with either of the raspberry sauces (page 494 or 495), or with Sauce Melba (page 495), or with bought Melba sauce. Stir a few spoonfuls of kirsch or maraschino into the sauce. In well-chilled parfait glasses, tulip champagne glasses, or large wineglasses alternate generous layers of coffee ice cream and raspberry sherbet with thin layers of the sauce. Freeze until serving time. Before serving decorate with whipped cream.

If you have candied violets or rose petals, place them sparingly on top.

Oranges in Rum, Cuban Style

4 TO 6 PORTIONS

6 large seedless oranges
2 tablespoons sugar
¼ cup dark rum
⅓ cup guava jelly, red currant jelly, or marmalade

Peel and section the oranges (pages 468). Place the sections in a wide bowl. Sprinkle with the sugar and rum. Turn gently to mix and let stand for about 1 hour, turning occasionally. Drain the fruit and reserve the syrup.

Over moderate heat stir the jelly or marmalade to soften. When smooth, mix it with the reserved syrup and pour over the orange sections.

Cover and refrigerate, stirring occasionally.

Serve in large brandy snifters or wineglasses that have been in the freezer for about ½ hour. Serve quickly while glasses are still frosty.

Note: In Havana each portion was topped with a few small pieces of guava paste.

Ice Cream Ambrosia

Vanilla ice cream
Grated coconut (see Note)
Oranges in Rum, Cuban Style (page 483)

In each chilled dessert bowl, large brandy snifter, or wineglass, place a scoop of vanilla ice cream. Top generously with grated coconut. Circle with the Oranges in Rum, Cuban Style.

Note: This is best if made with fresh coconut, which is now frequently available in many frozen-food sections. If you use canned or packaged coconut, try to get that which is moist-pack, and preferably unsweetened.

Raspberries Niçoise

Fresh raspberries
Vanilla ice cream
Strawberry Topping (page 493)

I do not wash raspberries. They hold water if you wash them.

In each chilled, individual dessert bowl, or in a large wineglass, place a scoop of ice cream. Circle with the raspberries and top generously with the Strawberry Topping.

Pineapple and Strawberries Creole

4 TO 6 PORTIONS

1 ripe pineapple
3 to 4 tablespoons kirsch
Sugar
Strawberry Topping (page 493)

Peel the pineapple. Cut lengthwise into quarters and remove the core. Cut each quarter lengthwise into very thin slices. Place them on a large flat tray. Sprinkle with the kirsch and a bit of sugar, about 2 to 3 tablespoons depending on the sweetness of the pineapple. Cover and refrigerate.

On each chilled, flat dessert plate, place several overlapping slices of pineapple. Spoon a generous ribbon of the Strawberry Topping across the pineapple slices. Serve with a knife and fork.

Sauces

CUSTARD SAUCE 490
Rum Cream Sauce 491
Grand Marnier Custard Sauce 491
Chocolate Custard Sauce 491
Lemon Custard Sauce 491

RICH CUSTARD SAUCE 492
Rich Bourbon or Rum Sauce 492

APRICOT SAUCE 493

STRAWBERRY TOPPING 493

RASPBERRY SAUCE 494

FRESH RASPBERRY SAUCE 495

SAUCE MELBA 495

SUZETTE SAUCE 496

FORTNUM AND MASON SAUCE 497

BUTTERED RUM SAUCE 498
Old-Fashioned Lemon Sauce 498

BOURBON-HONEY SAUCE FROM MISSISSIPPI 499

GINGER CREAM 499

OLD-FASHIONED WALNUT-CHOCOLATE SAUCE 500

BITTERSWEET CHOCOLATE SAUCE 501

HONEY CHOCOLATE SAUCE 502

HOT FUDGE SAUCE 503

COFFEE SAUCE 504

PEANUT BUTTER SAUCE 505
Charlie Brown Sundae 505

Many of the recipes in this book suggest which sauce to serve with them. But instead of saying after each sauce recipe "serve with fruit" or whatever—and as I don't really have any cut-and-dried rules about it—I suggest that you experiment and try your own combinations.

A jar or two of good sauce is a joy to have on hand. Served with ice cream or fruit, or both, you have a quick special dessert. Or try some of these with pound cake, or sponge cake, or un-iced chocolate cake squares. The combinations are endless and delicious.

Custard Sauce

2²/₃ CUPS OF SAUCE

> 1 cup milk
> 1 cup light cream
> 4 egg yolks
> ½ cup sugar
> Pinch of salt
> 1 teaspoon vanilla extract

In a heavy saucepan over moderate heat, scald the milk and cream.

Meanwhile, in the top of a large double boiler off the heat, stir the yolks lightly with a small wire whisk just to mix. Gradually stir in the sugar and salt.

When you see steam rising from the milk and cream, a wrinkled skin forming on top, or tiny bubbles around the edge, remove it from the heat and very gradually stir it into the yolks.

Place over hot water, which must not touch the upper section of the double boiler and should be simmering gently, not boiling hard.

Stir the custard mixture constantly with a rubber spatula, scraping the sides and the bottom of the pot until the mixture thickens slightly or will coat a metal or wooden spoon. (This rather difficult moment to ascertain is easy with a candy thermometer: 180 degrees. It might take about 10 minutes.)

Remove from heat immediately to stop the cooking and strain into a bowl or container. Stir in the vanilla.

Cool uncovered, stirring occasionally. When cool, if sauce is not absolutely smooth, strain again through a fine strainer. Cover and refrigerate. Serve very cold. Stir briefly before serving.

Note: To use a vanilla bean instead of the extract: Slit a 6- to 8-inch vanilla bean the long way. Scrape the seeds into the milk and cream and add the pod, also, before scalding. Leave it in until the sauce is strained.

Rum Cream Sauce

Whip ½ cup of heavy cream. Gradually fold in 1 cup of cooled Custard Sauce (above) or Rich Custard Sauce (page 492) and 3 tablespoons of dark rum.*

Grand Marnier Custard Sauce

Prepare the preceding recipe for Custard Sauce (page 490), substituting ¾ cup heavy cream for the 1 cup light cream. When cool, stir in 3 tablespoons Grand Marnier.*

Chocolate Custard Sauce

Prepare the preceding recipe for Custard Sauce (page 490) with the following addition:

Before scalding the milk and cream, add 6 ounces of coarsely cut-up semi-sweet chocolate. Cook, stirring occasionally with a small wire whisk, until the chocolate is melted and the mixture is smooth. Continue to cook, stirring occasionally, until the mixture comes almost to a boil.

Continue with the rest of the recipe as is.

Chill 8 hours or overnight.

Optional: Stir about 1 tablespoon (or a bit more to taste) dark rum into the cooled sauce.

Lemon Custard Sauce

Prepare the preceding recipe for Custard Sauce (page 490) but eliminate the vanilla. Cool the sauce to tepid, then stir in 3 tablespoons of lemon juice. Cool completely, cover, and refrigerate.

*Other liquors or liqueurs may be substituted and you may use either more or less, to taste.

Rich Custard Sauce

1 1/2 CUPS OF SAUCE

1 cup light cream
6 egg yolks
1/4 cup sugar
Pinch of salt
1 teaspoon vanilla extract

Using above ingredients, follow the procedure and directions for previous Custard Sauce (page 490). However, due to the large amount of egg yolk in this recipe, it will thicken at a lower temperature, or at about 168 to 170 degrees.

This should be strained through a fine strainer, stirred frequently until cool, and then, if not absolutely smooth, it should be strained again through a fine strainer. Cover and refrigerate. Stir briefly before serving. Serve very cold.

Rich Bourbon or Rum Sauce
Stir 2 tablespoons of bourbon or dark rum into the above Rich Custard Sauce.

Apricot Sauce

1 GENEROUS CUP OF SAUCE

1 cup apricot preserves
1 tablespoon water
¼ cup light or dark rum, or kirsch

In small saucepan or skillet over moderate heat, stir the preserves and water until preserves are melted and come to a boil.

Remove from heat. Stir in the rum or kirsch and press through a strainer.

May be served warm or at room temperature. (This may also be kept refrigerated and warmed just slightly before serving.)

Strawberry Topping

2 CUPS OF SAUCE

1 pint strawberries
¼ cup sugar
2 to 3 tablespoons curaçao, kirsch, Cointreau, or Grand Marnier

Rinse the berries briefly in cold water. Pick off the stems and leaves and drain thoroughly on toweling. Slice each berry lengthwise in about three slices and place in a large bowl. Sprinkle with sugar and turn gently with a rubber spatula. Add liqueur to taste and mix gently. Cover and let stand at room temperature for 1 hour, stirring gently a few times. Refrigerate for at least 1 hour or more.

Serve generously over ice cream, custard, pudding, or sliced fresh peaches.

Raspberry Sauce

> **2 packages (10 ounces each) frozen raspberries (in syrup)**
> **¼ cup sugar**
> **2 tablespoons cornstarch**
> **Pinch of salt**
> **¼ teaspoon almond extract**

Thaw berries, drain them, and reserve the syrup. Add enough water to the syrup to make 1½ cups. In a medium-size saucepan mix sugar, cornstarch, and salt. Gradually add syrup and water mixture, stirring with a rubber spatula until smooth. Cook over medium heat, stirring slowly and constantly with the rubber spatula. Stir gently, do not beat. When the mixture thickens and begins to turn somewhat transparent and has just barely come to the boil, let it simmer gently for 1 or 2 minutes. Remove from the heat. (Overcooking or overbeating would thin the sauce.) Add almond extract and gently stir in the drained raspberries.

Refrigerate and serve cold.

Fresh Raspberry Sauce

1 1/2 CUPS OF SAUCE

2 cups raspberries
2 tablespoons sugar
1 teaspoon lemon juice

Either mash and force the berries through a large strainer, or puree them in a food mill or a food processor and then strain to remove seeds. Mix in sugar and lemon juice. Refrigerate. Serve cold.

Note: This may either be a smooth sauce, as above, or you may reserve a few whole berries to stir in.

Sauce Melba

Fresh raspberries
Red currant jelly

For every 2 cups of raspberries use about 1/3 cup of jelly.

Either mash and force the berries through a strainer, or puree in a food mill and then strain to remove seeds.

Stir the jelly over moderate heat to melt. When smooth, mix with the raspberry puree. Chill and serve cold.

Suzette Sauce

1 1/4 CUPS OF SAUCE

T his will keep almost indefinitely in the refrigerator.

1 orange
½ lemon
3 tablespoons sugar
2 tablespoons butter
1 ounce (2 tablespoons) each kirsch, rum, maraschino liqueur, curaçao

Pare and sliver the orange rind following directions on page 468. Place in saucepan. Squeeze the juice of the orange and the half lemon and add to saucepan. Add the sugar and stir over moderate heat to bring to a boil. Simmer for about 10 minutes. Add butter and stir until butter is melted. Add kirsch, rum, maraschino, and curaçao. Bring to a boil and remove from heat immediately.

Serve warm.

Fortnum and Mason Sauce

2 CUPS OF SAUCE

2 large, bright-colored oranges (see Note)
12 ounces (1 cup) red currant jelly
1 tablespoon lemon juice
¼ teaspoon cinnamon
¼ cup curaçao or Grand Marnier
2 tablespoons dark rum

Use a vegetable peeler with a swivel blade to peel the very thin, orange-colored rind of the oranges—it must be thin. Squeeze the oranges to make ⅔ cup of juice and set aside. Cut the rind into slivers, following directions for paring the rind and cutting it into slivers (page 468). Place in a saucepan with the ⅔ cup of orange juice, currant jelly, lemon juice, and cinnamon.

Cook over moderate heat, stirring occasionally, until mixture comes to a boil. Adjust heat so that the sauce simmers slowly. Simmer uncovered without stirring for 15 minutes. Remove from heat and set aside to cool.

Stir in curaçao or Grand Marnier and rum. Refrigerate and serve cold.

Serve over vanilla ice cream, orange sections, or a combination of both.

Note: The sauce will be bitter if the oranges are greenish, or if they are pared too deeply.

Buttered Rum Sauce

1 ⅓ CUPS OF SAUCE

½ cup sugar
1 tablespoon plus 1 teaspoon cornstarch
⅛ teaspoon salt
1 cup hot water
2 tablespoons butter, at room temperature
2 tablespoons heavy cream
1 teaspoon vanilla extract
2 tablespoons dark rum

Mix the sugar, cornstarch, and salt in a rather small, heavy saucepan. Gradually stir in the water. Cook over moderate heat, stirring gently and constantly with a rubber spatula, for about 5 minutes until mixture is thick and clear. (Overbeating or overcooking would thin the sauce.)

Remove from heat. Add the butter and stir gently until it has melted. Stir in the cream, vanilla, and rum.

Serve warm, at room temperature, or refrigerated.

Old-Fashioned Lemon Sauce

Follow the preceding recipe for Buttered Rum Sauce with the following changes:

Eliminate the heavy cream, vanilla, and rum. In their places substitute the finely grated rind of 1 lemon and 2 tablespoons of lemon juice.

Bourbon-Honey Sauce from Mississippi

3/4 CUP OF SAUCE

Simply mix ¼ cup bourbon into ½ cup honey. Bourbon may be increased or decreased to your taste, but this is not meant to be a mildly flavored sauce. Make it strong or don't make it. (Rum may be used in place of bourbon.)

Try it over coffee ice cream with a sprinkling of toasted, sliced almonds.

Ginger Cream

2 CUPS OF SAUCE

1 cup heavy cream
2 tablespoons confectioners sugar
½ teaspoon vanilla extract
2 tablespoons Grand Marnier or curaçao
2 tablespoons crystallized ginger, very finely cut, or drained preserved ginger

In a chilled bowl with chilled beaters, whip the cream, sugar, vanilla, and Grand Marnier or curaçao only until the mixture holds a soft shape. Fold in the ginger.

Old-Fashioned Walnut-Chocolate Sauce

3 CUPS OF SAUCE

½ cup light cream or coffee cream
1 cup sugar
2 ounces unsweetened chocolate
2 ounces semisweet chocolate
¼ pound (1 stick) butter
2 egg yolks
1 teaspoon vanilla extract
3½ ounces (1 cup) walnuts, cut or broken coarse

Place the cream and sugar in a heavy 1½- to 2-quart saucepan on moderate heat. Stir with a rubber spatula, scraping the sides of the pan, to dissolve the sugar and bring the mixture to a boil.

Add both chocolates and the butter. Cook, stirring with a small wire whisk, until very smooth. Remove from heat.

In a small bowl stir the egg yolks briefly just to mix. Gradually stir in a few spoonfuls of the chocolate mixture and then stir the egg yolks into remaining chocolate mixture.

Cook over low heat, stirring gently and scraping the saucepan with the rubber spatula, for 3 minutes. Remove from heat.

Stir in the vanilla and walnuts.

Serve slightly warm or at room temperature.

This sauce may be kept warm over warm (not hot) water, stirring occasionally. It may be refrigerated and then reheated over warm water.

Note: To prepare Plain Old-Fashioned Chocolate Sauce follow above recipe, eliminating the walnuts. This will make 2 cups of sauce.

Bittersweet Chocolate Sauce

1 $^1/_3$ CUPS OF SAUCE

½ cup heavy cream
¼ cup sugar
4 ounces unsweetened chocolate
½ cup apricot preserves
2 tablespoons Grand Marnier, bourbon, or rum

Place cream, sugar, chocolate, and preserves in the top of a small double boiler. Place over hot water on low heat. Cook, stirring constantly, until everything is melted.

Remove top of double boiler. Stir in Grand Marnier, bourbon, or rum.

Press through a fine strainer.

Serve hot or warm. This thick sauce will thicken even more as it cools.

Note: The sweetness may be adjusted by substituting semisweet chocolate for all or part of the unsweetened chocolate. It is an equally lovely sauce either way.

Honey Chocolate Sauce

1 CUP OF SAUCE

> 1 ounce unsweetened chocolate
> 1 ounce semisweet chocolate
> ¼ cup honey
> ½ cup heavy cream
> Finely grated rind of ½ large orange
> 2 tablespoons rum, dark or light

In a small, heavy saucepan over moderate heat, bring both chocolates, honey, and cream to a boil, stirring occasionally with a small wire whisk. Reduce heat and, stirring constantly, simmer for 2 to 3 minutes. Stir in the orange rind.

Remove from heat. Cool to tepid and stir in the rum. Serve at room temperature.

Note: This may be refrigerated or frozen. If it is frozen, it should be stirred briefly over hot water to soften.

Hot Fudge Sauce

1 CUP OF SAUCE

A note of warning! As soon as this sauce touches cold ice cream it turns to chewy, caramel-like fudge, most especially appreciated by teenagers or others with strong teeth.

2 ounces unsweetened chocolate
1 tablespoon butter
⅓ cup boiling water
2 tablespoons light corn syrup
1 cup sugar
1 teaspoon vanilla extract

Place the chocolate, butter, and boiling water in a 1½-quart saucepan. Cook over low heat, stirring until the chocolate is melted and the mixture is smooth. Mix in the corn syrup and sugar.

Raise heat to moderate and stir occasionally until it comes to a boil. Stop stirring and let boil moderately for exactly 8 minutes. Remove from heat and immediately place saucepan briefly in cold water in order to stop the boiling. Stir in the vanilla.

Use sauce while it is still warm, or let it cool and reheat over hot water. This may be refrigerated and then reheated. It must be served warm, as it hardens when it is cold.

Coffee Sauce

1⅓ cups sugar
⅛ teaspoon salt
1 tablespoon plus ½ teaspoon instant coffee
⅓ cup light corn syrup
⅔ cup boiling water
1 tablespoon butter
1 teaspoon vanilla extract

In a 2½- to 3-quart saucepan, mix the sugar, salt, and instant coffee. Gradually mix in the corn syrup and then the boiling water.

Cook, stirring, over high heat, until the mixture comes to a boil. Reduce the heat slightly and continue to boil without stirring for about 10 minutes, until slightly thickened (about 228 degrees on a candy thermometer). Mixture will boil up high; if necessary, adjust heat so that it doesn't boil over.

Remove from heat. Add butter and stir until melted. Place the bottom of the saucepan briefly in cold water to stop the cooking. Set aside and cool completely without stirring.

When cool, with a spoon remove the skin that will have formed on top. Stir in vanilla.

Serve warm or at room temperature. May be reheated.

Peanut Butter Sauce

1¼ CUPS OF SAUCE

1 cup sugar
1 tablespoon light corn syrup
⅛ teaspoon salt
¾ cup milk
2 tablespoons butter
⅓ cup smooth peanut butter
½ teaspoon vanilla extract

In a 6- to 8-cup heavy saucepan, mix the sugar, corn syrup, salt, and milk. Stir over moderate heat until mixture comes to a boil. Insert a candy thermometer. Adjust heat so that the sauce boils gently, and let boil without stirring for 30 to 40 minutes or until the temperature registers 225 to 228 degrees. The sauce will have caramelized to a light golden color.

Remove from heat. Add butter and peanut butter. Stir briskly with a small wire whisk until smooth. Stir in the vanilla. Serve warm.

Sauce may be kept warm, or reheated, in the top of a small double boiler over hot water on moderate heat, stirring occasionally.

Note: Over cold ice cream the sauce thickens to a hard caramel consistency. Delicious.

Charlie Brown Sundae

Serve warm Peanut Butter Sauce over vanilla ice cream and top generously with coarsely chopped salted peanuts.

Or, for a Charlie Brown Banana Split, place ice cream over a banana, split the long way. Top with whipped cream, chopped peanuts, and Peanut Butter Sauce.

Etcetera

PEANUT BRITTLE 508

HONEY BUTTER 509

HOMEMADE APRICOT PRESERVES 510

CANDIED GRAPEFRUIT RIND 511

CHOCOLATE CONES 513

GRATED CHOCOLATE AND CHOCOLATE CURLS 514

CHOCOLATE LEAVES 515

CHOCOLATE SLABS 516

CHOCOLATE CIGARETTES 517

Peanut Brittle

This is not the usual peanut brittle. It is solid peanuts with barely enough brittle to hold them together. You will need a candy thermometer to make this. This is fun and easy and delicious. You're in for a treat.

1 pound (4 cups) dry-roasted, salted peanuts
1½ cups firmly packed light brown sugar
1 cup light corn syrup
⅓ cup water
2 tablespoons butter, cut into 6 or 8 pieces
1 teaspoon vanilla extract

Adjust rack to center of oven. Preheat oven to 350 degrees. Butter a 14 x 17-inch cookie sheet and set it aside. Also butter the blade of a large wooden spatula or the back of a large, heavy wooden spoon and set aside.

Place the peanuts in a large shallow pan and bake for 5 minutes, stirring them once or twice. Turn off oven heat but let nuts remain in oven to keep warm.

In a 3-quart heavy saucepan over high heat, stir the sugar, corn syrup, and water until the sugar is dissolved. Place a candy thermometer in the syrup and continue to cook without stirring until the temperature reaches 275 degrees. Reduce the heat to moderate and continue to cook until the temperature reaches 290 degrees.

Immediately remove from heat. Work quickly. With a large wooden spoon or spatula (not the buttered one) stir in the butter, vanilla, and warm peanuts. Instantly turn out onto the buttered cookie sheet. Now use the buttered spatula or spoon to spread and flatten the candy. The mixture will be quite firm. It will take considerable pressure to flatten it. Press as hard as you can to press the peanuts into a single layer.

Let the peanut brittle cool to room temperature, then with a wide metal spatula remove it from the cookie sheet in one piece. Wipe the bottom with a paper towel to absorb the butter. Break the candy into large pieces. Immediately store airtight.

Note: It is easy to remove the carmelized sugar from the utensils. Simply place them in the sink and let hot water run onto them until the sugar dissolves and washes away.

Honey Butter

For each ¼ pound butter, use ⅓ to ½ cup honey, depending on your taste and the strength of the honey—some honeys have a stronger flavor than others. Beat the butter and gradually add the honey, beating until smooth. Pack in a crock, jar, or individual butter dishes. Refrigerate until firm. May be refrigerated for a week or so, or may be frozen.

Serve with toast, as you would serve butter, or with pancakes, waffles, or popovers.

Homemade Apricot Preserves

1 QUART

Marvelous as these preserves are, they should not be used for recipes calling for apricot preserves to be made into a glaze. This doesn't have enough pectin to set or dry firmly. Use a commercial brand.

1 pound dried apricots
2½ cups water
½ cup sugar

In a heavy saucepan with a tight cover, over high heat, bring the apricots and water to a boil. Reduce heat to low and let apricots simmer, covered, until they are very tender—about ½ hour, depending on the apricots. The fruit should be very soft. The water should be partially but not completely absorbed.

Stir and mash vigorously with a wooden spatula, or press with a potato masher to break up the fruit somewhat, leaving some chunky pieces. Add the sugar and stir briefly to dissolve. Some apricots are more tart than others. Taste. If necessary add a bit more sugar, but this is best if it is not too sweet.

Remove from heat to cool. Pack in a covered container and refrigerate.

Notes:
1. Do not wash fruit unless necessary, in which case rinse quickly under cold running water.
2. Refrigerated this will keep indefinitely. If the preserves become too thick after a time in the refrigerator, just stir in a bit of water to correct consistency.

Candied Grapefruit Rind

ABOUT 2½ POUNDS

This is fabulous—classy—elegant. It takes a while to make it (it might take a day or two for it to dry sufficiently) but then, if you can resist eating it all, it will last for many weeks. I'm guessing—I was never able to keep it that long.

A jar of this makes a beautiful and much appreciated gift.

When I gave the recipe to Rochelle Huppin-Fleck, who was then the pastry chef at Wolfgang Puck's Granita in Malibu, she started serving a few slices of it along with almost every dessert. Everyone raved about it and they all wanted to take some home.

3 large, thick-skinned grapefruits (the very thick-skinned fruit is best for
    candying, although it will take more time to get it dry enough)
Sugar

Using whole grapefruit, cut through the skin and white underskin, cutting from top to bottom in large wedges. Peel off the rind and slice each wedge the long way into pieces about ½ inch wide at widest point.

Place the rind in a large saucepan. Pour boiling water over it to cover. Boil for 5 minutes. Drain and repeat three more times, using fresh boiling water each time (four waters, or blanchings, in all).

In a wide, deep frying pan or a wide, shallow saucepan, mix 2½ cups of sugar and 1½ cups of water. Place over high heat and stir until sugar dissolves. Let boil until syrup spins a thread (230 to 234 degrees on a candy thermometer). Add the drained peel. Stir well. Reduce heat so that syrup boils gently. Stir occasionally and let simmer, partially covered, for about 1 hour until peels are tender and have absorbed almost all of the syrup. Then uncover and cook slowly, stirring gently, until all the liquid has been absorbed or evaporated. Place peels in a single layer on cake racks set over a large piece of aluminum foil.

Without waiting, place 2 to 3 cups of sugar in a shallow bowl or tray and roll each piece of warm peel in the sugar. Then place on cake racks and let stand overnight only loosely covered at room temperature to dry.

If peel is still a little too wet, let it stand longer until dry. But if it is still very wet, place the racks on cookie sheets in an oven set at the lowest temperature for 30 minutes to 1 hour, but no longer than necessary. Peel is best when still moist inside. Reroll in sugar and let stand again to cool.

Store airtight. This will last for weeks. It makes a great gift. I always make this during the Thanksgiving and Christmas season when the best thick-skinned fruit is available.

Note: To use the rind of grapefruit halves (left over after serving half grapefruits) remove all the membranes but leave the white underskin on the peel. Cut the strips in the same manner as above; now each piece will be an elongated triangle half as long as if you had started with a whole fruit.

Chocolate Cones

This is not something to do when you are in a hurry. These take time. If they are made with real chocolate they should be stored in the refrigerator, if they are made with compound chocolate (see page xviii) they can stand at room temperature.

Cut wax paper into squares measuring 4 to 5 inches. The smaller they are, the more elegant, and the more difficult to handle. Cut each square in half to form two triangles. Form each triangle into a cone by rolling two outer points, one after the other, to center point and double-folding to secure (see illustrations). The tip must be tightly closed or the chocolate will run out.

In the top of a small double boiler over hot water on low heat, melt a few ounces (depending on the number of cones) of compound chocolate (see page xviii) or real chocolate. Remove the chocolate from the heat before it is completely melted. Stir until completely smooth. With a small, pointed paring

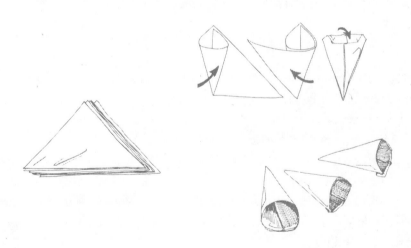

knife, spread the inside of a cone with the chocolate. Coat it completely, making sure not to leave any holes in the chocolate. (If the chocolate begins to harden while working with it, replace over warm water for a few minutes.) Place on a small plate and place in the freezer or refrigerator for a few minutes only until the chocolate is completely set and firm. Then gently, with a light touch, carefully peel off the wax paper, handling the cone as little as possible.

Chocolate Cones are used as a decoration. Generally, they are placed on a cake before the icing is dry—one cone to a portion. Place them on their sides with open ends pointing out and pointed ends toward the center. They may also be used on top of whipped cream on icebox cakes or other desserts.

Resist the temptation to fill them with a squirt of whipped cream or butter cream; it would hide their thinness and delicacy.

Chocolate Cones are exquisite and make an elegant and exciting presentation. If you are handy, you will find them easy to make and great fun. The following chocolate leaves are an equally beautiful creation, considerably easier to make.

Grated Chocolate and Chocolate Curls

Grated chocolate may be made with a coarse grater or with a swivel-bladed vegetable peeler. Very finely grated chocolate may be made in a small Mouli rotary grater. Use any chocolate you wish. Grate the chocolate over paper, then use a spoon to sprinkle it over the dessert. It may be stored in a container at room temperature.

Chocolate curls are very "iffy." If the chocolate is very fresh and if the room is not too cool and if you use just the right amount of pressure, they may possibly be formed with a swivel-bladed vegetable peeler. Use a piece of thick chocolate. Work over paper or directly over the dessert. Cut downward firmly against a smooth side of the chocolate. Try milk chocolate—it curls beautifully.

Chocolate Leaves

You may use any fresh, green leaves, preferably gardenia, ivy, or rose leaves. In choosing leaves, try to pick those that are firm (if leaf is too thin and delicate it will tear while being peeled away from the chocolate) and have the most markedly raised veins on the back. Separate the leaves, keeping enough stem on each one to hold it by. Wash and dry thoroughly, patting both sides with a towel.

In a small double boiler over hot water on low heat, melt a few ounces (depending on the number of leaves) of compound chocolate (see page xviii). Remove from heat before completely melted. Stir until completely smooth.

Hold a leaf in your left hand, upside down. With a small metal spatula spread a thin layer of the chocolate over the underside (or veined side) of the leaf. Be careful not to let the chocolate run onto the reverse side of the leaf. With a fingertip, wipe the edges of the reverse side to make sure there is no chocolate there. (If the chocolate begins to harden while working with it, replace it over warm water.) Place the leaf, chocolate side up, on a small plate in the freezer or refrigerator for a few minutes only until the chocolate is completely set and firm. Then, gently and carefully, peel away the green leaf, starting at the stem end and handling the chocolate leaf as little as possible. Immediately put the leaf on a plate or small tray. The chocolate leaves may be refrigerated or frozen.

If the green leaf has not torn it may be reused.

Chocolate leaves may be used to top any dessert, standing them on an angle or placing them flat on whipped cream, cake icing, or ice cream.

Chocolate Slabs

Melt 2 or 3 ounces of chocolate as directed in preceding recipe. While it is melt-ing, cover a cookie sheet with wax paper. Stir the chocolate until smooth and then turn it out onto the wax paper. With a long, narrow metal spatula spread the chocolate very, very thin. Do not worry about making it perfectly smooth, and do not fuss with the edges. Work quickly, spreading the chocolate thin before it starts to harden. Place the sheet in the freezer (or in the refrigerator if there isn't room in the freezer).

When you are ready to use it, remove from freezer. Quickly bend the paper backward to break the chocolate into large, irregular slabs. Handling the chocolate as little as possible, let the slabs fall haphazardly, directly on the dessert.

Chocolate slabs may be used on top of cake icing before it has hardened, and they are especially attractive on top of whipped cream.

Work quickly. These wafer-thin chocolates will melt quickly, which is all right after they have been placed on a dessert—but a mess if they melt in your hands.

Chocolate Cigarettes

These are long, thin curls of chocolate that are used as a decoration. They are very professional.

To make chocolate cigarettes: Coarsely chop about 8 ounces of compound chocolate (see page xviii). Melt it slowly over hot water. When partially melted, remove from hot water and stir until completely melted. Pour onto a marble work surface (or a large marble cheese board), forming a ribbon about 3 to 4 inches wide and 10 inches long. The chocolate should be about ¼ to ⅜ inch thick. Let cool at room temperature until it is no longer soft or sticky.

To make the curls use a long, heavy knife—I use a Sabatier cook's knife with a 12-inch blade. Hold it at a 45-degree angle across the width and right near the end of the chocolate. Cut down slowly and firmly. The chocolate will roll around itself as it is cut. Repeat, each time placing the blade very close to the cut end—the curls should be paper-thin. Transfer them with a wide metal spatula to a shallow tray. Cover with plastic wrap and store at room temperature.

Index

266–67

Gingerbread, Moosehead, 146–47

Gin Ice Cream, 457–58

Glacéed Strawberries, 479–81

glaze(s). *See also* icing(s)

  Apricot, for Apple Kuchen, 109

  bourbon, for Kentucky Pound Cake, 160

  chocolate

    for Capri Pastries, 287–88

    for Helen McCully's French Chocolate

      Torte, 20

    Thick, for Marble Loaf Cake, 141

  citrus, for Trinidad Torte, 93

  kirsch, for Danish Loaf Cake, 82

  lemon

    for Caraway Seed Cake, 129

    for Carrot-Nut Torte, 39–40

    for East 62nd Street Lemon Cake, 127

    for Swedish Almond Torte, 28

  orange

    for Orange Cake (Texan), 131

    for Spanish Orange Cake (Valencian),

      133

  red currant jelly, for Peace and Plenty (pie),

    365

  sugar

    for Aspen Rocks (cookies), 177

    for Budapest Coffee Cake, 73

    for Spritz Cookies or Pretzels, 250

    for Swedish Jelly Cookies, 248

    for Swedish Jelly Slices, 246

    for Trinidad Torte, 93

graham cracker crusts. *See under* crust(s)

Grandma Hermalin's Chocolate Cake

  Squares, 42–43

Grand Marnier

  in Chocolate Filling, for Black Velvet, 339

  Custard Sauce, 491

  in Deep South Chocolate Ice Cream,

    454–55

  in English Crêpes, Buckingham Palace,

    306–7

  in French Ice-Cream Cake, 464–65

  Parfait, 450

grapefruit, preparing (or oranges), 468

Grapefruit Rind, Candied, 511–12

Grated Chocolate and Chocolate Curls, 514

grating citrus fruit, xxv

grinding nuts, xxvi–xxv

guava, in Oranges in Rum, Cuban Style, 483

H

half-and-half, xix

hazelnut(s)

  blanching, xxvi

  Crescents, Hungarian, 240–41

  in Nut Cheesecake, 371

  Rusks, Almond or, 225–26

Health-Food Cookies, 182–83

Helen McCully's French Chocolate Torte,

  19–20

Homemade Apricot Preserves, 510

honey

  Butter, 509

  Cake, 136–37

  Chocolate Sauce, 502

  Parfait, 448

  Sauce from Mississippi, Bourbon-, 499

Hot Fudge Sauce, 503

  Walnut Fudge Pie à la Mode with, 48–49

Hungarian recipes

  Budapest Coffee Cake, 72–73

  Butter Biscuits *(Vajas Pogácsa)*, 186–87

  Dobosh Torte, 6–8

  Hazelnut Crescents, 240–41

  Walnut Torte, 24–25

I

icebox cakes. *See under* cake(s)

Icebox Rice Pudding, 412–13

ice cream(s). *See also* frozen desserts;

  sherbet(s)

  about, 446

  Ambrosia, 484

  in *Bananas Cubaine,* 477

  Cake, French, 464–65

  in Charlie Brown Banana Split, 505

  in Charlie Brown Sundae, 505

  in *Coupe Longchamps,* 482

  Deep South Chocolate, 454–55

  Gin, 457–58

  Jean Hewitt's Old-Fashioned Lemon, 447

  in *Raspberries Niçoise,* 484

  in Raspberry-Strawberry Bavarian, 442–43

  Walnut, 456

icing(s). *See also* glaze(s)

  buttercream

    Coffee, for Royal Viennese Walnut

      Torte, 31–32

    Rum Chocolate, for Rum Chocolate

      Layer Cake, 65–66

  Caramel Coffee 7-Minute, for Montana

    Mountain Cake, 59

  chocolate

    Bittersweet, for Small Walnut Torte, 25

    for Black Velvet, 340

    Buttercream, Rum, for Rum Chocolate

      Layer Cake, 65–66

    for Chocolate Cake Squares (Grandma

      Hermalin's), 43

    for Chocolate Cake Squares (Lydia

      Pinkham's), 45

    for Chocolate Pound Cake, 164

    Cupcake, for Chocolate Cupcakes, 290

    for Dobosh Torte, 8

    for Palm Beach Chocolate Layer Cake, 51

    for Palm Beach Chocolate Tube Cake,

      53

    for Queen Mother's Cake, 14–15

    for Rum Cream Layer Cake, 62

    for Sour Cream Chocolate Layer Cake,

      55

    for Sponge Cake, 117

    for Truffles Torte, 18

  coconut: Fluffy White, for Coconut Layer

    Cake, 68

  coffee

    Buttercream, for Royal Viennese

      Walnut Torte, 31–32

    Java, for Java Cake, 149

    7-Minute, Caramel, for Montana

      Mountain Cake, 59

    lemon, for Pecan-Coconut Bars, 213

    mocha, for Mocha Pecan Torte, 34

    Rum Chocolate Buttercream, for Rum

      Chocolate Layer Cake, 65–66

  sour cream

    for Palm Beach Chocolate Tube Cake, 53

    for Sour Cream Chocolate Layer Cake,

      55

  sugar

    Brown, for Buttermilk Spice Cake,

      124–25

    Caramelized, for Date-Nut Cake

      Squares, 91

    7-Minute, for Devil's Food Cake, 57

  whipped cream: Kumquat, for Chocolate

    Applesauce Torte, 22–23

Indian River Sweet Orange Bread, 134–35

individual pastries and petits fours. *See under*

  cookie(s)

ingredients, xvii–xxv

  and electric mixer, xxxii

  folding of, xxxi–xxxii

  heating, in double boiler, xxvi

  measuring of, xxvii

  procedure for adding, xxxii

  temperature of, xxxii

Irish recipes

  Almond Cakes, 281–83

  Caraway Seed Cake, 128–29

  Caraway Seed Wafers, 193

  Coffee Jelly, 444

Italian recipes

  Cornmeal Cat's Tongues, 174–75

  Pine Nut Macaroons, 194–95

  Rusks, Italian Style *(Biscotti all'anice),*

    223–24

J

Jamaican recipe: Pepper Pound Cake, 168–69

Java Cake, 148–49

Java Icing, for Java Cake, 149

jelly

  Cookies, Swedish, 247–48

  Irish Coffee, 444

  red currant

sunflower seeds, in Health-Food Cookies, 182–83
superfine sugar, substitute for, 256
Suzette Sauce, 496
Swedish recipes
    Almond Torte, 26–28
    Dream Cookies, 253–54
    Icebox Cookies, 229–30
    Jelly Cookies, 247–48
    Jelly Slices, 245–46
Syrup, Rum
    for Capri Pastries, 285
    for Peaches-and-Cream Rum Cake, 102

T

Tea Cakes, 184–85
temperature
    of ingredients, xxxii
    of oven for baking, xxvii
Texas, recipes from
    Fruit Cake, 76–77
    Orange Cake, 130–31
Thick Chocolate Glaze, for Marble Loaf Cake, 141
timing cakes, xxx
Toasted Almond Butter Cake, 80–81
Toni's Pound Cake, 157–58
topping(s)
    almond
        for Cottage Cheese and Pineapple Icebox Cake, 384
        for Irish Almond Cakes, 282–83
        for Linzer Torte, 5
        for Swedish Almond Torte, 27
    apricot, for Apricot Cheesecake Squares, 373
    coconut, for Pecan-Coconut Bars, 212–13
    cream, for Walnut-Peach Kuchen, 105
    peach, for Peaches-and-Cream Rum Cake, 103
    pecan
        for Pecan-Coconut Bars, 212–13
        for Pecan Squares Americana, 211
    Pineapple, for Pineapple Cheese Pie, 379
    sour cream
        for Cottage Cheese and Pineapple Icebox Cake, 384
        for Cottage Cheese Kuchen, 386–87
        for Cream Cheese Pie, 378
    strawberry
        for Cream Cheese and Yogurt Pie, 380
        for Peace and Plenty (pie), 364
        in Raspberries Niçoise, 484
    sugar
        for Apple Pudding (Streusel), 418
        for Blueberry Crumb Cake, 96
    whipped cream
        for Black Bottom Pie, 361
        for Capri Pastries, 287

for Charlotte Russe, 336
for Chocolate Cream Cheese Pie, 382
for Chocolate Mousse Torte, 10
for Chocolate Rum Icebox Cake, 332
for Chocolate Soufflé, 323
for Coffee Buttercrunch Pie, 356
for Cold Apricot Soufflé, 435
for Cold Walnut-Coffee Soufflé, 433
for Dark Chocolate Sponge, 429
for Kentucky Chocolate Icebox Cake with Bourbon, 330
for Lemon Chiffon Icebox Cake, 327
Mocha, for Chocolate Mousse Heatter, 423
for Mousse au Chocolat, 425
with Nuts, for Black Bottom Pecan Cream Pie, 362–63
for Orange Cream, 439
for Peaches-and-Cream Rum Cake, 103–4
for Pumpkin Custard, 407
for Raspberry-Strawberry Bavarian, 443
for Rum Pie, 353–54
Soft, for Chocolate Icebox Cake, Country Style, 334
for Vanilla Cream Pie, 358
torte(s), 2–40
    about, 2
    Carrot-Nut, 38–40
    chocolate
        Applesauce, with Kumquats, 21–23
        Dobosh, 6–8
        Helen McCully's French, 19–20
        Mousse, 9–11
        Queen Mother's Cake, 12–15
        Small Walnut, 24–25
        Truffles, 16–18
    Linzer, 3–5
    Mocha Pecan, 33–34
    Royal Norwegian Macaroon, 35–37
    Royal Viennese Walnut, 29–32
    Swedish Almond, 26–28
Trinidad Torte, 92–93
Tropical Mango Cream, 440–41
truffles
    Black, for Ethiopian Truffles, 291–92
    Ethiopian, 291–92
    recipe for, in Truffles Torte, 17–18
    Torte, 16–18
Turin Loaf, 426–27
Twists, Almond, 319–20

V

Vajas Pogácsa (Hungarian butter biscuits), 186–87
vanilla
    Cream Pie, 357–58
    in Pots de Crème à la Vanille, 391–92
    sugar, xxiii, 241

Vanille, Pots de Crème à la, 391–92
Victorias, 276–78
Viennese recipes
    Almond Crescents, 243
    Royal Walnut Torte, 29–32

W

wafers, rolled. See under cookie(s)
walnut(s)
    in African Date Bars, 218
    in Apple Kuchen, 108–9
    in Brownie Crisps, 208
    in Brownies, 206–7
    -Chocolate Sauce, Old-Fashioned, 500
    -Coffee Soufflé, Cold, 432–33
    in Craters (cookies), 197–98
    crust
        for Coffee Buttercrunch Pie, 355
        for Linzer Torte, 3–4
    in Date-Nut Bars, 214–15
    in Health-Food Cookies, 182–83
    in Honey Cake, 136–37
    Icebox Cookies, Old-Fashioned, 233–34
    Ice Cream, 456
    Loaf, Coffee, 84–85
    in Mexican Wedding Cakes, 242
    in Mulattoes (cookies), 199–200
    in Oatmeal Cookies, 178–79
    in Oatmeal Wafers, 262–63
    or Pecan Pound Cake, 165
    in Palm Beach Brownies with Chocolate-Covered Mints, viii–xi
    -Peach Kuchen, 105–7
    in Pumpkin Cake, 94–95
    Shortbread, Scotch, 236
    in Southern Nut Cake, 74–75
    in Soya Date Bars, 216–17
    in Texas Fruit Cake, 76–77
    Torte, Royal Viennese, 29–32
    Torte, Small, 24–25
    in Trinidad Torte, 92–93
watermelon, how to prepare for Fresh Fruit, 470
Wedding Cakes, Mexican, 242
wheat germ, in Health-Food Cookies, 182–83
whipped cream. See also under filling(s); icing(s); topping(s)
    and electric mixers, xxxii
whipping cream, xix
Whole-Wheat Pound Cake, 166–67
wine, red, in Poires au Vin Rouge, 476

Y

yogurt
    Cake, 119–20
    in Orange Cake (Texan), 130–31
    Pie, Cream Cheese and, 380